A STILLNESS
HEARD ROUND THE WORLD

OTHER BOOKS BY STANLEY WEINTRAUB

Private Shaw and Public Shaw
The War in the Wards
Journey to Heartbreak
The Last Great Cause
Aubrey Beardsley: Imp of the Perverse
Whistler
Four Rossettis: A Victorian Biography
The London Yankees

A STILLNESS
HEARD ROUND THE WORLD
The End of the Great War: November 1918

STANLEY WEINTRAUB

T·T TRUMAN TALLEY BOOKS / E. P. DUTTON / NEW YORK

Published in the United States by Truman Talley Books • E. P. Dutton,
2 Park Avenue, New York, N.Y. 10016

Library of Congress Cataloging in Publication Data

Weintraub, Stanley, 1929–
A stillness heard round the world.

"A Truman Talley Book."
Bibliography: p.
1. World War, 1914–1918—Armistices.   I. Title.
D641.W36   1985   940.4'39   85-6775

ISBN: 0-525-24346-1
Published simultaneously in Canada
by Fitzhenry & Whiteside Limited, Toronto

Designed by Mark O'Connor

COBE

10 9 8 7 6 5 4 3 2

In memory of
Ewart Garland,
who flew over Flanders
on the final day,
and for the thousand others
who shared their memories
with me

CONTENTS

vii

"Bliss it was in that dawn to be alive."
—WORDSWORTH

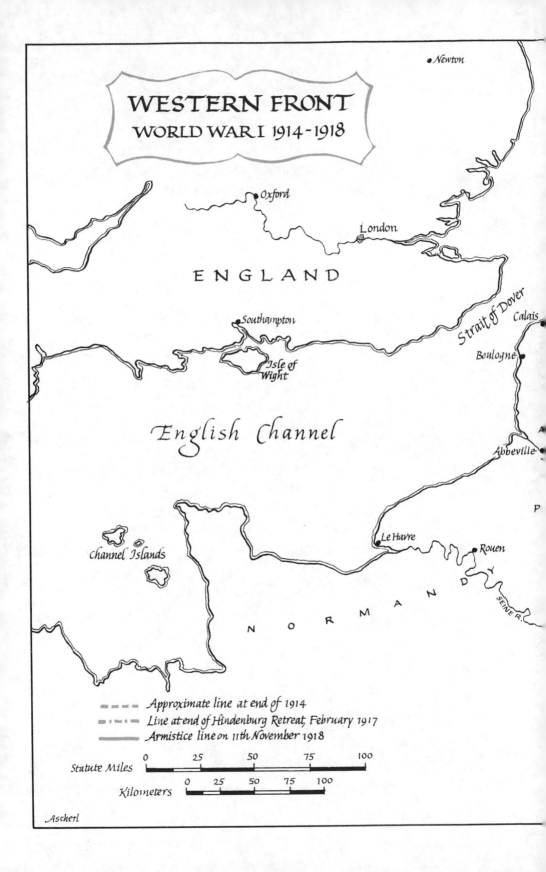

WESTERN FRONT
WORLD WAR I 1914-1918

• Newton

• Oxford

London

E N G L A N D

• Southampton

Strait of Dover

Calais

Boulogne

Isle of
Wight

Abbeville

English Channel

P

Le Havre

• Rouen

Channel Islands

N   O   R   M   A   N   D   Y

SEINE R.

- - - - Approximate line at end of 1914
-·-·- Line at end of Hindenburg Retreat, February 1917
——— Armistice line on 11th November 1918

Statute Miles   0   25   50   75   100

Kilometers   0   25   50   75   100

Ascherl

PROLOGUE:
ENDINGS

Oh, it's a cushy life, boys,
Really, we love it so!
Once a fellow was sent on leave,
And he simply refused to go.

Oh! Oh! Oh! It's a lovely war!
Who wouldn't be a soldier, eh?
Oh, it's a shame to take the pay. . . .

—"OH! OH! OH! IT'S A LOVELY WAR"

War is easier to make than peace. That the Great War of 1914—"the sausage machine," it was dubbed—might go on indefinitely began to haunt the mind as the carnage continued into its fifth year in August 1918. Circulating the trenches was a sardonic prophecy that the end would be signaled by four black flares rocketed invisibly into the night sky. Another grim forecast was that the war "will be finished when all the dirt in France has been shovelled into sandbags. . . . Then they'll have to quit, or fall through." Late in the war a German soldiers' saying echoed cynically the vanished martial spirit: *"Wir siegen uns zu Tode"* ("We'll conquer until we're all dead").

The commanding general of the 36th Ulster Division claimed that he knew exactly when it would be over: when a London bus could hold all the surviving men of his original unit. Not only did the grisly joke measure the price of the war—it suggested how the patriotic feeling with which both sides had begun the fighting had withered. In a similar mood was the wry calculation by a British officer that the pace of the Allied advance since 1914 would bring them to the Rhine in 180 years.

Whatever had exhilarated soldier and civilian in the beginning, privation and death had now ground down. In 1914 subaltern Rupert Brooke had lyricized that the purity of the Allied cause had made volunteers "swimmers into cleanness leaping." On the other side, intellectuals like Thomas Mann had exulted that *Kultur* would now be brought to the decadent West. According to which clergymen and home-front demagogues one listened to, God supported both sides—"our accomplice in murder and devastation," as Bernard Shaw put it. Meanwhile the reality rested in the elegy by Edward Thomas, who himself had died in the trenches, that the soldiers most blessed were "the dead that the rain rains upon," now beyond pain and freed from fear.

The hope for an end to fear and pain was seldom expressed in the flag-waving rhetoric of home-front patriots. Rather, after four years, soldiers measured their yearnings in the new credence they gave to tales of sudden and unexplained cease-fires. Some fiction, some fact, these multiplied among the men. Early in the war a drafted university student from Berlin wrote home about how, after a battle near Loos, men on both sides suddenly "walked about unconcernedly . . . in full view of the enemy, who was only a few yards away, and not a shot was fired. . . . I can imagine that the general war-weariness might at last reach such a point that it might lead to a similar *entente cordiale* between the opposing armies without any diplomatic preliminaries. Then indeed the World War, which began in such a flood of patriotic ardor, would end in farce; but I believe that the history of the world contains other tragicomedies of the same sort." The ultramilitarist Ernst Jünger, who would turn out fervid war novels in the 1920s, recalled another unexpected armistice. It was a rainy November night when dugouts filled with near-freezing water began collapsing, crusting weapons and troops with icy mud. Yet to emerge meant becoming instant targets.

> Suddenly a cry echoed across to us. On the other side of the barbed wire and hardly distinguishable from the background of the clayey wasteland, figures appeared in long yellow [rain]coats. They were English soldiers who, like us, were forced to vacate their trenches. This was really a relief for we were at the end of our resources. We went toward them. . . .
>
> We had remained underground so long it hardly seemed thinkable to us that . . . one might walk above ground with such unconcern and speak to the other fellow with human speech instead of with the language of machine guns. And now a great common need showed that it was a very simple and natural thing to meet in an open field and shake hands. We stood among the dead who were lying in this area of No Man's Land and we marveled at all the troops who seemed to appear. . . .

Soon conversations were going; then men began exchanging souvenirs. "It was Fritz here and Tommy there," and the disappearance of tension created the atmosphere of a grotesque fair. "It gave us," Jünger recalled, "an inkling of the happiness and purity implied in the word *peace*. It did not seem unthinkable that some day the best men of all nations would come up from the trenches because of sudden impulse and moral insight to clasp each other by the hand and to be finally reconciled as children who had been fighting." But as rain gave way to sunlight the situation grew awkward, and men withdrew into their own zones to renew the struggle.

Spontaneous truces were most likely to occur in bad weather, and men emerging from flooded trenches often were not shot at by the other side even when orders to fire were in effect. During the winter of 1916–17 the 7th London Territorial Battalion reacted to the terrible cold by lighting fires at night in their trenches and openly moving about on their parapets to keep warm. On the other side the Germans ignored the British and lit their own fires, and the shooting did not begin again until a visiting British brigadier insisted that the war continue. Burial truces were other opportunities for stopping the shooting, and were often initiated locally despite orders to the contrary. There was always the concern that the cease-fire might be used unscrupulously by the other side—perhaps also that the truce might spread out of control.

The best known of the cease-fires had been the earliest, when on Christmas Day 1914, Germans, English, and French, without prior negotiation, left their trenches all along the 475 miles of the line to meet in no-man's-land and exchange drink, food, cigarettes, even addresses back home. A company from the 2nd Battalion, Lancashire Fusiliers, even played football with a unit from Saxony, winning 3–2. An officer of the London Rifle Brigade found the Germans "really magnificent in the whole thing, and jolly good sorts." Another officer, finding Scots, English, Prussians, and Württembergers showing each other photos of their families and singing Christmas songs, declared the scene "absolutely astounding. . . . If I had seen it on a cinematograph film I should have sworn it was faked." General Sir John French was appalled at the apparent disintegration of the "fighting spirit," writing that he had been informed of "unarmed men running from the German trenches across to ours holding Christmas trees above their heads. . . . I issued immediate orders to prevent any recurrence of such conduct, and called the local commanders to strict account." The next Christmas, to prevent "slackness" in discipline, the British command ordered a slow, continuing artillery barrage through the day.

Every spontaneous truce meant a loss of command control over the war, and at least once the war nearly ended one-sidedly at Verdun. Casualties had been so ghastly by early May in 1917 that whole divisions mutinied. What the French later called "collective indiscipline" would spread to fifty-four divisions—half the French Army—and would be suppressed in the newspapers and suppressed brutally in the line. In *A Fable* (1954) William Faulkner would invent, perhaps based upon Verdun, a surrealistic vision of an uncalled armistice in May 1918—"that curious week's holiday which the war had taken which had been so false that they remembered it only as a phenomenon." In the novel a French regiment, on a Monday morning, refuses to carry out a suicidal attack; the reaction becomes so contagious, that by Tuesday evening all gunfire in France on both sides stops in an impromptu recess in the war. Like the actual French mutiny, Faulkner's Passion Week fable ends with brutal punishment of the peacemakers, and the bloodletting resumes.

Reports that an armistice was at hand, or had flickered briefly somewhere and vanished, surfaced with the ebb and flow of hope. One version concerned three priests—two younger ones and a frail, elderly prelate—who had used a *laissez-passer* to make their way into the silent limbo beyond the last French post. "Please," said the old man to the curious soldiers huddled in the zigzag trench, "please, my children, let me pass." He unfastened his muffler and greatcoat; recognizing him, a gaping *poilu* jumped aside as the little man walked to the fire step and mounted the ladder.

"*C'est le Pape!*" the other soldiers cried when they beheld the white soutane. "*Le Pape!*"

"Yes, I am the Pope, my children." His voice switched in pitch as he stood atop the parapet, exposed to enemy fire. "In the name of Christ, I call upon you; let there be peace! Peace! *Friede!*" He tore the crucifix from his breast and held it high.

"The war is over!" he insisted in French and then in German. "*La guerre est finie! Der Krieg is beendigt.* I declare peace on earth for all, for everyone, in the name of Jesus Christ!"

In the suddenly mistless early morning light men knelt at his feet, officers and soldiers, friend with enemy. They kissed the tatters of his cassock, torn by barbed wire. "*Pater noster,*" cried the Holy Father in the sudden hush, "Hallowed be Thy Name . . . Thy Kingdom come . . ." A babble of voices took up the prayer in French, in German, in Breton, in Flemish, in the Bavarian dialect. "Thy will be done on earth as it is in heaven . . ."

Suddenly the Pope fell silent. He clutched at his throat and fell backward. The tall young priest who had followed him out of the trenches caught the limp figure in his arms and carried him down into the trench. Machine guns rattled. The men who had gathered had already vanished. A *Minenwerfer* projectile exploded, throwing up an old man's shoe and burying it under a shower of mud.

Had Benedict XV slipped out of the Vatican? Had there been a false Pope, or an aborted peace? Whatever it appeared to be, it existed only in the hopes of men who saw nothing less than a miracle as the way out of a war that seemed to have no end. Yet even the wish ended badly—another black flare into the long night.

Another myth of no-man's-land suggested that the war would end when the bands of cellar-pale, hoary-bearded deserters and escaped prisoners who allegedly lived in underground lairs between the lines were forced to emerge after the stalemate which sheltered them had evaporated. For four years a shifting desolation barely fifty yards wide wound from the Channel coast through Belgium inland to the French frontier with Switzerland, bounded by barbed wire and a maze of trenches. After each of the inconclusive but bloody battles, it was whispered, long-missing men issued forth— Australians, Canadians, Germans, Austrians, English, and French in a bandit league of horror—to rob the dying and the dead. Both commands would have to order the ghouls gassed when the shooting stopped. Among the moldering dead their inhuman cries (so soldiers believed) mingled with the snarling of carrion dogs. Once, a tale went, a French unit at Fresnes had put out as a trap a basket of food, tobacco, and whiskey, but the next morning found the bait unsampled. A note in the basket was alleged to have read, "Nothing doing!" Since the war would never end, they had no need of supplies: the dead and dying would continue to provide.

As the war ground on, a story by a London rifle brigade officer appeared in the September 1918 issue of the popular English monthly *The Strand.* Britten Austin's "Peace" foresaw a field in Flanders where American troops were poised for the signal to advance. Across the silent trenches a still-tough German unit was dug in. The hammer tap of a machine gun, the crack of a rifle shot, the whine of an arcing shell "left no register on their consciousness; they were part of their habitual environment, as normal as the song of birds to the ploughman." It was dusk; the first stars were emerging in the moonless sky when a flare went up across the line, then died away. In the stillness which followed, men waited for the artillery barrage which the flare usually signaled, but heard only a murmur of voices at the far end of their communication trench.

A runner from battalion headquarters, brandishing a message as if he knew its contents, came into view. Seizing the folded sheet, the *Leutnant* tore it open and flashed his lamp upon it cautiously. "PEACE! PEACE!" he read aloud. "All offensive operations are cancelled. It's all over!" His laugh was vacuous, as if his mind had gone. "The war is over! Peace is signed! Do you hear?" His voice rose wildly, and the men stared at him. Then, pulling himself together, he reassumed the disciplined tone of authority.

"Sergeant, the sentries will be posted as usual. No man is to be allowed out of the trenches. No shot is to be fired except under the direct orders of an officer. . . . The strictest discipline will be maintained in your section."

"*Zu Befehl, Herr Leutnant,*" the sergeant acknowledged, saluting.

Then he stared after the officer, who was hurrying around the traverse of the trench. "So!" he said, turning to his men.

No one spoke. They gazed into the sudden silence which had spread across the enemy trenches. Through the night "not a gun spoke. . . . *They had heard the last shell.* The memory of its sear across the dark sky was suddenly vivid in them with its full significance— *the last!*"

Digging into their stores, the Germans illuminated the night sky with soaring white flares. Cheers rose and fell with each, but with the other side strangely quiet, the Germans spent the hours of waiting in anxiety that something had gone wrong. Finally a German soldier, seizing a megaphone, shouted into the stillness, "Hi! You Americans! It's Peace! Peace!"

A megaphoned reply boomed back hollowly, "We know. We won't hurt you!" But then came further silence, until, in the approaching dawn, slouch-hatted Americans emerged to retrieve their dead. Leaving weapons behind, the Germans cut through their own barbed wire and streamed out to find their own casualties, sensing, in their first moments in the open, the strangeness of silence and unthreatening exposure. The war was over, not only for the dead, but for the living.

The end would not come quite that way, yet the storyteller was a better prophet than the generals. By the time that "Peace" appeared in print, some sort of conclusion hovered in the near distance. Aware that they had already lost the war, the Germans hoped only that dragging it on might gain them more palatable armistice terms. Allied forces assumed that it would still take a spring offensive in 1919 to defeat an adversary still everywhere on captured soil.

Perhaps the only soldier who was certain he knew when the shooting would stop was Gunner John Thomson of the Seaforth Highlanders, a Scot from Penicuik. Exhausted after a heavy shelling in July 1918 on the Ypres front, Thomson had fallen asleep, he claimed, when an apparition cloaked in black appeared before him and told him not to worry. All would go well for him and the war would end on the eleventh day of the eleventh month. On awakening he made the mistake of confiding in the men in his battery. They reacted with banter, yet began to lay bets on the prophecy. In his next letter home he mentioned his experience. In Thomson's small town of casualty-stricken homes south of Edinburgh, where the Cowan Institute tower was blacked out and the parish church clock had not pealed the hours for four years, no one took the vision seriously.

That the war would indeed end on the eleventh day of the eleventh month, and on the eleventh hour at that, has teased the imagination since. Occultist Aleister Crowley even claimed that his magical *Book of the Law* forecast the date and time, and he established an intricate juxtaposition of Greek, Hebrew, Tarot cards, and numerology which, he observed confidently, "ought to suffice the most sceptical." Some parts of the world still mark the day and hour solemnly, and in his 1979 novel of a Nazi-occupied Britain in a later World War, *SS-GB,* Len Deighton begins page one with a Scotland Yard puppet official stamping a document "11 Nov. 1941." The date retains its resonance, but in the months before that memorable November it was universally accepted that the war would never end, except for the individual soldier who "went west" (or "under"), or who received "a nice blighty one." *Blighty* was an all-purpose word. Capitalized, it was the paradise of one's former existence in an England now nostalgically unreal; uncapitalized, it was the fortunate wound which did not maim but which was sufficient to cause one's evacuation home. (As an adjective it was a general expression of approval, even of the ideal.) Without the good fortune of a nice blighty one, a soldier might expect to be in the line forever, as cartoonist Bruce Bairnsfather suggested in his "A.D. Nineteen Fifty," in which two soldiers with Rip Van Winkle beards muse over a newspaper while shells scream over their trench. "I see the War Babies' Battalion is a coming out." There was even deeper resignation in a caption in which his war-weary "Ole Bill" is asked how long he is "up for."

"Seven years," sighs Bill.

"You're lucky," says the other. "I'm duration."

THE FALSE ARMISTICE

As they followed after George,
At dear old Valley Forge,
Our boys will break that line.
It's for your land and my land
And the sake of Auld Lang Syne,
Just like Washington crossed the Delaware,
General Pershing will cross the Rhine.

—1918 SONG BY HOWARD JOHNSON
AND GEORGE MEYER

From Ypres in Flanders to St. Mihiel in Lorraine, German machine gunners and artillerymen were staving off the end by little more than a stubborn refusal to concede defeat. Also, their lines had shortened, while the devastation of the countryside made Allied resupply difficult; and a combination of natural forces, from rain and fog to mud, forest, and river, further slowed the advance. The outcome, however, was not in doubt. In the name of the High Command, Field Marshal Paul von Hindenburg had appealed to Berlin for "an immediate peace offer." It was urgent, he explained, "to break off the struggle in order to spare the German people . . . useless sacrifices. Every day's delay will cost thousands of brave soldiers their lives."

A peace government headed by Prince Max ("Max Pax") of Baden had taken office late in October, leading to the dismissal of the architect of thwarted victory, General Erich Ludendorff. Once he had been virtual dictator of Germany; now he kept out of sight—and out of mind, he hoped—in a flat in Berlin. Even the Kaiser realized, early in November, that his throne hung on the thread of an immediate armistice, and when Prince Max—his cousin—pleaded for sufficient time to prepare the people for defeat, Wilhelm answered stiffly, "The Supreme Command requests it, and you have not been brought here to make difficulties. . . ."

To survey what lines might be held through the approaching winter, Wilhelm Groener, who had been on the Russian front until he suddenly succeeded Ludendorff as First Quartermaster General, had made a hurried visit to the crumbling front. Looking more like a businessman than a general, despite his long officer's greatcoat, he commanded respect rather than the awe to which his predecessor had been accustomed. But Groener knew how and when to cut his losses. Only in Alsace, German just since 1870, had the Fatherland been penetrated. Although everywhere to the north his troops still held precariously to French and Belgian soil, he knew why he had been called upon to replace the legendary tactician. Groener was a transportation specialist. Someone would have to organize a massive withdrawal, in peace or war.

Hardly had he arrived when the lines in the north began to crack, leaving Germany, he knew, soon to be as helpless on the Western Front as it was becoming within. He raced back to Spa—the Kaiser's headquarters in Belgium—with the dread but not unexpected news. The Kaiser was even there. To insulate Wilhelm from pressures to abdicate, his entourage had rushed him to the *kaisertreu* atmosphere of Spa on October 29. There, the cautious and elderly

Hindenburg, Groener's only military superior, was deaf to the rising clamor for abdication. "What will the Kaiser Do?" the Berlin *Vorvarts* had already asked on its front page. Loyally, Hindenburg ignored the inevitable, persuading Groener that the person of the Kaiser was all that stood between order and anarchy. Still, admitting that the Army was defeated, and that all that remained unsettled was the extent of the catastrophe, he sent Groener to Berlin. It was Tuesday, November 5.

To Prince Max's cabinet, Groener first reported Hindenburg's views—that the Field Marshal "would look on himself as a scoundrel if he deserted the Kaiser." Then Groener added, "Gentlemen, I think the same and so do all other honorable soldiers. . . . If the agitation against the Kaiser does not cease, the fate of the Army is sealed. It will fall apart. The wild beast in man will break out in the disorganized groups of soldiers pouring back into the Homeland." Nevertheless Groener knew that the Allies would never negotiate with a government headed by Wilhelm II. Groener and the Cabinet also knew that the previous Sunday, Admiral Reinhard von Scheer, with the watchwords "Vanquish or perish honorably," had ordered the fleet into the North Sea to give battle rather than surrender their ships. A "death ride" for the sake of a slogan failed to rally men tired of war. Mutinying, many crews murdered their officers and raised red flags from the gaffs of ships at Kiel and Wilhelmshaven. Revolutionary feeling had been smoldering, and the reaction ignited a movement. Rebel sailors took trains southward and fanned out through Germany, visible symbols of discipline giving way to disintegration.

Germany's allies, rotting anachronisms less a bulwark than a burden, had already crumbled. Once a sprawling, still-feudal empire, Turkey had quit the war on October 30. Austria, with its old domains breaking away through nationalist risings, had sued for peace on November 3. The armistice terms forced on the former dual monarchy, said *The Times* of London on November 5, "leave her disarmed and helpless, and place her territory, her communications and many of her resources at our disposal for the prosecution of the war against her late ally. They may be assumed to foreshadow the nature of the terms on which the allies will grant an armistice to Germany when that Power makes up its mind to sue for one."

By Wednesday the sixth, the Kaiser was telegraphing Groener in Berlin to urge that the Army approach the enemy about armistice conditions. Consulting Prince Max, Groener agreed that they "must cross the lines with a white flag."

"But not for a week, at least," urged Prince Max, hoping for a miracle in the interim.

"A week is too long a time."

"But still, not before Monday," the Chancellor pleaded. By the eleventh, Max hoped, some new pressure might be brought upon the enemy to ease what were expected to be harsh armistice terms.

"Even that is too long to wait," said Groener. "Saturday is the very latest."

At a meeting of the Cabinet the Quartermaster General explained the urgency of a quick cease-fire. "I too had hoped that we could wait eight or ten days, until we had established ourselves in a new line. After all I have found out about Kiel, the Tyrol, and morale at home, particularly in Bavaria, with its far-reaching political consequences, I am convinced that we must take the step, however painful it is, and ask Foch."

The authorities in Berlin would have been horrified had they known how easy it had been to make a revolution in conservative Bavaria. Everyone was weary of privation and of mourning, and the climate of defeat paralyzed the will. The catalyst had been a war-protesting drama critic, who with his wild hair and beard, and unkempt clothes, was the caricature of a Bohemian coffeehouse Bolshevist. Kurt Eisner easily worked up the disillusioned Munich crowds, inevitably including radical sailors, to march on local barracks, each of which immediately hoisted red flags. Ousting the flabby Wittelsbach dynasty proved even easier. The figurehead Ludwig III (all real decisions came from Berlin) had few enemies, and even fewer friends. While he was strolling in the English Gardens a passerby told him that his life might be in danger. By the time Ludwig returned to his palace, the grounds were packed with people demanding his abdication. Unobtrusively, he strolled to the back entrance, retrieved his ailing queen and four princesses, salvaged a box of his favorite cigars, and begged a ride from a passing car. *"Macht euch euren Dreck allein!"* ("Take care of your own filth now!") he was reported to have shouted at the mob. By the time the car ran off the road into a potato field in the twilight fog, Eisner had been acclaimed Chairman of the Workers' and Soldiers' Council in the Parliament building, which his supporters had managed to get the custodian to reopen. A Bavarian Republic was proclaimed, and the next morning people went about their business as if Ludwig III had never existed.

In a Munich suburb novelist Thomas Mann, throughout the war an apologist for Imperial Germany, noted in his diary that whether Ludwig had escaped was unclear, but that the city was quiet. Having married into a prominent Jewish family, he was anxious. "Munich as well as the rest of Bavaria is being governed by Jewish scribblers. How long is it going to put up with this situation? . . . The main actors on this stage are almost exclusively Jews." In Mann's *Doctor Faustus* (1947), related by its narrator in the closing months of the 1939–45 war, but about the parallel period in the 1914–18 war, the comparisons are deliberate. There the fictional Serenus Zeitblom echoes the carefully laundered memories of Mann. "If I were a novel-writer," Zeitblom claims, he could make a "most lively picture" out of his "tortured recollections." And he does, evoking the naive and futile Munich revolution "misbegotten" by "lunatics, dreamers, clowns, flibbertigibbets and fly-by-nights, plotters and small-time philosophers."

In Berlin, General Groener hesitated revealing to a coalition Cabinet which included Socialists and republicans that he needed an armistice in order to march the Army home to extinguish the flames of radicalism and revolution. He could only carry on the struggle, he explained, if Germany withdrew behind the Rhine, giving up great chunks of the Homeland. To bargain for peace, however, meant preventing, in the interim, a general collapse of the front. That meant initiating talks no later than Friday, November 8—which required that an armistice delegation leave Berlin within hours. Just before noon on Wednesday the Cabinet approved the decision unanimously. The High Command in Spa quickly seconded it.

Rightly or wrongly, said Social Democrat leader Friedrich Ebert before the meeting broke up, the people held the Kaiser responsible. He would have to go by Thursday at the latest, especially if the enemy were to take the peace offer seriously. One of his younger sons could become nominal head of state. "The Crown Prince is now impossible," Ebert insisted, "because he is too much hated by the masses." Someone, Ebert's SPD colleague Philipp Scheidemann added, must convince His Majesty to "draw the consequences of defeat."

Depriving the Army of its Supreme War Lord, Groener insisted, was unthinkable. The discussion bogged down in theoretical issues about monarchy until Scheidemann returned from the telephone. Shaken, he told the others, "The abdication is no longer a matter for discussion. The revolution is spreading. Sailors from Kiel have taken control in Hamburg and Hanover also. Gentlemen, this is not the time for further discussion; it is time to act. We do not know whether we will be sitting in these chairs tomorrow."

Although a Socialist, Ebert pressed Groener to arrange for the succession of one of the Kaiser's sons. Groener refused. He had been authorized to declare that all the princes had taken pledges to refuse the throne if their father were forced to give it up. "Under these circumstances," sighed Ebert, "there is no point to further discussion. Events must now take their own course." Turning to Groener, Ebert added, "We thank you for these frank words, and will always remember with pleasure our work with you during the war. From now on we go our separate ways and who knows whether we shall ever see each other again." With that the meeting adjourned.

News of the armistice mission would come as no surprise at home. It was well known that messages about peace, barely concealing German desperation, had been exchanged by Prince Max with President Wilson. Cautiously, he had relayed them to France and then informed Berlin that Marshal Ferdinand Foch would receive, under prearranged conditions, "properly accredited representatives." Unaware of the extent of the German collapse, however, Foch had become extremely cautious about German intentions. Few Allied leaders trusted anything emanating from Berlin or Spa, and suspected some trickery which would furnish the enemy with the pause it needed without any subsequent peace. Fewer, still, accepted the possibility of a revolution in Germany which would be more than a facade to permit peace overtures. Revolution seemed contrary to traditional Teutonic discipline.

If even a brief pause in the fighting came, Foch could not be sure that the exhausted French could be brought up to fighting pitch once more. Further, the Americans replacing them were inexperienced. As a result, on November 7, once German approaches had been made, American commander John Pershing received a message from him: "It can happen that the enemy may spread rumors that an armistice is signed in order to deceive us. There is nothing in it. Let no one cease hostilities of any sort without information from the Commander-in-Chief." If the Germans could lull them into hoping too much, Foch worried, the Allies might relax the pressure as well as the price.

That Thursday, as the semiofficial Wolff Telegraph Agency in Berlin carried the news of the departure of an armistice commission, the *Rapide* from Paris arrived at nine in the morning at Brest, chief Atlantic port for American troops and supplies. Getting off the train

en route home was Roy W. Howard, the mustached, youngish head
of United Press. As a Very Important Personage he was met by
Lieutenant Arthur Hornblow, Jr., intelligence officer on the staff of
the AEF commandant at Brest. Later an eminent Broadway and
Hollywood producer for forty years and the host, with his wife,
Myrna Loy, of legendary parties, Hornblow would never produce a
spectacle to match the event he would help spawn that day, and
never preside over a party as emotional as the one he would attend
that evening.

Since Howard was due to sail for New York at two, he had little
time, he explained to Hornblow. On shipboard there would be too
much time—two weeks. "I'd like to make better speed if possible.
Want to catch President Wilson in time to come over here again in
his party." Impressed by Howard's inside information, Hornblow
went to a telephone and quickly arranged for alternative passage the
next day on the much faster *Leviathan*—the seized former *Vaterland.*
Howard could save a week by waiting a day. Then came the matter
of killing time advantageously. Howard suggested dropping in on
Rear Admiral Henry B. Wilson, American Naval chief in the area,
and Hornblow agreed. They turned from the rue du Château into
the renamed Place du President Wilson, and saw an excited crowd
in front of the offices of the Brest daily, *La Dépêche*, examining a bulletin. It was the Wolff Agency dispatch. Rumors seeped through the
bystanders that an armistice had already been signed, but the
Americans could get no corroboration in the newspaper office. Still,
Howard was a welcome guest: United Press used the *La Dépêche* lines
from Paris to the Brest cable center for American transmission.

In Brest harbor, an old, roach-infested freighter rechristened
the U.S.S. *Kermoor* only seven days earlier, arrived from Wales with a
cargo of coal. A launch filled with French sailors approached, all
wildly waving tassled caps. *"Finie la guerre!"* they yelled. Ship whistles blew, American sailor William Seuter remembered, and guns
boomed and echoed. It sounded authentic.

Roy Howard had cabled the beat to America. With Admiral
Wilson's aide, Ensign Sellards, Howard had rushed to the *postes,* but,
en route, to make sure that his message would not be garbled by a
French cable operator, he decided to type it out. The best place for
that was the nearby telegraph room of *La Dépêche*, where he explained what he wanted. The excited telegraphist offered to type it
himself, and using his own instrument he tapped out the few historic
sentences, then tore off the tape, pasting it helpfully on a cable form.
When Howard then filed it, the message looked exactly as if it had

been transmitted from Paris, where all UP cables were censored before being wired further. But wasn't the news official? Hadn't the
message been shown to Howard by the admiral, with the comment
that here was something which might possibly interest him?

Once Admiral Wilson had an aide post a copy of the message in
the square, where the Navy band was presenting its weekly concert
that afternoon, shouts of rejoicing began surging through Hornblow's window. Then Howard himself materialized in Hornblow's
office with his copy of the greatest scoop of the war, the cable to
United Press in New York:

URGENT. ARMISTICE ALLIES GERMANS SIGNED ELEVEN
[THI]SMORNING HOSTILITIES CEASED TWO [THI]SAFTERNOON.
SEDAN TAKEN [THI]SMORNING BY AMERICANS.

It was signed "Howard-Simms." Simms was the UP man in Paris,
and Howard had graciously added his name to let him share in the
beat. But adding his colleague's name inadvertently speeded the
message through the cable office and the naval censor in Brest, for it
was assumed to be a message originating in Paris. When it was
turned into press copy in New York it read so officially:

PARIS, NOV. 7.—The Allies and Germany signed an armistice at 11 o'clock this morning. Hostilities ceased at 2
o'clock this afternoon.
    The Americans took Sedan before the armistice be-
came effective.

"My cable will get there in time to catch the afternoon editions," Howard said, counting confidently on the five-hour difference in time. "There's a day in history for you!" Less confidently,
Hornblow wondered to himself why American intelligence in Paris
hadn't independently informed his outpost in Brest.

With Howard still in the office, Hornblow telephoned Paris to
check. Sounds of celebration spilling through his windows filtered
over the wires to Paris as he listened to his colleague's astonishment
and denials. No such news had reached Paris—nothing more than
that enemy emissaries were scheduled to meet Marshal Foch that
afternoon at five. Howard's confidence was unshaken. Probably the
embassy received the news before military intelligence. His beat was
all the bigger. No newsman in Paris seemed to have had it.

That evening a military party which Howard and Hornblow

joined floated off for supper to La Brasserie de la Marine amid a pandemonium of gaiety. Everywhere the doughboy phrase *finie la guerre* rang out; the brasserie was festive with confetti, streamers, and flags; two pretty girls danced on a narrow table, cheered on by their Yankee escorts; nearby a French officer, nearly incoherent with champagne, exhorted the unlistening crowd not to stop the war. Then overcome more by alcohol than by emotion, he began weeping into his tablecloth. Ignoring him, the crowd rose and sang the *"Marseillaise."*

Hornblow had left word to have any wire from Paris delivered to him wherever he was, and through the chaos he saw a Signal Corps orderly making for his table. "A feeling of chilling apprehension seized me as I grasped and opened the message. . . . I felt Howard's eye on me as I read. . . ." The message was from his superior in Paris, Major Robertson, and had to be sight-translated slowly from its code:

> Armistice report untrue. War Ministry issues absolute denial and declares enemy plenipotentiaries to be still on way through lines. Cannot meet Foch until evening. Wire full details of local hoax immediately.

It was not a "local hoax," although Howard would be widely blamed, and in anticipation he spent the night trying to get information from his Paris office to explain how his beat had turned sour. One fact appeared certain: for most people the news had emanated from the American Embassy. Early that afternoon, *Saturday Evening Post* correspondent Will Irwin, for example, had met a British Army nurse he knew, Kathleen Burke, on the rue Scribe, near the American Express Office. "Heard the good news?" she challenged.

"What news?" he asked. And she reported that she had just come from the American Embassy, where it had been announced that an armistice had been signed at eleven that morning, to take effect at 3:00 P.M.

"No kidding!"

"No kidding," she insisted. "They got the news by telephone only twenty minutes ago." Joyfully, Irwin kissed Miss Burke and hurried on; overtaking an Australian officer, he took the officer's arm and told him the news. The closest bar was the Café de la Paix, where they stopped for a drink and, in the tradition of great occasions, exchanged hats. Having spread the news, they moved to Ciro's for another drink and to pass along the glad tidings. Then it was Harry's New York Bar in the rue Danou, where they shouted, "The war's over! Everyone have a drink!" Men in assorted uniforms, and two Red Cross girls, joined in singing songs which progressed from "Pack Up Your Troubles in Your Old Kit Bag" to "Mademoiselle from Armentières, Parley Voo." The Red Cross girls exchanged hats with a lieutenant and a corporal. Yet outside, Parisians remained so calm that Irwin decided to check with the American Embassy himself. A clerk answered and said that the announcement was a mistake. Someone had telephoned the embassy and identified himself as a high official at the Foreign Ministry, but the news he offered had not checked out.

Irwin put down the telephone and made amends for the news with another round of drinks. Exchanging hats, he and the Australian then went their separate ways. But Paris was still full of the rumor. A boy, aged seventeen and certain to be called up soon if the war went on, was walking through the Tuileries Gardens when a man dashed by shouting, "The Armistice has been signed!" The happy teen-ager was André Malraux. His first brush with history would be a false one.

That the armistice report was premature would take a long time to filter down to others all over France who had begun celebrating. At the British base in the north of France where former balloonist and parachutist Elizabeth ("Dolly") Shepherd was a WAAC automobile driver for an officer she would later marry, soldiers left their posts and hurried to the messes, carrying Dolly and other WAACs on their shoulders. While the lower ranks were making merry, four Scottish officers requisitioned her to drive them to whatever drinking places were open. When they failed to reappear, Dolly went looking for them. "I remember those men," she recalled many years later, "lying in the road."

Gassed and restricted to noncombat duty, Lieutenant John Boynton Priestley, a ruddy Yorkshireman, had been sent to a factory building on a back street in Rouen, where a dapper colonel who was all English gentleman and had never heard a shot fired in anger officered the Labour Corps Depot. The building, the future playwright and novelist discovered, was "a lunatic labour exchange. There we had only to receive, in correct triplicate, an indent for any form of labour, and we would supply it. Entertainers were our favourite commodity." The sergeants were "real professional soldiers" intent upon polished brass buttons and rigid salutes, "waiting for this monstrous amateur affair, this bloodthirsty melodrama of bomber bank clerks and machine-gunner gardeners, to blow itself to pieces." During dinner, an elaborate affair foreign to Priestley, "a report came of an armistice, and the little colonel bought us all champagne on the strength of it, and was furious when the report was denied." Listlessly, the men returned to the "mad factory" to furnish comedians, conjurers, and female impersonators to the rear areas. The troops doing the fighting had no time for such entertainment. They were still chasing Germans and wondering what the armistice reports meant, since they could see and hear that the war was not over.

"The news is good," American cartoonist Will Judy, then a field clerk with the 33rd Division, wrote in his diary. "Frenchmen pass along the streets shouting *'Finis le guerre, pas encore'*" ("The war is ended—never again"). Closer to the action at Bellenglise, just north of St. Quentin, British Lieutenant John Ventham, with the 168th Brigade Royal Field Artillery, had just been ordered to the 1st Battalion of the Dorset Regiment as forward observer to check covering fire for troops about to cross the Sambre-Oise Canal. As he set off with two signalers, his battery commander said, "I'd better tell you the latest rumour. Back at Divisional Hq. where they have a small wireless receiving set, they have picked up some Morse signals in French which give good reason to believe that an armistice is being arranged between the German High Command and our own through contacts in Switzerland. It even mentioned a point at which the German plenipotentiaries would probably cross the Allied lines—not too far from the 32nd Division front." The rumor, Ventham considered, was "really not [one] to take with me to the Dorsets." Nevertheless, stories such as the one he had heard abounded, causing premature celebrations and a relaxation of interest in being the last soldier maimed or killed. When Ventham reported to a Dorset company commander, Captain W. F. Lipscomb, who was sitting in a small cellar beneath a pile of rubble which had once been a house, his feet resting on bricks which kept him above the two inches of water which covered the floor, he could not resist passing along the rumor of an armistice. Lipscomb's laugh sounded hollow in the bare cellar. "Could anything be funnier?" he said. "My last subaltern has just gone sick; I have only half my company left; a sapper officer has just been here to tell me that all our petrol-tin rafts have been sunk by gunfire and I've got to make an attack at 7 o'clock tomorrow. And now you come to tell me that the war is going to finish! What a dream! Will it make any difference to what happens tomorrow?"

In some cases it would make a difference. The "Buckeye" U.S. Division—former Ohio National Guard troops augmented with other reserves, including a skinny sixteen-year-old from Oakdale, Nebraska, named Darryl Zanuck—was about to go into action along the Lys-Schelde Canal, then less a waterway than a muddy trench into which the withdrawing Germans had abandoned vehicles and guns. They had trained through the summer for the drive to Berlin, learning how to fire French weapons and flee French brothels. Some, Zanuck among them, were eager to kill Huns. He had lied about his age and drunk quarts of water to get his weight up for enlistment at fifteen. It seemed his big chance for fame. But just after the orders came to advance, they were countermanded by news of an armistice. It would prove false, but the division would remain in place. To his further frustration, back home his friends, still in high school, "had long since got bored with the war." Zanuck would live the shooting of Huns vicariously eight years later, writing the screenplay in Hollywood for Bruce Bairnsfather's comedy *The Better 'Ole.*

At Evacuation Hospital No. 8, at Petit Maujoy, six miles from Verdun, Frederick Pottle, a ward attendant (in hip boots, in the mud) later to edit James Boswell's papers for Yale, noted in his diary for November 7, "Heard from an official source of Germany's surrender." And in his diary the next day he added, confidently, "Officially confirmed." In the American lines in the Argonne Forest, the 309th Infantry Regiment of the 78th Division, pursuing the Germans toward Metz, heard similar news. Now miles from the rapidly changing front after being in action for two months, they were able to light comforting fires every few feet when they settled down to rest; but then came the unexpected sounds of firing, and shouts that the war was over. Sergeant Joe Latta of the Signal Platoon in Headquarters Company ran to his stock of "Chenille" signal rockets, large devices which ejected flares of various colors according to a prearranged code. But to get into the celebration quickly the arming of the rockets had to be improvised. After one malfunctioned and grazed the cook shack, and others wobbled up erratically, they switched to safer signal grenades, firing off their entire supply. Then they discovered that the war was still on.

In England reports of an armistice were greeted at command level with skepticism, but the news seeped into military camps and bases anyway. At the RAF Observer School in Manston, in Kent, troops at the aerodrome refused to take further orders and broke into the canteen, carting away pails of beer to drink in their huts. The next morning a parade would be called, with the commanding officer reminding the still unruly troops that no armistice had been signed and that they were to "behave themselves like men and not like beasts." In the Scottish evening papers which arrived in Penicuik late on the seventh was a report that a cease-fire had been signed earlier in the day. It was not taken seriously.

Premature reports of an armistice would disrupt staid English classrooms even where discipline had long held priority over learning. In Ford Madox Ford's novel *Parade's End,* physical instructress Valentine Wannop recalls the false alarm and the horror of the headmistress when the six hundred girls in the "Great Public School" abandon decorum and even begin to sing, unladylike,

> *Hang Kaiser Bill from the hoary apple tree*
> *And Glory, Glory, Glory till it's tea-time!*

Miss Wanostrocht had to chasten the girls. When the Great Moment truly came, she cautioned, it would not be a triumph, it would only be a cessation of hostilities. "It was their province as the future mothers of England . . . to go on with their home-lessons and not run about the streets with effigies of the Great Defeated! . . . It was their function to shed further light of womanly culture." Valentine, "for a mutinous moment," wanted to feel real triumph, but understood what was frightening the caste system which the headmistress symbolized. "If, at this parting of the ways, at this crack across the table of History, the School—the World, the future mothers of Europe— got out of hand, would they ever come back? The Authorities—Authority all over the world—was afraid of that. . . . Wasn't it a possibility that there was to be no more Respect?"

Even in more distant places armistice reports triggered wild celebrations. One raised cheering crowds in nonbelligerent Havana, Cuba. In the Argentine capital of Buenos Aires, where a junior officer on the British East India Company freighter *Omara* was preparing a shipment of mules for Army use, the populace took to the streets, but because of the large German population in the city it divided into two flag-waving factions. Cadet Ivor Lawrence remembered joining the pro-Allied procession going north on the Avenida de Mayo. Eventually it met the pro-German peace vanguard going south, and pent-up enmities flared. Lawrence and the other cadets from the *Omara*, with several nurses in tow, slipped into a side street, conducted the young women home, and rejoined their ship. Soon the ship's carpenters would begin dismantling the mule stables below decks, to prepare the holds for a substitute shipment of wheat, "a clear case," Lawrence thought, "of swords into plowshares."

In Australia, across the international date line, the news reached Sydney early on the morning of the eighth, as people were making their way to work. Trams, trains, and ferries exploded with joyous shop assistants, clerks, and factory hands, and the harbor shook with the cacophony of whistles, sirens, and hooters. City streets quickly clogged, and by noon the Minister for Education had issued a belated proclamation closing schools already emptied. Class barriers collapsed, with sedate businessmen parading noisily with clerks and secretaries, none of them very sober despite the early hour. At the Central Police Court the presiding magistrate celebrated by discharging, without hearings, the previous night's collection of drunks. At two that afternoon city authorities closed all places where alcoholic beverages could be served, but the carnival atmosphere persisted even as posters began appearing at newspaper kiosks that the happy news was false. An effigy of the Kaiser was burned, and the hysteria continued into the warm spring night.

The news was received at the Western Union cable office at 16 Broad Street in New York at 11:56 A.M. By 11:59 it had reached United Press offices on the third floor of the Pulitzer Building in City Hall Square. Seconds later the bulletin was on the UP wire, spreading across the continent.

On a Washington, D.C., streetcar with several friends was Evelyn Mae Shipman, who worked in the Aviation Section of the Signal Corps. A few blocks beyond Pennsylvania Station it seemed to her "as if everyone in the whole United States had suddenly dropped on Washington. The streetcar couldn't move because of the mass of humanity, so we got out and joined the wild, screaming mob—dancing, hugging and kissing everyone else." Eventually they found a taxi and squeezed into it to careen into the night, not discovering until the meter had escalated enormously that the armistice was yet to be signed.

Sitting at her sewing in a sun-flooded room, Ellen Slayden, wife of a Texas congressman, heard the whistles and sirens above the clatter of her treadle machine. "Could they be peace whistles?" her maid, Annie, asked. The phone rang. It was her friend Mrs. Gregg, who had a son in France and another about to go. Her voice quavered. The *Washington Post* had telephoned her husband that the Germans had surrendered. The women cried happily, and as soon as Mrs. Slayden put down her phone it rang again. This time it was Mrs. James Brown Scott to tell her that the surrender was complete: "The Germans had walked into No Man's Land carrying a white flag and surrendered unconditionally."

Eleanor McAdoo, at twenty-nine Woodrow Wilson's youngest daughter, found it a "thrilling adventure" to cross the crowded street between the gray Treasury Building, over which her husband presided, and the White House. Caught in the press of people shouting, singing, and dancing, she was embraced and kissed by an enthusiastic man who had no idea who she was. Entering the White House, she felt "like a chip on the waves." As bands played and crowds shouted for the President, Edith Bolling Wilson, his fortyish second wife, came into his study excitedly and begged him to come to the portico and greet the people. Thin-lipped and unsmiling, he refused. There was no armistice. It was impossible.

Despite her private knowledge that the burgeoning frenzy outside was for nothing, the excited First Lady would write later, "I simply could stand no longer having no part in it. In an open car I picked up Mother and my sister Bertha at the Powhatan Hotel, thinking we would drive down Pennsylvania Avenue and watch the crowds. No sooner was the car recognized than the throngs surged around us. I was glad that I had come out. . . ." But she told no one that the celebrating was premature, and her presence suggested that peace was real.

What Mrs. Wilson also did not realize was that after she had left the White House, her husband, despite his misgivings, emerged outdoors long enough to wave his luncheon napkin at the crowds who were shouting "Wilson! Wilson!" and to show a mouthful of white teeth, and withdraw. The gesture to the frenzied celebrants—the President smiled seldom, and with some strain—added a further credibility which he could not have anticipated. The news that the First Lady and then the President were participants raced through Washington.

War workers and government employees abandoned work, joining soldiers, sailors, and civilians in the streets, singing patriotic songs, waving flags, packing buses and trolley cars, which became impromptu mobile parties. Tin pans, horns, and bells were the most numerous noisemakers, but were drowned out by iron pipes pounded by sailors and laborers from the Washington Navy Yard. Trolley motormen clanged their gongs, and automobile drivers, either because they were trapped in traffic or wanted to contribute to the din, honked their horns without letup. And when nine airplanes from the Army's Langley Field circled the city and performed stunts above the crowd all afternoon, one even returning after dark to do dips and loops in the tracery of searchlights, it appeared that further official sanction was being given to the peace news, despite the lack of confirmation in the press.

With everyone who could possibly be there already in the streets, almost no one was available to listen to Secretary of State Lansing's statement at four that afternoon that the peace report was "not true," and that a reply to an inquiry to Paris, received at 2:04 P.M., confirmed "that the armistice had not yet been signed." At least one Washington bureaucrat who had not heard of the retraction telegraphed to Elizabeth, New Jersey, suspending further work on a million-dollar contract to build dwellings for laborers employed in war work in the district.

In defense of its original report the United Press office in Washington saw "great conjecture in official quarters here tonight as to why there is silence in the capitals of Europe on the signing today of the Armistice between Germany and the Allies. One reason advanced is that Germany asked one condition, namely, that she be permitted to announce the news of her surrender in her own way to her people before it was announced abroad. This, it was pointed out, would enable her to prepare her garrisons and military police forces to oppose the growing Bolshevist movement within her borders." The Germans, the UP added, may have been given as much as twenty-four hours to accomplish the necessary safeguards, which would explain the refusal of Allied sources "to confirm the signing." It was an invention to buy time.

However erroneous, news of the armistice was taking on a life of its own. In Northfield, Vermont, just after four that afternoon, a new second lieutenant, Richard L. Strout, was putting on his jacket to stand retreat with the student corps of cadets at Norwich University when the church bells began "turning somersaults" and the twin whistles in the quarry began to shriek. The two other lieutenants checked in, and then the unit's major, who asked, "Have they signed? Is it over?" The dean appeared in the doorway, imperturbable, white teeth shining through his black mustache. "A telephone call from Montpelier," he announced, "says the United Press declares Germany has signed." It was clear that the telephoned tidings were being spread further along the party line as a farmer began beating his improvised fire alarm, a disk saw hung from a maple tree, and a deeper bong sounded from the next farm higher up. "As the bugle blew and the flag came down at retreat," Strout, the future *Christian Science Monitor* Washington correspondent and "T.R.B" columnist of *The New Republic* remembered, "they unexpectedly fired the old campus cannon, though where they got the powder for this feat, God knows. It didn't explode. We wanted to meet history half way. The tumult of Yankee farmers had climbed into the hills now; the chain of exultation went over the mountain. And in New York, we knew, in Times Square, they would be rejoicing! People would embrace. All over the world."

In New York the UP stood by its first bulletin, which had put extras on the street by 1:00 P.M. What the UP office did not know is that Roy Howard, unable to validate his scoop from sources in Paris, had rushed a second cable warning that his earlier report was unconfirmable. This time the Navy censor had bypassed the UP and sent it directly to the Secretary of the Navy in Washington for handling, leaving the UP still out on its increasingly fragile limb. Having heard nothing further from Howard, UP General Manager Hawkins in New York reaffirmed the original report. "Nothing has been received either from Europe or from Washington," Hawkins said, ignoring Secretary Lansing, "to prove the story anything but true. The fact that nothing more has come from Paris tends to confirm our story, for it shows that the cable lines are crowded with official business. We believe that our Mr. Howard and Mr. Simms were able to slip their brief message, while other news agencies were less fortunate." In truth there had been another, independent report the same afternoon to the British Bureau of Information at 511 Fifth Avenue. It read, "The armistice has been signed and the war is over." It was released with a statement by Lieutenant H. C. T. Walker, a British officer attached to the bureau to oversee an exhibition of naval pictures at the Anderson Galleries. Tracked there by the press, he disclaimed any knowledge of the report, but another officer, Lieutenant Percy, said that he had seen the message in the Fifth Avenue office, and that it left no doubt in his mind that the war was over. The origins of the bulletin were never explained further.

No one in Manhattan seemed to know or care about the du-
biousness of the news being celebrated so lustily into the evening
hours. Offices had emptied quickly, and from Washington Square to
the Plaza Hotel, Fifth Avenue was a crush of humanity. The Stock
Exchange closed at 2:30 P.M., and a shower of ticker tape began
floating down from windows about Wall Street, supplemented by
emptied wastebaskets, shredded newspapers, torn telephone direc-
tories, and unrolled toilet paper. At the Metropolitan Opera a rehearsal of Verdi's *La Forza del Destino* was under way when diva
Geraldine Farrar broke it up by rushing onstage trailing red, white,
and blue streamers. Assorted stagehands, singers, and orchestra
members raised their voices with her in "The Star-Spangled Banner." From an upper floor of the Hotel Knickerbocker, Enrico
Caruso thrust his head out the window to see what the noise was all
about. Hearing that the war was over, he sang his own version of
"The Star-Spangled Banner" while crowds listened raptly below.
When he finished, Caruso was showered with roses and chrysanthemums tossed down from windows even higher up in the Knickerbocker. Hundreds of miles west, the Chicago Opera was in rehearsal
when a Belgian tenor rushed in weeping, "Stop! Stop! Peace has
been declared." The director ordered "The Star-Spangled Banner" sung, and then the anthems of the Allies, after which the rehearsal was adjourned and everyone poured into the street to
celebrate.

New York Mayor John J. Hylan, always ready to address a cap-
tive crowd, mounted the steps of City Hall and announced what he
was already powerless to prevent—that all city employees had been
given a holiday. Most of them were already in the streets, encouraged by a bright sun and blue sky. No one was listening, and
many couples among the mob were busy doing trench glides and
Western Front wiggles. "Be quiet and give His Honor a chance,"
yelled a blue-coated police sergeant.

The mayor praised everyone and everything, all to husky
cheers. Then he retreated to his office to complete plans for a huge
victory parade for that night, which he had announced he would
lead himself. But within half an hour Grover Whalen, his secretary,
emerged to tell waiting newspapermen that in view of conflicting
reports concerning the armistice the parade would not occur. An official procession was unnecessary and very likely would have proved
impossible. Police had already given up all attempts to keep traffic
or people orderly, yet there was little rowdiness amid the unre-

strained joy except in a bar in Yonkers, where Arthur Fritchy of Boston shot and killed Arthur Helwig of West New York during an argument over the authenticity of the armistice. A crowd then surrounded and pummeled the survivor.

The day was a bonanza for newsboys, who threaded through the crowds shouting, "Extra! Germany surrenders! Peace! The war is over!" From the Fifth Avenue dress-designing firm Lucile, the proprietor, Lady Duff Gordon, who had survived the *Titanic* because her husband had bribed a lifeboat crew, but then had to leave England because of the scandal, watched the hysteria from her window. Her girls were working on costumes for a Florenz Ziegfeld revue, and there was a deadline to meet. She offered them champagne to stay. "New York went mad, individually and collectively," she remembered. "Old men let off fireworks and waved flags, staid fathers of families kissed young women who were perfect strangers to them in the street, and other people threw down from their windows half their worldly goods, or at least such as were portable, on the heads of passers-by. The city streets were littered with stacks of paper thrown down from office windows . . . in the first exuberance of rejoicing. Some of them were of value to their respective firms, and it was funny to see grave, elderly head clerks rooting among the rubbish to try and retrieve them." To Elizabeth Stuyvesant Howard, writing to her fiancé, Lieutenant Robert Winthrop Kean, in France, New York was "a dozen New Year's Eves in one. . . . Many shops have closed for the day. One with 'Too Happy to Work Today. Come Tomorrow' on the window. Rogers Peet has on their window 'Who Can Work Today? Gone to Celebrate. Open Tomorrow.' The streets are packed with happy, good-natured crowds. Speeches are being made. People are parading—and above the din Grace Church chimes are ringing. It is a wonderful sight. I really cannot describe it. But I kept a grin on my face as I went about, although I kept mopping my stupid eyes now and then. If only it is true. . . ."

To the north in a Harlem brownstone on 129th Street opposite All Saint's Church on Madison Avenue, an Irish postman named David Langdon lay dying, another victim of the influenza epidemic. His family was gathered around the bedside, wife and daughters kneeling over their rosaries, sons standing behind them quietly. His eyes were closed, and it appeared that he had passed beyond prayer. Suddenly the streets nearby erupted into noise—church bells, automobile horns, sirens, neighbors exuberantly banging pots and pans. Langdon opened his eyes: an expression of distaste for the jubilation which had interrupted his demise crossed his face. Then he closed his eyes again.

As the afternoon waned and night approached, a few of the less hysterical among the jubilant crowds permitted themselves some doubts, for the evening papers carried no confirmation. Doubters began slipping away in the darkness.

On Broadway, officially still lightless, the Great White Way shone with prewar brilliance, and the flow of liquor in hotel bar-rooms and other saloons showed no sign of ceasing as the legal cur-few hour approached. This particular night, proprietors announced, they were going to issue all-night licenses to themselves. (From the police the tip had come that patrolmen would remain blind to lights which shone after one o'clock and deaf to sounds of revelry after that hour.) Crowds massed as far north as Columbus Circle, where a pickup band played, spilling north on Broadway from there, and despite city ordinances against outdoor drinking—or any drinking after hours—revelers who had begun to celebrate the dawn of peace intended to keep celebrating until dawn, even if the light of the new day proved to have removed their motive.

The hysteria of victory swept through settings soon to be silent morasses of unemployment. At the huge General Electric factory in Schenectady where 23,000 men and women were producing war materiel, the shrill steam whistle on building thirteen went off at 12:45, and within ten minutes the news had traveled down all the assembly lines "that the war is over and that Germany has accepted our terms." Work ceased, and employees poured out of the build-ings, somehow having found flags, cowbells, drums, and even empty vehicles—one truck quickly held fifty-three merrymakers—with which to proceed to the center of the city. Meanwhile the steam whistles continued to shriek, one man in overalls commenting as he joined the parade, "I hope they tie the whistle down till the string rots."

From the Dayton-Wright Airplane Company in Ohio, where work had suddenly stopped, flight pioneer Orville Wright, turning his enthusiasm to an idealistic key, wrote Signal Corps scientist Wallace C. Sabine, "We all rejoiced today to learn of the armistice just signed with Germany, which, no doubt, means the war is en-tirely at an end. The aeroplane has made war so terrible that I do not believe any country will again care to start a war; but I hope that the Allies will make another war absolutely impossible as a part of the peace terms."

In Massachusetts ten thousand shipyard workers at Quincy's

Bethlehem works on the Fore River, most of them to lose their jobs within weeks if not days, took their tools to use as noisemakers and marched through the city cheering and singing, with Mayor Joseph L. Whiton at the head of the parade. Similarly in South Boston the largest impromptu procession was composed of enthusiastic employees of the Army's supply base. Yet in New England there was an undercurrent of skepticism from people who did not credit the solitary UP report and kept the telephone lines to their newspapers busy with requests for confirmation. In Philadelphia, however, crowds gathered around historic Independence Hall, where Mayor Thomas B. Smith rang (with a small hammer) the venerable, and cracked, Liberty Bell. Fire bells rang, church bells tolled, and whistles blew; and at the huge shipyards along the Delaware from Philadelphia and Camden south to Chester and Wilmington, one hundred thousand men and women left the jobs they were about to lose in wild displays of joy.

In the small Pennsylvania town of Port Allegany, near the New York border, the pastor of the Free Methodist Church, Loyal L. Adams, was earning some needed extra money by painting the house of E. A. Roys on Broad Street. At two o'clock the whistles began to blow. "I walked out on the street to see where the fire was," he wrote in the tall ledger book he used also as a diary, "when Sister George [of the church] beckoned me. I waited until she approached, and [she] said, 'The war is over. The Kaiser has surrendered.' I went back in the house and in a little bit Little William came, out of breath, excited and warm, partly because the day was warm, and he had his overcoat on and he ran all the way up to tell me. He was the most excited I ever saw him. . . ." Abandoning the papering and painting, Adams and his son rushed off for "down town" to join in the celebration, on the way buying two flags and three horns from an alert peddler. The Reverend Adams carried the seventy-five-cent flag and blew a horn. Willie carried the ten-cent flag and blew two horns.

"Everybody," Adams recorded, "was in high glee, doing everything imaginable. We went to our parsonage and got Martha, Paul and the baby and all came up town together. . . . John Seltz, the hardware man, had Kaiser Bill laid out inside the glass front, with Uncle Sam standing at the foot of the pretended corpse with an epitaph written, AMEN—*The Kaiser is Gone.*" Although there had been as many as fifteen funerals a day because of the influenza epidemic, barns being torn down to find sufficient wood for the rough coffins and relatives forced through lack of gravediggers to inter their own

dead at whose obsequies Adams hurriedly officiated between painting jobs, the fear of crowds and contagion had temporarily been forgotten. A few hours later everyone in town was hungry. Jubilation
halted as if by common agreement. Everyone went home for supper,
then returned to town for an impromptu parade.

One who savored the memory of the day all his life was Thorn-
ton Wilder, then a young corporal in the Coast Artillery at Fort
Adams in Newport, Rhode Island. What he chose to recall appears,
with fictional refurbishing, as one of the last episodes in the last
novel he would write, *Theophilus North* (1973), in which the narrator
returns to his station via a Fall River Line boat. In the crowded saloon a watchman appears, swinging a lantern and sounding as well
as looking like a town crier of old. "Ladies and Gentlemen, quiet
please!" he shouts above the rumble of conversation. "Word has just
come over the wireless that the War has come to an end. . . . The
Armystiss—what they call it!—has been signed. . . . The skipper says
the Line offers a free drink to anybody that's sittin' up. . . ." Soon,
sloshed revelers begin to hurl crockery, and even to roll the heavy
brass cuspidors on their rims—and Theodore and Jenny (after her
initial protestations of outraged honor) go to her cabin to celebrate
between the sheets. As Theodore disembarks at Newport he sees a
great bonfire in Washington Square, and everyone around it "hugging and kissing everyone else," while the "apparatus of the Newport Fire Department [is] . . . dashing up and down the streets in an
ecstasy of uselessness. . . . In the little park . . . sporadic religious re-
vivals and scandalous orgies were contaminating each other. Nico-
laidis's All Night Café, having run out of coffee and frankfurter
buns, was jammed and was being looted by enraged customers.
Reader, it was gorgeous!"

The narrator finally disentangles himself "from the embraces of
a grateful populace" and walks the two miles to Fort Adams in the
light of early dawn, finding, at reveille, that 90 percent of the soldiers are absent without leave. "That," he observes, "was the famous
False Armistice."

As in Wilder's Newport, in some places the frenzy turned ugly.
In Newcastle, Pennsylvania, near Pittsburgh, what was described as
a bomb was set off, killing a fourteen-year-old boy and wounding
five others. And in another part of town Jack McDonald, a foreman
at a local tin factory, was beaten and shot by rowdies after a cele-
brant "recognized" him as a German who had allegedly defiled an
American flag.

In Louisville, Kentucky, the news, ignored by the Associated

Press, traveled to frenzied celebrants on brokers' wires. While factory whistles shrieked and church bells rang, women shoppers in mid-city stores sobbed in each other's arms. In nearby Camp Taylor, Corporal Thomas L. Stokes, later a widely read political journalist, was with the 48th Training Battalion. Recruits could hear the revelry although it was several miles away, and were eager to celebrate having been spared the Western Front. But camp officials "would not let us leave. . . . Instead of that, they herded us into an assembly hall and told us we were going to be sent to Russia. We gave them what was later to be known as the Bronx cheer." Britton Hadden and Henry Luce, fresh from the *Yale Daily* news and harboring dreams of battle command, felt crushed. Freshly minted second lieutenants, they would have to go back to college. (Later, Luce would fire his cannon in *Time,* which the pair would found in 1923.) A former ambulance volunteer in France now on his way to Camp Taylor, Malcolm Cowley refused to join the "rampaging" crowds, and only listened later to tales of "imbibulation, osculation, embracements, dancing in the streets."

The carnival atmosphere across the nation was a contagious explosion of emotions which official denials from Washington could not suppress. In the town of Bridgeport, Indiana, schools emptied, and excited teachers began to lead a march up National Road, with flags waving and "The Star-Spangled Banner" sung, past homes which displayed the red, white and blue emblem with stars indicating members of the household in military service. (In some windows the stars were gold, and draped in black cloth.) As the happy throng, increasing with each house it passed, approached the farm where young Homer Schnitzius lived, on the east edge of town, "the principal of the school came running up the road in an agitated frame of mind and stopped our parade. The war was not over, it was all a mistake. . . . Furling our flags, we straggled back to the school house in a deflated mood. . . ." In La Crosse, Wisconsin, Ralph Toland took his two small children, one of whom would be a biographer of Adolf Hitler sixty years later, downtown to witness a celebration which belied the town's considerable German population. "Free soda pop was passed out at Begun's Drug Store and at the newspaper office a straw effigy of Kaiser Bill was hung out a window and set afire." In the even smaller town of Newport, Arkansas, a parade materialized spontaneously. Ordinarily staid townspeople blew horns and fired guns into the air, while church bells rang and children banged on pots and pans. "I had a tin dish pan which I beat with a kitchen spoon," Lee Hays remembered; "after that day ... my mother was obliged to retire that pan from active service." At the courthouse, speeches were made, prayers read, and taps played. It was the next day before news filtered into Newport that there was no armistice.

Not far away, in Caldwell, Kansas, just above the Oklahoma border, nine-year-old Gordon Wallace, reading the daily news bulletin posted in the window of the stationery shop, discovered that an armistice had been signed, ending the war, but that no one seemed to have noticed it. "Let's go down to the mill," he suggested to his friend Earl, "and tell your father about it and get the mill whistle ablowing." They ran all the way to the railroad tracks, where the flour mill's foreman switched on the shrill, rising and falling wail, and the two boys swelled with pride and patriotism. But soon the siren stopped, and the celebration aborted. Contradictory news had come to the mill.

In Atlanta, Georgia, one newspaper carried the peace news; the others subscribed to the Associated Press wire service. Yet the single report was sufficient to empty the schools, parades beginning which quickly fell apart when later newspaper editions failed to corroborate the glad tidings. Even less enthusiasm was evident in Dallas, where the official prearranged signal for the end of the war was a giant siren, which did begin shrieking vigorously. When the Associated Press failed to confirm the story, the siren was quickly switched off, and few demonstrations arose in the atmosphere of disbelief. In Kansas City, however, despite disagreement among the newspapers, everyone took to the streets in good-natured frenzy, fathers carrying their small children on their heads and singing "Tipperary."

Nineteen and a lieutenant in the British Army, future playwright (*Evensong*) and novelist (*Down the Garden Path*) Beverly Nichols found the only action he would know in the war in Chicago, where he was shepherding a deputation of scholars. At the station they emerged to discover that "the peace treaty had been signed while we were still in the train. We entered a city that had gone mad. Snowstorms of paper fluttered down from the skyscrapers as the telephone books were torn to pieces. Bells clanged from every church. All the taxi-drivers were drunk and the pavements were littered with prostrate figures. When we reached the hotel where we were staying we had to step over recumbent bodies while our bags remained in the hall." A Chicagoan, Arnold Larsen, remembered the scene in "Bucktown," an enclave of Germans, Scandinavians, and Poles, where a crowd massed beneath the elevated train tracks from which an effigy of the Kaiser had been strung. Emotions were mixed, some of the Germans "venting their anger and disappointment toward the dangling figure above them, a bundle of rags in the shape of a man, slowly turning at the end of a rope." Wilhelm II had let them down. The weather, too, dampened spirits in Chicago, turning the Loop into a swamp of mud and soggy paper beneath the thousands of milling feet. And as the news turned sour, the sky wept with the throng.

Farther west, municipal restrictions against the gathering of crowds, because of the spreading epidemic of Spanish influenza, tempered celebrations. In Minneapolis, the parents of Mary and Kevin McCarthy, who had been taken off the train from Seattle dying of influenza, were buried, while six-year-old Mary, the future novelist, sick with flu as well as with pneumonia and unable to go to the funeral, remembered "bells ringing and horns and whistles blowing and a nurse standing over my bed and saying this meant the war was over." In Denver only the dashing of fire wagons through the streets clanging bells and screeching sirens suggested local enthusiasm.

In California in this last pre-radio decade the news spread by newspaper and by telephone from the East. Temporary health regulations forbidding crowds were widely ignored. Impromptu parades clogged Los Angeles business districts, while in San Bernadino the Kaiser was burned in effigy once more; and in Long Beach an aged woman who had been washing her hair when a friend came by with the news dashed delightedly down American Avenue, a cowbell in her hand and her long hair still streaming soapsuds. A newspaper reported that she was a Civil War widow with a son who was soldiering "over there"—which if true would have made him the most elderly doughboy in France.

At the Paramount Studios in Hollywood director Cecil B. de-Mille walked onto the sumptuous bedroom set of *Don't Change Your Husband,* in its first hour of filming, interrupting nineteen-year-old Gloria Swanson, who was packing a trunk. "Excuse me, Miss Swanson," he apologized; "forgive me. Wonderful! We're going to stop for today. Word has just come that an armistice has been declared. The war is over!" The studio emptied, employees thronging happily into the street. Miss Swanson looked at the clock. It was barely noon. She had not yet been told the title of the film she was making, nor had

The False Armistice: front page of the San Diego Sun, *November 7, 1918. In his excitement the compositor misspelled his headline.*

she seen the script. For silent films such technicalities were unimportant.

Describing itself under a bold EXTRA as a "full leased wire service United Press Association," the *San Diego Sun* headlined, "PEACE. FIGHTNIG ENDS. ARMISTICE IS SIGNED." In his excitement the compositor misspelled FIGHTING, but in any case it hadn't ended. To a crowd of more than a thousand who filled the City Hall rotunda, San Francisco Mayor James Rolph declared cautiously, "The United Press has been informed that the armistice has been signed. I have received no confirmation of this from the Associated Press, and until I do, I suggest that celebration plans be suspended." There were no parades.

Had all the reports a common origin? St. Nazaire received the news, as did Chartres, Bordeaux, Marseilles, Nice, Le Mans, and other cities, and Brest had been buzzing with the rumor before Admiral Wilson's message from Paris. The London press had it, but had prudently sat on it; and Holland had also received the news. Foch had even worried that false armistice reports might affect the troops. On November 8, General Pershing would send two related messages to his commanders in the field. The first relayed Foch's preparatory instructions that "hostilities will cease along the whole front beginning at date and hour not yet determined, Paris time." The second warned "that the armistice has not been signed and there is no cessation of hostilities."

"Please confirm and notify us of when we may publish armistice," Secretary of State Robert Lansing would cable the embassy from Washington. President Wilson's personal representative, Colonel Edward M. House, would reply, "Armistice has not yet been signed," and the next day a member of the embassy staff would cable, "Most of the officials in Paris and practically every non-official person here believed yesterday that the armistice had been signed. Captain Jackson, naval attaché at the Embassy, sent Admiral Wilson at Brest a wire to that effect."

Pershing's assistant chief of staff for intelligence (G-2) would investigate, too, and reported the next day that the first message received came at 11:30 A.M. on the seventh in a telephone call from Captain H. J. Whitehouse, acting director of the Army's liaison service in Paris, who declared that an armistice had been signed. G-2 had expressed surprise as well as doubt, and checked with its French counterpart. The officer in charge at Deuxième Bureau that morning had no such report, but Whitehouse insisted that the bureau was the source of his information. It would turn out that his informant was a member of the staff of General Alby, chief of French intelligence. Captain de Cartusac had received the message, among many others, early on the seventh, and passed it on to his American associate. Various officials of the Ministry of War had the news, too, and transmitted it to other ministries and even to Paris banks. Even the Netherlands Legation received a call, but officials there were skeptical.

Since the alleged signing seemed physically impossible, given the locations of the likely signers, Lieutenant Colonel Cabot Ward at G-2 had telephoned Pershing's headquarters and followed up the call with a telegram: "Rumor stated by responsible parties to have been received from Ministry of War states that Germany signed armistice terms at ten o'clock this morning. This is sent with all reserve."

How the message came to Captain de Cartusac was never explained, but it is possible that all of the premature reports had a common origin, especially since M. Audibert, who was editor of the Second Bureau's newspaper, *L'Information,* "confirmed" the news to callers. Nevertheless, the only actual cease-fire on the wires was a purely local and restricted one, beginning at three in the afternoon in the vicinity of Guise, and intended to last only until the German armistice delegates had passed through. The message may have been picked up and misinterpreted, but since no official bulletin appeared in confirmation, most quarters in Paris had reacted cautiously. By early afternoon the American Embassy was exercising caution, too, but it was too late.

Although it is possible that reports of an armistice were suggested by Foch's instructions to the French First Army to hold its fire in a particular sector during the period when the German armistice mission was expected to cross into the French lines, the premature news appears to have originated in the Paris office of the French Army's intelligence bureau. If it were not a German plant, it was as good as one. Arthur Hornblow, who found himself at the center of the "False Armistice" frenzy in Brest, later thought that the report was an enemy espionage effort to build up support for peace and weaken the "On to Berlin!" hawks. There were many in the American military who had just begun to fight and were not war-weary. But the "False Armistice" had succeeded mainly in America, three thousand miles from Foch's railway siding where the bargaining had yet to begin.

In New York journalist Gene Fowler remembered, "When it became quite clear to the street dancers that the bulletin was false a feeling of resentment took hold of them. They had been wasting their joy on a fake. . . . Their wrath burst like the flywheel of some huge machine gone awry. In Times Square they tore up the newspapers which carried the State Department's denial that peace had come. A seismic grumbling became the voice of the town. There was a sound of shattered glass as store windows gave way. The police, until now quite lenient with the disillusioned merrymakers, moved in. . . ." To Fowler the day and night of the false armistice "marked the true beginning of the age known as the Roaring Twenties." It was, he thought, a sudden change in the climate of human affairs in America, a complete break with the past—the opening of "Act II of this century."

To the service newspaper in France, *Stars and Stripes,* a soldier-correspondent cabled that that the aborted celebration was "no preconcerted affair. We did it at once without waiting for the other fellow to suggest it. We just got up and shook our jobs, whether baking, selling, street sweeping or housekeeping, and went forth. We filled every principal street of every city in America. We wiggled cowbells, tooted horns, backfired every motor engine, rang every church bell, let loose every whistle, kissed every willing girl, and altogether had a day we will never in the least be ashamed of. . . . Now we are like the kid that had Christmas ahead of time, but we don't care."

"When the real peace comes," asked the New York *Sun* the next day, "shall we have another celebration as good and joyous as these first hours of the false armistice?"

THE DINING CAR
IN THE FOREST

Nach Frankreich zogen zwei
    Grenadier',
Die waren in Russland gefangen.
Und als sie kamen ins deutsche
    Quartier,
Sie lassen die Köpfe hangen.
Da hörten sie beide die traurige Mär:
Dass Frankreich verloren gegangen,
Besiegt und geschlagen das tapfere Heer—
Und der Kaiser, der Kaiser
    gefangen!

—"THE TWO GRENADIERS,"
HEINRICH HEINE/ROBERT SCHUMANN

To France were marching two
    grenadiers
Who had been captured in Russia.
And when they came to the German
    frontier,
They hung their heads in shame.

And here they learnt the sorry tale
That France was lost forever,
Her valiant army beaten and smashed,
And the Emperor, the Emperor
    captured!

Could Germany hold out through another winter? Prince Max had posed that question before the First Quartermaster General knew that he was being relieved. "Only if we obtain a breathing space," said Ludendorff. With no military means left to create that respite, there were no more options. Allied pressure was building as American troops poured into France. Germany had nowhere to go for reserves but into the factories, where workers were infected by revolutionary propaganda. Such replacements, Ludendorff warned, "would cause more disturbance than we can stand." His aide, Colonel Wilhelm Heye, added, "For the Supreme Command not to hasten on the peace negotiations would be playing a mere game of chance. . . . Yesterday the penetration of our line came within a hairbreadth of succeeding."

Even before Prince Max had come on the scene, the Kaiser had named General Erich von Gündell to direct an exploration of armistice negotiation positions, and an atmosphere of unreality suffused the proceedings. Realizing that they would have to withdraw from territories once occupied with grand designs to absorb, they lowered expectations only to "The evacuation must be executed in such a manner that we are always ready to fight." Accepting the inevitability of the end of submarine warfare, they prepared nevertheless to hedge: "The cessation of submarine war must certainly be granted, but its resumption must be assured." To obey literally such instructions, the armistice commission would have had to bargain from a position of strength it did not have.

Since Major General Detlev von Winterfeldt had once been military attaché in Paris, and knew French, he had been named chief of staff to the exploratory group, all military men. It would have been unthinkable to include a civilian. Then, suddenly, the government was no longer manipulated from Spa by the General Staff. The need for peace was even more desperate, and no one wanted to have the enemy turn peace offers aside because it refused dealings with representatives of those who it claimed had made the war. A German agent in Switzerland had even sent to Spa a report on Allied plans for Germany which included "strict rejection of any negotiations with Ludendorff or any representative of the Supreme Command. But willingness to negotiate with a commission selected by the Reichstag. . . ."

"I was obliged to cover the armistice offer with my name," Prince Max explained later; and the military were spared the appearance of having sued for peace. "I thank your Grand Ducal

Highness in the name of the Supreme Command and in the name of the Army," the relieved Ludendorff had said. After the team of Hindenburg and Ludendorff had shared credit for toppling the sluggish giant, Czarist Russia, Theobald von Bethmann-Hollweg, then Chancellor, had boasted, "The name Hindenburg is a terror to our enemies; it electrifies our army and our people, who have boundless faith in it. Even if we should lose a battle, which God forbid, our people would accept that if Hindenburg were the leader, just as they would accept any peace covered by his name." With his spiked, Imperial pickelhaube, medals, and mustaches, the Field Marshal resembled a Wagnerian god. But behind the symbol of Hindenburg had been the vain and increasingly unstable Ludendorff. Now he was gone, and the German people would be asked to accept a peace for which the Field Marshal and the Prussian military caste were desperate, but for which they preferred to hide behind a civilian facade.

From fresh prisoners taken, German intelligence was aware that the Allies were preparing a vast offensive for November 14, predominantly with American troops, to push through Lorraine and break into the Saar, cutting off whole German armies. Only an armistice could forestall it. "We can hold out long enough for negotiations," Groener told the Cabinet on November 5. "If we are lucky the time might be longer; if we are unlucky, shorter. . . . But one thing must not be allowed to happen: the American army—or any considerable portion of it—must be prevented from advancing north of Verdun." The next day he had been even more grim, talking of retreating "behind the Rhine" if the war had to go on more than a few days longer. Still, like his predecessor, Groener was happy to leave the signature on what was bound to be a bitter document to a civilian—"to keep our weapons clean," as he would put it later, "and the General Staff unburdened for the future."

The officer corps was loyal; even veterans in the decimated ranks remained disciplined if not enthusiastic. But draftees, especially the later classes of reinforcements, had been difficult. On October 30 the 18th Landwehr Division had refused to go into the trenches in Lorraine, and disaffection continued to spread. On November 2 reinforcements for the Seventeenth Army, who had already fought on the Russian front, mutinied and had to be disarmed by a Storm battalion; the Army's chief of staff reported that he could not count on his troops to withstand another attack. On the fourth the 2nd Guard Division, a first-class assault unit needed desperately on the line, had to be diverted to Cologne to maintain order, as rear areas as far away as the Rhine were filling with thousands of wandering deserters who looted and lived off the land. On the fifth red flags were flying at most Baltic ports and the contagion was spreading into the interior.

When Prince Max had decided on November 6 to end the war as quickly as possible, his first civilian choices shrank from the armistice assignment. No one sought assured political death, and Konrad Haussmann, a secretary of state without portfolio and Prince Max's first choice, begged off on grounds of exhaustion, having just returned from the turmoil at Kiel. From the Foreign Ministry's representative at OHL, Baron Kurt von Lessner, came the suggestion that Matthias Erzberger head the commission, as he was familiar with the Wilson messages, and the Germans in any case wanted to send a mixed military-civilian team to validate the government's claims of democratization. A pillar of the Catholic party, forty-three, plump, and with a pince-nez, a rural schoolteacher turned politician who had become Director of Propaganda for Neutral Countries but had shifted through the war from annexationist to pacifist, he was safe. From the Foreign Ministry came the talkative Count Alfred von Oberndorff, Minister to Bulgaria until it had quit the war. For the Army, Detlev von Winterfeldt was considered—as only a divisional general—of sufficiently inferior rank to save the honor of the officer caste. The other delegates were even lower in visibility. Ernst Vanselow, a mere *Kapitän zur See*, would represent the Imperial Navy. Still, Vanselow since September had commanded the battleship *Kaiser*—no mean assignment—at Kiel, missing the mutinies earlier in the week because he had been detached to Spa for the exploratory armistice consultations chaired by General Gündell. (Counting his blessings at not having to represent the Navy in defeat was another captain at Spa—Erich Raeder, commander of the cruiser *Köln*. As a Grand Admiral he would run the Nazi fleet until January 1943.)

Erzberger's special train to Spa was to leave Berlin at five minutes after five. At three that afternoon he still had no documents authorizing his mission and even was unsure of the identities of the rest of his party. The Foreign Office was nearly empty, but he was referred to Herr Kriege, the head of the Legal Section. Kriege complained about not having been consulted and said that he was engaged in a dispute with the head of the Political Section about whether a Foreign Office could authorize the signing of a military armistice. "The entire course of world history," he objected, "knew no precedents for making out the kind of document which was required." The pedantry made Erzberger furious. "There were no precedents for a World War in the Foreign Office files either." At 5:05 the train was getting up steam, but he refused to board. At 5:10 Count von Oberndorff appeared. At 5:15 a messenger arrived with the papers, headed "Full Power," which authorized the delegation

> to conduct in the name of the German Government with the plenipotentiaries of the Powers allied against Germany, negotiations for an armistice and to conclude an agreement to that effect, provided the same be approved by the German Government.

Erzberger did not even have full powers to commit his side and wondered whether he would be acceptable should he survive as far as the French lines. Yet there was an added admonition from Prince Max: "Obtain what mercy you can, Matthias, but for God's sake, make peace."

Fortunately, given his mission, Erzberger felt as if he no longer had any political ambitions. Three weeks before, his son Oskar had died of influenza at the officers' school at Karlsruhe. To avoid thinking about it, Erzberger kept his mind on his mission. As the train moved out through the suburbs and across Germany in the quickly darkening evening, he began to make notes which emphasized the mutual acceptance of Wilson's Fourteen Points as the equivalent of a pre-armistice contract. Also, as a last gesture of royalist loyalty, he scribbled arguments to refute the contention that peace was predicated on the Kaiser's abdication. He had not been a propaganda chief for nothing.

General Groener was returning to headquarters on the same train. Late in the evening the two met in the dining car for a late supper, glumly discussed the military situation, then parted for their last lengthy sleep for several days. The train was halfway to Spa when, shortly after midnight, Paris time, Foch received the radio message he had been expecting:

> The German Government having been informed by the President of the United States that Marshal Foch was invested with full power to receive its accredited representatives, and let them know the conditions of the armistice, informs him of the names

of its plenipotentiaries, and asks him to indicate the place where they can reach the French lines. In the name of Humanity they also ask for a cessation of hostilities.

At 1:25 Foch sent back his answer—via the Eiffel Tower transmitter—that the delegation should present itself "at the French outposts on the road Chimay-Fourmies-La Capelle-Guise. Orders have been given to receive and conduct them to the place selected for the meeting." In response to the plea for cessation of hostilities, he announced a temporary cease-fire in the area for the hours during which the delegation would be picking its way through the lines, and German headquarters answered that the truce delegation would be preceded by a road-repair company to patch what was left of the cratered La Capelle road. Through all the exchanges Erzberger and Groener slept, arriving at Spa at eight in the morning.

Flourishing amid sixteen mineral springs, the town had long before given its name to similar resorts. "There is only one Original Spa," went the advertisements for its bubbly elixir then as now. "It comes from springs in the Belgian Ardennes that gave the world a word for healthy water." Frequented by royalty since Peter the Great in 1717, it consisted largely of hotels and lodging houses and an Establissement des Bains. Colorful shops which once tempted the tourist with souvenirs now catered to soldiers. Bands had entertained strollers under the magnificent old elms when the sky was fair; in unfavorable weather, musicians had played in the Galerie Léopold Deux. Since August 1914, however, only troops in German *feldgrau* paraded the pleasant promenades, and military bands continued the Spa tradition. There were no officers' wives to share the healing waters—even the ailing Kaiserin remained in Berlin, leaving the ornate hotel lobbies to ladies of the evening. Still, the waters bubbled at a constant fifty degrees Fahrenheit, warmer than the drenching rain which darkened the windows of the Grand Hotel Britannique as OHL mechanics prepared automobiles for the journey and Erzberger assembled his delegation. Of a dozen volunteers he had selected two Army captains to accompany the four senior members. As the vehicles sputtered, Hindenburg emotionally embraced Erzberger. "Go with God's blessing and try to secure what you can for our Fatherland."

The five vehicles, emblazoned with Imperial eagles, left at noon, a delegate in each (although all could have fit in one car), with the two aides sharing the last. (They would show the French some Imperial style.) But even with bulging headlamps ablaze, visibility was poor and the road surfaces slick. Soon the first vehicle, hurrying around a curve on a narrow road, smashed into a house. Following too closely, the second lurched into the rear of the first. Both were abandoned, the delegates crowding into the three remaining cars. The accident, Oberndorff mourned, was an unfavorable omen. Erzberger found a helpful German proverb: "Broken glass brings good luck."

The truncated convoy needed some luck. Rain had turned day into night and concealed the crevices and craters in the roads, already clogged with columns of retreating German soldiers who gazed with puzzlement at vehicles traveling west. By six the cars had only reached Chimay, just east of the French frontier, and there the commanding general insisted that they could proceed no farther that night, as trees had been felled across the roads to cover the withdrawal of his men. Erzberger found a field telephone and reached German corps headquarters in Trélon, on the French side of the border. The barriers were moved, and by 7:30 the convoy had churned into Trélon. There Erzberger learned that a mine-clearing unit would precede them and that officers with white flags would go ahead to secure an extension to the cease-fire, which had already expired.

At Trélon the weary corps commander told Erzberger of the valor of his troops. Without hope of relief they had been in action for six weeks. One division had shrunk to 349 men and another to 437. (The paper size of a German division in 1914 had been 16,000.) They had shown superhuman courage, he said, but had been forced back to the lines of four years before. He knew little of the turmoil in Kiel or Berlin or Munich and begged Erzberger to say nothing about it to his officers.

On the signal that the roads had been cleared, the convoy started up its motors, Erzberger first making sure that a large white flag—actually a towel—was mounted on the first car. Also, he secured a trumpeter to sound their progress to the French in four-note blasts as they left German-occupied territory. At the last German outpost a soldier who turned out to be, like Erzberger, a Swabian, asked in his provincial dialect, "Where are you going?"

"To conclude an armistice," said Erzberger.

"Do you really think," the Swabian asked incredulously, "that just the two of you can bring that off?" In the darkness he could see only the forward automobile. It took millions to make a war. Could only two end it?

At 9:20 P.M. that Thursday night Erzberger, remembering his visit to his dying son, penned a note about the fog-shrouded crossing into French territory. "My feelings on the journey to Karlsruhe, which any father can understand," he wrote, "were no more depressed and painful than my feelings at the present moment. The words of the Schumann song about *The Two Grenadiers* went through my head." And he added the lines from Heine which Schumann had set, about soldiers hanging their heads in shame as they crossed the frontier, realizing that their country was beaten. The words had referred to the troops of Napoleon, but the parallel needed no explanation in Erzberger's diary.

It was nearly midnight (German time) when the automobiles, moving as slowly as a funeral cortege, arrived at Haudroy, the German trumpeter still hanging on to the first vehicle, wobbily sounding his four lugubrious notes. About 150 meters beyond the German lines the first *poilus* appeared, from a battalion of the French 171st Infantry, and brought the vehicles to a halt in a flood of lanternlight. An officer stepped forward, and Winterfeldt emerged from the leading car to identify his group. A Captain Lhuillier squeezed into the car to direct it, and ordered a French bugler corporal to replace the German trumpeter on the running board. Then they continued through the mud to La Capelle, the bugle piercing through the rain and fog while the occupants of the car sat in silence. As one of the German delegates remembered it, the "motor tour" was very likely intentionally prolonged "in order to drive us all over the devastated province and prepare us by what we saw for what was shortly to be put before us in the way of hatred and revenge in the extremely severe armistice conditions. Now and again a Frenchman pointed accusingly at heaps of ruins, or identified a place—'Violà St. Quentin.'"

At La Capelle were Major the Comte de Bourbon-Busset, representing General Debeney, and Major Ducorne, commanding officer of the 19th Chausseurs à pied. Winterfeldt apologized for the delays. "We are prepared," he confided to Bourbon-Busset in excellent French, "to sign one of the most shameful capitulations in History. We are obliged to, because of the revolution. We don't even know if there will be a Germany tomorrow." Erzberger recalled soldiers coming up to the car to ask, *"Finie la guerre?"* and, forgetting discipline, to beg for cigarettes, which the nonsmoking plenipotentiary did not possess. And he recalled scattered applause greeting the cars as harbingers of the war's end. Yet most soldiers (there were a few cries of *"Vive la France!"*) were guarded in their emotions.

The French had reoccupied the town only that afternoon, and

as the party rode in the rain to Bourbon-Busset's command post, a farmhouse, Erzberger could see in the glare of headlights the still-standing German signposts in Gothic script, and on one building, in large letters, *"Kaiserliche Kreiskommandantur."* At the Villa Francport the delegation found the three German officers who had preceded them and made possible the extension of the cease-fire. There they waited, Winterfeldt trying to appear cool and dignified, Erzberger unable to keep from fidgeting. The room—General Debeney's—was filled by a large round table under a shaded lamp which hung from the high, pitched roof, lighting a map of the front which was so detailed that it covered two walls at a right angle.

At one in the morning they were invited to have a brief supper—Army fare of soup, salt meat, and peas. They had had nothing to eat since leaving Spa. Replacement automobiles—one for each plenipotentiary and French escort—drew up, and after photographs were taken by the light of magnesium flares, which glared off balding Captain Vanselow's high-domed head, the cars rolled off, the Germans hearing a voice rise from the crowd of returned villagers teasing, *"Nach* Paris!" The going was slow as cars bumped over roads rougher than in the German sector. Erzberger's hat was dented; his glasses tumbled from his nose. When he grumbled to himself about the heavy going, Bourbon-Busset reminded him that the Germans had been responsible. Then, Erzberger growing silent, the major made conversation, explaining how far they had to go (fifty kilometers), and how to pronounce Foch's name.

At three, French time, the procession arrived in the ruined town of Tergnier, south of St. Quentin. "Where are we?" Erzberger asked.

"At Tergnier."

"But there are no houses."

"True. There *was* a town here once."

At the railhead, lit by torches, a company of *chasseurs* presented arms. Amid the wreckage Foch's sense of theater began to emerge. A special train was getting up steam—an old locomotive and three carriages, a dining car, sleeping car, and a coach upholstered in green satin and ornamented with an *N* capped by a crown. It had been the personal coach of Napoleon III, whom the Germans had defeated in 1870 at Sedan, and from whom the Germans had seized Alsace and Lorraine. (Winterfeldt's father had helped to settle the terms of the French capitulation.)

Late in 1917, when the Germans were imposing a drastic peace settlement upon once-Czarist Russia, Hermann Labude, a soldier and former philosophy student, wrote from Dunaburg, on the East-ern Front, that he had watched a briefcase-laden Russian delegation arrive by rail under terms of a temporary armistice. "During the past years," he wrote home, "we have often, as a joke, asked any-body who came in from a forward observation post, 'Well, comrade, did you see Peace passing by?' Now, on this Sunday, I really did see her, and this is what she looked like: telegraph-wires, dispatch-cases, and a special train!" Now the situation was reversed, and the logis-tics nearly a mirror image of Private Labude's vision. But by then peace of a different sort had come to Labude. Transferred on Gen-eral Groener's efficient railways to the Western Front, he had been killed on March 29, 1918, near Beaufort.

As Erzberger's party entered the train Winterfeldt noticed a huge shell hole beside the track. "That was a delayed-action shell," Bourbon-Busset explained. "It exploded three weeks after the Ger-mans left. I hope there are none under our train. I don't wish to blow you up, or to be blown up with you."

Aggrieved, the general insisted, "The High Command has never ordered destructions of this sort, which are very regrettable and must be ascribed to isolated persons."

Once the six Germans were offered brandy and permitted to sink into the venerable plush, they realized that the blinds were down, and would remain down. Until the train came to a halt in the early morning light, the delegates, still in the clothes in which they had traveled, dozed on and off while Major Bourbon-Busset and a few of his men remained watchful. They had jolted onto concealed railway artillery trackage near Rethondes, in the forest of Com-piègne, only forty miles from Paris. Erzberger asked, but was not told, where he was. (Soldiers in attendance claimed not to know.) When the blinds were raised he could see another train much like his own on a parallel siding about a hundred yards away. Again three carriages—a parlor car, a saloon car for dining, a *wagon-lit* for sleeping. Clearly the delegates were to remain there overnight or longer, watching the few sodden leaves still left fall from the trees. It was seven o'clock. At nine, said Bourbon-Busset, they were to meet the other side in its saloon car. That was little time to recover a sem-blance of dignity.

Nine o'clock. Ten by Berlin time, which had been carried west by German troops to the now-receding front lines. A plank platform led from one siding to the other. Crossing it nervously, the supplicants were led into the saloon car by wiry, weasel-like General Maxime Weygand, Foch's chief aide. The Allied contingent had been in the forest through the night, having left the Paris suburb of Senlis at 5:00 P.M., once the British delegates had come aboard. There were only British and French representatives, First Sea Lord Admiral Sir Rosslyn Wemyss and his staff largely there for naval matters and to show the Union Jack. Foch intended to run the negotiations (or at least appear to run them) the way he had attempted to run the last months of the war—by himself.

Rosie Wemyss, a descendant of one of William IV's illegitimate children, had, according to economist Maynard Keynes, "a comical, quizzical face and a single eyeglass," and was "pleasure-loving, experienced and lazy." But he was not too idle to keep a record of the proceedings, beginning with the journey into the forest, when the Marshal, "quiet and confident," told him that he proposed to do as little talking to the Germans as possible. He would let them have their say, and then hand them the terms of the armistice. Foch and Wemyss had dined together in the saloon car, which doubled as conference room, while the proposed text of the armistice, which had undergone small technical changes, was being retyped nearby by the General Staff's secretary, Henri Deledicq. After arriving at Rethondes they kept in touch with the progress of the German delegation via radio messages until they saw, through the mist, the red lights of the train from Tergnier, being shunted backward into its siding.

The Germans found the wooden coach on the other siding dominated by a wide table with four places identified by place cards on either side, hand-cranked telephones set nearby, and table lamps glowing under quaint pink shades. Charts of the front line lay open. Weygand motioned them to one side of the table, where they stood, uneasily, waiting for the remainder of the Allied contingent. "In a few minutes," Erzberger recalled, "Marshal Foch appeared, a little man with hard energetic features. . . ." The white-mustached Foch, sixty-seven, looked older. Even the bluish-gray bags under his tired eyes were deeply lined. Erzberger was seeing Foch's reputation rather than the man.

Giving the Germans a military salute and curt bow, Foch doffed his *kepi* and put it on the table. The Germans bowed in return, discovering with surprise that the other side consisted only of French Army officers and British Navy equivalents. No American, Belgian, or Italian was present. The session would be, Erzberger assumed, Foch's stage-managed affair.

Asking first for the German credentials, the Marshal silently retired with his staff to an adjoining compartment to examine them, Erzberger worrying that although the documents announced that the delegates had what was declared to be "full power" to negotiate, Foch would quickly realize that any agreement remained subject to government ratification. Returning, Foch motioned his group to the conference table and nearby chairs, and asked Erzberger to introduce his delegation. Winterfeldt, white-haired and thin, in a major general's *feldgrau* tunic. Vanselow, balding and stocky, in the naval uniform in which he had made the journey. Oberndorff in a diplomat's blue suit, with bowler in hand. Erzberger, plump and shabby, looking like a weary commercial traveler. Geyer and Helldorf, the two aides, rigid and masking any emotion.

In turn Foch identified his own delegation and staff, including the English and French interpreters, Bagot and Laperche. Then he opened the proceedings with an icy question to his interpreter which the Germans could only receive with astonishment.

"Ask these gentlemen what they want."

"We have come to inquire into the terms of an armistice, to be concluded on land, on sea, and in the air."

"Tell these gentlemen that I have no proposals to make."

Foch half rose from his chair, as if to suggest that haggling over *proposals* subject to negotiation was not what he had in mind. Quickly Count von Oberndorff intervened. Leaning across the table he appealed, in French, to Foch. "Monsieur le Maréchal, surely this is too serious a moment to quarrel over words. How would you like us to express ourselves? It is a matter of complete indifference to us."

"It is for you gentlemen to say what you want."

Erzberger permitted Oberndorff to go on. "As you are aware, M. le Maréchal," the Count continued, "we are here as a result of a note from the President of the United States. If you will allow me I will read it." And in English he read from Wilson's reply to Germany of November 5, which concluded that Foch had been authorized to furnish armistice conditions to a German delegation. "If I understand this aright, it means that you will communicate to us the armistice terms."

Stubbornly, Foch insisted, "I will *acquaint* you with the Allies' conditions when you have asked for an armistice. *Do* you ask for an armistice?"

"*Ja!*" Erzberger and Obendorff exclaimed in relief.

Foch finally appeared satisfied, instructing Weygand to read the terms which had been worked out at inter-Allied conferences a few days earlier. Handing Erzberger a copy of the document (in French, which Erzberger did not understand), Weygand began to read out the thirty-four catastrophic clauses of the armistice, interrupted only by Laperche, who repeated the crushing conditions in German. The Allies wanted all occupied lands, including Alsace and Lorraine, evacuated in fourteen days. Within twenty-eight days all of Germany west of the Rhine would be occupied, as well as bridgeheads on the other side to a depth of thirty kilometers. Heavy guns, field guns, machine guns, trench mortars, aircraft as well were to be given up in numbers so ruinous that in some cases the figures represented more than remained in use. Five thousand locomotives and 150,000 railway cars "in good repair" were to be delivered within thirty-one days, and ten thousand trucks—hardly time to utilize them to retrieve the Army. Return of cash and gold from occupied banks, reparations for war damage, surrender and disarming of all submarines and surface warships. And despite near-famine in Germany, clause twenty-six declared the blockade of German ports indefinitely in effect.

Couched as reparations, the economic clauses would deprive Germany of most of its merchant ships as well as its railway cars and motor trucks still in operating condition. They would be just the beginning of the economic reprisals which the Versailles treaty would mandate to make Germany "pay for the war." Unconcerned that bad economics makes bad politics, France wanted a devitalization of the traditional enemy, and England the elimination of a commercial rival.

According to Weygand there was complete silence, and faces on both sides struggled to conceal emotions. At the reading of the clauses providing for occupation of the Rhineland, Captain Vanselow could not suppress the tears which rolled down his cheeks. The Germans, Weygand announced finally, would have seventy-two hours in which to accept the terms.*

---

* A story about the reading of the armistice conditions which has only one source and may be apocryphal is told by one-time Scotland Yard chief Sir Basil Thomson: "Prince Max told me . . . [that] one of his cousins was a member of the German delegation which came to Marshal Foch to ask for armistice terms. When these were read to them the German officers could scarcely believe their ears and went cold with dismay. When the reading ended, their leader stammered, 'But—there must be some mistake. These are terms which no civilized nation *could* impose on another.'

Erzberger who had listened in silence, hid the terrible document in his pocket and asked to be heard. Might not hostilities be immediately suspended? His plea, he said, was based upon the disorganization and indiscipline seeping through the German Army, and the spread of revolution through the nation as a result of the people's sufferings. He described, Foch remembered, "the difficulties which he and his fellow delegates had encountered in passing through the German armies and in crossing their [own] lines, where even the order to cease firing was executed only after considerable trouble. All these circumstances led him to fear that Germany might soon fall into the grip of Bolshevism, and once central Europe was invaded by this scourge, western Europe, he said, would find the greatest difficulty in escaping it. Nothing but the cessation of Allied attacks would make possible the recovery of discipline in the German Army and through the restoration of order save the country."

The Marshal was cold and unhelpful. Early in the war, as Foch was leaving the XX Corps at Nancy to take command of a new Ninth Army hastily assembled to defend Paris, he had received the news of the death in battle of his only son, Germain. Fallen with him on the same day, near Yprecourt, on the Belgian frontier, had been Captain Bécourt of the 26th Chasseurs à Pied, Foch's son-in-law. "The cruel sacrifice we are making," Foch had written then to his old chief, General Millet, "ought not to remain sterile." Now he would not even give the enemy, however supplicant (or civilian), the minimal recognition of a glance. His steely eyes gazed straight ahead, as he spoke, into nothing, perhaps, but his memories of 1914.

"At the moment when negotiations for the signing of an armistice are just being opened," he told Erzberger, looking at him as if the Marshal did not see anyone there, "it is impossible to stop military operations until the German delegation has accepted and signed the conditions which are the consequence of those operations. As for the situation described by Herr Erzberger as existing among the German troops and the danger he fears of Bolshevism spreading in Germany, the one is the usual disease prevailing in beaten armies, the other is symptomatic of a nation completely worn out by war.

" 'I am very glad to hear you say so,' replied Foch gravely. 'No, gentlemen, those are not our terms. You have been listening to a careful translation of the terms imposed upon Lille by the German commander when that city surrendered. Here are my terms.' And he handed to them the written armistice conditions."

Western Europe will find means of defending itself against the danger."

Winterfeldt had prepared a statement on behalf of the Supreme Command. During the period when his government and military authorities were being urgently consulted, he begged in French, "The struggle between our armies will continue, and it will result, among both soldiers and civilians, in numerous victims who will die in vain at the last minute and who might be preserved to their families. Therefore, the German Government and the German Supreme Command have the honour to revert to the proposal made by them in their wireless message of the day before yesterday: that Marshal Foch be kind enough to consent to an immediate suspension of hostilities for the entire front, to begin today at a certain fixed hour, the very simple details of which could be decided upon without loss of time."

Weygand whispered something to Foch, probably telephoned instructions from Clemenceau, after which the Marshal declared himself unmoved by the confession of German desperation. He was only the representative of the Allied governments, he insisted. "These governments have decided upon their terms. . . . I am likewise desirous of reaching a conclusion and therefore I shall help you as far as possible towards this end. But hostilities cannot cease before the signing of the armistice." He was not inventing his own responses. While the conference was in progress the dining car in the forest remained in direct communication with General Henri Mordacq at the War Ministry in Paris, who in turn relayed messages to and from the Premier. Speaking for Clemenceau shortly after ten o'clock, Mordacq, responding to a query from Weygand, had instructed Foch that he could not discuss peace conditions, but only the armistice. The German plea for an immediate cease-fire was also brought to Mordacq, who quickly reported that Clemenceau remained firm—the signing had to come first. Even new demands were being raised outside the forest as the delegates met. At 9:30 Mordacq had telephoned Weygand that Italy, eager for spoils, had insisted on the withdrawal of Bavarian troops from the Austrian Tyrol.

Given the difficulties of communication, could they have, Erzberger asked, a twenty-four-hour extension of the time limit for a reply? Again Foch was unmoved. He was only the spokesman for the governments he represented. Yet, despite his parting assurances from Prince Max, Erzberger was less sure that he could speak for *his* government, divided as it was between Berlin and Spa. Might not the Supreme Command reject draconian terms and fight on? Was there any objection, he asked, to members of his delegation conferring with the Allied delegates? Or to his sending messages to his government? Erzberger was guessing that Weygand, an Alsatian who had behaved correctly if not warmly, and the two Englishmen might be more responsive.

Foch looked at him with eyes that suggested a blind man. Weygand and Hope, he said, would discuss any details his side wished to raise. Further, Erzberger was welcome to Weygand's good offices to make contact with his government, although the time limit, Foch cautioned, would remain seventy-two hours from the point at which the sitting had risen, which—he checked a large watch on a chain— had been eleven o'clock that morning, French time.

The Germans huddled in brief discussion in their dining car; then Winterfeldt walked back across the planks at 11:30 with a radio message in Erzberger's name. To Spa he explained the time frame for making a decision and confessed failure to effect an immediate cease-fire. "A German courier bearing the text of the armistice conditions," he added, "has been sent to Spa, there being no other practical mode of communication. Please acknowledge receipt and send back the courier as soon as possible with your final instructions." Weygand pored over every word before approving the transmittal. It was better, Erzberger told his colleagues, than transmitting the full text of the imposed armistice, with all its implications for Germany, *en clair,* as any radio operator could pick it up and inform disaffected soldiers and civilians from the Rhine to the Russian border.

At one o'clock Captain von Helldorf left, accompanied by Major Bourbon-Busset as far as the French advanced lines. There they found no arrangements to pass the captain into the German lines, the local French claiming that disorganization on the other side had prevented contacts. Possibly the Germans were deliberately heading off Helldorf. Their own soldiers, he would report afterward to Erzberger, "fired like the very devil" and for five hours ignored his white flags, soundings of the prearranged bugle call, and even his exposure to their volleys. When night came Helldorf had still failed to penetrate his own lines. (In Berlin the English-born Princess Blücher, whose husband had Foreign Office connections, noted in her diary that the courier "has just radio'd from the front that he cannot get through the German lines, as the fire is still continuing.

They have radio'd back, informing him that the firing has been caused by an ammunition dump exploding accidentally. . . . So now he will be hurrying towards us. . . ." The explanation was an unlikely one.)

French outposts were in communication with Rethondes, and the difficulty had become known before dark. Since the weather had partially cleared it was decided to fly another courier, this time Captain Geyer, who, with a French pilot and promised safe-conduct, took off from Tergnier in a two-seat Breguet biplane. For Geyer it was the low point in a young military career that had looked for a time as if he were fortune's favorite. He was the junior officer who had conceived the infiltration tactics and written the guidelines on which the German Army had been trained for the spring offensive earlier in the year which had aimed at defeating the British and French before America could get its troops in the field. It had almost worked.

To the High Command, Winterfeldt had sent a wireless message which asked for a safe aerial route and altitude and marks of recognition for the airfield. "Allied machine," he noted, "will carry as distinctive marks two white streamers." In his urgency he identified von Helldorf as the courier, rather than Geyer.

Meanwhile, from Spa, where Erzberger's first radio message had arrived, Foreign Secretary von Hintze telegraphed Berlin with a further Erzberger transmission, this one having been painstakingly put in cipher because of its sensitivity. It is unlikely, he reported, that Germany would be permitted any substantive counterproposals, but Erzberger hoped to modify those conditions affecting internal order and the possibility of famine, and hoped, too, to secure a reduction in the amounts of material to be surrendered. He would try to gain whatever concessions he could, and in accepting the armistice would declare it impossible to carry out all the conditions imposed. "In case a refusal is not determined upon," the key phrase went, "request express authorization to sign at once with whatever modifications in the matter of practical execution of the terms we may be able to attain here."

That afternoon, as attempts were being made to get detailed information back to Germany, Erzberger and his colleagues huddled in their own saloon car to plan strategy for modification. Oberndorff and Winterfeldt saw Weygand about military concessions and Vanselow saw Admiral Hope about relinquishing ships and softening the blockade. Since the blockade would be continued, the Kaiser's captain asked, would his country be starved during the armistice? (George Hope told Wemyss, whose reaction was, "Such is their mentality, so I suppose that is what they would have done had the cases been reversed.") When Hope said that he wasn't prepared to discuss the subject, Vanselow suggested that the Allies were making the same error into which his own nation had blundered in its treatment of Russia, having behaved as a conqueror toward the Bolsheviks, although they were only the successor government to the defeated one. Now, he said ruefully, Germany was the conquered nation. "It is he who has the wind in his sails who wins," observed Hope. Vanselow wondered whether any returning submarines would be sunk during the armistice, and about using German ships holed up in Belgian ports to ferry troops home. Hope listened and reported back to Wemyss.

For Weygand, Winterfeldt drew a dramatic picture of wholesale disintegration, which seemed to belie the intense resistance which the defeated Germans were putting up along most of the front. According to him the vaunted Prussian discipline had evaporated; orders were disobeyed and soldier soviets appearing. Roads and railways, always a model for efficiency in Europe, were chaotic with retreating troops, and the Germans were forced to withdraw through difficult country with scant means of communication. The troops resembled flocks of sheep. Local revolutions were breaking out, and a total Bolshevist takeover was to be feared. It was absolutely necessary that the Allies permit a portion of the Army to remain intact, as it was the only means of maintaining order. For that, Germany needed to retain equipment from machine guns to railway cars. Weygand listened but kept his own counsel. (A permanently weak Germany was what France wanted, and Bourbon-Busset had reported to him that the Germans were surrendering wholesale, and when retreating were even abandoning their field kitchens.) Weygand's conversation went on into the evening, and would be continued the next morning, with Oberndorff.

According to Foch, who presumably relied on Weygand's notes, Oberndorff made the point that there was no deceit in Germany's wish for an armistice. "The fact that her delegates are here proves that no other course is open to her. Hence, it may be assumed that the delegates are sincere." It would be, he continued, "to the advantage of everybody that the German Army marched back to Germany in orderly fashion; to do this the time limit fixed for the evacuation must be extended. It is not a case of allowing merely additional days, but weeks." The Allies, he conceded, had a right "to secure by the terms of the Armistice, as a minimum, the continued possession of all advantages won," but

> Germany, if driven to despair, would oscillate between two extremes. Either there would be a revival of bellicose passions leading to a resolute fight to the finish, whose result could not be foreseen; or Bolshevism would triumph and turn the country into a chaos like Russia's. In case of renewed fighting France risked the further devastation of her countryside; in case of Bolshevism the danger of contagion and the loss of Germany's solvency for payment of reparations. It seemed to me that France had a real interest in preventing the triumph of Bolshevism in Germany. But this required an orderly withdrawal of the German troops and a guarantee of adequate food supplies for the German population. The contemplated evacuation deadlines and the simultaneous surrender of all of our rolling stock made both of these protections against Bolshevism completely impossible.

"Guard against your natural compassion," Shaw's Inquisitor in *Saint Joan* would caution her clerical judges. Allied negotiators needed no such warning. They had not paid the heavy price already exacted only to permit the Germans to withdraw during the safety of a cease-fire to more defensible frontiers, at which point Allied will to resume the fighting might be drained. Weygand himself wanted no armistice which was only "a kind of vigil at arms . . . to allow preparation for the future."

While he talked with Winterfeldt and Oberndorff, and their two aides explored ways to carry the armistice documents into Germany, "great nervousness" (according to Mordacq) prevailed in Paris about whether the German leadership could afford to accept so drastic a truce. There was even the question of whether Clemenceau could afford to agree to one, as his political enemies, including Raymond Poincaré, President of the Republic, wanted total victory. Poincaré had even written him, bluntly, "Everyone steadfastly hopes that there will be no question of hamstringing our troops by an armistice, however short."

As early as noon on Friday, Foch had informed Paris that everything was proceeding favorably. He was sending a courier with details. By three Mordacq had more information for Clemenceau, who was waiting in his office on the second floor of the War Ministry with Stephen Pichon, the Minister of Foreign Affairs, and René Renoult, who chaired the Committee on the Army in the Chamber of Deputies. "Good news, Mr. President!" Mordacq had announced, tendering the message in which Foch predicted, from the manner in which the terms had been received, that acceptance would follow. Clemenceau "had hardly finished reading the report," Mordacq wrote afterward, "when I saw him staring at me long and fixedly. His eyes moistened, and, taking his head in his hands, he began to weep silently. Never, either before or during the war, had I seen him prey to such emotion. After a moment he pulled himself together and cried, 'It's absurd, but I am no longer the master of my nerves; it was stronger than I, but suddenly I saw 1870 again, the defeat, the shame, the loss of Alsace-Lorraine, and now all of that is wiped out. Is it a dream?' "

Foch's confidence had been reinforced by the impotence he recognized in the occupants of the Napoleon III saloon car. It confirmed what he sensed from the field. If the Germans would not sign, he had confided to Wemyss, he would have "the capitulation of the whole lot in three weeks." Further, he insisted, he would make them leave everything behind. And he would not permit them to evacuate Belgium by ship, via Antwerp, as Vanselow had asked Admiral Hope, for Foch wanted them to get home only with the utmost difficulty. Furnishing Wemyss a public excuse, he suggested that if the Allies were in a hurry to relieve hunger in central Europe, German ships might have to be used.

On Saturday morning, having spent much of the previous night drafting what they expected would be spurned counterproposals, the German delegates breakfasted glumly in their dining car, starved of news about what was going on. Foch had seen to it that they heard only what he wanted them to hear; and there had been no response from Spa or Berlin. Erzberger would not know until much later that the long message he had coded to the Foreign Office would take twenty-six precious hours of the seventy-two with which they began negotiations just to reach Berlin. The authorities in any case had much else on their minds. The situation at the front was only precarious. In the interior on the ninth it was nightmarish.

From General Max von Gallwitz's Army Group came a report that a train with five hundred soldiers who were trying "to force their furlough" had been disarmed at Arlon, in the southern tip of Belgium just west of Luxembourg. Another report, from Composite

Army C, was that ten thousand mutineers had taken control of Metz and formed a Soldiers' Council. Meanwhile the 20th Pioneer Battalion, en route to the front, refused to travel beyond Arlon, and arrested its officers. From Hindenburg came an appeal (OHL* 11373, Secret) to the field armies on the Western Front to keep peace and order.

Events the day before had confirmed to Prince Max what lay in store. "On the morning of November 8," he recalled later, "the following reports of revolution lay before us: Brunswick had gone Red at seven in the evening; during the night Munich had gone Red, and [the Bavarian] War Ministry had been occupied by a Workers' and Soldiers' Council. A republic had been proclaimed [in Munich] and the abdication of the King was demanded by twelve noon. In Stuttgart the . . . Council had seized control of the government. During the night a trainload of soldiers had been derailed at Paulinenaue and the sailors had started for Berlin on foot."

On Saturday the situation would become even worse as, almost simultaneously, most major cities, rail centers, and supply depots fell into the hands of the revolutionaries. Prince Max had toiled through Friday to force the Kaiser's abdication before there was no government at all. Since the Social Democrats appeared ready to join the revolutionary movement in an attempt to keep the most extreme radicals from power, the Chancellor hoped for some arrangement whereby the form of the monarchy could be salvaged. As remote from reality as he was from Berlin, the real Germany was, to the monarch himself, his feudal circle of paladins at Spa, rather than the unseemly chaos of his own cities and towns. To Herr Drews, Prussian Minister of the Interior and personal emissary of Prince Max, the Kaiser announced that a descendant of Frederick the Great had "no intention of quitting the throne because of a few hundred Jews and a thousand workmen. Tell that to your masters in Berlin!"

That night, while Erzberger and his harried associates huddled over armistice strategy in their isolated railway carriage in the forest, the Imperial Chancellor was telephoning the Kaiser. An aide in Berlin took down Prince Max's half of the conversation:

> The advice I have sent your Majesty by Herr von Hintze I must repeat to you as a relative. Your abdication has become neces-

---

* OHL: Oberkommando das Heeresleitung (Military Supreme Command).

sary to save Germany from civil war and to fulfill your mission as the peace-making Emperor to the end. The blood that is shed would be laid upon your head. The great majority of the people believe you to be responsible for the present situation. The belief is false, but there it is. If civil war and worse can now be prevented through your abdication, your name will be blessed by future generations. . . .

Whatever step is decided on, it must be taken with the greatest possible speed. This sacrifice, if made after blood has once flowed, will have lost all its power for good. . . . Otherwise republic and revolution are imminent. If the troops could be depended on, things would be different. . . .

I speak to you today as your relative and as a German prince. This voluntary sacrifice is necessary to keep your good name in history. . . .

The disembodied voice which crackled over the wires sounded as stiff and unyielding as the Kaiser always appeared in person. He would return at the head of his Army, which he still relied on, even to fight the civilian population in his behalf. And he would not permit the Prince to resign. "You sent out the armistice offer; you will also have to accept the conditions."

Although Prince Max agreed to remain in office, he telegraphed to Spa new information received. German princes, dukes, and lesser kings were fleeing everywhere. Thrones had toppled, or had been renounced, in Bavaria, Brunswick, and Mecklenburg-Schwerin, and Workers' and Soldiers' Councils were in control; in Berlin the Cabinet had voted to recommend abdication as the only means of staving off civil war. If he could no longer command a majority in the Reichstag, which seemed likely, Germany would be "without a Chancellor, without a Government, without a parliamentary majority"—and without any legal authority even to conclude an armistice. By the time the appeal arrived the Kaiser had gone to bed and no functionary would disturb him.

What neither the Kaiser nor Prince Max knew was that just after the futile telephone call, Hindenburg, Groener, and General von Plessen had discussed the Kaiser's plan to lead the Army home and suppress the revolutions. Had it any chance of working they would have recommended it, but they knew that even the crack division selected for its dependability to cover the rear of General Headquarters against the revolutionaries, after it had reached Aix-la-Chapelle from Cologne, had defied its officers and begun to march home. Only Plessen in the face of such evidence was unwilling to confess the hopelessness of the Kaiser's dream. But all three did nothing except go to bed.

As the ninth of November dawned, Social Democratic leaders in Berlin were still anticipating the abdication which Prince Max had failed to elicit. When the Chancellery could only report that it continued to expect the news at any moment, Philipp Scheidemann resigned from the Cabinet. Then, at 9:15, Hintze telephoned from Spa that the Supreme Command had decided to inform the Kaiser that the Army would not support any effort to put down the revolution. Assuming that this meant the Kaiser's imminent abdication, an undersecretary to Prince Max telephoned Friedrich Ebert with the news and a request to delay the planned street demonstrations in Berlin.

"Too late!" said Ebert; "the ball has been set rolling. One factory has already gone into the streets."

Berliners by the tens of thousands were already flooding into the central boulevards, some with signs demanding abdication. Others, anticipating a violent response from the military presence in the capital, carried placards appealing, "Brothers, don't shoot!" Rumors were spreading of attacks on barracks and casualties on both sides, although it was quickly apparent that many soldiers had joined the workers in the streets. At any moment, Prince Max realized, a demagogue among the mutinous masses needed only to proclaim the Kaiser dethroned to eliminate any benefit which might be gained from an orderly abdication. Again he struggled to reach the Kaiser's residence in Spa. There were only busy signals. Both telephones were off their hooks.

In the forest clearing, a Major von Bapst turned up with a safe-conduct through the French lines. He had come, he announced, from the OHL in Spa, where he had been with the transport service. Weygand received him before he was permitted to see his compatriots. Revolutionaries, the major claimed, held all the bridges across the Rhine; not a single supply train could reach the left bank, leaving the Army in effect bottled up in Belgium. (None of it was true, although his source had been General Groener.) To Laperche, Foch's interpreter, Bapst confessed ruefully, and probably with Groener's careful preparation, to arouse—or heighten—Allied fears of encroaching Bolshevism from the east, "Just a year ago we were stationed opposite the Russians at Brest-Litovsk. We were then the victors, and we dictated a victorious peace. 'Bolshevism is among us,' said one of the Russian delegates to me one day. 'Look out! Tomorrow it will be amongst you.' When he prophesied that I laughed at him, so absurdly remote did the idea that Bolshevism could ever menace Germany seem. . . . A year ago, Brest-Litovsk; today, Rethondes! What a terrible collapse!"

With no news from German officials in the interior, Allied authorities busied themselves with contingency plans. The enemy might sign, it was felt, but the government accepting the armistice might have difficulty getting it obeyed. If so, Clemenceau told Wilson's deputy, Colonel Edward M. House, "Foch will continue his march forward." And House added, in a cable to Wilson, that the delays experienced by the German couriers could mean that "we will probably not receive any definite news until Sunday night or Monday morning."

All that the German delegation could do while waiting was to press its detailed objections to the armistice terms, which Erzberger had spent the morning drafting and much of the night before in working out with his colleagues. The document was entitled "Observations on the Conditions of an Armistice with Germany" and took so long to compose that it was 3:45 on Saturday afternoon before Oberndorff and Winterfeldt handed the bulky treatise, heavy on details about withdrawal difficulties and weapons surrender, to Weygand, who promised a response in writing. Foch, he did not tell them, would discuss the appeal by telephone with Clemenceau.

In the documentary novel about the negotiations by Thomas Keneally, *Gossip from the Forest* (1976), the reaction of the Count (named Maiberling in the novel, because of the Oberndorff family's objections) to the General is, "You see, all that writing is futile."

"Please," says Winterfeldt, "I don't want to hear any more about what's futile. . . . Do you think a soldier considers the question of futility? Nearly all a soldier does in peace is futile. And in war the odds mount in favor of futility."

"*You* shouldn't talk that way," says the Count. "You're a Prussian."

At 3:25 P.M., just twenty minutes before the carefully detailed "Observations" had been delivered to the other siding, American Expeditionary Force Headquarters had intercepted a Berlin wireless:

The Kaiser and King has resolved to *renounce the throne*. The Imperial Chancellor will remain at his post until decisions have been made on questions connected with the Kaiser's abdication, the Crown Prince's renunciation of the Imperial and Prussian thrones, and the creation of a regency. He intends to propose to the regent that Reichstag representative Ebert be named Chancellor and that a bill be enacted for the immediate calling of general elections for a German constitutional assembly, upon which would rest the responsibility for the final formation of a government for the German people, including those groups of people that might wish to be included within the Empire.

Toward evening the news reached the forest. Unaware that the abdication message had been composed without the Kaiser's help—or knowledge—Clemenceau questioned whether the delegates in the other dining car had any authority left. Then he left the War Ministry for his home in Paris and went to bed. "It would appear that the [German] plenipotentiaries have no longer any powers," Admiral Wemyss wrote, "and one would think that Erzberger at any rate has no longer any standing."

Weygand had a copy of the German wireless delivered to the Napoleon III railway coach. Erzberger read it and wondered whether his credentials to end the war were still valid. And if they were, he did not know whether he was representing an empire or a republic. Nor, in fact, did anyone else.

ARMISTICE EVE

We are Fred Karno's* army
Just come across the sea:
We cannot fight, we cannot shoot,
No bloody good are we.
But when the war is over,
The Kaiser he will say,
"Hoch, hoch! Mein Gott!
What a bloody fine lot
Are the British infantry."

—BRITISH DRAFTEE SONG IN 1918

Darling, I am coming back
Silver threads among the black.
Now that peace in Europe nears,
I'll be home in seven years.
I'll drop in on you some night
With my whiskers long and white.
Home again with you once more,
Say in Nineteen fifty-four!

—DOUGHBOY SONG IN 1918

---

* Fred Karno was a music-hall low comedian who specialized in absurd ineffectiveness and incompetence. Charlie Chaplin followed in his tradition.

The rain in the Argonne, American correspondent Damon Runyon wrote, is "finely woven and as clammy as a funeral garment." Officially it rained every day in 1918 in sectors of the Western Front where the Union Jack flew, for whenever British brigade commanders would certify that the weather was inclement, a rum ration could be issued. The dark, syrupy fluid, decanted from stone jars marked *SRD* (popularly translated as "soon runs dry"), arrived without fail from Army stores at Deptford, where it had aged since the Boer War, and by regulation was issued in the presence of an officer. The teetotal American forces were not so fortunate.

Rain did fall almost incessantly during the last week of the war. Only on the ninth was the sun visible, but it had disappeared by late afternoon. Dirt roads turned into gluey streams of mud, choking the movement of troops, equipment, ammunition, and supplies. On the German side the weather was the same, but their supply lines were becoming shorter, and they had not been chewed up by four years of warfare over the same ground.

Disorganized in their advance as well as in their motley method of resupply, American forces north of Verdun moved forward in amiable confusion over uncongenial terrain. Rear areas, so recently the front lines, seemed filled with stray elements from the 1st, 6th, 42nd, and 80th divisions, half-famished and exhausted men who had lost their units and their way. Stragglers were so numerous that squads of military police continually combed rear areas to keep men moving forward. Two confused companies from the 307th Infantry Regiment found each other in a field west of the Meuse and made a meal of cabbage they had found unpicked, while a battalion commander implored headquarters, "My men, with the exception of [a] few who went through towns, have had nothing to eat today, with no prospect of anything tomorrow."

Contributing to the confusion was the devastation. It was difficult to locate one's position from any known landmarks, as Corporal Horatio Rogers, 101st Field Artillery (26th Division) discovered. His battery was being shifted to support the 16th French Regiment, and he followed, on horseback, a *poilu* who guided him up a hill. "He said the place was called the Forêt d'Haudromont, but no trees were visible. All I saw was a wide panorama of bare hills pocked with shell holes." Lieutenant Lee Harrison, Jr., of the 111th Machine Gun Company, remembered a mission platoon returning, "guns and all," after having been missing for three weeks. He "strung them out in a line, as they should have been," and broke the platoon sergeant to private. Three weeks was too much. Besides, he could not forget that when they first moved up to the front at Xammes, "one platoon got lost and some of the recruits threw away their rifles."

With roads, poor enough at best, bottlenecked with motor trucks, horse-drawn vehicles, and soldiers slogging among and around them, frustrated couriers on motorcycles struggled half a day to bring orders from GHQ to corps headquarters. At times they did not get through at all, and orders in any case were often based upon inaccurate data. Wireless radio was in its undependable infancy, and telephone lines easily interrupted.

Field officers confidently ordered lost infantry out on new missions, although company commanders puzzled over the whereabouts of their men. Everywhere troops hastened to occupy farms and forests from which the Germans appeared to have withdrawn, only to be slowed down by pockets of machine gunners left to block the way; and roads and bridges and trackage were regularly mined to impede passage. A few months later Bernard Shaw could write Frank Harris in New York—the censorship had been lifted—about the "heartrending" way "in which the American boys slaughtered and defeated themselves by rushing on machine guns ... while Haig's men, who had learned their lesson, got off with a tenth of the American casualties." Americans—some drafted as recently as June or July—were too innocent of war to mop up the enemy before moving ahead.

In some ways a Charlie Chaplin film which was the current sensation in film palaces across America mirrored the way Americans saw their role in the war as well as the way it was. In *Shoulder Arms,* war's discomforts and dangers were bearable and the Germans easy to master—but films appealed to wish-fulfillment fantasies. That wars could be won even by so complete a *klutz* as the splay-footed Charlie appealed to the Yankee concept of an unprofessional civilian army. The British Tommy could sing that he was part of Fred Karno's army, yet each replacement Tommy had been fed into a unit which had been fighting for years. Doughboys who had barely learned how to salute were little removed in imagination from the film's Charlie. Shipped to France, with an identity disk forebodingly numbered thirteen, he would go over the top in a uniform augmented by several knapsacks, a blanket, tin bathtub, coffeepot, egg beater, cheese grater, and mousetrap, and capture thirteen *Boches*. Asked how he did it, Charlie shrugs, "I surrounded them." A master of disguise, he goes out on a patrol looking like a tree trunk; and on another mission, this time in German officer's uniform, he captures the Kaiser and the Crown Prince, delivering the Kaiser with a well-aimed kick to the Imperial arse.* But the cheering of his fellow Doughboys turns out to be only the efforts of his buddies to waken him from his heroic dream. It would be the only way the Allies would take the Kaiser—and Charlie Chaplin had done it.

The Germans were relinquishing ground grudgingly, Chaplin's film notwithstanding. Machine gunners were usually the last of the thinning troops to leave, and afterward the hammering of German artillery would take up the slack. As contact diminished, the Allied advance was held up less by enemy fire than by the consequences of its own forward momentum. Vehicles, field pieces, soldiers, and horses backed up at each water barrier. New bridges had to be improvised under fire, and the pontoons and planks for them had to be trucked over roads which had become near-marshes. With pursuit so handicapped, Foch was not getting the rout he wanted, and wondered whether an army which was shortening its front and its lines of supply, perhaps even to the Rhine, might—if an armistice failed—fight on until the Allies grew weary and divided.

As if confirming these concerns, an American military intelligence agent sent to his headquarters the assessment of the military critic of the Vienna *Neue Freie Presse,* who was clearly purveying propaganda from Spa. "German troops," the unnamed critic had written, "are still offering strong and stiff resistance. They are still deep in enemy country and it is obvious that [the Allied] High Command has deceived itself as to [the] fighting ability of [the] German army. It is a difficult problem to attack Germany through Austria considering the difficulty of advancing through the Alps. The Germans need expect no serious action from this direction during the next three months. If the German West Front continues to make as good a stand as heretofore, the German Army will be able to carry on very well through the winter and this is something which should give the Entente food for thought." Since Allied supply and communications lines were growing increasingly chaotic as they lengthened, General Staff officers in Spa did have tantalizing thoughts about buying "breathing space" for a stand into 1919 on the Antwerp-Meuse line. Yet even without disorder at home, resis-

---

* *Shoulder Arms* would be banned from postwar Germany because the scene in which the Kaiser is taken prisoner was deemed insulting to German honor.

tance could not have been prolonged more than another few months, hardly enough to moderate Allied terms, but enough to bring devastation into the Rhineland.

While the delegates in the other dining car, who had no thoughts of prolonging the war, had retired to prepare their responses to the Allied peace conditions, Foch telegraphed the French, British, and American commanders to maintain the pressure. "The enemy, disorganized by our repeated attacks, is giving way along the whole front. Our advance should be kept going and speeded up. I appeal to the energy and initiative of the commanders-in-chief and their armies to render decisive the results obtained."

Some British and American generals hastened to comply, yet Foch knew that costly efforts to convince the High Command in Spa were unnecessary. Few troops sensed that the war might end in a day or two, but few were unaware that cease-fire negotiations were going on at the very moment that they were being ordered to push on. Any unit with a receiver could pick up wireless exchanges suggesting the splintering within Germany. A Soldiers' and Sailors' Council, in possession of the powerful radio station at Metz, communicated with similar revolutionary committees all along the front and at naval bases on the North Sea. Anywhere a wireless could be appropriated, German radicals aired messages of exhortation and defiance.

Foch's instructions were transmitted at 2:30 P.M. on Saturday, November 9, more than twenty-four hours after the armistice delegates had been handed a list of conditions and a seventy-two-hour limit. On the fifth the French Fourth and Third Armies had maintained a front of eighty-one miles. By the time they reached the west bank of the Meuse they had reduced their area of contact with the enemy to forty-two miles, relieved by a shortening of lines and by American divisions. The French First Army, on reaching the la Chapelle-Avesnes road, reduced the number of divisions in its front lines from twelve to four. To Castelnau's Army of Lorraine the telegram from Foch was merely rhetoric—a manifestation of patriotic enthusiasm. In Alsace and Lorraine the French were not eager to further destroy lands they intended to annex, nor to endanger inhabitants who would be living under the Tricolor. Their advance was measured to the liveliness of German resistance and the efficiency of German withdrawal. They would watch and wait and then move.

* * *

In a Belgian farmhouse British troops of the First Army found a report dated November 8, from the headquarters of a division in the army group of Bavarian Crown Prince Rupprecht. "The division," it read, "can only be considered as unfit for battle. Owing to the extremely heavy casualties, to sickness and to numerous desertions, the average strength of regiments is under 600." (On paper a regiment consisted of 3,000 men and 64 officers.) "Still more important as regards efficiency in battle," it went on, "is the shortage of officers, of which no regiment . . . has more than twelve, and one regiment has only nine. Almost all the machine-guns in the division have been lost or are out of repair, and half the guns in the artillery are deficient. Owing to lack of horses, less than half the transport of the division can be moved, and if the retreat continues, many guns and vehicles will have to be abandoned. Owing to lack of petrol, much of the motor transport of the division cannot be moved. The division has not received rations for two days, and the condition of the horses . . . is becoming very bad, because owing to constant movement there is no time to collect supplies from the country, and forage for them is not arriving."

A soldier in the German 79th Infantry Regiment wrote, on November 9, in a letter that would never get home, "We have had some bad days behind us and before us as well. We must remain constantly in the open, and we [can only] dig ourselves in about one meter deep. The Americans are shelling us almost constantly, and to increase our discomfort, it pours rain every day, wetting us through and through." Erich Maria Remarque's *All Quiet on the Western Front* (1929) has its narrator observe at the end, "There are not many of the old hands left. I am the last of seven fellows from our class. Everyone talks of peace and armistice. All wait. If it again proves an illusion, then they will break up; hope is high, it cannot be taken away without an upheaval. If there is not peace, then there will be revolution." A twenty-year-old conscript three times wounded, Remarque was there and kept a diary.

The young Germans shipped to the front as replacements were inadequately trained and unmotivated by 1914-vintage patriotism. Even so, they were sometimes shocked by the depth of the disenchantment they encountered among troops fighting glumly on. One seventeen-year-old, reporting to the 13th Infantry Regiment in Münster, was told by a veteran soldier, "You damned lengtheners of the war ought to be stood up and shot." Trains would arrive in the West with many of the reinforcements supposedly within having already slipped away at interior stations. A troop train in Limburg as early as June 13 had borne the words, "We're not fighting for Germany's honor but for the millionaires," and from a train at Stettin on October 23 soldiers had waved red flags and shouted, "Down with the war. Long live France!" At Minden on October 25 the same words were scrawled on a troop train, while at Liegnitz the stationmaster found, to his horror, a slogan scrawled on a railway car passing through: "Down with the war! Kill the fat brutes! Hurrah for the revolution!" On trains mutinous officers and soldiers alike would urge men to refuse to fight, while replacement troops were being greeted by retreating units with such insults as "strike-breakers" and "war-prolongers."

In the 9th Battery of the 10th Foot Artillery Regiment, incensed soldiers shouted threateningly to their beleaguered battery commander, "Are you still firing? If you fire again as you fired this morning, we shall do for you." They were not eager to be killed by return fire on the verge of going home; yet Hindenburg later would suggest that with a few "fresh" divisions, "great deeds might still have been done." And indeed there were newly commissioned officers like the lieutenant in Regensburg awaiting orders to a front-line machine-gun unit, which in the November confusion would never come. "I'll never lose my resolve," the die-hard monarchist Heinrich Himmler wrote home, "even if there is a revolution, which is not out of the question." Not all future Nazi leaders were so militant. The cautious Martin Bormann had joined the 55th Field Artillery Regiment in Naumburg in June at age eighteen, apparently a draftee. In November he was still there, safely—an officer's orderly.

Among the replacements surrendering in the final days were former prisoners of war in Russia. On their release they had been taken to Warsaw, in columns of a thousand men each, for reshipment to the West. There, according to interrogations by III Corps Intelligence, the dazed and frail men were given physical examinations to prevent the introduction of disease into Germany and given eight weeks' home leave. One prisoner explained that he was from a group of six hundred who had reported to the 129th Ersatz [Replacement] Battalion for two weeks of retraining, after which they were added to other troops ordered to front-line divisions. "The 600 ex-prisoners refused to leave for the front and were punished by eight days' solitary confinement and then forwarded to Mons to the recruit depot of the 117th Division. There they again refused to bear arms . . . and were at first sentenced to hard labor for the duration of the war. But this order was changed and they were forced to join the

450th Regiment with instructions to the Commanding Officer that they be used for front-line duty on all possible occasions. The 600 were distributed through the elements of the 117th Division in such a manner that not more than two entered the same group or squad."

Even the commanding general of the 117th, General Hoeffer, exemplified the German predicament. Earlier in the war he had been wounded and captured by the French. His right arm was amputated, which later made him eligible for an exchange of disabled prisoners. All disabled returnees had to attest that they would not fight again. Nevertheless, he was back in action, personally inspecting his beleaguered outposts every night and vowing "that he will keep his division in the line despite reverses until no more men are left than can be fed at one field kitchen." Attrition was leading toward that. As Colonel George Marshall had observed in a report to his chief, emphasizing what American numerical superiority was doing to the enemy, "The gaining of ground counts for little; it is the ruining of his army that will end the struggle."

Many soldiers returned to the German lines as fit for combat duty were pitiful shells of their former selves, yet were felt to be more reliable than politicized or defeatist draftees from the seething cities. Hospital orderly and future playwright Bertolt Brecht saw "how they patched people up in order to ship them back to the front as soon as possible" and wrote a grotesque satire of the situation which he sang to his own music. In his "Ballad of the Dead Soldier" the corpse of a soldier who had already died a hero's death is exhumed by medics and pronounced fit, whereupon he is "reinducted," filled with brandy "though his flesh had putrefied," and led off to combat. A priest ("knowing corpses well") swings some incense in the air "to cover up the smell." And the soldier goes off to do battle against France once more, and again dies a hero's death.

Fresh soldiers, General Hermann von Kuhl complained, were "contaminated and spoiled" by defeatism; but he acknowledged that his forces had no tanks, and that "hostile tanks were decisively effective against the thin lines of exhausted German troops." What von Kuhl did not know is that the Allies were also without the dreaded yet inefficient weapon. By November 5 the 40 percent casualty rate—more than half of that resulting from mechanical failure—had reduced the British tank force to eight vehicles. On the Argonne and Champagne fronts the Americans and French had lost 437 tanks, most of their operational vehicles, in October. The final week of the war would be fought without tanks.

* * *

On November 9 the 2nd Battalion of the Coldstream Guards advanced to a line just east of the Maubeuge-Mons road, returning to the district where the British Expeditionary Forces had first fought in 1914. The country was well suited for a German delaying action. The ground on both sides of the Mons-Condé Canal was intersected by a network of drainage ditches and covered by miles of willows. To the north were woods, dark even in daylight; to the south were coal mines, great slag heaps often more than a hundred feet high, villages of humble houses dilapidated even in peacetime, small farms, and half-destroyed cobbled roads. At one farm where Captain Alex Wilkinson of No. 1 Company billeted his men after the Germans had quietly withdrawn, the liberated farmer dug up "a couple of bottles of excellent claret" which he had buried in August 1914. "The usual disciplines of the trenches were enforced," Wilkinson recalled. "The farmer insisted that I should sleep in one of his spare beds, but as I could not take off my boots, one of our [Guards'] rules, I put sandbags over them."

To cover withdrawal with the fewest possible men, the Germans employed well-disciplined snipers and machine gunners. There were few places where abandoned supply trains or caches of weapons in working condition suggested revolutionary chaos, despite Winterfeldt's warnings in the railway car at Compiègne. Where the Germans had begun surrendering in large numbers, it was to secure food, shelter, and sleep somewhere remote from the rolling artillery barrages. It took no political radicalization to want that. Questioning the prisoners taken in the Cambrai-Maubeuge sector, the 62nd West Riding ("Pelican") Division's intelligence officer, Captain Thomas Robbins, heard over and over again the admission, *"Nur nach Hause—alles ist kaputt!"* ("Let's go home—it's all finished!")

Prisoners often uttered defeatist talk because it was what their captors wanted to hear. It was now accepted with less suspicion; and referring to the stubbornly kilt-clad Scots battalions, the Germans declared with believable gratitude that they were relieved to be out of the reach of "the women from Hell." In his diary, Arthur Wrench, a soldier in the Seaforth Highlanders, noted that prisoners "declare now that Germany cannot win the war."

One sign of defeat was that the Germans preferred to leave their wounded for the enemy. Medical supplies were low and there was little transport. Besides, if the war were soon over, the men would be cared for and returned. To artilleryman Jock Marshall of the British First Army, "winkling out" the enemy wounded from reoccupied villages was now the usual thing, but it did not mean an end to the chances of being wounded. On the night of the ninth, long inaccurate bursts of fire were exchanged, but as dawn came on the tenth, thick mist settled across the countryside, and under its cover, German rear guards made another effective and silent withdrawal. "The battle line was now getting shorter with each advance," Marshall would write, "and at various points along the British front some of our divisions had to fall behind owing to their fronts being crossed by the divisions on their flanks. This is what had occurred on our . . . front. We came to a halt on a line through the village of Beaufort. . . ." Their own advance had put them out of action.

The Third and Fourth British Armies had to battle their way across the seventy-foot breadth of the Sambre on the tenth. The 1st, 25th, and 32nd Divisions established three of the four bridgeheads attempted in three hours of heavy fighting in a cold mist. At Catillon a twenty-three-year-old (and ten-times-wounded) subaltern in the Irish Guards, in command as a temporary lieutenant colonel of the 16th Lancashire Fusiliers, directed repairs on one bridge the Germans had shelled apart, then was killed while leading his men across.

In most sectors of the British and Commonwealth front there was little action other than with the German rear guards. For Arthur Boyd, with a field ambulance of the 56th London Division, there was little to do in the final days except to scout each night for a place to sleep which had been occupied by the *Boches* the night before. On the evening of the ninth, however, the boredom was broken when, a few kilometers west of Mons, a brigade major in "splendid uniform" galloped up to the line and announced, "The news is good, boys. The Kaiser had abdicated." It was not just the announcement, but the panache with which it was done that raised a cheer from the troops, for few believed it. Then the major went on. From his immaculate uniform this appeared to be the farthest into the line he had ever been in the war. At Aulnoye, on the Maubeuge-le Cateau road, the 38th Division's 33rd Machine Gun Battalion caught the end-of-war contagion of other units in the area and held a one-franc sweepstakes about the exact time of the armistice. Helmets passed and were filled with francs, which in turn gave each Tommy a minute of his own to watch for.

After going through German-evacuated Valenciennes with the 311th Field Artillery Brigade, Captain Stuart N. Whibley's C Battery, diverted from the main road to Mons several times to support infantry movements, was attached to a Canadian battalion. First the Canadians went forward until held up by machine-gun fire; then C Battery would shell until the German shooting stopped. Very few big German guns were still in action, but on the night of the ninth "one of them dropped five or six shells right in the middle of our horse lines, killing or wounding over twenty animals. Next morning, as soon as it was light, a great number of Belgians from the surrounding district came with knives and buckets and baskets to cut all the flesh they could from the dead animals. It was a very horrid and distressing sight to the Drivers, but we felt we could not stop them as they had been so long without meat. However I made the Mayor of the nearest village bring a gang of men to dig a vast pit in which they buried the carcasses." Not everyone could go on toward Mons. Instead, the Norfolks returned to bury their casualties of several days earlier. At Ghissingnies an English platoon in an orchard had been wiped out to the last man. The faces of the dead had been mutilated by a knife lashed to a stick. "The news of the impending Armistice," Captain Guy Chapman remembered, "was accepted with a shrug."

"Rumours that an armistice had been concluded were current on the 10th," according to the official British *Military Operations France and Belgium 1918*, "and this had been a factor in the desire of the troops to press on and kill as many Germans as possible 'before the whistle blew.' " There is little evidence of such popular enthusiasm, but orders to continue operations were in effect, and they continued. Lance Corporal Alfred Billequez, with a Lewis gun battery in the South Staffordshire Regiment of the 2nd Division, remembered crossing the old stone bridge in the village of Romeries, where his platoon officer announced, "Every man for himself and we will meet on the other side." It not only sounded ominous in its theological suggestion but was also optimistic in the extreme, since the Germans were shelling the bridge heavily. To its own surprise, the unit crept across without casualties, spending the night of the ninth in cellars in Romeries and the night of the tenth in a church near Villiers Pol in which the Germans had kept their horses, it seemed, only hours before. Cemented into the stone walls were iron rings to which the horses had been tethered, and there was straw on the stone floor. There were no pews, but the altar was still intact, and on it lay a large Bible. "Some pages were torn and some were missing.

The pages were beautifully printed with gold decoration." There was a sharp frost, and the building was a good place in which to bed down.

By then rumors of an impending armistice had reached Whibley's battery through his colonel, who added, on his morning visit to the battery on the tenth, that he was established in the very same château—still standing, unmiraculously, because each side wanted it—in which, as a Regular Army captain, he had been billeted during the retreat from Mons in 1914. Like many others, he was an "Old Contemptible." The Kaiser had scornfully called the puny force—the four divisions of the original, badly mauled BEF—a contemptibly little (*verächtlich klein*) army. For four years its survivors had worn the derogation like a badge of honor. Now they were back.

Almost a site for holy veneration, Mons—the last resting place for thousands of British troops—was again within reach. On the tenth its roofs and spires were visible. The German Seventeenth Army was loath to let the city go. Sentimental factors may have impelled the British and Canadians, but for the Germans, Mons was a rail junction which simplified withdrawal to the east. The city was also the point at which divisions were retiring through one another, an orderly method which kept retreats from disintegrating into routs. Disciplined rear guards from successive units would cover withdrawals through their own lines until they, too, had covering fire from the next unit for their own retirement. Against snipers and machine gunners supported by artillery concealed in the woods to the north and east, the 2nd and 3rd Canadians fought for every foot of canal, orchard, house, garden, and stream. In the process, German divisions slipped away.

Elsewhere in the British sector, the situation had become far quieter. On the tenth the Third Army took only 131 prisoners in its entire area. Its V Corps reported that patrols had not even been able to make contact with the enemy, and mounted troops of the IV Corps captured three abandoned trains loaded with machine guns and ammunition at Ferriere le Grand. Only the XVII Corps was encountering fire—much of it in the vicinity of the Mons-Maubeuge railway. The First Army, with its Canadian divisions, was continuing toward Mons, while in the fog and rain the Fourth Army, augmented by South Africans, moved forward toward the Thure, on the east banks of which the Germans had emplaced machine guns and artillery.

On the night of the eighth, General Birdwood's Fifth Army had discovered that its units could cross the Schelde, which wove north through Tournai to Ghent, unopposed, rather than wait to fight its way across on the eleventh as planned; and General Plumer's Second Army kept to the Fifth's left flank. The medieval fortress town of Maubeuge would fall, almost without a shot, at 2:00 A.M. on the tenth, to the 3rd Grenadiers of General Byng's Third Army, bolstered by four New Zealand divisions.

At Landrednes the 8th East Surrey Regiment had been squeezed out of the line by other troops moving toward Mons. Wet and weary, they tumbled into houses from which the inhabitants had fled. In one, First-Class Signaller Ben ("Chota" for *small*) Simpson and his linesmen, Chalky White, Billy New, Dicky Baird, and Puss Sunderland, discovered "a very good supply of women's clothing. Ladies' clean chemises, nightdresses, drawers and button-up boots. Couldn't be better, we thought, than exchange our dirty, lousy undergarments." Simpson saw a water butt outside. Into it they dumped their muddy, lice-ridden clothes. Then they donned lacy nightdresses and frilly drawers, climbed into clean beds, and went promptly to sleep.

On the road between Tournai and Ath, northwest of Mons, Lieutenant Vivian de Sola Pinto, with a detachment of about one hundred infantry and a few cyclists, paused to take cover as a solitary German plane swooped low. Leaflets, rather than bombs, fluttered down. In French on one side and English on the other, they read, "The German People Offers Peace." The new German Government, it declared, was democratic, and the will of its people was to "end the slaughter." Germany was ready for an armistice, ready "to evacuate Belgium and restore it," to come to "an honest understanding with France about Alsace-Lorraine," and to "withdraw all German troops back over the German frontier." Such promises, the leaflet assured, were not "mere words, or bluff, or propaganda"; thus

> Who is to blame, if an armistice is not called now?
>
> Who is to blame, if daily thousands of brave soldiers needlessly have to shed their blood and die?
>
> Who is to blame, if the hitherto undestroyed towns and villages of France and Belgium sink into ashes?
>
> Who is to blame, if hundreds of thousands of unhappy women and children are driven from their homes to hunger and freeze?
>
> The German people offers its hand for peace.

Pinto had just left a rare undestroyed town, ancient Tournai, completely intact and stocked with "such luxuries as cream cakes and pastries which it would have been difficult to obtain at that time in most French or English towns. We were told . . . that Tournai had been kept as a kind of pleasure city for German officers on leave." When his brigadier had visited, in the rain, Pinto—the "Velmore" of Siegfried Sassoon's novel *Sherston's Progress*—had asked, "Can I push on and take Brussels, sir?" Considering the size of his force, the one-time subaltern later regarded the jaunty question as "the highlight of my military career." But he was instructed to remain where he was and await the rest of his brigade as there were reports of a mutiny among the German troops in Brussels, "and we had better not get involved."

By then Captain Sassoon had been invalided to Blighty, where in hospital he was penning antiwar poetry. "Velmore," he would write in his fictional memoir, had put a year at Oxford behind him when he put on his uniform, and because of his spectacles "had the look of one who might someday occupy a professorial chair." (Pinto would, at Nottingham.) In *Sherston's Progress*, Sassoon remembered a late-summer visit to the "Flintshire Fusiliers" by "a bishop in uniform" just after "Velmore's" arrival, when the Allies in mid-1918 were still reeling from German attacks. "You must not forget," the bishop had thundered to a Church parade, "that Christ is not the effete figure in stained-glass windows but the Warrior Son of God who moves among the troops and urges them to yet further efforts or sacrifices." Sherston had "resolutely avoided" looking Velmore in the eye during the oration. Afterward he thought, "If [the bishop] had told us that the War would end in four months' time we should have charitably assumed that he was suffering from martial religious mania." Early in the morning Pinto's battalion continued its cautious advance along the main road, anxious about mines, and the occasional shelling.

East through Flanders, as the German troops melted away, Captain Ralph Hale Mottram, who had fought back and forth over that terrain since 1915, when he left his desk in Barclays Bank, was arranging for the return of civilians. "They had sown their potatoes and wanted to harvest them." For four years he had "handled the British who fought [there] and the civilians on the spot who made summary room for them. . . . The most striking features of that landscape were great solid old farmhouses we knew as billets, many of them called *Ferme l'espagnole* (the Spanish farm) because they had been built as blockhouses, in the sixteenth century, to accommodate Spanish troops of the medieval Austro-Spanish Empire to keep back the French. . . . The ghost of half-forgotten conflicts haunted that area, and . . . gave me a theme, and I wrote of it all as *The Spanish Farm.*" (The sensitive and now underrated novel would win the Hawthornden Prize for fiction in 1924.)

In *The Spanish Farm*, Captain Geoffrey Skene, the Umpteenth's Clearing Officer, enters a once-occupied Flemish manufacturing town, with its core of old marketplace, cathedral, and town hall. Shopkeepers and womenfolk "who had heard but never seen the English soldiers fighting for them all these four years, suddenly saw in their own streets khaki and tin helmets. . . . Sober twentieth-century people, from offices and shops, wearing the shawls of mill-hands, the bowlers and black coats of a labourious life, danced, shouted, wept and wrung the hands of officers and men. Ladies with every appearance of invincible propriety kissed perspiring R[oyal] E[ngineer]s putting up the bridges the Boche had destroyed. . . . Struggling to his billet in the front room of a miner's cottage, [Skene] sat . . . over a bottle of whiskey, waiting for news of the Armistice terms that had been sent to the Boche. It was the evening of November the tenth."

Private Harry Smith remembered the scene at Jurbise, a Belgian coal-mining town nine kilometers north of Mons, where troops were "showered with everything that could be given us, including bottles of vin blanc, cognac, and devil knows what. We weren't sober for three days." He had been driving a Lewis gun limber with a pair of mules, and assumed that the celebration meant that the war was over. Yet the Germans were making a stand nearby, the beginning of the Second Battle of Mons. To spare the venerable city and its working mines, Canadian General Sir Arthur Currie planned to pinch off Mons. The 2nd Division was to occupy the heights to the south and east, the Bois la Haut, from which the Gordon Highlanders had been driven with staggering losses on August 23, 1914. The 3rd Division was to encircle Mons via the northern suburb of Nimy.

Helplessly, fourteen-year-old Georges Licope saw his house in Mons used as a German headquarters and guarded by soldiers who could not resist raising their rifles to aim at low-flying planes. After five or six shots, an officer rushed outside, warning that the firing would only give away their position. At noon on the ninth, the family sat down to lunch "almost as calmly as in peace time. In the veranda some officers had spread out maps which they were consulting. Suddenly we heard an enormous explosion. Two panes of a window in the room in which we were sitting flew into splinters and fell just behind my father, whilst five other panes on the veranda were smashed . . . by shell fragments." A shell had exploded about fifty yards behind the house, but the family did not take the time to check the impact point, fleeing to the cellar while the walls trembled from other bursts. Soon two soldiers joined them shouting, *"Zwei Kameraden kaputt,"* and soon the sound of machine-gun fire from the summit of Mount Panisel indicated how close the battle line had drawn. The Canadian barrage from La Bascule reached such a pitch that German batteries fell back hastily to the east, leaving only a few well-protected guns at key crossroads.

Officially, there was no shelling of Mons. Despite the difficulties of penetrating the almost continuous water barrier around the city which once was the moat system around the ancient fortress, and enemy machine guns sited in outlying houses which covered the approaches and made a daylight assault impracticable, Corps headquarters had forbidden any firing on the city, even on known gun emplacements, to protect the civilian population. A Canadian account published a year later by Major J. F. B. Livesay recalled, from a vantage point within sight of the great belfry of Mons, "frantic peasants" running out of their houses up the steep alleys to the Mons road. "There is a roar and a crash, and a lorry is engulfed in the smoke of the explosion. Swaying a little, it dashes on its way, but it has knocked down a civilian carrying a small boy, and he rushes wildly up and down trying barred doors for shelter. The child screams pitiably. Cries and moans come from down the alley. A shell has burst among a group of civilians. Two children are dead; a woman, clutching an infant, staggers to her feet and falls again."

At Battalion Headquarters, Livesay had heard news—"received with some skepticism"—that the Germans would have to sign an armistice the next morning. "Touch wood," said one listener.

For the Licope family the afternoon of the tenth would pass "in a fever of waiting." Finally, the Germans put on their equipment in readiness to march across the fields to the east after dusk. "Tomorrow," an officer confided, "your English friends will be here. We are beaten by a coalition of the whole world." In the early evening the silence was profound, and the family lay awake listening for sounds that would send them again to the cellar. Outside, the cold mist began to cover surfaces with a film of frost.

Immediately south of the Condé Canal was a break in the water barrier, and it was there that the 42nd ("Black Watch") Battalion intended to force an entrance into Mons. At 10:00 P.M. orders from Corps were that objectives for the eleventh remained the same as for the tenth. While the 19th Battalion was fighting to clear the Bois la Haut into the early hours of the morning, and the 4th Brigade was pushing on through the night to the Mons-Givry road, platoons of the 42nd began moving, under the covering fire of Lewis guns, into the railway yards on the edge of the city. It was 11:00 P.M. on the tenth. A second entry was made on an improvised plank bridge over the Derivation Canal, and a third, into the northwest corner of Mons, at 2:00 A.M.

Will E. Bird, of Amherst, Nova Scotia, had been with the Black Watch since 1916. Moving into the Mons suburbs earlier on Sunday, his company had interrupted a wedding, then went on, heaving grenades ahead of them. By 11:30 that night D Company had occupied the railway station, after a spray of parting machine-gun fire had ceased, and began filing cautiously down the street. "There was not a light anywhere, but suddenly we were confronted by an elderly Belgian in tall hat, striped trousers and swallow-tail coat. He . . . said that further along the street was an *estaminet* run by a lady who was hand-in-glove with the Germans."

He led them into the dark building. Although the German clients had fled, four of the eight beds in the cellar were still occupied by women without "a stitch of nightwear. They blinked in the glare of the flashlight as they sat up and viewed us, then lay down again. Our guide said they were imports."

As they turned to go upstairs "a blonde lady in a nightdress came down from above in a perfect fury. She almost spat at me and ordered me out of her establishment. I reached over with my rifle and swept about a dozen bottles of her stock to the floor." When she sprang at Bird another soldier lifted his bayonet, and she recoiled with screams up the stairs, blood running down her leg. "The Belgian was disappointed, we thought, that we did not shoot her."

Withering machine-gun fire continued to cover the retreat of the main German force to a line east of the Meuse. At major crossroads sappers dug great holes into which to bury mines and felled trees to further block passage. German aircraft had practically disappeared from the sky, making it possible for British planes willing to risk the gloomy weather to fly spotting missions almost unmolested. As a result the XIX Corps intelligence summary, headed NOT TO BE

TAKEN INTO FRONT LINE TRENCHES, at 18.00 (6:00 P.M.) on the tenth was able to identify preparations for blowing road craters at locations listed for advancing troops. Their pattern suggested the line of retreat. Aircraft also observed the removal eastward of supply dumps. Intelligence could fit those fragments of data to claims of prisoners that the Germans were preparing to withdraw to a line thirteen kilometers east of Brussels, where they intended to make a stand, as if no armistice were imminent. Yet it remained a puzzle as to why so few German machines were in the air, for the weather was the same on both sides of the line.

The last good weather for flying had been on the ninth, when a Belgian squadron had headed up the coast from Ostend to see where the Germans had withdrawn. In their two-seater Spad, Commandant Fernand Jacuet and Lieutenant Marcel de Crombrugghe, looking for new enemy positions, proceeded in cautious but widening curves eastward toward Bruges. Germans were hard to find, perhaps because they were moving to avoid entrapment between Allied forces moving north and east and the narrow southern projection of neutral Holland. Flying as low as possible because visibility was uncertain, the two Belgians found themselves over Leoringhe. Swooping over his own house, which he had not seen since August 1914, de Crombrugghe saw his mother and one of his sisters outdoors. They had survived the occupation. "His emotions," another pilot reported, "were indescribable."

The emptiness of the sky was evidence of the end approaching. For many Allied fliers it was a mystery that the air war had gone on as long as it had. One third of all the men who had flown on both sides had died. The Germans were running short of fuel and able to construct few new machines. The Allies appeared to have more and more of everything, and the enemy less and less. As early as October 14 rumors had surfaced at Captain Ewart Garland's aerodrome at Azelot, near Nancy, that the fighting was just about over. "The news is," he wrote in his diary, "that Germany has agreed to peace terms but the war seems to go on all the same." Despite few personnel reinforcements or replacement machines, the Germans fought as tenaciously as ever. Garland's 104th Squadron, in venturing on bombing raids as far into the interior as Essen, was meeting the heaviest antiaircraft fire it had yet seen. ("Archie was very hot," went a log entry.) On one raid all twelve intruders were shot up, a few limping back, the others spinning into the ground in flames. A surprise occurred on one "hot show" when "about 40 Huns" downed five

DH-9s. Something other than gunfire, Garland reported, had impeded navigation. "Just before crossing the lines [into Germany]," he wrote, "we passed through a maze of leaflets at 10,000 feet. On our return these were found to be peace messages from 'the German people.' It was a few minutes after flying through these pleas for cessation of slaughter that our fierce air fight took place." A fortnight later there was little enemy response.

Despite the mist and low fog, British bombers—wood-and-canvas Handley-Page biplanes powered by two Rolls-Royce engines—were airborne over Belgium on the night of the tenth with their loads of sixteen 112-pound bombs, dropping twenty tons by daybreak on the eleventh on facilities the Belgians would assuredly recover the next day. Louvain, with its railroad sidings and junction, was a major target, accounting for more than a hundred bombs, one of which set off a chain of explosions and fires on an ammunition train. "They were fine machines, and you sat out in the open," Lieutenant Anthony Kilburn recalled of the Handley-Page. "The distance of our raids was governed by our petrol capacity and the hours of darkness. Of course we had no wireless, no radar, no parachutes. . . ."

Kilburn was not on that final raid, having been recalled to England, to an aerodrome at Bircham Newton in Norfolk. Handley-Page had just completed the first monster bomber, a biplane powered by four Rolls engines developing 1,400 horsepower at 90 mph. The Super Handley V-1500, bigger than the Lancaster and Stirling bombers twenty-five years later in a far more sophisticated air war, had a wingspan of 127 feet and theoretically could carry a crew of six and thirty 250-pound bombs to Berlin and return. It was the reason some experienced pilots and observers had been withdrawn from the Western Front to the isolated base in Norfolk.

The new No. 27 Group had been waiting for sufficient planes to be ready. Nineteen had been manufactured by early November, with 206 more on order, but only three were flight-ready for the projected date, November 9. Colonel R. H. Mulock had sought and received written authorization "to carry out this operation on the lines you propose when you consider you are ready." A redheaded Canadian with twelve German planes to his credit, Mulock, who would become a major figure in the development of postwar Canadian civil aviation, counted on two crews to bomb Berlin and a third to hit Hamburg, all to cross the North Sea together. However, higher-ups in London reassigned him to the Air Ministry early in

November to prevent him from jumping off on his own. Only on the tenth had he been permitted to return. "As if by magic," Lieutenant Kilburn remembered, "our Mess suddenly filled up with brass hats and senior officers from all over the place, come to witness the start of this memorable raid! We young pilots and observers in the squadron had to be content with second sittings for our meals. Then suddenly something was found to be defective in all twelve engines. Mechanics and engineers worked feverishly all day and all night by searchlights, to correct the faults. At last all seemed ready and in order and only suitable weather conditions were needed."

According to H. H. Balfour, who had been promoted to major just a few days before his twenty-first birthday on November 1, "Actually the sandwiches were cut ready in the Mess on Sunday . . . when the bombing raid . . . was held up by orders emanating from the Foreign Office." At the time no one knew that. Kilburn thought that if weather improved over the North Sea, the Super Handleys would take off on the eleventh.

The British had yet another plan. On November 4 a conference of Allied government representatives in London included for the first time a representative of the Czech National Council, Edouard Beneš, who had been waiting in Paris. Following up its recommendations, Captain William R. Read's 216th Squadron in France was ordered to fly in conventional Handley-Pages to Prague, where the Czechs were already prying Bohemia from the weakening grip of Vienna and Budapest. At Prague they would improvise an airfield from which to bomb Berlin. Raiding large industrial complexes was nothing new to Read's force, and Autigny-la-Tour, in the Vosges, had been picked as a base because it was within striking distance of Cologne and similar targets. The son of a wealthy inventor, Read had inherited a fascination with complicated schemes. Two operatives would slip into Prague on the ground to prepare the way, he noted in his diary. "Crossfield has gone since he knows the country and Pring because he can talk Hungarian and German. . . ." Read would pilot the lead aircraft himself, taking off five hours before dawn and flying a route over Stuttgart and Pilsen to locate a landing site he would mark for the others with a large smoke fire and white circle fifty yards in diameter. Six other planes would follow. Slipping out of Flying Corps Headquarters on the eighth, writer Maurice Baring (of the banking family) met with a courier in Paris who had brought detailed maps of Bohemia from the British Museum. The date for the flights was fixed for November 11.

By November 10, when the cloak-and-dagger arrangements had been completed, a "mysterious message" arrived for Read: "One machine to be got ready at once. One observer will be supplied you. One rack of Cooper's bombs will be carried. As much petrol as possible to be carried. . . ." He guessed that the ministry "wanted to bring off a stunt trip of one machine." By telephone Read explained that the flight would be impossible on a Handley-Page's fuel capacity. Then, realizing that someone else would get the assignment if he turned it down, he rang up headquarters again. He would pilot and take an observer and a rear gunner.

American planning to carry the war into the German heartland was in the hands of Brigadier General William ("Billy") Mitchell, chief of the Army's Air Service in France. The farsighted but brash Mitchell, who would later prove that battleships were sitting ducks for aerial bombs and be court-martialed by opponents of air power for insubordination, was working on ways to drop poison-gas cylinders which would decimate German livestock herds and incendiary bombs to fire crops and forests. But his staff, bored with weather-related inactivity, used November 10 to prepare a mock communiqué which parodied past extravagant claims. According to "Bull No. 50"

> The dampness made the day impossible for flying. In spite of this, our planes were up in great numbers destroying numerous enemy planes and taking dozens of photographs in spite of the dense fog which rendered visibility impossible.
> Our scout patrol of three planes met 20 Fokkers. The Fokkers immediately burst into flames and crashed.
> The ceiling was so low that at times our planes were forced to run along the ground. In spite of this, we penetrated deeply into the enemy's territory bringing back invaluable information as to the location of towns, rivers and roads behind his lines.
> Lt. Cholmondelay Brown destroyed three enemy balloons in their beds by descending upon them so suddenly that they became tangled in the bed clothes and were unable to escape. . . .

While the mock communiqué suggested the switch to inactivity, there would be one more "kill" on the tenth. At 10:50 A.M. a 94th Squadron Spad-13 piloted by Major Maxwell Kirby ignored the rain and fog to go on what was labeled a "volunteer" patrol—for

planes were officially grounded by bad weather. Few German aircraft had been sighted. They had risen only for artillery spotting and
no longer challenged enemy lines. Emerging from a cloud bank at
150 feet, Kirby found himself almost atop a Fokker biplane. He
pushed down his plane's nose and fired a long burst. The Fokker
dived steeply and crashed into the side of a small hill near Mau-
court.

Mitchell, whose thinking had gone beyond jousts between small
biplanes, would have been interested in a scheme being hatched
back home. An American plan to bomb Berlin and the rest of the
German interior was much less advanced but far more imaginative
than the Bircham Newton scheme. Lester Barlow and Glenn L.
Martin, two aeronautical engineers, had been working on a system
by which a small plane would carry a detachable second plane—actually a flying torpedo—which would be released to fly on to a distant target while the parent aircraft returned to its base. Berlin, 800
miles from the front lines, was the goal. General C. O. Squier, chief
of the Air Corps, was at first skeptical. Four years later, Benedict
Crowell, who was then Assistant Secretary of War, revealed that
when General Squier became convinced of its practicability, "his
greatest fear was that the Germans might hit upon the same idea
and put it into effect before we could get the necessary equipment
across the Atlantic."

In September 1918 government orders to proceed immediately
with production had arrived at the Martin airplane factory in
Cleveland. (Martin had estimated that a thousand units could be
produced for the cost of one modern battleship.) "Under the plan as
adopted," Crowell recalled, "a fleet of flying torpedoes, each of 800
horsepower, would be piloted under cover of darkness from the
American lines to within a few miles of Berlin. The pilots would return while the flying torpedoes continued under mechanical control
to the center of the city. There the wings automatically would be
blown from the torpedoes, causing the whole mass to fall. On striking, the torpedoes, each of which would contain a ton-and-a-half of
t.n.t. or the equivalent of poisonous gases, would explode." To assure success, he added, a fleet of at least fifty had to be launched simultaneously and maneuvered to approach Berlin from several
directions. The German V-1 remote-controlled "Flying Bomb,"
which terrorized the south of England in 1944 and 1945, suggests
what might have been accomplished with the more primitive tech-
nology of 1918. But the order to the factory in Cleveland had come

far too late to be useful. Ruefully, Barlow remembered, the idea had come to the inventors as early as October 1915. The bureaucracy in Washington was then more interested in cavalry.

While the Allies were preparing to strike by air deep into Germany, the Germans were husbanding their forces for a desperation strike in the other direction. After October 30, when sixty-seven machines were shot down to a loss of forty-one of the enemy's planes, the *Jagd-geschwader** roamed less over the disintegrating front lines. Accord-ing to one pilot, "All available machines were concentrated in the northern-most corner of Flanders. Heavy bombers, scout and recon-naissance machines stood ready. . . . A huge air raid on England had been planned. It was a raid which would destroy everything which could be destroyed. . . ." There were Gothas, which had been bombing London intermittently for a year, and giant new Staaken R.XIVs, with five engines. Allied troops were closing in on the air-fields, however, and orders to wreck the big planes on the ground would arrive before orders to send them over the Channel.

The most ambitious coup was being planned in a large hangar at Poll, near Cologne, where a huge triplane was nearing comple-tion. Conceived in 1916 by Vilehad Forssman, a Swedish engineer with the Siemens-Schuckert munitions firm, it was being put to-gether, apparently, with the assistance of Mannesmann Werke, a manufacturer of steel tubing. Its top wing rose fifty feet from the ground, and top and bottom wings, twenty-two feet apart, were 102 feet long, with the center wing 165 feet. There were to be ten 260 hp Mercedes engines, in tandem pairs of pusher and tractor. The Poll Triplane was designed to cruise for eighty hours at seventy miles per hour—to bomb New York and return.

On November 9 the dream was interrupted by work stoppages all over Germany, even at the Krupp works in Essen, the holy of holies of German war production. Work ceased on the big triplane. All that remains is a boxy and cavernous cross section of fuselage and a single seven-foot nine-inch wooden wheel built to take an axle a foot in diameter. The relics of the "New York bomber" are in the Imperial War Museum in London.

A lone, "show" bombing of the American coast, even if the equip-ment had been ready on time and—against all odds—had worked,

---

* Pursuit squadrons, normally of twelve planes each.

would not have prevented the flow of men and equipment across the Atlantic. Poorly trained and inexperienced—a veteran had two months of combat behind him—American troops were unhesitating where the badly bled British and French were cautious. The French, sensing the end, were willing to risk someone else—their own white-officered Colonial Divisions and the fresh Americans. Joined by the American 5th and 79th, the 15th French Colonials were pushing east through the hills which separate the Meuse from the flat plain of the Woëvre. With the American 81st, 26th, and 33rd Divisions were the 2nd and 10th French Colonials, who were apparently also expendable on the eve of the armistice, and who, even before Foch's order to intensify the attack, had begun an advance on a wide front east of the Meuse.

Scheduled for the eleventh, the offensive had been moved up when Austro-Hungarian divisions had been withdrawn from the line. German troops, it was assumed, would be low in morale as well as precariously depleted in strength—and they *were* cardboard-thin. Opposite the American Second Army were only eleven German divisions, all of them woefully short in able-bodied troops. "Evidently the Allies are not going to relax a moment on war making, no matter how many armistice and peace talkers the Germans may send us," the Second Army's commander, Lieutenant General Robert L. Bullard, observed in his diary on the ninth. "My army is harassing the enemy and capturing men daily. It is going well. . . . Things will surely be popping from November 15th to December 15th if the Germans do not accept the armistice. I can see the signs." He ordered a general advance for the tenth, reasoning that although "we seemed on the verge of an armistice . . . the desire of the enemy to have an armistice had been brought about by fighting alone, so it was manifestly wrong now to desist from fighting."

Farther north, the German line of defense, running into Belgium, had shifted to the banks of the Schelde. An offensive to push the Germans out of their forward positions from the Moselle River to the Dutch border had been planned for the eleventh in an attempt to trap as many enemy troops as possible. To assist the Belgians and British were additional American divisions, some of which had hardly arrived in France before being rushed east. The last units of the 31st Division, made up of National Guard units from Georgia, Alabama, and Florida, had only landed in France on the ninth, but earlier arrivals were already in the Le Mans area, part of the 1,390,000 American soldiers who foreshadowed the inevitable future of the war to the military at Spa. Hindenburg and Groener were as bereft of replacements as the Allies would be surfeited with them.

Some locations were too suffused with symbolism for the Germans to give up willingly or for Allied forces to resist trying to retake, even though an armistice would make the case moot for both sides. One was Sedan, where Napoleon III had lost his throne in 1870. The American 42nd ("Rainbow") Division, commanded only since November 6 by the thirty-eight-year-old, controversial Douglas MacArthur, twice wounded in action, was poised toward Sedan. MacArthur, who refused to command from the rear, had been the subject of complaints to GHQ "that I wore no helmet, that I carried no gas mask, that I went unarmed, that I always had a riding crop in my hand. . . ." Pershing had called the carping nonsense and made Colonel MacArthur a division commander with a brigadier general's star.

About the same age was a temporary colonel—a captain until August 1917—who had also benefited, but just short of a star, by the burgeoning of the Army. Pershing had placed George Catlett Marshall, chief of staff of the First Army, on a list in mid-October for promotion to brigadier general and planned to make him chief of staff of a new corps. In Washington, Congress had put off approval until the Meuse-Argonne push had ended. Robbed of confirmation even of his temporary rank of colonel by the imminence of peace, Marshall would soon revert to captain. He would wait eighteen years—until he was fifty-six—for his first general's star.

Marshall was in his First Army office in Souilly when General Fox Conner, John Pershing's chief of operations, had entered to dictate a message for transmission that Pershing "desires that the honor of entering Sedan should fall to the First American Army. He has every confidence that the troops . . . will enable him to realize this desire." It sounded suspiciously like Fox Conner prose.

This, Marshall understood, was a matter of medals and promotions and professional glory. Sedan had lost its strategic value. It was a plum to be plucked in a day or two without a shot or a casualty. Besides, the French, remembering 1870, wanted it. "Am I expected to believe," he scoffed, "that this is General Pershing's order, when I know damn well you came to this conclusion during our conversation?" Conner saw no joke. "That is the order of the Commander in Chief, which I am authorized to issue in his name. Now get it out as quickly as possible." Relaying the order to corps commanders, Marshall added, "In transmitting the foregoing message, your attention is invited to the favorable opportunity for pressing the advance throughout the night." He knew that such a push would overlap the flank of the French Fourth Army, although he also saw reasons to ignore "a theoretical line drawn on a map" when a tactical advantage could be gained. To play safe, he took the proposed order to General Hugh Drum, the First Army's chief of staff, who agreed that it reflected Pershing's thinking and added a sentence: "Boundaries [between American and French forces] will not be considered binding."

Pershing's thinking may have been reflected in an unpublished memoir by General John C. H. ("Court House") Lee, then a colonel with the 89th Division. "He knew that if the campaign was not won in the Fall of 1918 he would doubtless be relieved by General Peyton C. March, the capable and ambitious Chief of Staff in Washington." And he remembered a conversation of Pershing's with General William Wright: "We have got to finish this job this Fall. What we need are two-fisted fighters who will push their way through regardless of cost. The French won't last another winter." Neither concern may have been valid.

From General Charles T. Menoher, who had left the 42nd Division to MacArthur when he took up a new corps, came a follow-up to his own units—Sedan was to be taken "even if the last man and officer drops in his tracks." Pershing, it later developed, had already given instructions himself to General Joseph T. Dickman of I Corps at five that afternoon to advance on Sedan, eager for its capture if only to be able to claim the superiority of the Americans over the French. Yet the one place where the French *were* moving was toward Sedan, where General Maistre's Fourth Army fought on the flank of the American First.

MacArthur had prudently postponed his attack because of darkness and "unfamiliar and rough ground." Other U.S. commanders did not, and pushed toward the Meuse with bizarre abandon, crossing into each other's fields of fire and even encroaching into the sector of the French 40th Division. Realizing the danger of friendly forces firing into one another, MacArthur set off to try to prevent it. In the process he was taken at the point of a pistol by a 16th Infantry patrol, which mistook his floppy hat and flowing scarf for *Boche* officer's garb. It was his last confrontation in France. After he was released with apologies, he discovered that his division was being relieved by the 77th and on the night of the ninth marched to reserve status near Buzancy. From Sedan the enemy fire was still intense, but MacArthur would see no more of it.

Ironically, the prize would elude both Americans and French.

A report from flying ace Eddie Rickenbacker, telephoned to First Army headquarters, that he had dropped newspapers to American soldiers in the streets of Sedan may have confused the town with its suburb of Wadelincourt; and the claim of the UP false armistice dispatch was as erroneous about Sedan as it was about the silencing of the guns. The Germans held it to the end.

Meanwhile the 2nd Division was trying to cross the Meuse. Since the two bridges which the Germans had wrecked were being kept that way by artillery fire, an engineer regiment had prepared makeshift footbridges to be floated down the river in sections. They were to be assembled after dark on the ninth at Mouzon, with the operation assisted by the 5th and 6th Marines* and the 89th. It was theoretically a weak spot—the boundary of the Crown Prince's Army Group and General Gallwitz's Army Group. Through the night the engineers labored to throw the bridges; before daybreak German artillery had zeroed in on the spot. Machine-gun fire prevented any alternative crossing. Overhead, once dawn came, German aircraft kept Allied planes from spotting active batteries, and return fire was too inaccurate to silence them.

"This being under shell fire," Private Allan Neil of the 5th Marines wrote his mother, "is one of the worst things about the war. You lie there in your dug-out and hear the shell coming about three seconds before it hits. It makes a whistling sound, like air-brakes . . . and then when it hits the ground it explodes with a terrific roar, throwing pieces of iron and dirt in all directions. One cannot dodge or do anything when the shells come, but hug down in his dug-out and pray the shell will not get close enough to get him. When you are under this for eleven days it gets very nerve-racking and it seems as if one would almost go insane, especially as you can do nothing to get back at the 'square-head' Heinies. . . ."

Many Marines had gone into action after all of four weeks' training in boot camp at Parris Island, South Carolina. The fate of one of them, Lance Corporal William Manchester, of Attleboro, Massachusetts, already wounded by a shell fragment which nearly ripped off his right arm at the shoulder, illustrated what often confronted an American unlucky enough to be hit in the confused last days. The surgeon at the clearing station, operating on the French *triage* principle that abandoned hopeless casualties in order to con-

---

* Battalions of the 4th Marine Brigade of the Army's 2nd Division, which was itself commanded by a Marine, Major General John A. Lejeune.

centrate on those worth saving, had Manchester carried into the "moribund" tent to die. There he lay unattended for five days, as the war ground to an end, his death certificate already signed to expedite his removal. From his father's memories, Manchester's writer-son described how "three civilians passed through the tent, representing the Knights of Columbus, the Red Cross, and the Salvation Army. The first, distributing cigarettes and candy, saw the Masonic ring on [the corporal's] left hand and skipped his cot. The Red Cross man tried to sell him—yes, *sell* him—a pack of cigarettes; Manchester had no money, so he got nothing. This outrageous exploitation of casualties was common . . . and the A.E.F. gave nothing away to fighting men who were so negligent as to get wounded. . . . It was the Salvation Army man who finally gave the penniless, suffering lance corporal two packs of Lucky Strikes and tried to cheer him up. As long as he lived, Manchester reached for coins when he passed a Salvation Army tambourine. . . . Eventually a team of Navy medical corpsmen, carrying out the dead, found one of the Marines still alive. They were astonished; he was indignant. Removed to surgery, Manchester was patched up, but his right arm would be useless, "a rigid length of bone scarcely covered by flesh, with a claw of clenched fingers at the end."

At a hastily called conference of field officers, Major Andrew D. Bruce (who would rise to lieutenant general in the next war), commanding officer of the 4th Machine Gun Battalion, with the 2nd Division, listened to Major General Charles P. Summerall, the V Corps commander, urge an eleventh-hour advance across the Meuse. "For every kilometer we gain, we enable our allies to move forward ten. We are swinging the door by the hinges. It has got to move. Rumors of enemy capitulation come from our successes. Only by increasing the pressure can we bring about his defeat. . . . Get into action and get across. I don't expect to see any of you again. But that doesn't matter. You have the honor of a definite success—give yourself to that." Summerall made it sound as if the war hung on the outcome, when again the matter was moot.

With units of the 89th Division and the 5th Marines, the 4th Machine Gun Battalion managed to effect a crossing despite machine-gun fire which raked the makeshift bridges. One pontoon span was destroyed twice by artillery fire and patched together again. As the 4th MG historian described it, melodramatically, "Companies dwindled away. Squads disappeared. Battalions shrunk. The ground flowed red—but the men kept on. . . . Replacements carried on the work of those shot away. . . . The bridge was damaged by enemy shells. Men held it together, lying under the hail of metal, until they were killed or dropped into the water wounded." Yet, before going into action, they had heard the rumor that it might be the last night of the war.

One of the two bridges at Letanne held, and more troops were ordered over it in the darkness under fire and despite precarious footing. Supported by floating logs, the bridge (according to the 2nd Division's *History*) was "like a railway track turned upside down," scattering into the stream whatever men machine-gun fire had not toppled there. Only a hundred could be assembled in the darkness on the far side of the Meuse, but after daylight on the tenth they were able to clear the bridgehead and bring reinforcements across. It was a heavy price for a crossing which everyone realized would be made at will in a few days at most, but on the tenth the Americans, at that point at least, held the right bank.

The 356th Infantry Battalion of the U.S. 178th Brigade (89th Division), also attempting to cross the Meuse, sent three patrols to swim to the opposite bank, losing half the men to exposure and gunfire. Eventually other patrols to the south made it with more losses, winning three Medals of Honor (one posthumous) in the process. In another battalion's sector, two patrols were driven from the shore by machine-gun fire, another abandoned its rafts—and the attempt—and the fourth gave up trying to swim the chill river. On the night when the ninth of November was fading into the tenth, some abandoned German pontoons, found floating down the river, were used for a crossing below Pouilly, where three Germans were taken prisoner; but the 355th Infantry, attempting to throw patrols across the Meuse, sent swimmers into the swift current. As they had to battle the cold and the current as well as German guns and grenades, the effort failed. More men died.

The 79th Division had been in the line, with little relief, since September, and had been given the task of taking a great bare crest rising sheer from the Meuse Valley, with a commanding view of the Argonne front—Hill 378 on American maps. After four days of costly fighting, La Borne de Cornouiller had been captured on November 7, and the division had pressed north into the Woëvre plain, and then east. The shallow but muddy Thinte had to be bridged to permit passage of artillery, and on the night of the tenth the 304th Engineers were ordered to throw five spans across, one for heavy trucks, the others for foot traffic. The footbridges were framed in sections near Etraye and moved in darkness. Enemy lines were close: the first sounds of hammering would have provoked machine-gun fire. In silence the bridges were lashed into place with rope and wire. Meanwhile, under cover of darkness, the stone bridge at Gibercy was being repaired with a twenty-six-foot trestle moved to the river-bank in sections. It was in place by 5:30 A.M. on the eleventh, which the Germans must have sensed, for gas shells were lobbed into the area—ineffectively, because of the blanket of fog. Under cover of the dense fog, the 79th renewed the attack. Crossing the Thinte would be easier than the Meuse.

Even after the Meuse had been breached, and villages on the east bank evacuated by the Germans, American troops found new haz-ards as they sought shelter in partially wrecked houses and cellars. The enemy had mined them. The authors of the *History of the 89th Division* saw the practice as characteristically European—and un-American. "A nation whose idea of the sport of hunting is to have beaters drive the game up to the concealed hunter for slaughter, could be expected to adopt the method of killing off their adver-saries with the minimum of personal danger. The feature which makes the use of concealed mines repulsive is that it does not give the victim a chance to engage with the individual who slays him—a chance which he has in fair, stand-up fighting in the open. . . ." Of the mines which the 89th encountered in Laneuville and Cesse, most were 77-mm shell cases filled with explosives, many in cellars, to be tripped by anyone entering, many more to be activated by a fuse left in the grate of a stove. A rain-chilled soldier thought little about in-fernal machines when diving for cover or attempting to thaw out.

A final massive crossing of the Meuse had been ordered for the night of the tenth. After inhabitants of the villages were warned by air-dropped leaflets, towns east of the river were repeatedly shelled. A fat, myopic, and unmilitary *Stars and Stripes* reporter, Alexander Woollcott, wrote, "It is not enough to say that . . . the guns were wheel to wheel. The cannon used in some areas could not all have been crowded in had they been placed wheel to wheel. . . ." While the German garrison in Pouilly huddled in cellars, the 178th Infan-try sent battalions across in rafts pulled across by ropes. Beginning at 9:30 P.M. on the tenth, the operation continued through the night, its goal the heights above Pouilly and Inor. It met no resistance. Meanwhile, orders for the 356th Infantry were late in arriving. It did not push off until 6:00 P.M. to join the Marine brigade of the 2nd Division in crossing a pontoon bridge emplaced before the Bois de l'Hospice. They met withering, accurate fire from machine guns and artillery. The 2nd Battalion's commander, Major Mark Hanna, nephew of the old Ohio politician, survived his first two trips through the barrage. He did not make it the third time. Many of his men were killed or wounded—256 according to Colonel John C. H. Lee—but the remnants went forward, while the 353rd Infantry looked for a way to cross north of Stenay, where another bridge had been demolished. One way or another—and whatever the price— the American command was determined to be east of the Meuse before the shooting stopped.

Also poised toward Stenay was the 90th Division, which received orders on the afternoon of the ninth to begin crossing. Engineers worked all day repairing the bridge at Sassey, to the south. By five, infantry units were moving across and up the Route Nationale, slowed by felled trees, wrecked roads, and anything else the Germans could fashion to delay movement of artillery. As Americans crossed the Meuse, headquarters radios picked up Prince Max's claim that the Kaiser had abdicated. Fighting continued, as the division's *History* put it, "severe and costly. It is probable that no other division in the Expeditionary Forces met with such stubborn resistance during the last hours. . . ." The Germans still had one first-class division in the area—their 20th—and fought for each kilometer through the night, leaving snipers behind when the main units withdrew. It was bitterly cold, and by dawn many men on both sides could barely walk. At six on the morning of the eleventh a "bare remnant" of the advance American battalion was still on the move. Its dead and wounded had exceeded two hundred. When patrols advanced cautiously in the first hours of daylight they found Stenay evacuated, its two principal streets barricaded "with the finest French furniture, rifled from residences." At a bakery where troops liberated two thousand loaves of bread and took prisoner seventeen stragglers, a little girl presented flowers to Major Souther and Captain Hennessey, the ranking Americans.

German planning for withdrawal and for maintenance of discipline went on despite Allied pressure in most sectors of the front. In the Meuse area a young artillery officer, Otto Brautigam, who a quarter century later would be deputy director of the Political Department at the Nazi Ministry for the Occupied Eastern Territories, noted in his diary that American "rolling barrages" had "played awful havoc" with his horses and guns "just at the very moment when we and our underfed horses had to start a fatiguing retreat of forced marches." Across from the American 2nd Division, artillery fire harassed German positions except where dense fog left American officers unsure where their men were. Up and down the line German observers reported unhappily that under cover of machine gun and artillery, American units had succeeded in crossing the Meuse with "weak forces."

As late as dawn on the eleventh, German artillery was still shelling possible new crossing points, but the German 70th and 174th Infantry Regiments were falling back from the river, returning fire as they withdrew. A message from the 31st Division, as the night of the tenth became the morning of the eleventh, suggests no lessening of fighting, or of fighting spirit. "The posts of the two left companies of the 70th Inf were pushed back on the M[ain] L[ine of] R[esistance]," the report went. "An outpost patrol of the 174th Inf seems to have been annihilated. In the 166th Inf sector most severe close range fighting with the Americans had developed approximately south of Senegal Ferme, the enemy having appeared here in flank and rear from the vicinity of Autreville, the regiment losing about two companies in this fight, due to extremely dense fog." By dawn on November 11 the 166th was down to 33 officers and 484 men, and the 174th to 29 officers and 298 men, less than a tenth of theoretical combat strength.

To relieve the pressure on withdrawing units, others were still counterattacking and forcing the Americans to retreat. "In the early forenoon [of the tenth]," a message from the German XXI Corps went, "the enemy suddenly attacked the front of the 192nd Inf. Div. in force and without artillery preparation. He succeeded in advancing, on a narrow front, approximately 2 km. beyond the main line of resistance. A counterattack by the divisional reserves and by the 211th Pioneer Bn. encountered a fresh attack by strong enemy forces and resulting in a deeper enemy penetration. Toward noon a second vigorous counterattack, under the personal command of the commander of the 183rd Inf. Regt. . . . threw the enemy back into the outpost zone. . . . The main line of resistance is again in our possession. Opposite the front of the 1st Landwehr and 15th Inf. Divs. enemy attacks in some force were also repulsed, at some points by counterattacking. . . ." Nothing in the report suggested that the cost was high and the gain certain to be of no value the next day.

In his autobiographical novel *Krieg* (1931), Arnold Vieth von Golssenau, who would write as "Ludwig Renn,"* remembered the last days of the war, when he was a nineteen-year-old sergeant. A soldier he named Höhle had told him, "People say that tomorrow at noon there will be an armistice, and today at six our position here is to be abandoned. There isn't any purpose in our being shot into cripples." With French artillery fire still withering, another soldier, Hanfstengel, complains, "What kind of sense does that make, to fire so heavily at these positions and not even attack? Is it just fun for those guys over there to kill a few more, as long as it's still allowed according to international law?"

"They probably want to use up their ammunition," Höhle suggests.

On the tenth the last radio report the British forces to the north had received about their French counterparts to the south had been that the French had crossed into Alsace and Lorraine almost unopposed, advancing fifteen kilometers at some points, seizing big guns and even abandoned railway trains. Although the Germans seemed only to be giving up territory they knew they would be relinquishing anyway, the real evidences of collapse appeared to be in the failure to render abandoned equipment worthless. Some officers in the field were beginning to realize that with the armistice they would be giving up heavy artillery and, despite orders, it was not worth endangering their men by delays to toy with hardware which would be obsolete the next time. "Once you clear out of here," a German industrialist would prophesy to Desmond Young before the year was out, "we will hunt the French home with sticks."

Between the Argonne and the Somme, where other French forces separated the Americans from the British in the north, the French appeared unable to move quickly enough to keep their front from being crossed by the Americans on their right. The Americans were taking risks and taking heavy casualties. On the tenth the 33rd Division reached the Bois d'Harville, east of the Moselle River, and took Marcheville, but the Germans counterattacked and forced the Americans to withdraw in what was no mere rearguard action. The 7th Division held a hill despite counterattack, while the 92nd took the Bois Frehaut, just east of the Moselle, although it was not able to

---

* In 1936–38, Renn, a Communist, would command the German "Thaelmann Battalion" of the International Brigade in the Spanish Civil War.

hold all its gains, and the 5th captured Jametz and cleared the Foret de Woëvre. In Flanders two American divisions attached to the French Sixth Army moved across the Belgian border despite intense fire and crossed the Escaut. The 92nd was a division of black draftees, its company-level officers coming from a segregated training camp in Iowa and its senior officers up to Brigadier General Charles C. Ballou pulled from white units. The only black combat division, it had been victimized in advance by inadequate training and shortages of equipment, from artillery to maps. Even in France its enlisted men had been pulled from training units to work as stevedores and on road-building gangs.

The Germans had no interest in the hue of their skins, having battled African troops from the French colonies since 1914, and the inexperienced division, by the tenth, had suffered a thousand casualties. In his diary General Bullard noted coldly that his line divisions "found the enemy everywhere" and "fought at it all day. The enemy seemed to strengthen from west to east, the ground being more favorable in the east. The 33rd Division . . . on the west, did well; the 28th Division next . . . had some but no great success. . . ; the 7th Division . . . had hard fighting but advanced some, perhaps half a kilometer; and the 92nd Division Negroes . . . gained a good deal of ground but did the enemy little harm."

To the north the 91st, a division of draftees from eight western states, crossed the Schelde under heavy fire between two less active French divisions. The 37th, composed mainly of Ohio National Guard troops, succeeded in crossing where French troops had failed, advancing two and a half miles beyond the river despite 1,612 casualties. Supporting the infantry of the 35th Division, the 309th Field Artillery had been urged on toward Sedan. Beginning at four in the morning of the tenth, they had trudged with their guns for twenty-three hours from Brinquinay to Eppionville through hard, steady rain on collapsed roads made even more treacherous by steep inclines and mud-concealed shell craters. On a mile-long hill to Apremont each field gun had to be hitched to twelve horses, and even then men were needed behind each wheel, inching the gun carriages upward at about a quarter mile an hour. Reaching the crest after four hours, at three o'clock in the morning, the men released their exhausted horses and, worn out themselves, went to sleep in the rain under trees, bushes, and wagons. The lucky ones found in the darkness a battered hog pen and the ruins of a barn. Officers slept under tarpaulins used to shield the guns. By ten in the morning on the eleventh, under low clouds but no rain, the march was resumed, in soggy clothes, with the rumble of guns to the east now growing more insistent. They passed shattered towns, and saw no sign of other units, but their orders were to push on, and they did.

In a memoir which he had ordered to be destroyed, perhaps because it evidenced how much the future Army chief of staff in World War II and distinguished postwar Secretary of State had yet to learn, George C. Marshall wrote that the last pushes were "a typical American 'grandstand' finish. The spirit of competition was awakened in the respective divisions to such an extent that the men threw aside all thoughts of danger and fatigue. . . . There were numerous cases where soldiers dropped dead from exhaustion, wonderful examples of self-sacrifice and utter devotion to duty. It requires far less of resolution to meet a machine-gun bullet than it does to drive one's body to the death. The men in the 6th Division, which lacked thousands of draft animals, substituted themselves for the missing horses and mules and towed the machine-gun carts and other light vehicles. In six days the army had advanced thirty-eight kilometers, and had driven every German beyond the Meuse from Sedan to Verdun. It was a wonderful and inspiring feat of arms. . . ."

In the Forêt de Woëvre, east of the Meuse, German resistance on the tenth was intense, with shells raining into the 5th Division's line with a precision that belied inferences, from prisoner-of-war interrogations, of imminent enemy collapse. Ordered, despite the hazards, to establish a forward command post, the 6th Battalion was sent into the forest under Lieutenant Colonel Courtney C. Hodges, who would be in France again as a general after D-Day in 1944. What roads there were had become bogs into which wheels and boots sank, but his units plodded on through shelling which would cause 142 reported casualties in the last twenty-four hours of the war. Supply convoys were sent around the south borders of the woods, where the mud was more manageable, but the weather had turned just good enough to permit German observation planes to direct the artillery, which became even more accurate, leaving men and animals sprawled on both sides of the road. A wagoneer of the 60th Battalion reached for his rifle and took a shot at one of the low-flying aircraft, which then turned back and riddled him with machine-gun fire.

At night engineers struggled to lash together a bridge across the fifty-foot breadth of the Loison at Louppy, and another at Jametz. Shelling continued, but the bridges survived. Only Lieutenant K. C.

Millspaugh, commanding the operation, was killed, as fog began descending on the valley. It was 2:00 A.M. on the eleventh.

As late as 2130 hours on the tenth—9:30 A.M.—divisional orders insisted upon continuing attacks and made no mention of a possible armistice. Yet GHQ surely knew that the enemy had only thirteen more hours in which to sign a surrender and had confessed, aboard Foch's railway car, that they had no other options. Many in the American officer corps approved pressing the attack until the last instant, whether to gain strategic position, postwar political advantages, or personal glory. One was a young lieutenant colonel, hospitalized since September 26 with machine-gun wounds of the leg and hip. He had passed the first week of November in bed working on papers dealing with night transport of that new weapon with which he had commanded a brigade, the tank (Renaults, since U.S.-manufactured vehicles had yet to arrive), and new strategies for attacking, using infantry behind tanks. The last one, dated November 10, warned, "While it is not the intention to make officers timid they must nevertheless conserve their lives until the supreme moment." Earlier, at Essey, however, to the awe of his troops, he had walked across a bridge to see if it was mined. ("If it had been," he wrote to his wife when it was all over, "it would not have hurt me at all as there would have been nothing left to hurt.") But he could no longer endure waiting to be declared fit for duty. He was thirty-three and the war might end before he could get back into it. Bribing an orderly, Colonel George Patton broke out of the hospital with Lieutenant Harry Semmes, appropriated a car, and took the road toward Stenay and Montmedy, clogged with troops marching east. It took them until morning on the eleventh to get as far as Verdun.

Except in Alsace and Lorraine, where the struggle seemed pointless and German troops were melting away to the east, the discontent and disorder about which Winterfeldt had warned in the forest became perceptible only in parts of Belgium where disciplined withdrawal contrasted with the milling of mutineers, deserters, shirkers, and stragglers. But such chaos had little to do with revolution and owed much to the decay of authority. Drivers sold their staff vehicles and men their weapons to Belgians for food and drink and civilian clothes. They opened the prisons as well as the prisoner-of-war camps; stormed warehouses and supply trains; compelled railway employees, at the point of a gun, to transport them eastward; packed stolen automobiles with plunder, and took to the congested roads. A fervid account by a veteran, Werner Beumelburg, *Sperrfeuer um Deutschland* (dedicated to Hindenburg, by then *Reichspräsident*), described the end from the perspective of the loyal troops. "At night the retreat continues. At road intersections and bridges the figures of soldiers loom, wrapped in overcoats. As soon as the last cannon, the last machine-gun, has crossed, they blow it up. A dark red flame, a muffled thud and a black cloud. The rear guards of the infantry follow the troops on the march. In the morning we are lying once again in dugouts, waiting for the enemy. The same game begins." Communications have broken down and they hear nothing from home but rumors they prefer not to believe ("We are not in Russia!"). On the evening of November 10, the withdrawing army approaches, "undefeated and still fighting in a grueling match, the line of Antwerp-Brussels-Charleroi-Givet-Mezieres-Stenay-Dun.* From there on down to the south, the old front of the four years of fighting remains almost unchanged."

To Beumelburg it was the civilian population behind the lines which had turned criminal. "The people, whose freedom and safety had been secured for years by the front troops with their lives, were robbing the provisions depots from which these very troops were supposed to exist during their march home. . . . They don't have anything more urgent to do than severing the arteries of the fighting army." Meanwhile, that army was still sustaining grievous losses. "Many are still being hit with lead and shell splinters. Many are still throwing their arms up and falling to the very ground over which the victory march of the German armies took place four years before. Yet weapons are still in the hands of the [surviving] infantrymen. Machine-gunners are still adjusting their sights. Batteries are still firing with discipline and order. . . . Worthy of its great past, this army persists up until the last minute. . . ."

Ludendorff, years later, claimed that the mushrooming Soldiers' Councils, "an institution prepared in long, systematic underground work," had undermined discipline and command, yet that December, at the General Congress of Workmen's and Soldiers' Councils, Richard Müller would observe that the revolution had come sooner than expected: "We had not reckoned with the old rulers' yielding their places to us so soon." The Soldiers' Councils were improvised affairs, men with almost no technical or military knowledge taking charge of communications, supply, and personnel

---

* Dun: a town on the Meuse (Maas), south of Stenay and north of Verdun.

matters. For the most part regular officers quickly moved into the vacuum, with a much-relieved *Soldatenrat* member only initialing or stamping a document. As a lieutenant colonel reported about a small railway office in Coblenz, on the Rhine, "One of the lads had a pile of transport reports and waybills in front of him and asserted that he was responsible for the strict control of the entire railway traffic. I endeavored to make clear to him that such work required not only technical knowledge but also administrative machinery. He understood this and abandoned his job with relief."

Somehow the instinct for order would prevail in most places as front-line troops moved east under march routes planned and communicated to units down to the battalion level "in case of an official ... armistice." Orders from General Adolf von Oven's XI Army Corps to the 28th Division on the tenth accounted for everything. "The mounted troops of the division, including field trains which will be called in," secret order no. 742 read, "will move on November 11 from the area: Ethe—Latour—Latour Halancy—Rachecourt, on November 12 into the area: Messancy—Athus, Pettingen—Dippach—Fingich, on November 13 to Luxembourg. Shelter will be arranged by the division in agreement with Z or Com Insp no. 5. The march of the mounted troops will be made in a closed body. It will be conducted personally by the C.O. of the F[ield] A[rtillery] regt. Immobile elements of the field trains will be left behind (keep roads clear), but all men will be taken along."

Preparing for the end, the major general commanding the 115th Division issued, on the tenth, with distribution ordered down to company level, an exhortation in which he addressed all his men as comrades and laid down the details by which Soldiers' Councils would be permitted in his command.

> After the final difficult fighting on the soil of France, from which we emerged rich in glory and honor, you have under my leadership reached this point. In this serious hour I once more wish to address a word of thanks and appreciation to you for the willingness to sacrifice and the heroic courage of which you have, at all times, during the long years of bitter fighting given proof.
>
> The mutual faith existing between leaders and troops, between officers and men, has been the basis for the successes of our division.
>
> It is particularly at this time, when the political events at

home seriously threaten good order and discipline in the Army
and the safety of our loved ones at home, that the tie between
subordinates and superiors must be drawn ever closer.

With masterly psychology, he proceeded to create the conditions by
which their revolutionary teeth would be drawn.

> ... I hereby decree that men from the ranks, who enjoy the
> confidence of the other men in their units, shall be delegated by
> them, after mature and deliberate consideration, to all head-
> quarters, from the battalion upward.

Such confidential representatives, although authorized "at any time
to go directly to their commanding officers to present to him the
wishes of their comrades" and urged to be "in touch with their comrades constantly," would be quartered and fed with the officers, thus
separated from the ranks and effectively co-opted. In place of revolutionary Soldiers' Councils, the general had created under the same
name an informal new level of officers whose "most dignified duty"
would be "to prevent the arising of any discord within the firmly
knit frame of our division and, where it has developed, to remedy
the same." To complete the subverting of his soldier soviets, "Trust
for trust" was the general's closing line above his name, rather than
the traditional "by command of" phrase. The covertly patrician
strategy would work more often than it failed, and could not have
been lost on other units, such as the XV Army Corps, where Major
Gerd von Rundstedt—a future Nazi field marshal—was at General
Staff Headquarters.

When they had to withdraw hastily to Tellancourt, north of Metz,
to a field half flooded by early winter rains, Oberleutnant Hermann
Goering recalled his men of the Geschwader No. 1 Manfred Freiherr
von Richthofen. Not many days before, the "Red Baron's" squadron, which had carried on after his death in April under the lean
young Goering, himself with twenty-one Allied planes to his credit,
had been located in Guise. There, Goering had addressed his officers
in the hangar and urged them to go on fighting for the Fatherland
and to ignore "absurd rumors that our beloved Kaiser is preparing
to desert us in our hour of need." The men had cheered. Now, while
rain drummed on the tin roof of their operations hut, he declared
that the squadron was ready and capable of any mission required,

but with the armistice negotiations in progress, he could not conceal the imminence of orders to demobilize.

Outside the hut, Oberleutnant Ernst Udet, later a *Luftwaffe* general under Goering, recalled, hung a blackboard, which had gone with them from aerodrome to aerodrome. "A broken piece of chalk lay in the tin groove. The black paint of the board was peeling and splintered. For a whole year the briefings had been chalked on it. Now the board was empty. While the sentries marched up and down outside, the officers sat in the mess. Their faces bore signs of weariness but no bitterness. That night they did not speak of the lost war."

The wiry, energetic Udet, who had scored his sixty-second victory on September 28 near Metz—downing an American plane— had been in Berlin not long before consulting with Dutch designer Anthony Fokker, for whom he had test-flown the newest aircraft. At the Adlon, Berlin's most fashionable hotel, the usual crowd had sung the old tunes to the accompaniment of a three-piece band when suddenly an officer pushed the pianist from his stool and began thumping out a revolutionary song. Others—clearly none of them officers of 1914—joined in the chorus:

Blood must flow, blood must flow, blood must flow,
Like hailstones, thick as fists,
Down with the dogs, down with the dogs, down with the dogs of Reaction. . . .
To the scaffold, to the scaffold, to the scaffold
With the princely brood.

Elsewhere in Berlin, Theobald Tiger's cabaret song, which might earlier have put him in prison, was catching on among soldiers, vowing "No more conscription, no more soldiers, no more monocled potentates, no more discipline, no more medals, no more reserve officers":

Keine Wehrpflicht! Keine Soldaten!
Keine Monokel-Potentaten!
Keine Orden! Keine Spaliere!
Keine Reserveoffiziere!

At the Adlon the horrified manager rushed into the room and ordered the waiters to close the windows, but only succeeded in having a glass forcibly pressed into his hand. Fokker and Udet went outside, and then along the Unter den Linden to the Hotel Bristol, where Udet was packing to return to the front the next morning. "We shan't meet again so soon this time," the Dutchman said. It would not be a Fokker, but a Junkers JU-87, with which Udet would return to action years later. Observing a primitive Curtiss dive bomber in America in 1933, he would push for development of the screaming "Stuka" aircraft which would power the *Luftwaffe* during the next invasion of France.

At Tellancourt on the morning of the tenth, mist again closed in the airfield. For four days no planes of the Richthofen Squadron had flown. Now, in the rain, the red-tailed Fokkers were axle-deep in mud. In Flanders, Oberleutnant Olden, at twenty-six the senior officer of a *Jagdstaffel*, returned from headquarters, where his pilots assumed he was receiving final instructions for the planned raid on England. He looked haggard, and his uniform was torn. Leaving his puzzled comrades standing, waiting for news, he went into his office and wrote out a statement for posting. "On my way back from H.Q. I was held up by a sergeant in command of infantrymen wearing red armbands and ordered to remove my sword-knot, cockade and shoulder-straps. When I refused, the men made a physical assault on me. In my own defense I drew my Browning, fired and wounded the sergeant in the arm." Then Olden ordered the whole of the thinning *Staffel* to muster. Eight pilots and seventy-eight others—mechanics, cooks, and clerks—turned out. *"Kameraden,"* said Olden, "the politicians of the belligerent powers have ordered an armistice!" The statement was premature but the lieutenant was facing the inevitable and already assigning blame away from the military, who had lost the war. "I hereby resign the leadership of *Jagdstaffel* 356. You must choose from your ranks a council of four which is to take the *Staffel* home and await further orders from G.H.Q." The four, he made clear, had to be enlisted men, since the revolution under way was demanding Soldiers' Councils: "Works foreman—ask your mechanics to make their choices."

The men stood silent. Olden looked ill, and one of his men touched his arm to get his attention. "Chief? Chief?" he repeated vainly. "By permission of the Dutch Government," Olden went on, "the *Staffel* will fly over Holland to Krefeld, and then up the Rhine to Mainz." He knew that it was useless to keep flying and fighting, even on "laundry" weather days as most now were, outnumbered eight to one and moving airfields almost daily, each time back another step toward the Rhine. "When we take off in the morning and fly over the ground where the front lines ought to be, according to our map," Leutnant Rudolf Stark of *Jagdstaffel* 35—a Bavarian squadron—had written in his diary, "We see English troops below us. . . . We have grown very lonely; in fact we feel that we are superfluous. . . . We are unable to help our infantry because we never know their positions. We feel that the end is near, but we dare not speak of it."

To Lieutenant Olden of 356 the politicians somehow were guilty, especially after the Bolshevist indignities he had just suffered. There were no revolutionaries, however, in a *Jagdstaffel*. In the grim days of German collapse, no ground personnel of front-line flying units were involved. Mutineers might say that the officer class picked safe staff positions and sent common soldiers and noncoms to their deaths. Flight crews could have no such reproaches for their officers, for mechanics lived in relative comfort and safety while flying officers fought and died. "The mechanics," Baumann, the works foreman, predictably insisted to Olden, "do not want any new leaders. The Herr Leutnant is our leader. All men of the same opinion step forward!"

With a click of heels the other seventy-seven took one step toward him in closed ranks. As they did, the only man still on duty—the telephone orderly—came running from the house which they were using as a headquarters, waving a paper and calling for the Oberleutnant. Olden read the message to himself, taking a long time. Then he read it aloud. "The German Republic has been proclaimed in Berlin. His Majesty the Emperor is on his way to a neutral country." While the men stared silently, Olden put his Browning pistol to his forehead and fired once. Then he sank to his knees, still grasping the pistol. When he crumpled to the ground and lay still, Baumann bent down and picked up Olden's cap.

All day and night, M. E. Kahnert remembered, troops marched along the road near their airfield, eastward from Flanders, some singing, some silent. They headed through Belgium toward the Maastricht panhandle to Holland, on the way to Germany. It was the end of *Jagdstaffel* 356.

Yet there never was a *"Jasta"* 356. The book which recounts its history, appealing, in the early 1930s, to German pride, honor, and sense of betrayal, includes several photographs of the slight, sharp-featured Olden, one with his chief mechanic, Baumann. The few copies which still retain their wrappers include a curious disclaimer: "Although the author has obviously given this *Jagdstaffel* a fictitious number and changed the names of the pilots composing it, the incidents related in this book have a genuine ring and will be recognized by anyone who has had the experience of flying on the western front. Whatever its real number may have been, *Jagdstaffel* 356 undoubtedly fought in the Flanders air in 1918." Only one flier is recorded as having committed suicide in 1918—Oberleutnant Fritz Ritter von Röth, who commanded *Jasta* 23 until the end, was credited with twenty-eight victories (Olden is given thirty-six) and, like Olden, was awarded the coveted *Pour le Mérite.* Whatever the author's fictionalizations, what happened to his squadron is likely to have been, but for the uncommon exception of its commander's end, the shared experience of German airmen in the last days.

On the tenth one of those fliers, Rudolf Stark, noted in his diary that his adjutant had returned at noon with what passed for the latest news and instructions. "It is the end," he wrote. ". . . Complete breakdown." Then he added the litany of armistice negotiations, mutiny of the fleet, Soldiers' Councils, revolution at home. "The *Staffel* receives orders to withdraw; we must at least try to save the machines. Perhaps we might manage to fly back to Bavaria. . . . We shall have to defend our frontiers against Italy. . . ." Later in the evening Stark added another note. "From outside the tramp of marching columns reaches my ears. A shuffle and a rolling—here and there shouts of abuse, and curses. The night swallows up the din. . . ."

One young officer pilot who would never fly against the enemy had only joined *Jagdstaffel* 35 in the first week of November, after being wounded in action two years earlier with a Bavarian infantry regiment and undergoing retraining after convalescence. The next time Lieutenant Rudolf Hess would take to the air in a combat aircraft would be on May 10, 1941, in a Messerschmitt 110 on a bizarre flight to Scotland.

Where there were spirited counterattacks, field bulletins about them were examined by some officers in rear areas with sorrow not at their futility but at not being able to participate. Captain Heinz Guderian, crossing from defeated Austria into Bavaria after having been a German representative to the Austro-Hungarian-Italian armistice talks, recalled helplessly his lost victories with the cavalry at Amiens. Next time he would have tanks. While Captain Erwin

Rommel's former unit, the 6th Württembergers, were fighting their last engagements, he was a staff officer in the interior, not even close enough to be in reserve. He had earned the Prussian *Pour le Mérite* with a mountain battalion at Caporetto, when Italy suffered its worst defeat in the war, now reversed by the Austrian collapse. Rommel would finally fight in France in 1940 and become a living legend afterward not in mountain warfare but in the desert.

Another young officer in a rear area, just out of the hospital and with orders to return to the line, traveled west via Strasbourg, where an invalided former sergeant in his battery had opened a small tavern. The ex-sergeant urged Carl Zuckmayer not to go: he could be hidden there until the war ended. The future playwright refused. The next morning he rode a forage wagon into the Vosges, to his assigned unit. There he found other troops who had preceded him in the replacement regiment which was the funnel to the front. "These men knew me. They told me they were about to form a soldiers' soviet and would elect me to it. The top officers threatened to have us shot."

The next day the senior officers prudently packed themselves into a staff car and left the mutinous troops to themselves. "My men left me my epaulets and medals, tied a red armband around my sleeve, and handed the command over to me. Mounted on a tired nag for whom I pilfered oats in the towns of Colmar and Strasbourg, I led the remnant of our company across the Rhine bridge at Kehl. The Alsatians gave us hostile glares. We kept our eyes straight ahead. . . . None of these soldiers imagined in the least that we had lost the war because of a 'stab in the back.' That was an idea that was talked into people later. We knew that we had been defeated. . . . Starving, beaten, but with our weapons, we marched back home."

An army doctor in Alsace and Lorraine but unmilitary in the extreme, with his slight build, sloped shoulders, and thick, metal-rimmed glasses concealing nearsighted eyes, novelist Alfred Doeblin had found that his grim months within earshot of the guns at Verdun had dragged into years. During lulls in the fighting he had been working on a war novel, choosing, for both distance and irony, the Thirty Years' War. It would become *Wallenstein* (1920). Although a Jew, he was an officer in the Prussian service; but he detested the ossification of soul and the love of flummery in the officer corps. A specialist in hysteria and melancholia, he had witnessed much of both, and was furious with medical men who paraded the wards with riding crop in hand and chaplains who wished loudly among the dying that they could bear arms to defend their *heissgeliebter* (hotly beloved) Kaiser. Doeblin was not surprised to find himself suddenly stripped of his insignia by mutineers, while other red-armbanded soldiers, rebelliously bareheaded, or with caps deliberately crumpled, looted military stores, threw boots and clothes to people in the street, and carried their rifles "butt upward in the Russian style." Years later, his earlier books burned by the Nazis, Doeblin would novelize the experience in *Burger und Soldat 1918,* which he had to publish from exile.

Also in tumultuous Alsace was Seaman Oscar Ludmann, a native of the disputed border province whose French grandfather had kept a picture of Napoleon concealed behind a portrait of Kaiser Wilhelm II. Conscripted into the German navy, he had been in the North Sea port of Wilhelmshaven when the mutinies had broken out. Soon he had sworn allegiance to a *Soldatenrat* and boarded a train with a band of Alsatians who forced their way past loyal troops as far as the Rhine. Still on the German side, they filed off the train near a bridge and were reassembled by their elected commander. "We are at the door of our Homeland," he told them. "I cannot ask you to come with me, but we have one duty and that is to hold firm in our convictions and serve our country. . . . It is better now that we each go our own way so we will have a better chance to get through, as there are still troops fighting. . . . Each of you go home; get your friends together to protect your village. You will be needed when the front troops dissolve. Good-bye, boys; let's hope for the best."

After crossing the Rhine they had separated. Six of them, including Ludmann, arrived in Andolsheim late on the ninth. The streets were empty and dark except for sounds of marching feet coming from the main street. They slipped through side streets to their homes. "How long are you going to stay?" Ludmann's mother asked. "Forever," he said between bites of his first good meal in many days.

By the night of the tenth the Alsatian deserters in the town had formed a pickup detachment and went through side streets holding up German officers, stripping them of their epaulets, and inviting passing units of German draftees to join. In the main streets Imperial troops still came and went. Daylight on the eleventh found open revolt spreading. More brazenly, now, deserters mustered under an arched doorway at a street corner, sniping at the officers as each column filed by and inviting the enlisted men to sneak out of ranks and disappear into the narrow intersecting streets. Some units resisted to a man, and continued their withdrawal in good order. Nevertheless, it was a withdrawal. Even before the negotiators in the Napoleon III railway carriage could do so, Alsace was wiping out 1870.

IMPERIAL SUNSET

Remember that hour heavy with gloom,
Germany sinking to Communist doom,
Germany abandoned, betrayed, despised,
Street and square with blood baptized:
Don't you remember?

—"THE SONG OF THE LOST TROOPS,"
FROM NAZI GERMANY IN THE 1930S

In the fantasy world of Spa, General Groener seized upon the solution to the abdication dilemma. The Kaiser "should go to the front, not to review troops or confer decorations, but to look on death. He should go to some trench which was under the full blast of war. If he were killed, it would be the finest death possible. If he were wounded, the feelings of the German people toward him would completely change." No one had communicated that indiscreet suggestion to the Supreme Warlord, and on the morning of November 9, officialdom at the Supreme High Command was eager only to see the Kaiser go away.

Even in private, the generals discussed the problem obliquely. Abdication, dearly desired, went unmentioned, despite continuing pleas by telephone from Berlin. One strategy to remove the chief obstacle to armistice was to exaggerate the local situation. Officials suggested to each other that the Kaiser's person was no longer safe—that the revolutionary movement was sweeping toward Spa, that insurgent troops were already visible in the area, that roads to the front had been barricaded by mutineers. Spa, it was pointed out, was only sixty kilometers from the Dutch border, where a monarchy conveniently ruled. Further, some courtiers suggested, the Hohenzollern dynasty might be preserved for a son or grandson if appropriate steps were taken before it was too late.

In Berlin the Kaiser's repeated vows to return at the head of his troops to suppress whatever insurrections might be encountered along the way were taken seriously by both sides. Princess Blücher noted in her diary that her husband had seen "van-loads" of armed rebel soldiers cruising the Unter den Linden, and was told that the Kaiser was expected back, "and that the Socialists intended seizing the train and taking him prisoner, but do not intend to murder him." No such rumor penetrated Spa, which had been busy with Prince Max's telegram early on the morning of the ninth that without abdication there would be revolution and anarchy, and "the Empire will thus find itself without a Chancellor, without a Government, without any compact Parliamentary Majority, utterly incapable of negotiating [an armistice]." The Kaiser penned a contemptuous marginal note: "This is what has happened already." He was scornful of "the miserable embarrassment of a Government which has no initiative, strength or will to survive, and which simply lets events take their course."

One uprising was even then evicting a daughter of the Kaiser. On the eighth, Luise, Duchess of Brunswick, was in bed with Spanish flu when a Workers' Council contingent led by August Merges invaded her castle. Her husband, Duke Ernst, had known it was coming, for revolutionaries, the day before, had taken over the rest of Brunswick, releasing prisoners from their cells and occupying civic offices. All the Duke could do was lock his doors.

The next morning the locks gave way to mutinying soldiers demanding to see the Duke. He asked whether they were Brunswickers. Only his own people would be entitled to an audience. The authentic Brunswickers among them poured out their grievances, and the Duke commiserated in friendly fashion but pointed out, to their astonishment, that he had possessed no military authority since the beginning of the war. Sheepishly, most began shuffling out, one pocketing a cigarette box. When others noticed he was forced to put it back.

Then came the red-cockaded and red-armbanded council leaders with Merges at their head. All the top officials in the duchy, they announced, had been arrested. "If you want to do all that," said the Duke, "believe me, it's a great relief to be absolved of responsibility." The wan Duchess, having crawled out of bed to find out what was happening, understood that her husband's airy dismissal would not delay the inevitable. Ordered to leave the state, they were permitted only a side trip to the country to collect their children (one of whom would become Queen Frederika of Greece) before running the gauntlet of sporadic gunfire, work stoppages, and angry mobs at each railway station en route south to quieter Bavaria.

To those with something to lose, a Communist takeover of all Germany seemed possible. A general amnesty a few weeks earlier, intended to relieve tensions and unify the nation, had released from prison a small, insignificant-looking intellectual with tight curly hair and tiny wire-rimmed spectacles. A fiery, hyperactive Marxist, Karl Liebknecht had quickly found himself the temporary beneficiary of the planning of Adolph Joffe, the Russian ambassador, whose duties, it emerged, had exceeded diplomatic niceties. When a packing case with embassy immunity was ordered to be "accidentally" dropped at a Berlin railway station, it proved, as expected, to be filled with insurrectionary propaganda. Joffe was quickly expelled; yet even without Moscow's clumsy interference, revolutionary feeling was strong throughout the country. Much of it was not doctrinaire Bolshevism, although the vacuum of leadership was often filled by professed Reds. What people in the streets wanted, and what the red armbands and banners meant, was that the system which had lost the war and left them hungry had to be replaced. Even where cities had already fallen under some form of Leftist control, the risings lacked a fulcrum. Radical groups and leaders positioning themselves to inherit the remnants of power could not or would not coalesce their interests. Under several layers of rhetoric lay the despised old order, unaffected.

In Berlin, as elsewhere, red-flagged trucks filled with laborers and soldiers singing the *"Arbeitersmarseillaise"* rumbled through the streets hailing the revolution, but no one was sure, from vehicle to vehicle, which revolution. Officers and burghers alike kept out of sight. Few in Berlin believed that the weekend would conclude without a change in government and the Kaiser's fall, for the general strike called by both the Socialists and Liebknecht's Spartakists was bound to force other parties, especially the anti-Bolshevist Social Democrats of Ebert and Scheidemann, to do something.

By early morning the strike was on. Scheidemann had submitted his resignation from Prince Max's shaky coalition, and Berliners waited to see whether the Kaiser would abdicate before he was deposed. Through the morning officials at the Chancellery tried desperately to reach the Kaiser by telephone, but no one could get through to the fog-shrouded Château la Fraineuse. Anticipating such pressure, he had disappeared for a walk in the black pinewoods with Lieutenant Colonel Alfred Niemann, his aide, but they were back by the time Hindenburg and Groener arrived from headquarters. Evasive through days of discussions about the future of the throne, the old Marshal surprised Groener when, in the car on the way to the château, he announced that the news from Berlin and from the front had finally convinced him that the Kaiser had to abdicate and leave Germany. The two of them, he told Groener, had to recommend that to His Majesty.

At fifty-one, in the Army since he was seventeen, Groener had everything to lose. He was finally at the top. Defeat could topple him; disloyalty to the Throne would compound his disrepute among hard-line Prussians. The Kaiser, he realized, would be propped up in his resolve by grandees whose universe would vanish with their sovereign; and in fact when the generals were admitted at 10:00 to the drawing room overlooking the garden, where a wan log fire flickered, a number of retainers were already present.

In a voice choked with sorrow, the Marshal began by asking that his resignation be accepted. As a Prussian officer and *liege* he could not tell his King and Lord what he was forced by unhappy circumstances to recommend. As an officer of the army of Württemberg, on the other hand, Groener was a Swabian and Wilhelm was not his king.* Thus the First Quartermaster General could use language forbidden to a Prussian subject. Hindenburg had stage-managed his role well. His hands would be clean.

Whether or not Groener appreciated the feudal subtleties, he was motioned to speak. To the Kaiser, standing with his back to the fireplace, his left arm, withered and nearly useless since birth, as usual tucked behind him, Groener explained the few alternatives. As a colonel early in the war, Groener had been one of the few officers about whom the Kaiser spoke with real warmth. "The General Staff tells me nothing and never asks my advice," he once said at a dinner party in a rare case when he let the mask drop. "If people in Germany think I am the Supreme Commander, they are grossly mistaken. I drink tea, saw wood, and go for walks, which pleases the gentlemen [of the OHL]. The only one who is kind to me is the chief of the Field Railway Department, who tells me all he does and intends to do." While the Emperor was kept remote from reality by courtiers and generals, conducted to safe sectors of the front, and rarely permitted public appearances in the capital because of his penchant for uncontrolled utterance, Groener had moved closer to the war. And he was still frank in the Kaiser's presence, however unwelcome his candor. The front-line situation, he explained, was hopeless, and deteriorating daily. A military operation against mutinous troops in the interior was impossible. Transport, communications, and supply depots were in the hands of revolutionaries, and most major cities were in rebellion, including Berlin. An armistice, he concluded, had to be accepted on whatever terms were offered, and made effective as soon as possible.

Without saying it, the General had made it obvious that there was no other course for the Kaiser but abdication, to ease the necessary course of events.

Later the Crown Prince, who was then en route to Spa, would complain that Groener was "inaccessible to those considerations of decency which a few moments before had prevented the old Marshal from speaking. . . . Roughly and brusquely he swept away the most ancient and honorable traditions and thought of nothing but going straight to his goal and delivering the blow which it was his

---

* Under the Imperial Constitution the King of Prussia was President of the German Confederation with the title of Emperor (*Kaiser*).

mission to deliver." Having said what all responsible military experts at Spa thought, but none would own up to, Groener would later earn the reproaches of Rightist politicians while the venerable Hindenburg would take on an aura of saintliness.

Turning to his retinue, the Kaiser asked Count Friedrich von der Schulenburg, who (as a major general) was chief of staff of the Crown Prince's Army Group, for an opinion. The Count refused to share Groener's pessimism. Although exhausted, the troops were showing the utmost heroism, and at the front at least were completely loyal. If an armistice could furnish them with breathing space—"time to sleep and delouse themselves"—they could be motivated to move against the Bolshevist mutineers in the interior by being told "how they had been disgracefully betrayed by the Navy and how their food supplies were threatened by a crowd of Jews, war profiteers, slackers and deserters."* One could extinguish the revolution (and preserve the monarchy), he suggested, by picking a few highly visible places to retake, like Cologne, using "all the most modern equipment, smoke bombs, gas, bombing squadrons and *Flammenwerfer.* . . . They would be able to restore order."

In their unreal world far from the dining car in Compiègne, the gaudily uniformed *kaiserliche* retinue had selected their scapegoats and dreamed that favorable armistice terms would leave them in control of their aircraft and advanced weapons as well as with a blank check to reverse the political changes in progress. The Kaiser was encouraged, and his seventy-seven-year-old Adjutant General, Hans von Plessen, who still thought as if Bismarck were Chancellor, rushed to express the same unrealism. "His Majesty cannot purely and simply capitulate to the revolution. Everything must be done to restore order." He wanted armed expeditions to unruly home cities organized at once.

---

* Schulenburg knew what the Kaiser preferred to hear. Wilhelm had written a confidant a few days earlier that he would "write my answer on the pavement with machine guns, even if it means shooting up my own palace. There is going to be order. . . . I wouldn't dream of abandoning the throne on account of a few hundred Jews and a few thousand workers." Yet the only important man in Germany who would opt not to live in a world bereft of the Kaiser would be a Jew, Albert Ballin, head of the Hamburg-American Line. When a Workers' and Soldiers' Council materialized in Hamburg, and it appeared likely, with revolution and abdication imminent, that he would be arrested as a backer of the Kaiser's war, Ballin committed suicide. He was pronounced dead at one in the afternoon on November 9, the very hour newspapers headlined the end of the Empire.

Groener put a stop to the insanity. The Army could not be counted on. As far as its loyalties went, he told the Kaiser, "Sire, you no longer have an army. The army will march home in peace and order under its leaders and generals, but not under the command of Your Majesty."

While the Imperial advisers buzzed with murmurs about Groener's audacity, Wilhelm said, coldly, "I must request that you confirm your statement in writing." Yet it was already eleven o'clock, and revolutionary forces were gaining momentum in Berlin as elsewhere in the Empire. Schulenburg's summary to the Kaiser as they went into the garden finally touched upon the unmentionable: His Majesty had only two alternatives, either to restore order at the head of his army, or bow to the revolution and abdicate. Yet no one brought up another unmentionable: the Allies were unlikely to agree to an armistice which left the Kaiser in power. More war would ravage Germany itself.

Accompanied in the garden by his generals, Wilhelm received the latest news from Berlin from the Foreign Office deputy, Paul von Hintze, and Baron Wernher von Grunau, who represented the Chancellery. The atmosphere was one of unrelieved despondency, hardly alleviated by Grunau's pressing Prince Max's message—that the Kaiser's greatness would be demonstrated best by his self-sacrifice. Still, he appeared ready to acquiesce until General von Plessen broke in to suggest that a distinction be drawn in the abdication message between the Imperial crown and the hereditary throne of Prussia.

Schulenberg seized at the subtlety. "In any and every circumstance the Emperor should remain King of Prussia. He should gather his Prussians around him, and then see what the nation would do!! If the Emperor's abdication was inevitable, the crown of Prussia should be saved from the wreck. This was a purely Prussian question. . . ." Hindenburg grasped the ambiguity happily, and the Kaiser's most devoted adherents assumed that the inevitable had been averted.

By then the Crown Prince had arrived from his beleaguered Army Group headquarters at Waulsort, a Belgian border town just north of the Meuse. Emotionally, Schulenburg rushed to him to explain the dilemma. Prince Friedrich Wilhelm's face was pale and drawn with fatigue and anxiety, but he came forward with what he described as "the simple mentality of a soldier from the front." His views were uncompromising. "See what you gain by widening the

Government? When the process is complete you are shown the door." And he asked why the mutinous sailors had not been "stood up against a wall."

Once the Kaiser had explained what was known from Berlin, the Crown Prince modified his position. If abdication as Emperor had to be, he insisted, "my father should at least remain indisputable King of Prussia."

"Obviously," the Kaiser agreed.

It was not yet one o'clock when General Groener returned with Colonel Wilhelm Heye, who from 1926 to 1930 would be chief of the covertly rearming *Reichswehr*. Heye's mission had been to summon to Spa as many officers of regimental rank as could make it to the OHL in time and poll them as to whether the Kaiser at the head of his troops could "reconquer the Fatherland by force of arms" and whether the Army would fight the Bolshevists "on the home front." Heye reported his findings. "The troops remain loyal to His Majesty, but they are tired and indifferent and want nothing but rest and peace. At the present moment they would not march against Germany, even with Your Majesty at their head. They would not march against Bolshevism. They want one thing only—an armistice at the earliest possible moment. For the conclusion of an armistice every hour gained is of importance."

A melancholy silence greeted Heye. They all watched the Kaiser for some suggestion as to what he would like to hear them say, but no emotion flickered across his face. The generals shifted from foot to foot and looked at each other. Finally, Schulenburg questioned whether German troops would abandon their "War Lord" and their oath to the colors. Groener rushed to answer before Heye could—not directly to the Kaiser, as some later accounts have it, but to the elderly Adjutant General. "Oath to the colors? War Lord?" he questioned sadly. "These are only words, an idea." It was not revolutionary sentiment, but a hard military assessment. Schulenburg, who knew the world of the War Lord's paladins at Spa and similar headquarters units, where well-fed and smartly clothed officers wore the wine-red trouser stripes of the General Staff, assured Groener (who had been a division and corps commander in France in 1917) that he did not have his finger on the pulse of the Army. After all, he had only arrived from the Eastern Front on October 30, and it was "in the trenches and under fire" that one got to know the troops, whose "high sentiments of duty are coupled with a profound sense of religion." Although exhausted after four and a half years, such an

Army "would be incapable . . . of breaking its oath and deserting its King."

The gulf was unbridgeable. As Colonel Heye observed, backing Groener, "If Your Majesty wishes to *march* with them the troops will ask nothing better and be delighted; but the army will *fight* no more, either abroad or at home." Schulenburg eagerly took this as positive, agreeing that even if the Army would not fight, "His Majesty could well return to the Fatherland at the head of his troops." Admiral von Hintze, a veteran royalist, saw that solution as unreal. "His Majesty has no need of an army in order to take a walk. His Majesty needs an army which would fight for him." And as if to prove his point, a call came through for the Admiral. It was Prince Max, again urging that the Kaiser "save a desperate situation by abdicating." What the Chancellor did not confide—it was already 1:15— was that he had already announced the abdication.

With the others standing mute, the Kaiser was forced to some response. The elderly among the group dreaded the *Herumstehen.* Uninterrupted standing was a ceremonial imperative as long as the Kaiser took no notice of it, and he could pace nervously for hours while septuagenarian bureaucrats swayed. He sought the gray eyes of Hindenburg, but the old Marshal evaded contact. "Hoarse, strange and unreal was my father's voice," the Crown Prince recalled, "as he instructed Hintze . . . to telephone the Imperial Chancellor that he was prepared to renounce the Imperial Crown, if thereby alone general civil war in Germany were to be avoided, but that he remained King of Prussia and would not leave the army." As Hintze set off for the telephone, Schulenburg insisted that a written statement be read to Prince Max, and while aides went off to draft one, the others sat down gratefully to an improvised lunch. (The Kaiser normally took his meals in the Imperial railway train.) "After a good lunch and a good cigar, things will look better," said the Crown Prince without conviction.

Around a table decorated cheerfully with fresh-cut flowers, few ate anything, and that in silence. When the group arose and went into the drawing room, Schulenburg arrived with his draft, which stressed Wilhelm's intention to remain "in August Person" with the troops of Prussia, whose King he would continue to be, and included his assent to "empowering the Armistice Commission, now with the enemy, to conclude an agreement immediately, even before the armistice conditions have become known. . . ." While the document was being put to the Kaiser for signature, Plessen came in to report that Hintze had a further and more discouraging message from the Chancellery. Then the door of the adjoining room opened again and an agitated voice called, "Sire, would you be so good as to come here for a moment?" It was Hintze, still on the telephone to Berlin, with news that the Wolff Agency had already announced the Kaiser's abdication of both thrones. Wilhelm had been left a spectator to his own catastrophe.

"Over my head," he would recall bitterly, "the Chancellor had himself proclaimed my abdication, which had not yet been decided, and the renunciation of the succession by the Crown Prince, who had not been approached in the matter. He had handed the government over to the Socialists and had made Herr Ebert Chancellor! The wireless was spreading the news everywhere. The whole army had heard it. Thus they took out of my hands the decision whether I would stay or go. . . ." Struggling to maintain his dignity, he wondered aloud in a faltering voice whether the news could be true. "It is a coup d'état," said Schulenburg, "an act of violence to which Your Majesty should not yield. The crown of Prussia belongs to Your Majesty. . . ."

When Count Hans von Gontard, his eyes filled with tears, announced the news in the drawing room, the entourage was stirred with indignation. Reappearing, the Kaiser cried, "Treason, Gentlemen! Barefaced, outrageous treason!" Seizing blank telegraph forms, he began scribbling a manifesto of protest, until the Crown Prince entered to announce that he was leaving for Vielsalm in Luxembourg, to which he had withdrawn his headquarters. "I had no idea when I shook his hand," said Prince Wilhelm later of his father, "that I should not see him for a year, and then in Holland."

In Berlin, as the clock ticked toward noon, crowds gathered in the streets to await news either that the Kaiser had abdicated or that the Left had deposed him. It was no different elsewhere in Wilhelm's realms. The tension could not be contained to the capital. Confined (as enemy alien) to Leipzig by police permit, Caroline Ethel Cooper, who lived (for "convenience and economy") with a Hungarian pianist, Sandor Vas, at forty-three thirteen years her junior, wrote to her sister in Australia that revolution seemed as infectious as the Spanish flu. She tried to give Emmie Carr, in Adelaide, some idea of the trepidation in Germany: "If you can imagine 75 million members of the Salvation Army massed on the South Coast [of England], seeing the heavens above them torn, and waiting for the good God to fall with a splash into the English Channel, you may have some idea of the atmosphere here. The heavens are torn, *something* has happened to the 'All-Highest,' and they are waiting breathless for the splash." Then, knowing that the letter could not be mailed, she hid it, with others written since 1915, among the extra leaves of a friend's dining table.

"All-Highest," both women understood, was a term that referred as well to the Kaiser, and on the apocalyptic final Friday of the war, Caroline Cooper realized that his end had come. "My dear Emmie," she wrote, "I have seen the red flag! . . . I was on my way to lunch, and coming into one of the main streets [I] saw a dense crowd coming towards me and at the head of it a great red flag. I must say I stood rooted, with my heart in my mouth. As you know, I have waited for it for weeks, but when one first sees it, it takes one's breath away." Things would get worse, she knew, before they would get better, and she was already frying with lamp oil, brewing strawberry-leaf tea, and making biscuits of scarce ground potato. She added the letter to the collection in the table panels, and waited.

Prince Max, in Berlin, knew what the red flags meant also, and preferred the All-Highest's abdication to his violent overthrow. With the waning of the morning, he had run out of time. His chief confidant, Walter Simons, a legal expert and head of the Chancellery staff, the Prince would explain years later, "urgently advised me to disregard formal considerations at a moment when it was perhaps still possible to save the Monarchy." Prince Max was groping at a way to salvage the vestiges of the old system if only through a label. He or Hindenburg might be named, temporarily, Imperial Deputy for some Hohenzollern pending the restoration of peace and order. Simons, when President of the Federal Supreme Court, explained that for him "it was a question of deciding whether the Government should pass peacefully into the hands of Ebert or whether the Spartakists should get control after a bloody revolution. The latter would have spelt the destruction not only of the Monarchy but also of the Army. . . . Only if the civil servants of the old regime put themselves at Ebert's disposal, was the army to be saved; and I knew that Ebert had no objection of principle in the Monarchy. If the Spartakists had taken over, it would have meant not only a revolution *à la* Moscow, but also a complete breakdown of the administrative machine."

The administrative apparatus, despite rumors, remained in good order, for the general strike was unlike any other mass demonstration that had ever gone by that name. Factories had indeed shut down, and the military for the most part had ignored its officers and put itself and its arms at the disposal of the SPD—the Social Democrats—as well as more radical elements, depending upon which had importuned the unit first. But the order for the strike issued by the Workers' and Soldiers' Council included a list of exemptions from participation that was longer than the roll of participants. "Those in fields of trade, communication and transportation" were to keep working, as well as "butchers, bakers, brewers, employees in public eating places." (Only coffee-house workers, among food and beverage handlers, were permitted to strike.) Also exempted from striking in the order were "essential state and community services (in particular, gas, water, electric power, canals, street cleaning, garbage removal, and such)," and even "custodial and nursing personnel, including domestic workers." The Chancellor's functionaries had claimed to Spa that every minute counted because Berlin was already "flowing with blood." They may even have been led to believe it, but what was going on was a very bourgeois revolution. The Council had not authorized the chaos and anarchy which might have radicalized Berlin but would never happen.

Shortly after noon, when Prince Max's announcement became known, an SPD delegation headed by Ebert appeared in the Chancellery to announce their readiness to take over—that they regarded it "as indispensable for the avoidance of bloodshed that the Government be now entrusted to men who possess the full confidence of the people." They had won over, Ebert said, the Independent Socialists; and Scheidemann added, "All the garrisons and regiments of Greater Berlin have gone over to us." Konrad Haussmann asked for proof, adding, "Are you even sure you can still control the movement and that it is not passing out of your hands?" Scheidemann invited him to see for himself. "I propose that Herr Haussmann should take a motor and drive past each of the barracks in the company of a member of the party. . . ."

"I must refuse to appear in public," Haussmann retorted, "under circumstances which would make it seem as if I supported the movement."

Max and several of his aides had retired to another room to discuss the mechanics of transfer of power when his War Minister, General Scheüch, arrived with a message, dated 12:30 P.M., from General von Linsingen, commander of the Brandenburg (Berlin) District. When the troops had formed Workers' and Soldiers' Coun-

cils and announced their refusal to fire on the masses of people who
appeared ready to seize government buildings, Linsingen had
quickly issued an order: "No weapons to be used." Guards were
withdrawn almost everywhere, yet crowds of revolutionaries who
forced entrances to government buildings were interested largely in
compelling officers to remove their badges of rank and to sport red
cockades. "This was rather a fiasco," Admiral Georg von Müller,
Chief of the Naval Cabinet, noted about the Navy Office in his
diary, "because nearly all the officers in the building were in civilian
clothes."

The atmosphere was far different from that when a younger
and more cocky Wilhelm II had addressed the officers of the Emperor Alexander Regiment at the dedication of their new barracks
in 1901. To the assembled officers as well as the curious citizens who
thronged the farther reaches of the square, he had declared, recalling the revolution of 1848, "The Emperor Alexander Regiment is
called upon ... to stand ready as bodyguard by night and day, if
necessary, to risk its life and its blood for the King and his House;
and if ever again the city should presume to rise up against its master, then I have no doubt that the Regiment will repress with the
bayonet the impertinence of the people toward their King." Now
the *Frechheit* of the people had unseated the Kaiser and King, while
few if any bayonets had been lifted in his behalf anywhere in the
Reich.

In the Chancellery, Ebert's deputation waited for Prince Max's
summons. When it came the Prince asked Ebert if he were prepared
to accept the office of Imperial Chancellor. "It is a hard task," he
said, "but I am prepared to take it on."

"Are you prepared," asked Foreign Minister Wilhelm Solf, "to
carry on the Government in accordance with the Constitution? Even
with the Monarchical Constitution?"

"Yesterday," said Ebert, thinking of the mobs in the streets, "I
could have said yes, absolutely; today I must first consult my colleagues."

"Now," suggested Prince Max, "we must solve the question of
the Regency."

"It is too late for that," said Ebert; and his deputation behind
him chorused, "Too late! Too late!"

Prince Max's government had frantically searched for a plausi-
ble way to save the throne via a temporary regency, first thinking in
terms of evading the unpopularity of the Kaiser's own sons by nam-

ing the eldest of his grandsons, then twelve. Since the Hohenzollerns
had lost the war, and with it the faith of their subjects, such a game
of musical chairs was unlikely to alter the direction of events. Yet
Max's under secretary of the Ministry of the Interior, Herr Lewald,
had as a contingency prepared a draft proclamation dated October
31, 1918, which announced the abdication of Wilhelm II as well as
the renunciation of succession by the Crown Prince and the appointment of Prince Eitel Friedrich as deputy "for the carrying on of
Affairs of State," but it is unlikely anyone ever had the courage to
show it to the Kaiser. Ebert would not only become Chancellor
without a regent, but without authority to hold his office. (No
Chancellor had the right to name his successor.) Nevertheless, Ebert
was Chancellor in fact, and took over the old government, including
most of its ministers. Wireless messages to Spartakist leaders from
Moscow, intercepted in the Foreign Ministry, had included one
which Count Bernstorff, ambassador to Turkey until its collapse, recalled had greatly impressed him: "If you wish to make the Revolution complete, you must get rid of all the old officials. If these
remain, the Revolution will fail." The results would prove Moscow
right.

While Secretary of State Arnold Wahnschaffe still struggled to
get through on the telephone to the Kaiser, Ebert began interview-
ing prospective members of his new government and drafting proclamations which could be quickly distributed as leaflets to crowds
milling in the streets. The first, to "Citizens of Germany," announced that with the agreement of his Cabinet, Prince Max "has
entrusted me with the conduct of all the business of the Reich
Chancellor. . . . Fellow citizens! Leave the streets! Preserve law and
order!" The second, to all civil authorities, urged them to stay in office and offered them legitimacy. "I know that *for many* it will be *difficult to work with the new men* who have taken over the Government of
the Empire, *but I appeal to their love of our people.* A breakdown of organization in this grave hour would hand Germany over to the extreme of anarchy and misery. Join me therefore in helping the
Fatherland by *working on fearlessly and tirelessly each man at his post,*
until the time comes for him to be relieved."

Confident that there was a place for him in the government,
Philipp Scheidemann had gone off to have lunch in the restaurant
at the Reichstag, expecting Ebert to follow. While Scheidemann
spooned at his bowl of watery potato soup, people were swarming in
Parliament Square shouting "Down with the Kaiser!" and "Down

with the War!" Other than the roughing up of officers who were slow to remove their insignias, there was little violence, although reports that blood coursed through the streets of Berlin had reached other cities and towns. Petty brutality, however, was common, as an elderly, white-haired general discovered when he made the mistake of driving down the Königgrätzerstrasse in an open cab. Young toughs pulled him into the street while he protested, "I am no longer active. I have taken an honorable part in three campaigns. Give me leave to go home." In uniform, and bemedaled, he was a hated symbol of authority and suffered a battering as his epaulets and decorations were ripped off, and he was left to find his way home on foot through the thronged streets.

Looking for the SPD leaders, some of the crowd filtered into the Reichstag, warning that they had heard that Karl Liebknecht had invaded the nearly vacant Imperial Castle and was about to announce a Soviet Republic from the balcony. One implored, "Philipp, you must come out and speak!"

Scheidemann put down his spoon and hurried through the ornate corridors to the balcony of the reading room, overlooking the masses of people and red flags in Parliament Square. In the crowd was a Reichstag member from Schleswig, Hans Peter Hanssen, who had been watching the well-disciplined files of workmen wearing red boutonnieres and led by marshals with red armbands. Red banners were everywhere, and breaking through the revolutionary songs were chants for a Socialist Republic. "It will have to be here," Scheidemann called to Hanssen. "Hold me by the feet." Leaning precariously over the balcony rail with Hanssen hanging on to his ankles, Scheidemann shouted, "Workers and Soldiers! The cursed war is at an end! Most of the garrisons have joined us. The Hohenzollerns have abdicated. The people have won all along the line. Long live the new! Long live the great German Republic!" In his eagerness to foil Liebknecht, Philipp Scheidemann had altered the course of Germany by impulsively removing the last vestige of its monarchical base.

It was two o'clock. At four Liebknecht would indeed proclaim from the palace a "Free Socialist Republic of Germany." Not a Soviet one. "The day of liberty has dawned," he began. "A Hohenzollern will never again stand at this place." And then he would do little more than make a few more impassioned speeches at other locations, move into the vacated offices of the *Lokal-Anzeiger,* which he took over for his own *Die Rote Fahne* (*The Red Flag*), and agree the next day to join Ebert's government. But because of the threat his presence out of jail implied, the damage had been done. Confronting Scheidemann, who had returned to his bowl of cold soup, Ebert, red with anger on being told what had happened, banged the table and demanded, "Is it true?" Scheidemann admitted that it was, and that he had only acknowledged the inevitable. "You have no right to proclaim the Republic!" Ebert shouted uselessly. "What Germany is to be—a republic or whatever—is for a Constituent Assembly to decide!"

In the meantime the Reichstag still sat, but the chamber had been invaded by revolutionaries who interrupted the proceedings. An army doctor jumped up on a chair and shouted, "Fellow party men! We have no confidence in the Reichstag. For four years it has had the hilt in its hand but has forgotten how to use the blade. Now *we* have the power. We are the representatives of the people. It is we who shall decide what is to be done. Upstairs that old reactionary gang is [still] sitting and will not release the reins. Let's go up and demand a reckoning!"

While a storm of approval rumbled, someone tapped Hans Peter Hanssen on the shoulder—the Viennese newspaperman Dr. Hofrichter. "Tell me," Hanssen asked him, "what kind of people are these?"

"Es is eine ganz wilde Bande," Hofrichter said—("They are an utterly wild gang"). To Hanssen they were fanatical Bolsheviks. Most of them were in improvised uniform, but even the civilians had carbines and cartridge belts slung across their shoulders. Following their leader, they began moving up the stairs to the room where Ebert and Scheidemann were attempting to form a government. Hearing them, Ebert stepped to the railing above them and called, shrewdly, "Fellow party men! It is impossible for us to receive all of you here. But if you will appoint a delegation which can bring your wishes before us, we are ready to receive it."

The mob argued heatedly among themselves. Few knew each other. How were they to choose? Finally one proposed that every tenth person should serve on the delegation. "And the gathering," Hanssen wrote in his diary, "arranged itself in rows, and like well-disciplined Prussians, clicked heels together." The militant who made the proposal stepped forward and counted rows of ten, stopping each time to ask whether anyone objected to the person becoming a member of the delegation. Few knew anyone else, and no one responded. "You are elected," he would continue. "Step aside!"

Through the mob he went, selecting about thirty men. Order had prevailed, and Ebert would confront a group he could manipulate.

With a smile Dr. Hofrichter turned to Hanssen and quoted the words of Kaiser Wilhelm I to his queen following the triumph at Sedan in 1870: *"Welche Wendung durch Gottes Fügung!"* ("What a turn of events through God's will!")

In the early afternoon the telephone call from Spa which belatedly offered the Kaiser's partial abdication had come. In his office, Wahnschaffe, although knowing nothing yet of the declaration of the Republic, was indignant. "What are you saying?" he screamed at Admiral von Hintze. "Abdicate as Emperor but not as King of Prussia? But that is absolutely of no use to us; it is constitutionally quite impossible. . . . Herr von Hintze must listen to what is being telephoned *to him!*" Prince Max took the phone himself and explained that partial measures were of no use; but from Spa came no additional move.

It would be three weeks before an abdication document would be signed by the Kaiser, and it would be only a technicality. As illegal as had been Prince Max's announcement, or his irregular handing over of his post to Ebert, or Scheidemann's false proclamation of a republic, all these had become facts. Ebert was still referring to himself as "Chancellor of the Empire," but the Empire had vanished.

In Kiel, where the revolution began, the *Kieler Neueste Nachrichten* the next day would headline, *"Abdankung des Kaisers und Thronverzicht des Kronprinzen,"* while the second most prominent story, *"Was Foch verlangt,"* detailed what was known of Foch's armistice demands, although nothing of the end of the monarchy itself. In Munich, Thomas Mann consoled himself in his diary that the Allied *Diktat* was meaningless. "I have the feeling that nothing really matters. . . . Forced obligations for Germany, in the long term, seem to be quite illusory." An "Artist- and Worker-*Rat,*" he had been told, had taken over the management of the theater in Munich. "Foolish and childish," he closed his entry.

In Kassel the next day, where pianist Artur Schnabel was to play Beethoven, "twenty or thirty thousand people," he recalled, gathered expectantly in the main square at noon, leaflets having been distributed which suggested that something important would happen. "A few minutes after twelve," he remembered, "a car rushed into the square at high speed. In the car were five sailors;

they looked very similar to the ones I had seen in Cologne—perhaps they were the same ones. There was also one civilian in the car. He stood up and said: 'The Kaiser has abdicated!' Then something quite indescribable happened, for these thirty thousand people reacted as if there now could be only a rosy future for all mankind. There was immediate relief in their faces and they seemed to believe that they would have a happy life from now on and no trouble need be expected any more." His recital went on as scheduled to a sold-out audience with no indication that anything had changed.

In Berlin the fact of the republic took hold quickly. Prince Heinrich, the sovereign's brother, affixed a red band to his sleeve and fled the city. At the palace in Potsdam the Crown Princess gathered her children and, remembering Russia, awaited the worst. Soon an old servant came to her and quavered that a representative of the Revolutionary Soldiers' Council of Potsdam wished to speak to Her Imperial Highness. Clicking his heels, he entered and said deferentially that he was not there to make an arrest. He had been instructed in the name of the Potsdam Council to ask whether the Imperial Highness felt safe enough and to report that ten revolutionary soldiers had been detailed for her protection. "It was typical of your whole revolution," one of the young princes—by then an ex-prince—would tell Ernst Toller.

At 2:30 that afternoon, only half an hour after Scheidemann's appearance on the Reichstag balcony, people milled about in the Schlossplatz, from which troops had withdrawn. A shopkeeper named Schlesinger pleaded with the crowd not to ransack the Imperial Palace, since it was now public property. To establish his point he hoisted a large red blanket to the main balcony to serve as a revolutionary flag.

In Theodor Plivier's documentary novel, *The Kaiser Goes, the Generals Remain* (1933), which would precipitate his flight from Hitler's new Germany, such revolutionary masses are the heroes. The villains are not only the monarchists and the military, but the less-than-revolutionary Social Democratic leaders, and the confusion and privations of the final days are emphasized. In one scene thousands of gaunt, gray Berliners wait in a food queue for meat from diseased cattle, and as even that supply gives out with seven hundred people still in line, several young Communists push their way through to affix a poster to a nearby wall, diagonally across a now-obsolete exhortation in ornate Gothic lettering to subscribe to the Ninth War Loan: *"It is no sacrifice to invest money at 5 percent where it is as safe as a ward in chancery."* The crude lettering of the Communist poster reads, "THE WAR IS FOR THE RICH! THE POOR PAY FOR IT IN CORPSES!" But the people remain patient.

Little in the ornate palace would suffer from the curious throngs, but Plivier describes a different reaction when the crowd penetrates to the cavernous kitchens below and gazes incredulously at the piles of abandoned provisions. "With all the greed of starving men they fall upon the Imperial hoard: 800 sacks of snow-white Ukrainian flour, countless bags of coffee, boxes of tea, preserves, thousands of eggs, pots of lard, bottles of sauce, rows of sugar-loaf, quantities of dried beans, chocolate, cigars, cigarettes. . . . The smell of the good things of which they have so long been deprived intoxicates the senses of these famished creatures—munitions workers, soldiers, wounded men—even more than does the food which they so greedily stuff into their mouths."

Most unguarded public buildings remained in peace. Workmen and soldiers who had taken up red flags and expected to march to their deaths against troops loyal to the Kaiser roamed unmolested. But in the arrogance of sudden power, some of the revolutionaries did their own molesting. Incidents in a few places—largely officers defending themselves against indignities—left an estimated fifteen dead. That there were any dead made threats from the more militant radicals sound ominous, and some seemed disconcertingly trigger-happy. At the Adlon Hotel, where Count Bernstorff had taken up residence to be close to the Foreign Ministry (and where a red flag was displayed for all of two hours during the weekend), a bullet smashed through the window and a mirror above the fireplace while he and his wife were standing in the room with the owner, Louis Adlon. Prudently, the Bernstorffs moved to rooms on the inner court, out of range of the Brandenburger Tor across the Pariser Platz, where armed revolutionaries maintained a barricade.

The hotel itself was invaded by red-cockaded rebels, led by a youth in a sailor's cap, searching, they said, for "war-mongers and weapons." Mounting a chair, the sailor announced to the staff, which had been rounded up in the lobby, "When I give the word, everyone is to shout 'Long live the Republic' three times, at the same time raising his right arm with the fist clenched. Go!" Once the clerks and chambermaids glumly raised their arms and approved of the Republic, the militants began a search of the Adlon for "officers and capitalists," warning Louis Adlon—who had denied any were there—that he would be shot for counterrevolutionary activities if any were found. Fräulein Hartmann, the staff supervisor, slipped away and managed to hide the only officer left in the building, setting Captain von Berger on his crutches and stuffing him into the laundry elevator, which the pair rode up and down until the enthusiasts had gone.

It remained less a day for dying than for fraternization. The railway stations and post offices were occupied, yet the professionals went on with their business; the prisons were entered, but the files properly consulted and only political detainees released. An air of improvisation hung about the revolution, which succeeded more easily and bloodlessly than anticipated. Even the mood of celebration was muted. People had long been hungry, and in mourning for their many dead. On the tenth Thomas Mann reminded himself in his diary that the Empire had only been "a romantic relic" anyway. Adjusting to the fact of change in Berlin he added, hopefully, "The German revolution is just a German one, even if it's a revolution. No French savagery, no Russian-Communist drunkenness.... I am cherishing kind and cosmopolitan feelings toward the 'new world' which I welcome. This world will not be my enemy and I won't be hers either." Then he put down his pen and took a walk in the park in the autumn sunshine.

Liebknecht's palace oration had ended with the call, "Those among you who want the world revolution, raise your hands and swear!" Thousands of arms had shot upward, but the enthusiasm for more violence was not there. As a young banker on the scene saw it, people were largely indifferent to the red-flagged truckloads of mutinous soldiers and sailors. "The Red revolutionists shouted, brandished their rifles, and generally threw their weight about. In among them, before and behind, the usual mid-day Potsdamerplatz traffic carried on. A very curious significant scene, expressive of Germany's disrupted condition—revolution in trucks, apathy in the streets." It was an education for Dr. Hjalmar Schacht, who would become the financial brains of the Hitler regime in the 1930s.

At four snow began to fall, deepening the autumn darkness. At police headquarters in the Alexanderplatz, where throngs had gathered, a left-wing Socialist, Emil Eichhorn, walked in and announced, "I am the new police president." The anxious police, relieved to be under someone's orders, offered no opposition, not even when Eichhorn went through the cellblocks and released the 650 prisoners who had been arrested during the demonstrations.

At five o'clock Prince Max returned through the crowds to the Chancellery to say good-bye. He was on his way to Prussian Saxony to meet his wife and go on with her to Baden. "I should very much like you to stay," said Ebert. The second-floor office in the nearly abandoned building on the Wilhelmstrasse was quiet, and street noises echoed through the corridors. The Prince asked what he could do. "I should like you to remain on as Administrator of the Empire," said Ebert, who may have been angling for some legal fiction to validate his succession from the Prince.

Max politely declined. At the door he turned back. "Herr Ebert," he said, "I commit the German Empire to your keeping!"

"I have lost two sons for this Empire," said Ebert.

At dinner the half-Irish Count Harry Kessler and the half-French René Schickele discussed the idea of using sailors to carry the revolution to Alsace, "proclaiming it a Red republic, and thereby saving it for the German nation." The fantasy struck them at the moment as practical, and they hurried to offer the idea to an SPD leader in the Reichstag, Hugo Haase. Now and then shooting would lighten the sky, but they had no difficulty in getting to the main entrance to the Reichstag, lit by the headlights of commandeered army vehicles. "Soldiers with slung rifles and red badges checked everyone's business. . . . The scene inside was animated, with a continual movement up and down the stairs of sailors, armed civilians, women, and soldiers. The sailors looked healthy, fresh, neat, and, most noticeable of all, very young; the soldiers old and war-worn, in faded uniforms and down-at-the-heel footwear, unshaven and unkempt, remnants of an army. . . ." They searched for Haase among the swarming people in the enormous formal rooms and corridors of the ugly, neo-Gothic hulk, and found him arguing with a young Bolshevik. Haase stopped long enough to listen to the proposal about Alsace and suggested a further conference the next day.

Two or three floors higher in the building Kessler found an office where a woman was issuing revolutionary identity papers. He received a document according to which, "as bearer of this credential," he was authorized "to maintain order and security in the streets of the city" and an identity card certifying on behalf of the Workers' and Soldiers' Council that he was "trustworthy and free to pass." Both bore the Reichstag stamp. He left, now able to pass through impromptu checkpoints and roadblocks. "I have become, so to speak," the Count noted, "a policeman in the Red Guard."

*　*　*

At Spa a meeting convened by Hintze began in Hindenburg's quarters at 3:30. The Kaiser's movements had to be planned. First, Hintze asked, could one annul the abdication proclaimed in Berlin? Hindenburg and Groener shook their heads. Force would lead only to civil war and would fail anyway, aggravating the disaster in the field. Second, Hintze inquired, would publication of a protest that the Berlin proclamation was made without the Sovereign's knowledge and consent be of any value? Again the response was negative. Third, the Admiral wanted to know, how was the safety of His Majesty to be assured, since a return to Germany was "inopportune" and "impossible"?

Holland and Switzerland, Hindenburg said, had been considered as alternatives, with Holland chosen as easier to reach and "monarchical" in sympathies. Breaking in, Schulenburg reproached the generals for taking the Kaiser's problems so lightly. Groener pointed out that they in Spa had no control over internal events. There were mutinous forces as close as Verviers, a Belgian city northeast of Spa, reportedly moving in the direction of the OHL. This fact—if it were one—settled the matter for Wilhelm's entourage. It was time to go.

Hindenburg agreed to undertake the melancholy business of informing the Kaiser, with Hintze, Groener, Grunau, and Marschall accompanying him to the royal villa. "My God," exclaimed the Kaiser, "are you back already?" Turning to Groener, he added sulkily, "You no longer have a War Lord." Ignoring Wilhelm's continued insistence ("Max has presumed too much!") that he would renounce only the Imperial crown, Hindenburg, who in 1920 would claim that the Kaiser made the "sacrifice" on his own, summed up the conference which had settled the Imperial future. "I cannot accept the responsibility of seeing the Emperor haled to Berlin by insurgent troops and delivered over as a prisoner to the Revolutionary Government," he said. "I must advise Your Majesty to abdicate and proceed to Holland." Only a few months had passed since Czar Nicholas II and his family had been murdered by revolutionaries, but the Kaiser, tense with anxiety yet furious that a decision had been made to get rid of him, shouted, "Do you by any chance think I am incapable of remaining with my troops?" No one responded; then Baron von Grunau appealed, "I earnestly beseech you not to lose another hour. Going over to Holland is the only solution in this confusion."

With no choice, the Kaiser instructed Hintze (who had in fact already done so) to make the necessary overtures to the Dutch government. Then Admiral von Scheer and his staff were admitted to say their farewells. Scheer had taken no part in the proceedings, and the Kaiser asked Hindenburg to repeat to the Admiral what he had said. The Marshal did, concluding, "Would to God, Sire, it were otherwise." He turned away.

"I am still King of Prussia," Wilhelm insisted to the helpless Scheer, adding that the Navy had failed him. "I no longer have a Navy." Ushering his retainers out, the Kaiser announced loudly that he would remain the night at the villa. But he had already decided to leave La Fraineuse and decamp aboard his special gold-and-white train, perhaps to foil any plans to kidnap him. Hurriedly he dashed off a note to his ailing wife in Potsdam, that they must go "to a neutral State, Holland or elsewhere, where merciful Heaven may permit us to eat our bread—in exile. God's hand lies heavily upon us!"

In the automobile which took him to the railway siding he told the officers escorting him, "Plessen and Hintze have just put a pistol to my head. I was to leave this evening for the Netherlands. In the heat of the moment I agreed, but . . . I am remaining with the army as King of Prussia. . . . Even if only a few men remain loyal, I will fight with them to the end, and if we are killed, well, I am not afraid of death. . . . No, it is impossible! I am staying here!"

Despite the brave words he then boarded the train. It was 7:40 P.M.

The son of a tailor, and once apprenticed to a saddlemaker, Friedrich Ebert, goateed to add some statesmanlike distinction to his stocky frame, now at forty-eight held, in Germany, the title if not the powers once held by Otto von Bismarck. He was not even sure of the title's legality, or what the revolution in the streets would permit him to do. Suddenly office telephone 988 began to ring. No telephone call should have gone through, as he was alone and there was no one at the switchboard somewhere below. He searched for the right telephone, picked it up, and discovered that it was a secret direct line from Spa, once installed by Ludendorff.

"Groener speaking," said the voice.

Cautiously, Ebert asked how Spa was dealing with the crisis. The response was reassuring. The Kaiser, now aboard his private train for the night, had agreed to be conveyed to Holland.

"Was the Government willing to protect Germany from anarchy and to restore order?" Yes, said Ebert; it was. "Then the High Command will maintain discipline in the Army and bring it peacefully home."

Ebert wanted to know what the Army's attitude was toward the Soldiers' Councils, and Groener reported that orders had gone out to deal with them in a friendly spirit.

"What do you expect from us?" the Chancellor asked.

"The High Command expects the Government to cooperate with the Officer Corps in the suppression of Bolshevism, and in the maintenance of discipline in the Army. It places itself at the disposal of the Government for such purposes. It also asks that the provisioning of the Army be assured and that all disturbance of transport and communications be prevented." Hindenburg, the crisp military voice from Spa added, was willing to remain at the head of the Army.

"Convey the thanks of the Government to the Field Marshal," said the relieved Ebert.

The new Chancellor, who hardly represented the radical spirit of the Soldiers' Councils or the throngs in the streets, had repaid the High Command for thrusting the canker of the Kaiser from Germany. And while General Groener committed the defeated Imperial Army to protecting Germany from the extremists who might undermine the Republic, Friedrich Ebert committed the shaky new Republic to the maintenance of the Officer Corps. In the end the General Staff would control the Republic from behind the scenes, until it could drop the mask and run the country overtly. Ebert believed that he had saved democracy in Germany from civil war or suicidal revolution; looking into the far future, Groener was intent not only on preserving order in the interior and suppressing Bolshevism, but in maintaining the central position of the army hierarchy in the nation. That Germany would call itself a republic was immaterial to him. Ironically, it was a Württemberger, not a Prussian, who had strangled democratic institutions before they could even be born, but it would be years until anyone would know how it happened, or even that it had happened. "We have not had a revolution in Germany, but we've had a counterrevolution," satirist Kurt Tucholsky would say, for the rhetoric of social and political reform at first suggested more change than in fact occurred.

As an earnest of his cooperation, Ebert, on behalf of the government, telegraphed instructions for the Soldiers' Councils, ostensibly as orders to Hindenburg, for representatives from the councils were to meet in Spa the next morning. "We request," it went, "that you issue an order to all field forces . . . that military discipline, peace and strict order must be maintained in the army under all circumstances. Therefore, orders of military superiors must absolutely be obeyed by all troops until the moment of their discharge. . . . Officers will retain their arms and insignia of rank. Wherever soldier councils or committees have been organized, they will without reservation support the officers in their efforts to maintain order and discipline." The councils were to restrict themselves to exercising an "advisory voice" in maintaining confidence between officers and the enlisted ranks regarding such matters as food and leave. Although the signatures (Ebert, Haase, Scheidemann, Dittmann, Landsberg, Barth) ranged the revolutionary gamut, it is likely that the most radical members of the ruling council never saw it.

When the delegates arrived they discovered that they had become rubber stamps for the Supreme Command. Fully expecting to withdraw to the Rhine under an armistice, the OHL had Lieutenant Colonel Wilhelm Faupel demonstrate to the Soldiers' Council representatives, using a huge detail map, the complex logistic problems involved in bringing the defeated Army, still fighting desperate rearguard actions to safeguard its lines of retreat, home to Germany within the time span likely to be allotted. (Captain Geyer had flown the shocking details to Spa.) Any soldiers not withdrawn in time, the delegates were to warn their men, would become Allied prisoners of war, likely to spend months, if not years, doing rehabilitation labor in the devastated lands. Were they really prepared, Faupel asked confidently, to complicate the handling of this colossal problem by interfering in the work of the officers who had the responsibility for organizing and leading the march home?

The delegates, whose political militancy in many cases did not go deep and was of recent origin, received the charge with stunned silence. Then Faupel produced the telegram from Ebert, which cut any remnants of revolutionary zeal from beneath their feet and proposed, in line with the Chancellor's telegram, that the Soldiers' Councils should set up a committee to assist the Supreme Command in maintaining discipline and obedience. They readily agreed. The orderly march home was assured. The Red extremists in the interior would not realize it for several months, but they had already lost. And Faupel would rise to Lieutenant General and Nazi representative to General Franco in Spain during the Civil War, which the Germans would help Franco win.

There had been last-minute hesitations about the departure to Holland, but by the time the delegates had gathered, the Kaiser was no longer a factor. Aboard the Imperial train, His Majesty explained the flight to the Dutch frontier in a letter to the Crown Prince. Since Hindenburg, he wrote, "can no longer guarantee my safety, and can no longer vouch for the troops, I have decided after severe internal struggles to leave the wreck of my army. Berlin is completely lost. . . . I suggest that you should remain at your post in order to maintain good order among the troops until their departure for Germany. If God wills, *auf Wiedersehen.* . . ."

At a military hospital in Pasewalk, eighty miles north of Berlin, a pastor making the rounds to comfort the patients came upon a gaunt Austrian corporal whose broad mustache in better days had been neatly pointed at the ends. To Adolf Hitler and the others in the crowded ward the pastor announced sadly what Hitler would later brand "the greatest villainy of the century." The Kaiser had abdicated; the Fatherland had become a republic; the new government was suing for an armistice. To the stunned occupants of the ward the elderly clergyman eulogized the Hohenzollerns but went on to say that the war was lost and indeed had to be ended, and that Germany had to throw itself on the mercy of the victorious Allies. "Everything went black before my eyes," Hitler wrote later in *Mein Kampf.* "I tottered and groped my way back to the dormitory, threw myself on my bunk and dug my burning head into my blankets and pillow. . . . So it had all been in vain. In vain all the sacrifices . . . in vain the death of two millions. . . . There followed terrible days and even worse nights. . . . In these nights hatred grew in me, hatred for those responsible for this deed. In the days that followed, my own fate became known to me. . . . That night I resolved that, if I recovered my sight, I would enter politics."

At four-thirty in the morning of the tenth, before the first light of near-dawn, the Kaiser's train left its siding without any signal. Two red lamps on the rear of the last carriage were the only sign that the Imperial presence was being removed from Germany. When the train finally stopped in a secluded area miles away, the Kaiser was transferred to his chauffeured car, which had followed. At 7:10 A.M. the four-vehicle procession reached the Dutch border near the village of Eysden, south of Maastricht. The last German sentinel shouted "some coarse words."

On the Dutch side, chains barred the road. No frontier guard was on duty, as it was Sunday; it took repeated hooting of horns to rouse a drowsy sergeant from the customhouse. Identity cards with illustrious names failed to move him: he knew the rules and demanded passports. The Imperial party walked about shivering in the early morning chill and smoking cigarettes while someone telephoned higher authorities. *"En voyage à Paris?"* (Are you on your way to Paris?") a Belgian in the crowd jeered. ("The place was filled with hostile Belgian deserters," the Kaiser's aide, Count Detlef von Moltke, would explain.) Finally the party was escorted to the Maastricht railway station, and the Imperial train, which had covered the same route, was permitted to roll across the frontier. But of the seventy men in attendance upon Wilhelm, German Ambassador Friedrich Rosen turned back forty. (The reluctant Dutch welcome had its limits.) Reboarding his carriage, the ex-Kaiser moved clear of the gathering onlookers shouting insults—the news had spread quickly—and awaited formal authorization for asylum from the Queen of the Netherlands.

Sunday the tenth dawned quietly in Berlin. Citizens strolled in the *Grünewald;* trams and underground trains ran on time; newspapers appeared on schedule—although several now had revolutionary mastheads. In Unter den Linden red flags hung limply from staffs which once carried the Imperial colors, but the streets and squares were relatively empty. In Berlin's factories the machinery was still, but workmen gathered to elect representatives to an afternoon meeting in the Busch Circus which would establish a government. Revolutionary shop stewards who had organized the voting quickly found that they could not control the way the rank-and-file voted. The first issue of *Die Rote Fahne,* over the bold headline *"Wahl der Urbeiteräte"* ("Election of the Workers' Council"), had urged the installation of its adherents, but to counter the radicals the SPD printed thousands of leaflets, and its newspaper, *Vorwärts,* passed from hand to hand in the factories, had editorialized, "No Fratricidal War."

The day before, one of strikes, marches, and meetings, had exhausted popular feeling about revolution. The Kaiser had fled; the war would be over as soon as the new regime sent its acceptance to Erzberger; the Republic had materialized without riots and with little bloodshed; the fear of imminent civil war had largely vanished. It had been, Alfred Doeblin would say, "a well-ordered *petit-bourgeois* event magnified to enormous size." To die now for anything more seemed foolish in the warm November sunlight of the new day, and the elections were only a mixed victory for the organization of Revolutionary Shop Stewards. Further, a mass meeting of soldiers from Berlin units in the courtyard of the *Vorwärts* building ended with the troops, more conservative than their comrades in the factories, sending representatives to fill the front rows of the Circus. Finally, at 1:30 P.M., after hours of wavering, the Independent Socialists, recognizing how bleak were their chances of toppling Ebert now that he had army backing, decided to offer three "People's Commissars" to Ebert's cabinet, and lay down conditions. Confident that he could control events, Ebert accepted the candidates and the conditions.

In the November dusk the Busch Circus—the largest indoor arena in Berlin—filled with politicians and would-be politicians, and adherents of every political shade of the Left. Both principal sides, a German historian of the period, Sebastian Haffner, wrote, "fought under false flags. Ebert assumed the guise of a revolutionary. The revolutionaries assumed the guise of parliamentarians. The decision about who won or lost was in the hands of a mass meeting such as Germany has never seen before or since: in the front rows some thousand men in field grey uniforms, a firmly disciplined block; above them, towards the cupola, a thousand or two workers, men and women, blurred in the half-light—a world of feverish, care-worn faces. . . . In the arena, at improvised wooden tables, sat the panel . . . from Ebert to Liebknecht." Only a minority wanted to hear about the revolution; a mention of reconciliation would bring cheers. At the inner rim of the arena the restless troops chanted, "Unity! Unity!" The more radical the speaker, the longer the speech, until, when it was long past suppertime, the assembly "carried a previously prepared resolution with a lot of ornate and beautiful words about the Socialist Republic and World Revolution. . . . Then they sang the 'International' and at last—night had fallen— the Busch Circus began to empty."

Ebert had agreed to call the new coalition "the Council of People's Commissars" ("only words, an idea," as Groener had said about something else), but the radicalization of the revolution had been reversed. *Spartakus*—the *Gruppe Internationale* would adopt that name on November 11—knew it could not then muscle aside the SPD; and Liebknecht and the lame, intense Rosa Luxemburg would both be murdered by Rightist army officers two months later after a radical uprising had been crushed. It would prove what Ebert already knew in the first hours of his compromise—and compromised—government—that his real power lay with the Army, and that it was vital to get it home intact. "We consulted with each other every evening about the necessary measures," the Quartermaster General would reveal later, "using a secret line between the Chancellery and the High Command. The pact proved itself."

At his home Theodor Wolff, editor of the *Berliner Tageblatt*, received a telephone call on his own private line from the editorial and technical department: "Adolf Hoffmann speaking. I am in your composing room and wanted to tell you that my comrades and I have taken over your *Berliner Volkszeitung*, which will appear tomorrow as our organ, the organ of the Independent [Socialist]s and the Workers' and Soldiers' Council." The newspaper, owned by the same company as the *Tageblatt*, was produced in the same building. The takeover was a joke, Wolff said. No, Hoffmann insisted. Liebknecht and his faction had taken over a paper, and the Independents needed one themselves. "The only law was the law laid down by the Revolution." In that case, Wolff insisted, Hoffmann "should at least state at the masthead of the paper, for the information of its perplexed subscribers, that the Independents had commandeered the paper and made it into their mouthpiece, against the will of the owners. He agreed. . . ." It was, for the most part in those early days, a polite and orderly revolution, although the anonymous author of *"Das rote Jahr"* saw another face to change:

> When the cannons ceased to sound,
> Bullets at home took their place,
> For that was the greeting of freedom.
> Freedom awakened all around,
> And whoever thought otherwise
> Was beaten to a pulp instantly.

That evening, worried about possible danger in the streets, Austrian writer Theodor Däubler attempted to check in at a Berlin hotel. When he registered as "Austrian" the manager refused to have him because a foreigner required identification papers. "There was a scene," Count Harry Kessler noted in his diary for the tenth, "until I, as a delegate of the Workers' and Soldiers' Council who on the score of my credentials am responsible for maintaining law and order, intervened and commanded the manager to keep Däubler. The manager bowed in the good old Prussian way to discipline, even though of revolutionary origin, and allotted him a room." The revolution, Kessler would write, seemed little more "than an eddy in the ordinary life of the city which flowed calmly along its customary course. . . . The colossal, world-shaking upheaval has scurried across Berlin's day-to-day life much like an incident in a crime film."

THE SIGNING

La Moisson maudite est mûre	The cursed harvest is ripe
Qui, depuis quatre ans,	Which for four years has been
mûrit. . . .	mellowing. . . .
Tous tes chefs-batteurs arrivent:	All your "threshers" are coming:
Castelnau, Pétain, Gouraud;	Castelnau, Pétain, Gouraud;
Fayolle, Humbert, Mangin	Fayolle, Humbert, Mangin
suivent;	are following;
Et Degoutte, et Berthelot;	And Degoutte, and Berthelot;
L'Italie et la Belgique,	Italy and Belgium,
L'Angleterre et l'Amérique	England and America
Vont, te suivant pas à pas;	Are coming, following step-by-step,
Sans regarder en arrière,	Without looking back.
Fais ton oeuvre justicière:	Do your work of justice,
Fauche, Foch, à tour de bras!	Reap, Foch, with all your might!
Enfin, ta tâche achevée,	Finally your task is finished,
Tombés les derniers epis. . . .	The last kernels have fallen. . . .
Fauche, Foch, à tour de bras!	Reap, Foch, with all your might!*

—*Le Grand Faucheur*
  ("THE GREAT REAPER"), 1918

---

* The song *"Le Grand Faucheur"* is a play on the words *Foch* and *fauche*, which are pronounced almost the same. The verb *faucher*, of which *fauche* is the imperative, means *to reap*, while *le faucheur* is *the reaper*.

Foch awoke on the tenth, a Sunday, with the realization that he had to secure signatures to an armistice within twenty-four hours or press the war to a conclusion. The seventy-two-hour grace period expired at eleven the next day. He left the train to go to Mass in Compiègne.

Not until the previous evening, half a day after the news had been received, had he permitted the German delegates, isolated on their siding, to learn of the events in Berlin. Officials in Paris had wanted time to consider whether Erzberger's signature still had any value. Clemenceau, Foch, and Wemyss were all dubious, and wondered whether to do anything at all about the list of objections to the harshest armistice clauses, which the Germans had submitted on the afternoon of the ninth.

Foch himself considered the clauses less severe than the politicians in Paris had demanded. "We make war only for results," he had countered. "These terms will give us the desired results. That being so, no man has the right to cause another drop of blood to be shed." Wemyss's concern was to make one of the harshest terms seem less so without changing anything. Telegraphing Lloyd George that the German mission had protested that further blockade meant continued hunger, he proposed to tell the Germans only that "we should consider the revictualling of the country," and checked with Colonel House for Wilson's promise of assistance. Foch recognized how unpromising was the word *consider*. He did not intend to intervene: it was a British matter.

With nothing to do on Saturday while the Germans worked on strategies to make the terms slightly less catastrophic, Wemyss and Hope had motored to Soissons, once a tourist trip from Paris. Wemyss noted:

> Truly a dreadful sight—not one single house is habitable. The Cathedral is literally torn in two. Going through the streets gave one the impression of visiting Pompeii. We were shown some of the outlying houses which with great ingenuity and without any change in their external appearance had been made [by the Germans] into regular fortresses. The news which reached us . . . was tremendous and varied. The abdication of the Emperor—at first it was thought that Max of Baden had remained as Chancellor. Then a manifesto to the German people and the world, saying that a Socialist Democratic Government had been formed and that the functions of Chancellor had been taken over by Ebert. In the meantime a republic

seems to have been proclaimed in Bavaria. All seems to be confusion. It would appear that the plenipotentiaries have no
longer any powers. . . .

Whatever news there was turned up in the French morning
newspapers on Sunday, with headlines about the abdication and
melodramatic reports of revolution, Bolshevism, and bloodshed in
Berlin and other cities. While Foch was away, couriers brought early
editions of *Le Matin* to the siding and showed copies to the German
delegation. "We read no laughter, no triumph, in their faces," one of
the emissaries would write. ". . . The enemy maintained, in the persons of all his representatives, the same . . . coldness [which] was
mitigated by no single word that bordered on the human, as had
marked our reception by the Marshal. The English Admiral
adopted the tone of the French, and only from Foch's Chief of Staff,
who bore the Alsatian name of Weygand, did we perhaps receive
any greater politeness."

Thomas Keneally's novel about the armistice train imagined
Erzberger's begging a copy of the French newspaper from the
kitchen staff long enough to translate the appalling news to the
others:

> It says Scheidemann announced a republic at midday yester-
> day. . . . They say the soldiers from the Arsenal, from Reini-
> chendorf, Spandau, and Wedding have come in and pledged
> loyalty to the Soldiers' and Workers' Council. They make Ebert
> sound like a roaring Red, like Lenin's little brother. They say
> that the Kaiser and all his sons have skipped from the country.
> The King of Bavaria has abdicated and Kurt Eisner has taken
> the Cabinet over. Holy God, the list! The Duke of Brunswick,
> the Grand Duke of Hesse, the Wettins in Saxony. The Duke of
> Oldenburg deposed. Prince Henry of Reuss has renounced the
> throne in Gera. Can you take more? . . . Grand Duke Wilhelm
> Ernst of Weimar has renounced the throne on behalf of himself
> and his family. As a private citizen the King of Bavaria has
> joined his wife Maria Theresa in Wilsennath, where she is
> dying or dead. . . . I'm not good at participles.

It was Weygand who on the morning of the tenth had brought
to the other railway car a denial of most German objections. A few
modifications had been made, more for psychological reasons than
for their practical effect. Besides, there might be something to the

Bolshevist menace, although as a matter of policy the French preferred to ignore the danger publicly. Making conversation, he observed that he was worried about delays which might be caused by the change in government. No one, after all, had heard anything official from Berlin. Winterfeldt was unconcerned. They were dealing with the inevitable. "No matter whether the new chancellor be called Haase, Ebert, or whatever name you please," he commented to Oberndorff, as if he were not permitted to say such things directly to Weygand, "he will be compelled to sign, all the same!"

Although a statement from the delegates would have no legal standing, Clemenceau still worried over the powers which the Germans claimed to have and had Mordacq telephone Foch to demand a written declaration from Erzberger's group that they were the representatives of the new Berlin government and that they believed that government capable of guaranteeing the execution of the armistice conditions. It would be easy to get the first part, Foch said, but he was dubious about the second. Since it made no difference to the Germans, they promptly furnished both guarantees to Weygand. They had been "particularly conciliatory," Foch reported to Clemenceau, even offering to indicate to the Allies the locations of delayed-action mines in territory recently occupied by the French.

"Too polite to be decent," Clemenceau grouched suspiciously to Mordacq on receiving the offer. "If they are getting conciliatory, it is because they have received reports on the internal situation in Germany and know that at home matters are going none too well. In my opinion that is rather a good sign for us. Whatever it is, it is absolutely necessary to be on guard against people like that."

An even less expected message for the Premier arrived on the same morning—belated birthday greetings. His seventy-seventh birthday had occurred on September 28, six weeks earlier.

> *Dear Mr. President,*
>
> *I wanted to let the flood of congratulations which you received on your birthday go by before sending you my own. . . . I am not forgetful of the past and I have a faithful memory. But what I want to express to you today is the sentiment which we all hold . . . a sentiment which has led our soldiers to bestow on you the very charming nickname of "Father Victory."*
>
> *Please accept this expression of my loyal devotion.*
>
> ALFRED DREYFUS
>
> *Lt. Col. Dreyfus*
> *Commanding the artillery arsenal at Orléans*

As a journalist Clemenceau had once written in *Justice*, "Alfred Dreyfus is a traitor and I shall not insult any soldier by putting him in the same category as this scoundrel." Before long, however, he had taken up his powerful pen in support of Captain Dreyfus, who Clemenceau was now certain had been framed as a German spy by Rightists in the Army. Foch, too, had suffered during the Dreyfus affair, for persecution of Jews was followed by persecution of Catholics, and the devout Foch in 1901 had been banished to an artillery regiment in the small garrison town of Laon, his career in check and his promotion from lieutenant colonel delayed. The victory over the Germans would be a vindication for all three.

Isolated in the forest, the delegates were permitted to leave the train only to exercise. Much as if they were prisoners, they walked under the dripping trees, making small talk in the company of ten gendarmes. Something sensitive might be overheard by a *poilu*. Still, Erzberger thought, the railway carriage and environs were an appropriately modern venue for military negotiations. "The castles and fortresses of olden times have disappeared, even for such purposes. The train with its sleeping, drawing-room, and dining cars was very comfortable, and we were provided with everything we wanted. . . . But all the hostility and the fullness of hate for our country that now seems to be cherished in France came to expression in the form of the negotiations and the terrible nature of the conditions."

Erzberger and his compatriots understood that they were not parties to real negotiations, but potential signatories to an imposed peace—a *Diktat*, as the Germans themselves had forced on the Russians earlier in the year at Brest-Litovsk. Still, even a *Diktat* required a government which recognized their status to direct their signatures, and Ebert and his associates in Berlin had been too busy with internal matters to pay much attention to a sideshow in a forest in France. Hindenburg, nevertheless, had been pressing for action. "REQUEST SPEEDY DECISION ON THESE LINES," went one of his telegrams. The further the disintegration went, he thought, the less chance that the General Staff could hold the Army together. What he did not know is that the French, who in effect were dictating the armistice, would want the professional German Army to survive. "The Boches are good soldiers and have fought well," Foch had told a major on his headquarters staff; "we can leave them their army. The Austrians are slovenly fighters, and deserve general disarmament." Besides, an efficient army meant order.

At 6:30 P.M., Foch had a message signed by Weygand delivered to Erzberger, warning of the imminence of the seventy-two-hour deadline:

> According to the terms of the text handed to Marshal Foch, the powers of the German plenipotentiaries for concluding an armistice are limited by the fact that the approval of the Chancellor is necessary.
>
> As the time allowed for coming to an agreement expires at 11 A.M. to-morrow, I have the honour to ask whether the German Plenipotentiaries have received the acceptance by the German Chancellor of the terms communicated to him, and if not, whether it would not be advisable to solicit without delay an answer from him.

Just after receipt of the note the trains got up steam for the evening run to Compiègne to take on water, as the Rethondes station had no water supply. Both trains started at dinnertime, the French leading, the Germans following. There was little the Germans could do anyway but to keep waiting for responses from Berlin or Spa. As they pulled into Rethondes, en route, the station commandant ordered the trains stopped. General Desticker was telephoning from Senlis that a German radio message had been picked up, in clear: "German Government to German plenipotentiaries. The plenipotentiaries are authorized to sign the armistice." It was signed *"Reichskanzler Schluss* 3,084." Soon another radioed message reached the Allied train, with the same preliminary wording, but accompanied by a long list of protestations at harsh clauses which threatened to reduce the nation, including women and children, to starvation. Following that was a long message for the Germans from Hindenburg, this time in code, also protesting the terms but acknowledging, "If it is impossible to gain these points, it would nevertheless be advisable to conclude the agreement."

By nine o'clock the trains had returned to their sidings in the forest, and the French interpreter, Laperche, went over the duckboards to the German carriages to ask Erzberger if "Schluss" was the name of the new Chancellor. The gentleman, Laperche said, was "completely unknown to both the French Supreme Command and the government in Paris." Restraining his fury at the compromising of two days of negotiations by the naive or careless omission of cipher, Erzberger explained that *"Schluss"* at the end of a telegram meant "period" or "stop." (The number had been a verifying code.)

Soon Weygand asked, for Foch, whether the Germans were "at last ready to sign, and the sooner the better, if they truly desired, as they had not ceased repeating, to avoid useless bloodshed." When Erzberger asked for time to decipher and discuss the long messages from Hindenburg, Foch decided at eleven to snatch some rest. Tired of waiting, Wemyss was getting ready for bed when an aide arrived "and told me with the Marshal's compliments that he thought that the German envoys had received instructions and would probably want to see us tonight and would I therefore be ready." The Admiral decided to rest without getting out of uniform.

While the two napped, German OHL radio message no. 11397 to Army groups was being intercepted and translated by Allied signal units: "The Peace Delegation has been notified that the German Government accepts the armistice conditions proposed November 8. Time set for the beginning of the Armistice will be announced later." It was 11:35 P.M. by German clocks—10:35 French time. Whatever bargaining power Erzberger had brought with him from Berlin had now disappeared, but he did not know it.

At 2:05 A.M. on the eleventh, less than nine hours before expiration of the time limit, the German delegates, to no one's surprise, announced their readiness to conclude an agreement. Ten minutes later everyone was seated in Foch's carriage.

The Marshal asked Weygand to read a new text, into which had been incorporated minor modifications asked for by the Germans. Vanselow had observed, for example, that the demand for surrender of 160 U-boats was impossible, as the Navy no longer had that many. The formula "all submarines" was substituted. But the Captain had other objections. Was it admissible that the German fleet should be interned, he asked, when they had not been defeated? They only had to come out, said Wemyss, and this technicality could be taken care of. The plea was an ironic reversal of roles for Vanselow, who earlier in the year as Admiralty representative in Berlin had advised on how Russian warships, which by the sweepingly harsh Treaty of Brest-Litovsk had only to be neutralized or disarmed, could be seized by the Germans without breaching international law as well as the treaty. What Vanselow proposed was a bit of legalistic legerdemain, an apportionment of the vessels among the marginal German puppet states establishing themselves (with difficulty, because of Bolshevist pressure) on former Russian soil— the Ukraine, Tabriz, the Caucasus, and others—provided they lend the ships to Germany for the duration of the war in the West. Now

Captain Vanselow was being asked to put his pen to the seizure of his own navy.

A more realistic protest came from the delegates who claimed that the numbers of locomotives and airplanes to be delivered to the Allies exceeded actual quantities. The Army could not surrender 10,000 trucks, Hindenburg said; of the 18,000 it had, only half were usable. It would mean the complete breakdown of the supply system. He could not surrender 2,000 military aircraft when only 1,700 now existed. Foch accepted the figures as realistic, and also reduced the numbers of small weapons so that the Army could maintain order. As for the Germans in East Africa, who were still giving a good account of themselves, *capitulation* was replaced by *evacuation of all German forces.*

Among Hindenburg's requests (almost certainly dictated by Groener) was to have the Allies authorize the right (northern) wing of the German Army to march through the southern corner of Limburg (Maastricht) to prevent a bottleneck in the withdrawal. Foch refused, but Groener later paid no attention to the technicality and paid the price of having his troops disarmed by the Dutch as they passed into the neutral province. Another request, for extension of the withdrawal period, including the Rhineland, to two months ("otherwise the army will collapse") was modified to provide fifteen days to withdraw from occupied lands and sixteen more from German territory west of the Rhine—still only half the time the Germans claimed they needed. But Erzberger did succeed in narrowing the "neutral" zone on the right bank of the Rhine by ten kilometers, and in getting a promise that "nobody [in any evacuated territory] would be punished for participation in war measures prior to the signing of the armistice."

Three hours later the terms remained largely as first set—massive surrender of military equipment, ships, and rolling stock; withdrawal beyond the Rhine; immediate release of war prisoners; annulment of all agreements and treaties in conflict with the armistice. "I tried with each separate article," Erzberger would write, ". . . to get even milder terms and mentioned particularly the advantages of a smaller . . . army of occupation. . . . The most lively argument arose in connection with . . . the continuation of the blockade. We struggled over that article for more than an hour. In detail I pointed out that by means of this article an essential part of the World War was being continued." Prolongation of the blockade, he and Oberndorff had insisted, was "not fair," which prompted

Admiral Wemyss's "Not fair? Why, you sank our ships without discrimination!" Still, Wemyss claimed intentions to feed Germany during the armistice, a move afterward accomplished with all deliberate lack of speed. He permitted Article XXVI, which continued the blockade, to conclude with the line, "The Allies and the United States contemplate the provisioning of Germany during the Armistice as shall be found necessary." Recognizing the weakness of the commitment, the Germans protested that such drastic terms would result in the starvation of tens of thousands of women and children. In truth the Allies (excluding the United States) did not even "contemplate" sending food to Germany, and the pious lie—as the Germans realized it was—was to placate the idealistic Wilson. No food would be permitted into Germany until nearly five months later. What provisions there were, no longer controlled in distribution by the rationing machinery of the wartime government, would be hoarded and bootlegged, becoming increasingly unavailable to the poor and even to the straitened middle classes. The British and French blockade would even be expanded to include the Baltic fisheries, further pinching innocent civilians, already without adequate heat, light, or food.

When the new German Foreign Minister, Ulrich von Brockendorff-Rantzau, got his opportunity, on May 7, 1919, to respond to treaty conditions laid down at Versailles, he would observe, "I ask you when reparation is demanded not to forget the armistice. It took you six weeks till we got it at last, and six months till we came to know your conditions of peace. . . . The hundreds of thousands of noncombatants who have perished since November 11 by reason of the blockade were killed with cold deliberation after our adversaries had conquered and victory had been assured to them. Think of that when you speak of guilt and punishment." Wilson would dismiss the charge as "tactless."

In the railway car Foch brushed off the allegation that the continued blockade was inhumane. "My responsibility ends at the Rhine. I have no concern with the rest of Germany, which is your own affair. I would remind you that this is a military armistice, that the war is not ended thereby, and that it is directed at preventing your nation from continuing the war. You must also recollect a reply given to us by Bismarck in 1871 when we made a similar request to what you are making now. Bismarck then said, 'Krieg ist Krieg,' and I say to you, 'La guerre est la guerre.' "

There was nothing left to say. At 5:12 A.M. the discussions were declared concluded, and Foch moved that, for convenience, the effective date be rounded off to five o'clock, so that the armistice could go into effect six hours later, on the hour. Then he asked that the delegates sign the last page of the agreement before the other pages were revised, again to save time. Weygand showed the Germans the improvements in the text—fourteen days for withdrawing from occupied territories amended to fifteen; twenty-five days altogether for evacuating the Rhineland extended to thirty-one; 10,000 trucks to be given up in fifteen days curtailed to 5,000 in thirty-six; 1,700 airplanes rather than the nonexistent 2,000; 30,000 machine guns surrendered modified to 25,000; return of German prisoners to be settled at the conclusion of preliminary peace talks.

At 5:30 Foch and Wemyss signed; after them the Germans. "There were tears in the eyes of our two brave officers, General von Winterfeldt and Captain Vanselow," Erzberger wrote, "when, under hard compulsion, they took up their pens."

Erzberger then asked permission to speak, having drafted a "Declaration of the German Plenipotentiaries on the Occasion of Signing the Armistice." His government, he said, would endeavor to fulfill its commitments, but the inadequate time permitted in which to execute the armistice conditions and the surrender of so much rolling stock would affect its ability to achieve the letter of the agreement. *"Nous verrons, je vous assisterai"*—"You try, and I'll assist you," broke in Foch skeptically. Further, Erzberger went on, his voice faltering, execution of the armistice conditions could drive his prostrate nation into famine without adding to Allied security. Finally, he had an unrepentant peroration prepared. "The German people, which held off a world of enemies for fifty months, will preserve their liberty and their unity despite every kind of violence. A nation of seventy millions of people suffers, but it does not die."

"Très bien," observed Foch. But there would be no handshakes as the two delegations parted, the Marshal waving the Germans to go with *"Eh bien, messieurs, c'est fini, allez."* After 1,564 days the worst war in history was over.

Within minutes a message was transmitted to all fronts by radio and telephone, ordering hostilities to cease at 11:00 A.M., Paris time. "Until further orders," it went on, "Allied troops will not go beyond the line reached this day and hour." A precise report was to be made on the line reached, and no communication or fraternization with the enemy was to be permitted pending further instructions. Then

Foch breakfasted while waiting for the documents to be copied, stood for a photograph (briefcase containing the armistice in one hand, cane in the other) with his delegation before the railway carriage in which the signing took place, and then motored to Paris. Clemenceau had already heard of the conclusion from Mordacq. Tension had kept Clemenceau sleepless, and he was still up at six when Mordacq arrived. Overcome with emotion, and unable to speak, he clasped the general in his arms. But before Mordacq left, to go on to Poincaré, Clemenceau confided that he wanted to keep the signing a secret until he could announce it himself to the Chamber of Deputies that afternoon. Too many people already knew, he was told: the plan was impossible. Colonel House had known at 5:30 A.M. and noted that "at last our dead on the *Lusitania* are avenged." Despite French clauses on reparations and nonreciprocal prisoner-of-war release, and British clauses on sea supremacy and continuation of the blockade, all of which undermined Wilson's Fourteen Points and would guarantee a bitter peace, House's assistant, Walter Lippmann, responded to the signing with an emotional note. "I must write you this morning because I couldn't possibly tell you face to face how great a thing you have achieved. Frankly I did not believe it was humanly possible under conditions such as they seemed to be in Europe to win so glorious a victory. This is the climax of a course that has been as wise as it was brilliant, and as shrewd as it was prophetic. The President and you have more than justified the faith of those who insisted that your leadership was a turning point in modern history. No one can ever thank you adequately."

As a courtesy to Wilson's representative, House wrote in his diary, Clemenceau (who had excluded an American representative from the armistice train) "sent one of his generals around to give me exact information. I received him of course in my bedroom *en deshabille*, and did not tell him I had already gotten the news."

At 9:30 the Premier greeted Wemyss and Foch in the War Ministry to accept the armistice document, according to Wemyss, "taking my right hand in his left and the Marshal's left hand in his right" as they congratulated each other. "My work is finished; your work begins," said Foch. But, according to Foch, the aged Tiger had first asked suspiciously, as if he had not been apprised of every jot in the agreement as the negotiations progressed, "What have you yielded to the Germans?" The Marshal had then handed Clemenceau a copy of the articles, observing that cannon should salute the armistice in Paris at the appropriate time.

"Well," said Clemenceau, "let the guns be fired at eleven o'clock."

Lord Derby, who had devised the notorious English "attestation" plan which had been a military draft by another name, arrived at the Premier's invitation, just as the Marshal was about to go, and offered his congratulations. "Foch very much moved," Derby would write Foreign Secretary Arthur Balfour, "though I feel in his heart of hearts he regrets the armistice coming quite as soon as it did, as he told both of us that within another fortnight the German Army would have been completely surrounded and would have been obliged to lay down their arms."

Although it would have taken far longer than a fortnight for that—perhaps even another winter and spring of war, fought on German soil, where resistance might be ferocious, one can see why France and Britain, aside from their own exhaustion, were willing to end the shooting when they did. Wilson's idealistic Fourteen Points, on which basis the German people thought their government had sued for peace, and which Britain and France parried and pruned in the armistice document (and again at Versailles the next year), did not reflect what the major Allies considered their vital interests. France, Britain, and even America had fought on the Western Front largely with weapons manufactured on the other side of the Atlantic from Detroit, Pittsburgh, or Chicago. American troops were still green; their leadership lacked experience; their logistics were laggingly inefficient. By the Armistice the United States was reaching its war-making potential, and by the spring of 1919 it would have placed enough men and materiel not only in France, but in the line, to be acknowledged as the principal factor in Germany's defeat. With that, Wilson might command the real as well as the moral force to reconstitute Europe west of the Russian frontier along the lines he wanted. "I want to go into the Peace Conference," Wilson told his Cabinet, "armed with as many weapons as my pockets will hold so as to compel justice." Had America visibly won the war, it might have dominated the peace. The governments of Clemenceau and Lloyd George would prevent both on November 11, 1918.

As a result the terms would be both less punitive, and more punitive, than would be useful—an ineffective accommodation of the two positions. Foch appears to have understood. At 10:30 the Marshal called on Poincaré and told him (according to the President) "that the Germans accepted the conditions that he gave them, but that they did not declare themselves vanquished and the worst is that they do not believe that they are vanquished."

In England, Ford Madox Ford's Mark Tietjens, wartime Minister of Transport in the final volume of *Parade's End*, is so wrought up about the failure of the armistice terms to bring the consciousness of defeat into the heart of Germany that he has a stroke which leaves him paralyzed and speechless. "The last words he had spoken," his longtime French mistress Marie Leonie recalls, "had been whilst one of his colleagues at the Ministry had been telephoning to tell her, for Mark's information, what the terms of the Armistice were. At the news, which she had to give to him over her shoulder, he had made some remark . . . to the effect—in English—that he would never speak again. . . . At the news that the Allies did not intend to pursue the Germans into their own country—she had felt herself as if she could say to the High Official at the other end of the telephone that she would never speak [a] word to him and his race again. . . ." Her own feeling is that it is "betraying her country to have given those assassins an armistice when they were far from their borders," but it had been an Allied, not an English, decision. Mark, she remembered, in arguing over armistice conditions with his colleagues, had "stuck to his point that to occupy Berlin was not punishment, but that not to occupy Berlin was to commit an intellectual sin. The consequences of invasion is counter-invasion and symbolical occupation, as the consequences of over-pride, is humiliation. . . . To abandon that logic was mental cowardice. . . . We dare not put the enemy nations to pain because we shrank from the contemplation."

An enemy, the fictional Mark Tietjens felt, had to be psychologically as well as militarily defeated. The Fatherland had not lost a single inch of its historic soil in combat. The end came with Germans in control of every inch of their national territory. Only via German signatures on an armistice would an Allied soldier be permitted into Germany. Or at least so it appeared, and appearances were reality.

Were the armistice terms a covert German victory? Privately the OHL thought so, despite vindictive and even rapacious aspects of the peace which would be further legislated into the Versailles treaty the next year. Germany would be pruned, plundered, and punished, but as long as the nation and its infrastructure remained largely intact it could begin the process of circumvention while its citizens were still seething over the alleged unfairness of the settlement. "The armistice terms were humiliating," thought Louis

Botha, the Boer general who had become Prime Minister of South Africa. "I felt sorry, when I read them, that any nation should stoop so low as to accept such terms. Even barbarians will not surrender their cattle without a struggle. It would have been more dignified had the Germans said, 'We will not agree to your terms. You must do what you think best.' " What the Germans knew, however, was the kind of peace they would have imposed on the West. By comparison the Allied terms at their least charitable were benevolent.

Captain Geyer, who had already flown back and forth to Spa during the negotiations, picked up the German copy of the armistice terms and signed a receipt for it. At noon the German train pulled out of Rethondes to return to Tergnier. The French train, without Wemyss and Foch, left for Paris at 12:15. At Spa, with its own *Soldatenrat*, like so many other towns still in German hands, but now also festooned with the Belgian national colors, the returned delegates would find Hindenburg eager to thank them for the "extremely valuable services" they had rendered to the Fatherland. By 1924 Hindenburg could promise an audience of students, "And you, my dear graduating class, will one day occupy Paris as the victorious conquerors. . . !" Of course he was an old man and not to be taken seriously, yet a year later he was the venerable President of the Republic, and was still dodderingly in office in 1933 to appoint Adolf Hitler as Chancellor.

Without confiding that the General Staff would seek every way to evade the armistice terms, Groener would tell Erzberger that the results "exceeded our wildest expectations." They had been close to surrender in the field, without conditions.

In preparation for an announcement of the actual time to lay down arms, Hindenburg had already issued an order to all regimental and battalion commanders "in the West":

> The armistice agreement is being concluded with all possible speed. Thus the sanguinary struggle is to find an end. The longed-for moment is near when every one of us may return to parents, wives and children, and to brothers and sisters. At the same time revolutionary changes are taking place in the political conditions at home. The men who are at the head of the movement state that peace and order are to be maintained under all circumstances.
>
> That applies in an even greater degree to the Army as well.

No one may leave his organization without orders and everyone must obey his superiors as in the past. Only then can the Army be moved back to the homeland in orderly fashion. The railroads, now interrupted, must again be placed in regular operation. GHQ does not wish to see new bloodshed or civil war. In agreement with the new government authorities it will strive for peace and security, and save Germany from the worst fate that could befall her. The use of arms against fellow Germans will be resorted to only in self-defense or in case of common crime, or else to prevent plundering.

For Erzberger the thankless job would not end with the signing. He would be pressed into the chairmanship of the commission to implement the Compiègne terms, thus joining the new government. He hoped to help establish order and make possible a credible German stance in the coming peace negotiations which would remake the map of Europe; but as with the others in the delegation, the experience in the forest would be a permanent liability. Oberndorff had served his last diplomatic mission. Within a year both Winterfeldt and Vanselow would be retired, careers over, Winterfeldt having enjoyed a last moment of importance as the military official overseeing the German side of the armistice. In a cabinet meeting in which Chancellor Ebert would defend the retention of the High Command in place on November 11, he would insist, "We need the technical officers, in particular General Winterfeldt, who has been able to obtain the best conditions for us."

Unwilling to turn his back on the events in which he had just participated, Ernst Vanselow at forty-three would take up law, earning a doctorate in 1921 from the University of Freiburg, in Baden, with a thesis on blockade and international law (*Verkehrssperre und Völkerrecht*). Years later, still committed to the subject which had closed his naval career, he wrote an *Introduction to International Law,* and then coauthored a book on the rights of neutrals in wartime (*Neutralitätsrecht*). On the title page he refused to ignore his past, identifying himself as "Kapitan z. See a. Dr. Ernst Vanselow."*

In 1920, pursued by Rightist fanatics who labeled him a traitor, Matthias Erzberger would survive one assassination attempt but not

---

* His last recorded Berlin address was in 1944; he may have left in time to escape the carnage of 1945. On March 8, 1949, he died in Hildesheim.

the second. Only in 1957, after another world war, were the murderers tried.

Life would be sunnier for the OHL officers who wore the wine-red stripe. Major Fedor von Bock, of the Crown Prince's staff, would be a Nazi field marshal. Many majors and lieutenant colonels at Spa would become generals under Hitler. Being a *Schreibtischoffizier* in Supreme Headquarters was no drawback. Although being chairborne made medals for valor hard to come by, one learned a lot about intrigue and personal advancement. Ambitious and unscrupulous, Kurt von Schleicher, who became Groener's personal assistant for the last two weeks of the war after being a nonentity in Ludendorff's Press Department, would become chief of the Army and, briefly, Chancellor before Nazi triggermen would do away with him. Werner von Fritsch would become Army chief in 1934, until intrigue brought him down. He killed himself by deliberately becoming a target for Polish gunners in 1939. Karl Heinrich von Stülpnagel, a veteran of Verdun and later a major at Spa, as a general would become military governor of France and would return to Verdun in July 1944 to attempt to commit suicide rather than face a Nazi court for complicity in the belated bomb plot against Hitler. Shooting himself in the head would only blind him. He would be found, taken to Berlin, and strangled to death in Ploetzensee Prison.

Also at Spa was a legalistic young naval officer named Ernst von Weizsäcker, who worried over whether Prussian officers "owed the Kaiser the allegiance of vassals—that is to say, whether we were bound to follow him on his abdication. The problem was solved in a simple and natural manner. I was able to report to [Admiral von] Scheer that Hindenburg had undertaken to lead the Army back to Germany after the Kaiser had released the armed forces from the oath of loyalty to his person." With his line of thinking he was on his way to major achievements, becoming State Secretary at the Foreign Office and Hitler's drafter of the Munich pact of 1938 through which Britain and France sold out Czechoslovakia.*

The *Generalstaboffiziermentalität,* carefully preserved and cherished through the Weimar Republic years when the military renaissance of the Reich was being camouflaged by former captains and majors

---

* Ernst von Weizsäcker's son Richard would become President of the Federal Republic of Germany in 1984.

and lieutenant colonels who were staff officers at the armistice, would be turned to Hitler's purposes in the 1930s. The General Staff, largely driven underground by the peace terms, had little administrative function and could concentrate on planning for the future. Enforced disarmament freed the military from the burden of weapons obsolescence which might have bound Germany to old methods and traditional strategies. Divided and defeatist, immobilized since the early 1930s by the thought of renewal of the war with Germany, seen only as a horrendous repetition of 1914–18, France conducted its foreign policy and maintained its army accordingly. When the nation fell to the resurgent Germans in 1940, its army chief would be Foch's deputy at Compiègne, the sclerotic Maxime Weygand, who had opposed mechanization and remained smugly certain of the future of horse cavalry. Many planes and tanks were never used, and while some soldiers fought bravely and hopelessly, others did not fight at all. Whether misled or self-deluded, Frenchmen psychologically confronted a nightmare vision of the juggernaut of the Kaiser's war.

In the year of defeat, waiting impatiently in Bordeaux, where he had fled German tanks and dive-bombers, for news of his armistice delegation, Weygand finally received a telephone call on the night of June 21. French General Charles Huntziger was on the line. "Where are you?" Weygand asked, assuming that the Germans had chosen Versailles as the place in which to reverse November 1918.

"I'm in the wagon!" Huntziger confessed.

"Mon pauvre ami!" cried Weygand. He understood that it was Foch's own *wagon-lit,* which had been displayed in a museum built for it in the forest. German Army engineers had used pneumatic drills to cut out a wall and nudge the symbolic dining car back onto the rusty tracks. To eighty-four-year-old Marshal Philippe Pétain, the hero of Verdun who would become the puppet head of the rump French state at Vichy, his staff aide Major Fauvelle would say, *"Monsieur le Maréchal, l'armée allemande de 1939 a battu l'armée française de 1918"* (". . . the German Army of 1939 has beaten the French Army of 1918").

In 1940 the prostrate French were given less than twelve hours to sign an imposed armistice. Erzberger in 1918, they pointed out, was allowed seventy-two hours in which to receive instructions. Generals Keitel and Jodl refused to extend the period, and the French signed. In 1918 the spot in the forest known only to Clemenceau and Foch had been selected to spare the adversary from public humiliation and, as Weygand put it, "to place the conference out of reach of indiscretions." In 1940 he thought, "talion law had led the German Chancellor to choose the same place," but a different spirit had motivated the choice. "Every sharpening of humiliation had been devised for the one whom the fortune of war had brought low—a crowd, music, cinema. . . ." There, for the international media, Field Marshal Wilhelm Keitel, a young staff officer at the 1918 armistice, read a vindictive statement which emphasized the symbol which the Napoleon III *wagon-lit* had become:

> It was on November 11, 1918, in this same coach, that there thus began the Calvary of the German people. Every element of dishonour, moral humiliation, and material human sufferings that can be imposed on a people had its origin here. . . .
>
> France is beaten. The French Government has asked the Government of the Reich to make known to it the German conditions for the conclusion of an armistice.
>
> To receive these conditions, the French delegation has been invited to come to the historic forest of Compiègne, and this spot has been chosen to efface once and for all, by an act of justice and reparation, a memory which, for France, was not an honourable page in her history, but which was considered by the German people as the deepest dishonour of all time.

A marble block stood where the train had been. Its lettering had been equally provocative, the victor's revenge on the vanquished:

HERE ON THE ELEVENTH OF NOVEMBER 1918 SUCCUMBED THE CRIMINAL PRIDE OF THE GERMAN EMPIRE . . . VANQUISHED BY THE FREE PEOPLES WHICH IT TRIED TO ENSLAVE.

Before it a gleeful Adolf Hitler smiled broadly for the cameras and stamped his foot. British propaganda experts acquired a copy of the film and, according to Len Deighton, "looped the sequence to make it look as though a demented Hitler were dancing a jig." Three days later he ordered the marble block blown up and the dining car moved to Berlin, to be a Nazi museum prize.

In the massive British air raids on Berlin which reduced much of the city to rubble, Foch's *wagon-lit* became one of the casualties.*

---

* The car now in the clearing in Compiègne is a replacement for the original.

The wreck symbolized what had happened to German aspirations, but Hitler would insist, late in 1943, "No matter how long this war lasts, Germany will never capitulate. Never will we repeat the mistake of 1918, of laying down our arms at a quarter to twelve." And in 1945, although he did refuse to permit the High Command, at a quarter to twelve, to seek an armistice which would have preserved the Reich from the horrors of invasion, again there would be proponents of a new *Dolchstoss* legend. The "November criminals" of 1918 had allegedly stabbed Germany in the back by ousting the Kaiser and the monarchy and signing an armistice. The new legend would attempt to keep alive the *Führer* myth, that only the defeatist and dissident elements in the Army which had carried out the failed assassination attempt of July 1944 prevented the final triumph of Hitlerism. But this was largely residual Nazi thinking: the *Generalstaboffiziermentalität* which November 11, 1918, had preserved would be in far greater shambles after the *Götterdammerung* of 1945, when a general named Alfred Jodl signed, at Rheims, a German unconditional surrender. He, too, had been a young staff officer at the time of the Armistice.

LAST SHOTS

La guerre est finie pour les milliers partis,   The war is over for the thousands gone,
La paix éternelle pour les milliers partis,   Eternal peace for the thousands gone,
La fin de la peine et la peur,   The end of pain and fear,
Et le fin de tout désire,   The end of all desire,
Le fin de l'orgeuil et de la gloire,   The end of pride and glory,
Tout étient dans le feu. . . .   All vanished in the fire. . . .

—*La Guerre est finie,* AN OLD FRENCH SONG
   PREDATING MODERN WARS,
   SUNG AGAIN IN 1914–18

A correspondent trudging up a road toward Stenay saw a little wood in which a six-inch artillery piece was parked. Looking up from cleaning out the barrel, one of the crew announced, "We fired the last shot at 10:55." It was Battery C of the 56th Coast Artillery, from New York, but there would be thousands of claimants to have pulled the last lanyard or squeezed the last trigger.

Astride heights overlooking the Woëvre plain to the east, in the valley of the Meuse, the 129th Field Artillery (35th Division)—the peacetime 2nd Missouri Field Artillery—was supporting Senegalese troops of the 2nd French Colonial Corps who were softening up the area west of Metz. Battery D, commanded by Captain Harry S. Truman, a bespectacled unmilitary sort, was dug in astride a railway tunnel through which, in better times, the Verdun-Metz line ran. (The Germans controlled the eastern end.) The battery was in place and firing at 8:21 when the armistice news arrived, although he thought, erroneously, thirty-six years later, that it was only 5:30 A.M. when Major Newell T. Paterson at the 129th's headquarters called. "I can remember," President Truman told Jonathan Daniels in 1950, "that on November 10 we got our orders to move down the following afternoon into the valley of Verdun. That next morning some units did move down. Some men I knew, and that I thought a lot of, got killed that morning. If we had moved down, some of us would have got it."

In a memorandum to himself written on Armistice Day 1954, nearly two years after he left the White House, Truman noted that Major Paterson had told him—almost certainly on higher authority—"that I was to say nothing about the cessation of hostilities until 11 A.M. My battery fired the assigned barrages at the times specified. The last one toward a tiny little village called Hermeville eleven thousand meters from my position. My last shot was fired at 10:45. When the firing ceased all along the front lines it seemed not so. It was so quiet it made me feel as if I'd suddenly been deprived of my ability to hear."

His counterpart in Battery B, Captain Theodore Marks, also sent over his final round at 10:45, recording that enemy answering salvos were still falling. But soon there was silence. "The men at the guns," Truman's memo goes on, ". . . looked at each other for some time and then a great cheer arose all along the line. We could hear the men in the infantry a thousand meters in front raising holy hell. The French . . . behind our position were dancing, shouting and waving bottles of wine."

Up in the air, Harry Truman's old Battery F friend, Lieutenant John Broaddus, was in a 35th Balloon Company "sausage" directing artillery fire. Below "people went so wild celebrating that they forgot to pull me down . . . & I sat there for two hours." Broaddus had a primitive parachute for emergencies, but with other hazards now passed—and one hairy experience of jumping in practice—he preferred to twist slowly in the wind until someone remembered him.

The 76th Field Artillery (3rd Division), supporting the advance into the Forêt de Woëvre, refused to quit until the last moment, determined to unleash the last historic salvo. Harry Croft, with Battery D, remembered, "Oh, man, everyone in my outfit wanted to fire the last shot. We decided each of us would put a hand on the lanyard and pull at the same time. And that's what we did, at 10:59. . . . That was a racket: all up and down the line guns were [still] firing from both sides. As I look back on it, I realize how stupid it was. Americans and Germans must have been killed by that last barrage. But that's what happened."

According to Frank Sibley, with the 26th Division in the last minutes of the war, "There seemed to be little hate in that last morning's barrage. The guns weren't pointed anywhere in particular; they were just headed in the general direction of Germany and turned loose as fast as they could be fired. . . . In one battery each man took a shell and waited in line for his turn to fire the gun. In another battery, five officers took hold of the lanyard, and all fired the last shot together. In still another a long rope was made fast to the lanyard of each of the four guns. Some two hundred men got hands on each rope, and one man, with a watch, went out forward. At the hour he dropped a handkerchief." Eight hundred men could claim to have fired that "last shot."

Also in the Woëvre, where German shells rained through the night into the 5th Infantry Division lines, plans went ahead to push toward Montmedy and Languyon as soon as there was light enough. Despite deadly artillery and sniper fire, the bridges lashed across the Loison at Louppy during the night had held, but a heavy fog lay over the river and delayed movement against the strongly held hills above. At nine, as the sun began dissolving the fog, infantrymen and machine gunners of the 11th Battalion were crawling forward under its cover toward suspected German positions. Colonel Robert H. Peck had a Chemical Warfare unit in readiness to throw a curtain of gas into the enemy sector, but when the lingering fog evaporated with a suddenness that left American positions exposed, the Ger-

mans reacted not with further firing but with an even greater surprise. A white flag was raised, and an officer came forward speaking
good English and asking to be conducted to the commanding officer. "My God, sir," he said, "what are you doing? Don't you know
that the Armistice goes into effect at 11 o'clock?"

"No," said Colonel Peck; "is that so? Then that spoils all my
schemes!" Only then did a message reach him from 10th Infantry
Brigade commander, Brigadier General Paul Malone, calling off the
attack.

Some scheduled attacks were not rescinded. On the morning of
the eleventh, near Haumont, under cover of the same fog that had
briefly enveloped Colonel Peck's force, Lieutenant Francis Reed
Austin of the 28th (Pennsylvania) Division led a platoon of machine
guns and mortars against a German strong point defended by ten
machine guns. Heavy fire forced them back. According to the posthumous Distinguished Service Cross citation, "Exposing himself in
order to place his own men under cover, Lieut. Austin was mortally
wounded but he directed the dressing of wounds of his men and
their evacuation before he would accept aid for himself." By the
time the Armistice had taken effect at eleven, he was dead.

Few German units were in any condition to further prolong the war.
His men, a German company commander opposite the British
Fourth Army wrote, in a letter home, "have been in the same clothing, dirty, lousy, and torn, for four weeks, are suffering from bodily
filth and a state of depression due to living continuously within
range of the enemy's guns, and in daily expectation of attack. The
troops are hardly in a fit state to fulfill the tasks alloted to them. . . ."
Still, with army loyalty and morale in mind, Hindenburg had announced the end to German forces almost as if it were a victory.
They had borne their arms with honor, and with devotion and a
sense of duty had "achieved mighty deeds." Through "victorious attack" and "stubborn defense," he assured them, "you have kept the
enemy away from our boundaries and shielded the Homeland from
the terrors and devastations of war." The "collapse of our Allies . . .
together with ever-increasing food and economic problems, have
forced our Government to accept severe Armistice conditions." They
were ceasing the struggle "against a world of enemies" with "up-
rightness and pride" that they had defended "our Country and our
Honor to the last." Now, he warned, the terms of the Armistice
forced them to march back to the Homeland without delay. "In

view of existing conditions, this will be a difficult task, which will require self-discipline and devotion to duty on the part of every one of you. It will be a severe test of the morale and steadfastness of the Army. In battle you have never failed your field marshal; I continue to rely upon you even now!"

Supplementing Hindenburg's exhortation, individual commanders issued their own. The Fifth Army's, drawn with masterly psychology, praised the courage by which lines had been held to the end and guaranteed the gratitude of the Fatherland. "Upon our return home" it concluded, "we will find many things changed, and not to everyone's liking. The important thing now is to adapt oneself to the new conditions and to cooperate in the reconstruction. That will be possible only if we will take back with us to the homeland from this war of long duration, the good soldierly qualities of sense of duty, manly courage and love of order. . . . Everyone must strive for sensible understanding and farsighted self-restraint! As a proud remembrance take with you on the road back and to the hearths of your homes, the excellent reputation of the army . . . which has so often been glorified!" There would be just time enough to bury the dead.

To furnish no excuse for Allied retaliatory fire, OHL had issued instructions not only that shooting was to stop, but for the march "to the Homeland [to be] under firm control and in good order. To assure systematic crossing of the Rhine," the message continued, "pioneer units [engineers] and bridge units are to be placed in front of the organizations of the first line." Opposite American troops at Conflans, *Vize-Feldwebel* Max Spiegel—an "officer aspirant" although not an officer, despite his engineering experience, because he was a Jew in a Prussian division—had been given withdrawal orders while the last artillery shells were still falling. He was "to start the march back the same afternoon," his platoon getting "the job to lead the whole army group back as in case of destroyed roads . . . a technical unit would be required." They would march across Luxembourg, along the Moselle and the Rhine, to Rüdersheim, where trains would take them into Westphalia. "We had told our men that the better they behaved in a traditional military way, the quicker they would be able to get home. And that was indeed the case."

It was not always the case. In Hamont, a town in northeastern Belgium on the Dutch border, August Velser, a young Belgian impressed into the German Army, watched troops in the last hours of the war throw their weapons aside at the border as the price of escape into neutral Holland.

Also passing through Hamont were mutinous Austrian sailors long blockaded in Antwerp and now determined to make their way through Germany to join the revolution at home. Finally, there was a company of German soldiers reluctant to accept the fact of the Armistice who on the eleventh began marching in disciplined ranks to join other loyal troops massing in Liege for withdrawal to the Fatherland. As a last blow at the enemy they mined the Hamont railroad station before their departure, assuming that the last train carrying German troops from Antwerp had arrived. But only at midnight, long after the Armistice, did the train steam in, triggering an enormous explosion which blew some railway cars nearly one hundred feet from the tracks. Almost eight hundred soldiers were killed and others wounded, while the waiting room, stacked high with abandoned weapons, was turned into a tangle of wreckage. Fragments of glass from the shattered train windows injured Velser's mother, who lived near the station. Only after the war had officially ended had it come with all its violence to Hamont.

Another facet of the morning of the eleventh is mirrored in Odon von Horvath's play *Don Juan Comes Home from the Wars* (1936), never performed in the Nazi years. At 11:40, Berlin time, in a makeshift dressing room near the Flanders front, two aging and once-pretty actresses are the very face of defeat. "The war's over. We've lost," says one. "I can't find my red wig," says the other.

"The reserves have mutinied and that fat colonel's been cashiered," adds the first *soubrette*. "There aren't any more officers. The general's a sergeant."

". . . Do you think there'll be a show this evening?"

"God knows. Main thing is, peace is on the way. . . . It's a historic day, today. At twelve o'clock the Armistice starts."

"Another twenty minutes, then." (*Away in the distance, a grenade explodes.*)

"I wonder how many more men are going to die. . . ."

Too young to be a soldier, thirteen-year-old Victor Queulin-Caille was working on a Flanders farm. As the sound of gunfire inched closer the German occupiers "made me and some other boys drive a huge herd of cattle onto the road to Luxembourg." Preparing to fall back, the Germans ensured their food supply for the long march while devastating the economies of the undestroyed farms. "At 11:00 A.M. the occupying soldiers left. Immediately we made a

French flag with whatever material we could find. . . . The last German soldiers, about ten of them, walked past it. *'Vive le France'* one of them shouted."

To achieve an orderly return, Allied forces had to be kept from penetrating German supply lines and march routes. To maintain Route Nationale No. 64 open to the east, the 88th Division, dug in along the Meuse, struggled against the Americans until the last minutes of the war. As Major General von Beczwarzowsky, its commander, reported, "Everything depended on delaying the enemy for hours [so that the infantry divisions which were to withdraw through the protective support of the 88th could get through]. If this had not succeeded, a catastrophe would have been unavoidable. In the woods east of the national road, with its steep slopes and its bottomless roads, the division, and especially the entire artillery, would have been captured by the enemy. . . ." It had been a difficult, dispiriting period for the division since its transfer from the Russian front. In a year it had enjoyed only one eight-day rest and had its massive losses—two thirds of its strength—replaced by the remnants of seventeen decimated infantry regiments rather than fresh troops. "Although it was raining almost constantly," the general explained, "no shelter was available. Real rest was hardly known. At night the regiments were moved up, alternately, farther to the front and in the lively nightly hostile searching fire suffered severe losses. . . . The number of those men, who during these last engagements like the bravest of the brave, Major Friebe, sealed their devotion to the Fatherland with their death on the field of battle, was high. . . ."

The final report of the 176th Brigade, 425th Infantry, from Blancchampagne Ferme, described what happened. The fog-shrouded American crossing of the Meuse at Létanne, which threatened the German withdrawal route, had been counterattacked at 7:15 A.M. on the eleventh, and the advance briefly stopped. "Unfortunately this success was dearly paid for with the death of Major Friebe, who fell, 3 meters in front of his opponent, with a bullet through his head." It had all been unnecessary, yet Friebe, who had led his detachment with shouts of "Hurrah!" until three paces from the enemy, had to have known what he was doing, and may not have wanted to face returning to a defeated Fatherland.

Despite orders against contact with the enemy, German negotiators had gone forward to ask about Friebe. The Americans turned over his body to the 425th Infantry, who buried him in the cemetery at Moulins before beginning the march home.

With the front quiet, mobile kitchens which had been held back because of the intensity of artillery fire could be sent forward to feed the weary troops. "Weather," the report ended: "Heavy fog, dreary, and raw."

On the Allied side, reactions to Foch's announcement of an Armistice ranged the emotional spectrum from elation to apathy. "Altho encouraging," an American sergeant observed in his journal, "it sounds like B.S. to me." A *Punch* cartoon showed an anxious army trainee among many in a field being warned by the drill instructor, "Never mind looking at yer watch, me lad. *I'll* tell yer when the War's over."

When it became known that although the enemy was to surrender all of his fleet and all of his aircraft, as well as much of his heavy war equipment, yet be permitted to march home in orderly fashion, shouldering personal arms, French General Charles Mangin objected that it was a blunder. "No! No! No!" he said, in tears. "We must go right into the heart of Germany. The Armistice should be signed *there*. The Germans will not admit they are beaten. You do not finish wars like this. . . . Who will see that the conditions are enforced? The Allies? A coalition has never survived the danger which has created it. It is a fatal error and France will pay for it!"

A British brigadier grumbled to a runner who had brought the news, "They've been allowed to get away with it; we haven't finished the job." The battalion adjutant, Hubert Essame, who would be a brigadier general in the next war, also "had an uncomfortable feeling that it would all have to be done over again."

An official copy of the Armistice agreement was to be hand-carried to British headquarters by Major Richard Meinertzhagen, who had served in Egypt and was a recent arrival in France. He ordered his staff car too far to the east, into an area not yet cleared of mines, and about an hour before the cease-fire was to take effect an explosion rocked the car and blew the driver apart. Shaken, but only superficially injured, the Major hailed a passing vehicle and reached General Haig five hours late, passing through a French sector where troops waved small Tricolor flags and yelled at him with delight. Feeling sore at the pit of the stomach, and not only from the "piece of iron" which had hit him there but not gone through, Meinertzhagen wanted only some brandy.

At General Pershing's headquarters in Chaumont, on the Marne, no one had wanted to retire on the night of the tenth. Officers sat up and speculated upon what would happen if the Germans did not sign. No one had any conception of how close the enemy was to surrender in the field. (Even more ignorant were front-line troops.) Occasionally the ringing of a phone would excite premature jubilation. Finally, at six o'clock there was a call from Colonel Bentley Mott, Pershing's aide at Foch's headquarters.

Pershing walked to the big detailed map on the wall and began to muse about the offensive to take Metz, now aborted. "I suppose our campaigns are ended, but what an enormous difference a few more days would have made!"

In Flanders on the morning of November 11, British artilleryman William Pressey was in a field repairing two guns. "We had parts of guns laid out on sacks. The fighting was still going on, but had left us behind. Then our section officer called for me. 'Take it easy, Pressey,' he said, 'we'll not shoot again. An Armistice has been signed. . . .' "

He walked slowly back to his mates. "What's up?" they asked. "It's all over," he said. The men felt cheated of victory. "Why the bloody hell," they complained, "couldn't we have chased him right through Berlin while we had the chance. . . ?"

Although a generation of young men had been expended since 1914, there remained some enthusiasm among the British for carrying defeat home to the Germans. Major E. E. Mockler-Ferryman, with the 129th Brigade of the 4th Division, heard the news at Nouvelle, just south of Mons, when an Australian cavalryman rode by and announced that there would be a cease-fire at eleven. His unit expressed doubts until the official message arrived, when "Of course everyone was pleased, for the battery was worn out, but on the other hand, having got so far it seemed a pity to stop before getting into Germany." At 10:30 he threw his helmet in a corner of a farmhouse at Asquillies, put on a soft hat to mark the occasion, "and strolled into the lines. At 10:45, however, the Boche started to shell the southeast corner of the village. . . . I retreated hastily to get my tin hat. I wasn't going to take any risks at that stage of the war. We began to wonder whether the Armistice had really been signed. However at 10:56 the Boche stopped, his last shell being a dud."

Australian signaler Bill Harney remembered how the last prisoners taken brought home to him the "stupidity of . . . the whole thing." The dazed and wounded lot were "people I had always reckoned were supermen." To cope with the burden he would call out, "Any of you chaps [who] know English come and pick up your mates—we can't carry them back." And those who could walk would come forward—"and they'd salute me, you know. Blimey, I'd never been saluted in my life! And they'd pick up these chaps and take them back. . . . I saw one thing—the most terrific thing. It was a chap—a big tall man—and he had his jaw shot away and he's got another bloke with broken legs or something—he's got this chap on his back. He's staggering back along the road and when they saw me they had to put up one hand [to salute], you know, and it made me ready to cry. I used to go up and pat them on the back and they'd point to their big bottle that they had and it was full of coffee and cognac and I'd have a drink and give them some and then they'd sit down and pull out their postcards and they'd show me photos of their wives and children and farms. And when I saw all these things I thought, 'Well, blimey, what's it all about?' "

The Germans were fighting little more than rearguard actions, to keep their remnants of divisions from being bottled up in northern Belgium. At the front the British, too, moved relatively small forces. "The days were long gone by," R. H. Mottram wrote in the closing pages of his *Spanish Farm* trilogy, "when a battalion was [a] recognizable entity. . . . Depleted to form Machine Gun Companies, the truncated battalions of the end of the war usually worked by separate companies, moving independently. There was some desultory firing in front, but [Lieutenant Dormer's] own posts had seen and heard nothing of the enemy. About nine he sent a runner to see if his orders had miscarried. Reply came, stand to, and await developments." It was the morning of the eleventh.

Soon Dormer's order arrives: "Cease fire." When he reads the instructions on the pink slip to his young platoon leaders, "they almost groaned. Late products of the at last up-to-date O.T.C.s of England, they had only been out a few months and although they had seen shell-fire and heavy casualties, yet there had always been a retreating enemy, and fresh ground won every week. The endless-seeming years of trench warfare they had missed entirely. The slow attrition that left one alone, with all one's friends wounded or killed . . . meant nothing to them. They had been schoolboys [in 1914] when Paschendaele was being contested. Cadets when the Germans burst through the Fifth Army [earlier in 1918]. They wanted a victorious march to Berlin."

When the message is read to the company, the men receive it "with ironical silence," but a sergeant, unhappy at being left with unexpended ammunition, complains, "Cease fire! We've got the same amount of stuff on us as we had two days ago!" Dormer muses that the Armistice had happened just in time. "If it hadn't come, would we have been faced with the spectacle of two armies making peace by themselves, without orders, against orders, sections and platoons and companies simply not reloading their rifles, machine-gunners and Trench Mortars not unpacking their gear, finally even the artillery keeping teams by the guns, and the inertia gradually spreading upwards, until the few at the top who really wanted to go on, would have found the dead weight of unwillingness impossible to drag?"

Small units like Dormer's had possessed the advantage of mobility over land where the ponderous armies common earlier in the war could not wheel. The chewed-up terrain and the network of canals and streams left without bridges by the departing Germans made the mass movement of men and equipment difficult. Lieutenant Cecil Lewis of 152 Squadron, flying SE-5s, remembered flying at three hundred feet for miles over the devastated fields east of Ypres and seeing "nothing but a featureless landscape of contiguous shell-holes. Now, with the winter, they were mostly filled with water, and in the evening light looked dun, rancid, slimy—an abomination of desolation." For the author of *The Spanish Farm,* the shooting stopped in just such a setting. "On the ruins of Meteren," Mottram wrote in *A Personal Record,* "my last shell of the war, fired from a great distance, flung its mud and stench over me."

Despite appearances from the air, there were still pockets of working farms and active villages, looking almost normal except that they were devoid of men. The war had passed them by in 1914. When British and Commonwealth columns began occupying villages from which the Germans had withdrawn without a fight, soldiers shouted, *"Guerre fini, guerre fini, Boche kapoo!"* Women and children rushed to them to tuck late-flowering red and white chrysanthemums in their tunics and in the straps of their helmets. Even horses, trucks, and gun limbers were decked with flowers. Long-hidden flags appeared in streets where earlier the display of Belgian or French colors would have brought quick punishment. And soon reappearing in the villages were gaunt survivors of the drafts of Belgian and French civilians whom the Germans had seized as conscript labor. Unable or unwilling to feed them adequately, the Germans had nevertheless kept them until they had no further use for laborers and then sent them flooding back through the lines.

Civilian slave laborers were not the only returnees. Warrant officer Frederick Taprill, with a field medical unit of the 5th Division, remembered seeing, at Jolimetz, near the Forest of Mormal, "a ragged band of men staggering through no-man's land towards us. These men were our men, almost skeletons, released by the enemy about to retire." Some prisoner-of-war camps became close to the line as it shifted east, and soldiers employed to dig coal in the mines around Mons merely walked away—if they could walk. And at the eleventh hour, Taprill remembered at age eighty-six, the commanding officer and second-in-command of his ambulance company were both killed "by a stray high-velocity shell."

Violence left some villages less easily. In R. F. Delderfield's chronicle-novel *A Horseman Riding By* (1966), the novelist borrows an incident of the last day intact, inserting one of his Devonshire characters, Smut Willoughby, into it:

> On the final day of the war his battalion was advancing on a village east of Valenciennes, where a wounded German officer told them the enemy rearguard had gone back before dawn. So they went in, some hundreds of them and were milling about the Square when two well-sited machine-guns opened up and Smut went down with a bullet in the hip. He would have been hit again, probably fatally, had not his poacher's sixth sense somersaulted him into a doorway where he was protected by the bodies of less experienced men while the last-ditch Germans, including the wounded officer, were rooted out and despatched with bayonet and bomb.

The incident had been remembered even earlier, in poet Herbert Read's *The End of a War* (1931), which turned it into a four hundred-line reflection on values and beliefs. Again the wounded German lieutenant informs an officer of the advancing British battalion that the village his infantrymen are approaching is undefended. But when the troops enter the square, machine guns open up from the church tower and other points. A hundred men are killed or wounded before the survivors can eliminate the snipers. An unwounded corporal dispatches the German officer, who meets his fate impassively. In securing the village the soldiers find the body of a young girl who had been violated and tortured. The British officer, sickened by what he has experienced, falls into a sleep of exhaustion, awakening late in the morning to the bells announcing the Armistice.

A twenty-five-year-old captain (and, like Mottram, a former

bank clerk) with three years' service in France in a Yorkshire regiment, Read had been returned to England in May 1918 after the last Somme retreat. Although he had not been at the scene he set to verse, he postscripted that the incident "is true, and can be vouched for by several witnesses still living. But its horrors do not accuse any particular nation; they are representative of war, and of human nature in War." His protestations aside, it is clear who is condemned. The "Meditation of the Dying German Officer"—part one of the poem—captures the fanatic loyalty to Fatherland with which he had "lived in the ecstasy of battle," exulting in a mystic concept of German supremacy. Part two, "The Dialogue between the Body and the Soul of the Murdered Girl," discloses that she had been caught spying upon the occupiers of her country; and the poet advises,

> So be content. In this war
> many men have perished not bless'd
> with faith in a cause, a country or a God. . . .

Finally, in the "Meditation of the Waking English Officer," the lieutenant is roused by church bells and by the voices of peasants chanting a litany of thanksgiving. It is the morning of November 11. How can God's bells ring out, he wonders, from the setting of such an unholy happening? How can there be glory in the strife, or joy in its conclusion? He had begun the war with a vague idealism which had quickly turned bitter, and cannot pray to "an infinitely kind Father whose will / can mould the world. . . ." But he must believe that man's destiny does not lead backward to savagery but to something finer as yet unconceived. Read's dramatic meditation voiced the intellectual dilemma of countless others who found traditional value systems untenable after 1918. That the war was won did not push the clock back to 1914.

Field Marshal Douglas Haig had waited for the signing before summoning his five Army commanders to a meeting at Cambrai. Symbolically, the meeting opened at eleven o'clock, and at a place as far forward as some of them had ever been. He was concerned now, Haig told them, about how to keep troops occupied in good discipline in peacetime, which he insisted was as much a duty of command as to train troops for war. His diary notes that after the meeting ended the group was "cinemaed" for the newsreels, with the only break in the seriousness coming when General Plumer stood

"A.D. Nineteen Fifty." In the trenches. Cartoon by Bruce Bairnsfather, 1917.
From *The Bystander's Fragments from France*.

An example of the congestion of supply convoys in the muddy roads and villages: Americans at Esnes, near the Meuse.

RIGHT: Marshal Foch's train at the station at Compiègne. Car 2419D, in the foreground, is the dining car in which negotiations took place.

FAR RIGHT: A German Armistice leaflet air-dropped to Allied troops, printed in English on one side, French on the other. From the collection of Stanley Weintraub.

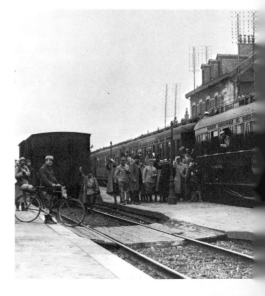

The German People Offers Peace.

The new German democratic government has this programme:

"The will of the people is the highest law."

The German people wants quickly to end the slaughter.

The new German popular government therefore has offered an

Armistice

and has declared itself ready for

Peace

on the basis of justice and reconciliation of nations.

It is the will of the German people that it should live in peace with all peoples, honestly and loyally.

What has the new German popular government done so far to put into practice the will of the people and to prove its good and upright intentions?

a) The new German government has appealed to President Wilson to bring about peace.

It has recognized and accepted all the principles which President Wilson proclaimed as a basis for a general lasting peace of justice among the nations.

b) The new German government has solemnly declared its readiness to evacuate Belgium and to restore it.

c) The new German government is ready to come to an honest understanding with France about.

Alsace-Lorraine.

d) The new German government has restricted the **U-boat War.**

No passengers steamers not carrying troops or war material will be attacked in future.

e) The new German government has declared that it will withdraw all German troops back over the German frontier.

f) The new German government has asked the Allied Governments to name commissioners to agree upon the practical measures of the evacuation of Belgium and France.

These are the deeds of the new German popular government. Can these be called mere words, or bluff, or propaganda?

Who is to blame, if an armistice is not called now?

Who is to blame if daily thousands of brave soldiers needlessly have to shed their blood and die?

Who is to blame, if the hitherto undestroyed towns and villages of France and Belgium sink in ashes?

Who is to blame, if hundreds of thousands of unhappy women and children are driven from their homes to hunger and freeze?

The German people offers its hand for peace.

Le peuple allemand offre la paix.

Le nouveau gouvernement démocratique de l'Allemagne agit en conformité avec le principe: »La volonté du peuple est la loi suprême«.

Le peuple allemand veut amener une fin rapide des massacres.

Le nouveau gouvernement du peuple allemand a pour cette raison offert

l'armistice

et s'est déclaré prêt à une

paix

du droit et de la conciliation des peuples.

C'est la volonté du peuple allemand de vivre honnêtement et loyalement en paix avec tous les autres peuples.

Le nouveau gouvernement du peuple allemand qu'a-t-il fait jusqu'à présent pour réaliser la volonté du peuple et pour prouver ses bonnes intentions sincères?

A) **Le nouveau gouvernement allemand a demandé au président Wilson d'amener la paix.**

Il a expressément reconnu et accepté les principes que le président Wilson a proclamés comme la base d'une paix de droit générale et durable parmi les peuples.

B) Le nouveau gouvernement allemand s'est solennellement déclaré prêt à

évacuer et dédommager la Belgique.

C) Le nouveau gouvernement allemand veut en toute loyauté s'accorder avec la France au sujet de

l'Alsace-Lorraine.

D) **Le gouvernement allemand a modifié la guerre sous-marine en ce sens que dès à présent les vapeurs servant au transport des voyageurs ne peuvent plus être attaqués, pour autant qu'ils ne transportent pas des troupes ou du matériel de guerre.**

E) Le nouveau gouvernement allemand a déclaré vouloir retirer toutes les troupes allemandes derrière les frontières allemandes.

F) Le nouveau gouvernement allemand a demandé aux gouvernements adversaires, de constituer des négociateurs pour s'accorder au sujet de la réalisation pratique de l'évacuation de la Belgique et de la France.

Voilà ce que le nouveau gouvernement du peuple allemand a fait! Y peut-on voir des phrases creuses? Est-ce là du bluff ou de la propagande!

A qui la faute, si dans ces circonstances l'armistice ne sera pas conclu?

A qui la faute, si tous les jours des milliers de braves soldats verseront encore leur sang et tomberont sous les balles?

A qui la faute, si les villes et les villages de la Belgique et de la France qui ont échappé jusqu'à présent à la destruction, tomberont en ruines?

A qui la faute, si des centaines de milliers de femmes malheureuses et d'enfants seront chassés de leurs domiciles et exposés à la famine et au froid?

Le peuple allemand tend la main pour la paix.

The white flags of Germany: Georges Scott depicts the German Armistice delegation moving through the night into the French lines. From *L'Illustration*, Paris, November 16–23, 1918.

ABOVE: The Kaiser (center) with Hindenburg (left) and Ludendorff (right).

RIGHT, TOP: Sailors flying the red flag in Berlin.

RIGHT, MIDDLE: Berlin, November 10, 1918: soldiers, sailors, and civilians with red armbands on the Unter den Linden.

RIGHT, BOTTOM: Brabant sur Meuse. American vehicles enter the devastated village.

Marshal Foch (white coat) at his headquarters with Field Marshal Haig (second from right).

Doughboys leaving a French village after the shooting has stopped: Norman Rockwell's sentimental version of such a scene for the sheet music of "Little French Mother, Good Bye!" From the collection of George Mauner.

Pershing (right) with Foch.

U.S. ARMY SIGNAL CORPS

IMPERIAL WAR MUSEUM, LONDON

ABOVE: Armistice Day, Paris.

BELOW: Paris, November 11, 1918.

Private Arthur Wrench of the Seaforth Highlanders cycling the Armistice news through Belgium, past the ghosts of his fallen buddies. Illustration by Arthur Wrench, reproduced from his diary.

L'ILLUSTRATION

Prix de ce Numéro : 5 Francs.　　　16-23 NOVEMBRE 1918　　　76e Année. — N° 3950-3951.

M. CLEMENCEAU A LA TRIBUNE DE LA CHAMBRE, LE 11 NOVEMBRE 1918

Clemenceau at the rostrum of the Chamber of Deputies, November 11, 1918. From *L'Illustration*, Paris, November 16–23, 1918.

Crowds in an English town on Armistice Day.

Crowds in Trafalgar Square at Nelson's Column.

The joy of Paris. Artist L. Sabbatier's rendition, somewhat more decorous than the real thing, of street celebrations in the city on Armistice Day. From *L'Illustration,* Paris, November 16–23, 1918.

ABOVE: *Czecho-Slovakian Army Entering Vladivostok, Siberia, in 1918*. Painting by George Luks. These were released and escaped prisoners of war who had formed themselves into a national army. From the Los Angeles County Museum of Art, Mr. and Mrs. William Preston Harrison Collection.

RIGHT: A page from Henry Williamson's *The Patriot's Progress*, illustrated by William Kermode. John Bullock, maimed and on crutches, greets Armistice Day.

FAR RIGHT: Lt. Guy Brown Wiser's drawing of the Armistice Day celebration in the *Gefangenenlager* at Landshut.

GEOFFREY BLES

George Luks
1913

The Kaiser and the Crown Prince reviewing troops in France.

before the camera trying to look smartly military "while Byng and others near him were chaffing the old man and trying to make him laugh." Then each returned to duty, Haig to prepare orders for the army of occupation, and for the withdrawal of unneeded divisions to available railheads.

. Lloyd George, who as Prime Minister had inherited his commander in chief, would write that Haig and his headquarters staff had never witnessed, "not even through a telescope, the attacks [they] ordained, except on carefully prepared charts where the advancing battalions were represented by the pencil which marched with ease across swamps, and marked lines of triumphal progress without loss of a single point. As for the mud, it never incommoded the movements of this irresistible pencil." Now, with the last desultory shots, some of Haig's smartest aides would sally forth to the front, one of them bursting into tears when he saw the mire and waste which had only been map coordinates on the wall of a comfortable château to the rear. "Good God," he cried, "did we really send men to fight in that?"

A battery commander with the 8th Division, John Wedderburn-Maxwell (who would be a brigadier in the next war), was in action on the Mons-Ath road, at Gyn, when his orders arrived. He read out the announcement to his men. "There was no wild excitement but a sense of shock and bewilderment . . . due to the sudden removal of the one objective in life." At seconds before eleven they fired their last salvo. Signaler W. Anderson Scott, with the 8th Division, remembered a dispatch rider bringing the news as they were proceeding toward Enghien to the sound of distant gunfire. The company sergeant read the message aloud, as their commanding officer had been wounded in the head the day before. "It's all over," he said; "an Armistice has been signed."

"What's an Armistice, mate?" a cockney asked.

"Time to bury the dead, mate," said another.

They continued on the Enghien road, encountering a battalion of German infantry marching toward them, white handkerchiefs fastened to their rifles and shouting, *Krieg endet! Krieg endet!*" Scott's company had marched through the cease-fire.

Gunner A. F. Marshall, a Scot in Y Battery Anti-Aircraft, Royal Artillery, was examining an Armistice notice posted by a dispatch rider at a village east of Valenciennes when a companion asked, over his shoulder, "Wot the 'ell's an armystyce?" He attempted to define "the puzzling word" for the Londoner as "a kind of truce, a temporary sort of peace." His own feeling was one of "sheer bewilderment," echoed and reechoed in the queries of comrades at the news. "Does it mean the war is over?" "Can it start all over again?" "Where do we go from here?" "Do I get my leave now? It's been a year since I had my last lot." Since there was no point in going forward, they pulled back to Raisnes, a village where the houses had roofs.

At 5:30 that morning Geoffrey Waugh was with a group about to jump off to try to seize the Jurbise railway station two miles away. Seventeen days before, he had been on a troopship that was also taking Prime Minister Lloyd George to France, and as Waugh stuffed fifty extra rounds into his bandoleer, together with three hand bombs, red artillery-spotting flares and two days' rations, he recalled the Prime Minister's jaunty farewell: "Cheer up, boys, it will all be over in a fortnight." Hardly had his five-man section begun moving up when it was halted by news that the fighting would stop at 11:00. Then at seven they were sent off anyway, and a mile ahead he could see smoke coming from the station, apparently an artillery hit. He passed a German corpse, and soon after a wounded *Boche* who asked, in English, "Is the war finished, Jock?" The station proved abandoned, but it was "a fine dry floor to sleep on."

Private Harry Smith of the Royal Scots Fusilliers remembered being halted at 9:45 close to Jurbise, where the Germans were trying to protect the railway line to the east. A British plane swooped low as they huddled in a meadow, and a message fluttered down. The adjutant sent his orderly to pick it up. "Attention!" it read. "The War is over. Everyone stay where he is. Armistice is signed as from 11 o'clock this morning."

One of the sergeants jumped up and exclaimed, "Right! Give us one of the guns." He wanted a Lewis gun and a forty-eight-round pan, to finish the war with a flourish. "Let's fire it!" he begged.

"No," said the adjutant, thinking of the men lost to German fire the night before. "Don't you take that gun off the limber. We're to stay where we are, not a shot to be fired. If you fire that, Jerry may be over the hedge. He'll lob something at us—we've had enough of these." And he pointed in the direction of the bodies they had passed in their march.

Just off the Mons-Maubeuge road, Private Thomas Lomax of the 8th Sherwood Foresters had been with a group which had lost contact with the English lines the night before and had crept under shellfire to a cottage where a thin crack of light indicated signs of life. "We rammed a bullet into the breech and tapped on the window. The house was occupied by three of our men belonging to a cycle corps. They told us of an Armistice we did not believe." The next morning two planes dropped confirming messages.

Despite poor flying weather on the final Monday of the war, Allied airmen ventured up, hoping to see history being made, or hoping to squeeze in a last sortie before the horrors of peacetime set in. Captain Eddie Rickenbacker's U.S. 94th Squadron, based with the 95th, was, like all others, ordered grounded on the morning of the eleventh, but he was determined "to see the war end." With the excuse that he wanted to test his engine, he hedgehopped under the low ceiling in the direction of Verdun, toward Conflans. Over the front lines before eleven, he collected bullet holes in his plane as the price of getting too close too soon. As eleven came he claimed to see all shooting in his sector stop. "It was almost as if lightning had struck everybody on both sides. I looked down from less than 1000 ft. altitude and you could see the helmets going into the air, guns being thrown into the air, hands being waved on both sides of no man's land. . . ."

Rickenbacker had arranged to have Lieutenant Jimmy Meissner of the 94th fly correspondent Webb Miller over the front lines at the moment of the Armistice. He told neither Miller nor Meissner that he was going himself, and when Miller checked in, Meissner told him, "There's fog all along the Meuse. . . . We couldn't see a thing. It would be useless. . . . I'll take you tomorrow if there's no fog and it's still worth a story." Miller had arranged for a car and driver in case the weather kept him on the ground, and took the main road to Verdun, where three lines of traffic squeezed along, unworried about enemy air activity. The middle lane was reserved for staff cars. Columns of troops going forward still choked one lane, while another was jammed with trucks returning for ammunition and supplies.

As they approached Verdun, intermittent, thunderous roaring indicated that a fourteen-inch naval gun, dismantled from an American battleship and brought by rail to be a surprise factor in the planned November 14 attack on Metz, was being fired every few minutes. There was no reason to use it, but the crew would not be cheated out of a few shots at the enemy. They fired at random, in the general direction of the German lines, and the Germans responded.

To avoid being caught in a crossfire, Miller and his driver

turned away from Verdun to Bras, still intending to get to the lines by eleven. A soldier directed him to a communication trench, ankle deep in mud, and he left the car to proceed on foot, able to see only about fifty yards ahead in the fog. Finally a captain emerged, and seeing Miller's green armband with "C" for correspondent, he asked, "What are you doing up here? There's nothing happening here."

"I've come to cover the end of the war—the Armistice."

"Good God," he exclaimed, "when is it?"

It was already nearly 10:45, yet the captain had not heard the news. Then the field telephone in the dugout jangled. The unit was finally receiving its Armistice instructions. "From the direction of Verdun the fog-muffled rumble of the cannonade gradually died away. . . . The men stood talking in groups." In the fog they could see or hear little, and there was little drama in the scene. He had heard bigger demonstrations, Miller wrote, "when a man rolled seven and won five dollars." The Army's reason for existence had ceased. "Wish I was in Cincinnati with my job back," said a private.

With a former Illinois National Guard regiment not far away, Sergeant Sol Cohen had been up since 2:00 A.M. on the eleventh, awaiting instructions to push off. At 3:00 they began moving forward in the darkness and fog, finally arriving at positions atop a hill, where they crouched and waited amid rumors which circulated from doughboy to doughboy that an Armistice was about to be declared. "There we were," he would write two days later, "ghostly creatures in the chill early morning, waiting, waiting. . . . And the cannons were firing away hateful things, cartloads of gas shells, and there was no end to the vile noise. A rumble away to our left indicated a[n enemy] barrage."

A few weeks before, one of their scouting parties had come upon a cache of abandoned musical instruments in no-man's-land and brought them back. One was a violin, which a company cook promptly fiddled upon so energetically that its bridge split and collapsed. Acquiring the mute discard, Cohen kept the bridge fast by tightening the strings. Now in the fog on the hilltop the precious violin lay with his pack, his gas mask, and his helmet. In the tension, as they listened to the boom of artillery and waited for orders to go over the top, Cohen's colonel strode over and asked him to play. "Ice-cold were my fingers, but I took the beloved instrument from its case. . . . The colonel stood above me, a queer smile on his face. Silent groups hovered around; the fog lifted a bit and gradually the grey cottages below us began to . . . show themselves, dismal ruined huts with soiled red roofs, [and] shattered sides. . . . One piece after another and my fingers grew warmer. I played myself into form and then the restless Yanks turned away. I replaced the violin in its case."

The music had not floated very far away, overwhelmed by the percussion of the big guns. It was 9:00 and the sun was groping through the mist. The jittery troops now increasingly exposed on the hill could not be soothed by a violin and had turned to weighing the chances of peace. "What do you think, sergeant?" one asked Cohen as he set down his violin case tenderly. "Oh, I don't know," he said. "I've given up thinking." And then the colonel returned. "Now, we don't want any shouting," he began quietly, "but the Armistice was signed early this morning. The artillery has been given orders to cease firing. The troops will remain in position."

Little knots of unbelieving Yanks formed. "Hell, it couldn't be over," said one. Yes, it was *fini*, said the French interpreter (there was an adjacent French unit). He had known of the signing for two hours, but had kept it to himself. There were no cheers. The Yank, Sol Cohen explained in a letter home, did not give a damn about victory. He "thought only of central Illinois and the girl back there, and the soda fountain and the billiard hall."

At the Azelot aerodrome, Captain Ewart Garland's 104th Squadron was grounded by fog. The day before, he had patrolled their sector of the empty sky in a precious new De Havilland-10 bomber, the only one of the new craft in combat service. Then he went off on his own at sunset to bomb an airfield at Sarrebourg. On the way back, having dropped his explosives, Garland was pounced upon by four planes, and his observer, Bottrill, "let off a few bursts from his double-barreled Lewis." Only then did they see that the pursuers were French-flown Spads. Other squadrons had not known of an operational DH-10, and "mistook it for a Hun bomber." With no German machines in the air, they were risking each other's lives on what Garland noted in his diary had to be "the last day of the war."

The supposition proved correct, as he recorded the next day. "So! It's over! I can scarce realize the stupendous event. Cease hostilities! Good Lord, it is really true? I am writing this at noon, having paraded the men to tell them—everyone has taken it very quietly, just as a Britisher would!"

Unlike the British and American pilots, the French were, with rare exceptions, relieved to quit combat flying. René Fonck had scored seventy-five kills, but the French had suffered nearly 12,000 pilot casualties and had few veteran officers left. France was grateful for the American-manned Lafayette Escadrille, now officially the U.S. 103rd Squadron, which had flown under the Tricolor before the U.S. was in the war. There had been other Americans, too, who flew for the French, among them Sergeant Charles Veil, once of Punxsutawney, Pennsylvania, a short, red-haired college dropout with three kills to his credit (he later claimed five) who learned his flying in Pau and went up with a French squadron, *Spad* 150, as a *pilote volontaire américain.* On October 9 he had technically become a first lieutenant in the U.S. Army, but with his partner from Vermont, Hank Stickney, stubbornly remained with the French. In the air early on November 11, Veil had no idea that he was on his last mission. "On our own hook," he wrote, "we wanted to see Charleville and Sedan." No enemy planes were in the air, but they did observe a German battery drop a shell on Italian troops working to repair a destroyed bridge. Diving down on the artillery position, they scattered horses and men with a fusillade, and then returned to their base.

"There was something queer about the landing field. . . . Stickney and I felt it from high in the air. Certainly bad news awaited us down there. . . . We settled to a stop. The *armurier* took the cartridge-belts out of our machine-gun magazines. He said not a word. . . . Commander Mény was waiting for us. Around him stood the [other] pilots, hands in their pockets. . . ." They braced themselves for news of flyers shot down.

"*L'armistice est signé,*" said Mény. "*La guerre est fini! Felicitations!*"

Veil understood the blank faces, the idle hands. "No more patrols, no more fights in the air. Nothing to do, nothing to live for. . . . I found my watch, brought it forth, threw it as far as ever I could. Time would never mean the same thing again. . . ."

They drank and felt sorry for themselves. The Germans, in their retreat, had abandoned an ammunition dump nearby. The pilots sullenly set it off, "a final conflagration of temperaments."

Most Allied flyers greeted the Armistice with surprise that they were alive to hear the news. In the 95th Squadron, Lieutenant Sumner Sewall of New York was typical. "Hell," he said, "we've lived through the bloody war." Major Harold Hartney, a Canadian who commanded the Americans of the 95th, felt the same. "A great weight was lifted from us. We had lived through it." When a brass band began to play, and cheering soldiers began firing pistols and guns in the air, there was some danger that, although they had out-lasted the war, not all of them would survive the celebration. Hart-ney flattened himself onto the aerodrome ground to avoid the ricocheting bullets.

Always the iconoclast, General Billy Mitchell, who had flown very little, felt more than relief at having outlasted the war. On the evening before the Armistice, he had picked up the radio intercept from the OHL which authorized the German delegates to sign, but at Toul he discovered the American Second Army headquarters busy preparing an attack for the next morning. "This, it seemed to me, was a rather foolish proceeding as it would lead to no benefit to us and would kill a great many men because the Germans would certainly resist. . . . The Division to be used was the 92nd, composed of colored troops who had very little experience. . . . The attack was actually carried out the following morning with disastrous results." Mitchell, responsible only for air support, had not been asked for an opinion.

Early on the eleventh he visited the commanders of air services for the U.S. First and Second Armies to congratulate them on their work. Not remaining to see the last shots fired, he went back to his own quarters to prepare a final report. On the morning of Novem-ber 11, 1918, he would write, American forces had 740 combat air-craft, most (528) manufactured in France. Only 196 were American-made. The self-proclaimed Arsenal of Democracy, the United States had not put a single home-manufactured tank into ac-tion, nor had any American-made airplane flown against the enemy. And only about 500 of the 3,500 artillery pieces used in action by the AEF were U.S.-made.

At the 8th Squadron, flying Bristol Fighters under the command of Major Leigh Mallory (later Air Chief Marshal) out of Malincourt, west of Mons, the news arrived before daylight. Lieutenant Stephen Horscroft remembered that few officers troubled to dress, but most got out of bed, and although the ground was white with frost they pulled a derelict German wagon into the village pond, doused it with petrol, and set fire to it, dancing and shouting and setting flares off into the waning darkness.

At the 217th Squadron, flying De Havilland-4 two-seater bombers, Lieutenant R. N. Bell had just returned from being hospi-talized with influenza (along with thousands of other troops on both sides). Ironically, the 200,000 Chinese coolies whom the French had imported for such labor as the building of airfields and laying of trackage may have brought with them the virus, mislabeled "Spanish influenza." In the last weeks of the war Spanish flu had laid low more troops than shot, shell, or shrapnel and contributed to the slackening of momentum and the weariness with war. Bell himself still felt too weak to fly when orders arrived, late at night on the tenth, that pilots and observers were to stow their gear in rear cockpits preparatory to getting airborne at dawn to occupy an abandoned German aerodrome a few miles from Bruges. Despite the rain, they took off and straggled "in a flock rather than a formation" behind their flight commander through low clouds and drizzle. Only when they arrived did they discover that the war was over.

"The day before," Lieutenant Ralph Donaldson of the 40th Squadron recalled, "when we approached Mons we had been greeted by German machine-gun fire, and the streets were deserted. On this morning the streets were jammed with people and all of them seemed to be waving Belgian flags. So we continued east looking for signs of our troops or retreating Germans." At an altitude of 150 feet they flew over abandoned artillery pieces pointing west and finally saw some khaki-clad men near a grassy, level stretch. Captain Chidlaw-Roberts wagged his wings to signal a landing, and the planes rolled up to a group of Canadian infantrymen "who wanted to know what was up. We told them there was to be an Armistice, but they wouldn't believe it. 'The big shots wouldn't dare call off the war,' a sergeant said, 'when we've finally got the sons of bitches on the run.'"

Just then, to Donaldson's surprise, "an officer on horseback came galloping across the field. He was carrying a long spear, to the end of which was attached a red pennant. No, it wasn't Sir Galahad from King Arthur's court; he was from divisional staff headquarters, and he was bringing official orders to the ground troops to cease fire at 11:00 A.M." The airmen, their story now accepted, returned to the machines, took off, and climbed to 12,000 feet, "scarcely believing that Archie* no longer would be taking pot shots at us, or that a Richthofen circus would not suddenly make its appearance out of the sun, diving in our direction. Just to make sure, we kept a close watch on our tails until we were safely on the ground."

Lieutenant Colonel L. A. Strange could not even find an airplane to fly on "the last day." When an orderly had awakened him

* Enemy antiaircraft fire.

with the message, "Hostilities will cease from 11 A.M. today. No machines to cross east of the balloon lines," he gave instructions to have the message delivered to the squadrons of his 80th Wing. Later in the morning he drove to the aerodrome at Grand Ennetieres, "as they had always looked after my Sopwith Camel, and I thought I should like just one more flight over the lines before the war was due to stop."

Despite the rain, he could not find a single serviceable plane on the ground. Even his own Camel was gone. The flight sergeant mumbled something about someone testing the guns. Strange went on to other aerodromes in his wing, finding aircraft beginning to return at about eleven. "When I questioned several of the Australian pilots, they said they had not seen any balloons, and asked most innocently how far east the balloon line was supposed to be. But I noticed that their bomb racks were empty. At noon some belated Snipes and S.E.5's put in an appearance, and when asked to give an account of themselves, the pilots said they thought it would be all right for them to go out and look for Smith, the man who had been missing since the Enghien raid. But their bomb racks were empty, too."

In the air at eleven, Captain A. Cunningham Reid was groping through the mist "for the shape of a landing ground" when he saw a Very flare rocket upward. Relieved, he was sure he was being guided down, and began descending, only to encounter a burst of colored lights, and no aerodrome. "For a moment I thought I was in a nightmare," he recalled, and then realized that troops had begun celebrating. He took evasive action and flew on.

Farther north, where flying weather was slightly more favorable, British Captain F. O. Cave was watching mechanics get the engine going on his machine for a 9:00 A.M. patrol when a plane from another unit appeared overhead and released a signal flare warning him not to take off. "Wash out the patrol" was the message on landing; "the war is over." Once the messenger left, planes went up anyway. "I contour-chased to Baupaume," Cave boasted in his diary. Then the aviators took a Crossley tender into Amiens to buy a newspaper, where they learned of the Kaiser's abdication and the revolution in Germany and watched an Australian band march through the streets, with crowds of civilians following. At a restaurant "the whole room broke out with 'Tipperary.' A French colonel then got up and sang a French song. . . ." Soon there were more songs, and everyone left the tables to march around the room. When they left for the aerodrome they found it was raining, but the weather no longer made a difference.

Across the Channel at Bircham Newton, where suitable weather was awaited for the bombing run over the North Sea to Berlin, word was that conditions had improved. But in the large hangar where a crowd of VIPs had gathered for the send-off, already once postponed, Colonel Mulock climbed atop a packing case and read an order from Air Chief Trenchard: "Hostilities will cease at 11:00. You will not carry out operations without orders from this HQ but preparations are to proceed." That meant, Mulock said, that if the Germans tried any funny business they would continue to be ready for a "special demonstration." The thwarted Berlin raiders streamed out to celebrate. The visiting brass hats vanished.

At W. R. Read's 216th Squadron deep in the Vosges, the message which arrived that morning was that no machines were to leave the ground. Their Berlin show was also off. In his diary the next day, Read would add, ruefully, "No more will our Handleys be used for the honourable purpose of war. We are postmen." In a handwritten autobiography he left at his death, at eighty-seven (in 1972), he confided that it was just as well that the Handley-Pages did not try to cross Germany. "The Armistice came," he wrote, "and so fell through a very interesting trip which was destined, in all probability, to end in disaster. I say 'disaster' because . . . only Pring returned and reported to the Air Ministry. Crossfield disappeared, Pring said, and nothing more was heard of him. It was thought that he had sold us to the *Boche*."

THE STILLNESS

Good-bye-ee! Don't-sigh-ee! . . .
Bon soir, old thing!
Cheerio, chin-chin.
Na-poo!* toodle-oo!
Good-bye-ee!

—THE HIT OF THE MONTH IN ENGLAND
IN MAY 1918 (AND IN FLANDERS IN
NOVEMBER 1918)

---

* *Na-poo* (or *na-pooh*): finished, empty, gone; *chin-chin:* a toast implying general goodwill, bottom's up.

At First Army headquarters Colonel George C. Marshall had been telephoned at six. He rushed from bed to cancel orders for four divisions scheduled to push off at six-thirty. Two of the divisions were already on the march, and it took him two hours to turn them back. Then he went back to sleep, assuming that he had done all that was to be done in his sector to stop the shooting on time.

Breakfast for his staff awaited his reawakening, and did not begin until ten-thirty. Between bites the French liaison officer announced his unhappiness that he could not go into Germany, shooting, at the head of a regiment of Moroccans. As his British equivalent began to air his grievances about freedom of the seas for the Germans, there was a tremendous explosion just outside the only window in the room. Marshall was thrown against the wall, stunned. "I thought I had been killed," he remembered, "and I think each of the others had the same idea, but we picked ourselves up and found that aside from the ruin of the breakfast, no particular damage had been done. A few minutes later a young aviator hurried in to see what had happened. He explained that he had been out in his plane with some small bombs, all of which he thought he had released, but . . . one stuck to the rack and as he sailed down just over our roof to make his landing in the field beyond our garden wall, the remaining bomb jerked loose and fell just ten yards outside our window." It was just thirty minutes before the Armistice. Had the walls of the old farmhouse been less sturdy, a different chief of staff would have led the American Army in the next war against Germany.

At Pershing's headquarters at Chaumont, breakfast had long been over. Time passed slowly, with no one eager to make small talk. At one minute to eleven they heard a tremendous salvo of cannon to the east in the direction of the Meuse. Then silence.

In some areas of the front the orders to stand fast *after* 11:00 were interpreted by overzealous commanders to mean that as much ground as possible could be contested until the deadline. If the Armistice broke down, one wanted to be in the best possible strategic position. On both sides, too, a final revenge on the enemy, using ammunition which would otherwise be valueless, was a motive, as was the desire for one last moment of personal glory. More realistically, some Germans on the line would resist furiously until the cease-fire, fearing that to become prisoners of war at the last moment might condemn them to years of servitude in French reconstruction battalions. Although some field pieces had to be set in almost liquid mud, artillery

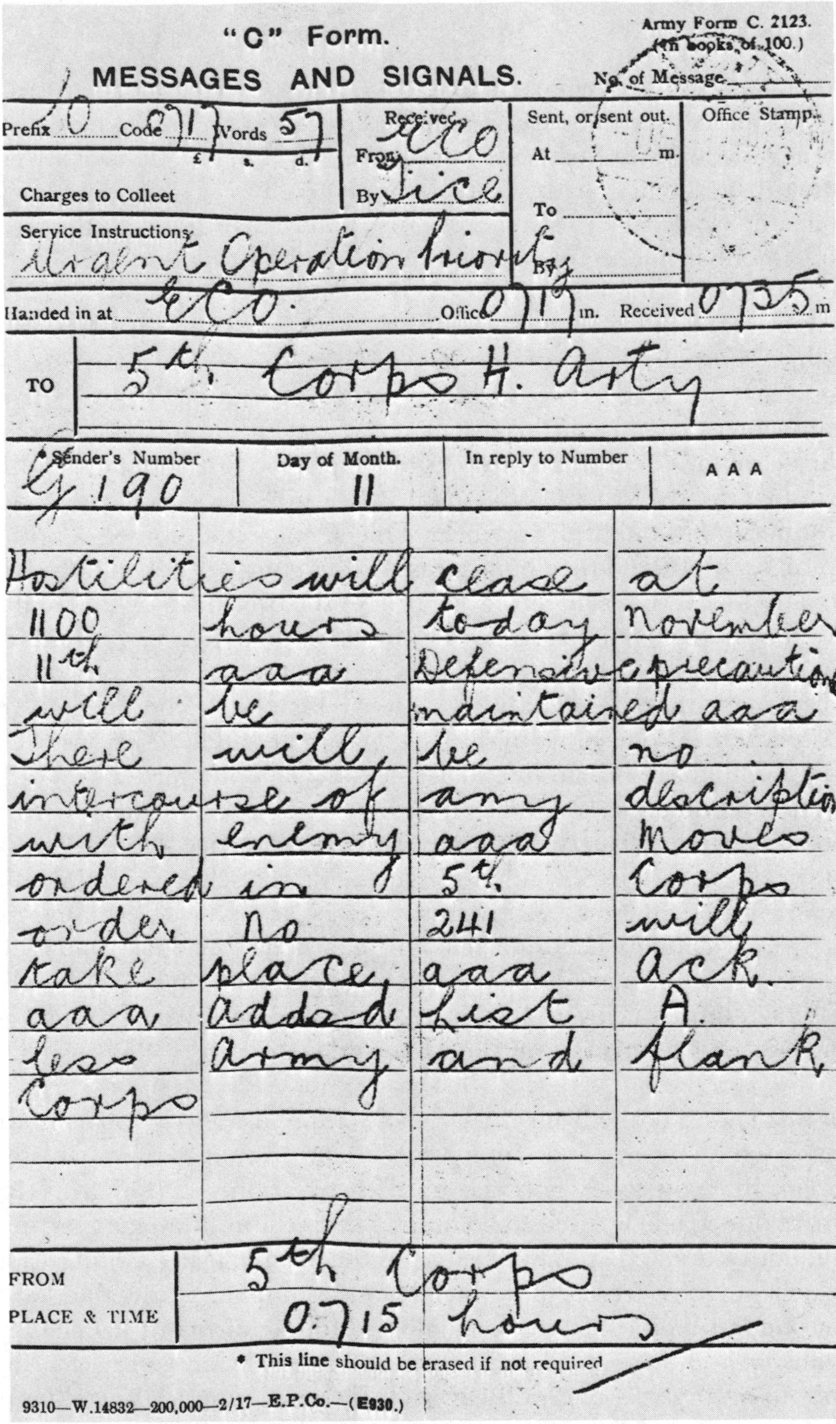

"C" Form.

MESSAGES AND SIGNALS.

Army Form C. 2123.
(In books of 100.)

No. of Message

Prefix	Code	Words 57	Received	Sent, or sent out.	Office Stamp.
Charges to Collect	£ s. d.	From ECO By Vice	At ___ m. To ___ By	

Service Instructions: Urgent Operation Priority

Handed in at ECO. Office 0715 m. Received 0735 m.

TO 5th Corps H. Arty

Sender's Number	Day of Month.	In reply to Number	A A A
G 190	11		

Hostilities will cease at 1100 hours to-day November 11th aaa Defensive precaution will be maintained aaa There will be no intercourse of any description with enemy aaa Moves ordered in 5th Corps order no 241 will take place aaa ack. aaa Added list A. less Army and flank Corps

FROM PLACE & TIME   5th Corps   0715 hours

* This line should be erased if not required

9310—W.14832—200,000—2/17—E.P.Co.—(E930.)

U.S. ARMY SIGNAL CORPS

The cease-fire message transmitted early on the morning of the eleventh by the 5th Corps, U.S. Army.

pounded away through the morning. On both sides casualties from the barrages were senseless.

At La Folie Ferme, the 1st Battalion, 70th Prussian Infantry, received cease-fire orders just as its counterattack was gaining momentum. Hostilities jarred to a stop on both sides forty-five minutes ahead of schedule, as if some gentleman's agreement had been reached. "Not a shot is fired," its commander reported from the farm. "Among our own men quiet, depressed mood, and quiet joy. . . ."

There had to be joy in having evaded maiming or death, even on the German side, for there had been little letup in the fighting in that sector. They had been heaving as much iron into the air as their artillery pieces could handle, and they knew the response would exact a price. "My battery," Otto Brautigam recorded in his diary, "had shot quite a few shells across the Maas, to avoid having to drag them home. Evidently the Americans gave the order, 'Barrels free!' shortly before twelve o'clock, for three minutes before noon a volley came over killing two of our infantrymen who were already en route to their quarters. . . . That's fate. According to the conditions of the Armistice we were not allowed to take the field guns back. So we left them in position."

At one such position Captain John Bagot Glubb of the Royal Engineers (50th Division), decades later the commander of the Jordanian Arab Legion, found "a park of German guns, with the words *ultima ratio regis*—the king's final argument—cast in the metal above the breech." But the irony then meant less to him than the news that the war was over. "A dreadful blow!" he wrote in his diary. "I was just beginning to enjoy it, and this will finish my dreams. . . ."

The noon report of the 31st Division, transmitted at 11:50 A.M., Berlin time, ten minutes before the Armistice was to go into effect, described heavy fighting in dense fog in which American forces "annihilated" patrols and even companies caught near the Meuse. The last hostile firing, its report noted, occurred at two minutes before the cease-fire, and the Germans continued to defend themselves until then, even taking prisoners from the American 2nd and 89th Divisions. After that it became crucial to ready themselves for the march to the Rhine.

Although staff officers knew the extent of American penetration in the last days, troops had been told little except to hang on. The Antwerp-Meuse line, they were assured, was impregnable. "Later," Otto Brautigam would write, "it was often said that the army was stabbed in the back, as if the . . . revolution had brought about the breakdown of the front. . . . The soldier at the front rejected the legend of the stab in the back from the beginning. In an honest fight, which had lasted for years, we succumbed to the superior strength of our enemies and to the lack of indispensable equipment caused by the blockade. . . . The Command had failed repeatedly, but the troops fulfilled their duty to the last."

Gratefully, the adjutant who composed the final war diary entry for the 27th Royal Württemberg Division noted, "At 12.00 noon the western front died." So had additional men. Throughout the night American forces had been attempting crossings of the Meuse, and German units had been resisting with everything they had. In several places the Americans had succeeded in the morning fog. Yet while the Germans were either fighting back or withdrawing under fire, they were receiving orders, depending upon commanders, that they were to stop fighting anywhere from 11:45 to 11:55 Berlin time, some minutes before the Allies had orders to stop shooting. A typical order, from General von Oven, an hour before the cease-fire was to become effective, insisted, "Armistice starts at 11.45 A.M. Put order through immediately to all concerned. Firing must cease by that hour without fail. Regimental commanders and others will be instructed to speak to the men, to admonish them to remain quiet, to warn them not to leave their organizations and not to meddle with ration supplies as the subsistence of the entire army would be endangered."

Maintaining discipline was difficult under the pressure of the last hours. The American Second Army was attacking all along its front through the morning, and a bulletin from the German 124th Infantry reported that one of its companies escaped capture between Inor and Malandry "only by the fact that a dense fog makes it impossible for the enemy to orient himself." Fighting to hold the east bank of a canal at the Bois de Soiry, the 120th Infantry Regiment of the Royal Württembergers lost contact with supporting troops on its right and began, with the 123rd, to retreat to the edge of the woods, leaving uninformed outposts behind. "The situation was extraordinarily critical," it reported, "and orders had already been issued to withdraw the artillery, by echelons, to the rear of the Chiers sector, when, as if by a thunderbolt, the division was suddenly freed of all worries when news was received at 10:00 A.M. of the Armistice. . . . The last shot fell on Inor at 12:10 P.M., which unfortunately took the life of a valiant officer, 2nd Lt. Thoma of the 5th Troop, 19th

Uhlans. He was shot by an American detachment which had not yet been reached by the Armistice order as he was making an attempt to inform them."

Although admitting that the 3rd Battalion of its 356th Infantry Regiment had not received word of the cease-fire until 12:15, the American 89th Division had a different version of the incident. When a party of three Germans, Lieutenant Thoma, Sergeant Benz, and Corporal Schweiker, were about to enter Inor from the north, an American company, unaware of the Armistice, fired, wounding Thoma, who "drew his pistol and ended his life by shooting himself through the head." In the confusion the corporal was taken prisoner and the sergeant escaped. Later in the day the battalion commander, Captain Dale D. Ernsberger, met a German officer of the 123rd Grenadier Regiment to express regret; yet although the incident occurred after the cease-fire hour, the German Armistice Commission as late as April 1919 was still vainly asking for the release of Corporal Schweiker.

Other American units also took prisoners after the Armistice, releasing them when German headquarters complained to Foch. As late as four that afternoon, Paris time, five hours after the Armistice, American GHQ received word from General Weygand that he had heard from the German side "of failure of Americans to stop firing at Stenay, Beaumont, and above the Meuse." The river crossing had cut some units off from communications, but others had merely paid no attention to the clock. The right of the American 89th and the left of the 90th had both reached Stenay, once the headquarters of the German Crown Prince, in the morning hours, and both divisions claimed the town, "particularly," Colonel George Marshall understood, "as everyone was looking for a dry place to sleep. After examining the map, I telephoned up instructions that a certain east-and-west street would divide the town between the two divisions so far as billeting was concerned. . . ." Even later an American platoon entered the village of Cervisy, beyond the Armistice line, its lieutenant ordering a German major and his troops to vacate because the village was wanted for beds and washing facilities, "the men having been without these greatly desired things." Again German protests forced the cease-fire violators to desist.

The zeal of some commanders surpassed anything which strategy required. At 9:00 A.M., Paris time, Major General Joseph E. Kuhn followed up Foch's Armistice message with tough and unyielding instructions to his 79th Division, supporting the French II

Colonial Corps near Chaumont, between the Marne and the Meuse, to the south. After acknowledging the Armistice he added, "Until that hour the operations previously ordered will be pressed with vigor."

The 79th's war would slacken in intensity through the morning only because fog prevented the laying down of supporting fire for the infantry. Although fog also interfered with the accuracy of enemy fire, both sides continued to suffer casualties. Northeast of Gibercy a company of the 315th Infantry Battalion received the Armistice news from a runner, then went on and captured a German field piece. The 314th slogged through "terrific artillery fire," which for the most part "struck deep in the boggy ground, hurling great columns of water and mud when exploding, but doing little damage." According to the 79th's official history, General Kuhn's cease-fire message reached the 314th by messenger only at 10:44, but "at the same time the American artillery seemed to roar with more terrible concentration . . . to inflict as much damage as possible on the Boche before the arrival of the Armistice hour. Right ahead of the 313th were German machine-gun nests being defended to the last. On the right of the line, at 10:59, Private Henry Guenther, Company A, charging headlong upon an enemy weapon, was shot to death, and, almost as he fell, the firing died away and an appalling silence prevailed."

The 79th's *History* listed fourteen dead during the final hours after dawn. When the shooting stopped, some men in forward positions stood up to gaze curiously upon the silent enemy lines while burying details from both sides went out to retrieve the dead and help the wounded. The 90th Division reported that its last casualty was Mechanic Carl Sheffield, 360th Infantry, killed at 10:30 A.M. at Mouzay. Yet there were casualties in other units closer to 11:00.

In the Troyon sector of Lorraine, where the divisions of the Second Army were commanded by Lieutenant General Robert L. Bullard, news of the cease-fire arrived at 6:30 A.M. Troops were about to cross the Meuse to pursue the Germans to the Moselle or had already effected crossings in the face of heavy artillery and machine-gun fire. Bullard let the attack continue, even sending other units over the top to engage the Germans if they could find any resistance. According to Captain Wendell Westover of the 4th Machine Gun Battalion, "The advance was still being forced at ten-fifty." They "knew no time" and were "ungoverned by protective barrage." But at eleven there was "an awesome hush. . . . The ear strains for the sound of [artillery) 'arrivals,' the tattoo of a machine gun, the crack of a rifle. The lack of exploding missiles becomes oppressive. Minutes pass by unheeded. Then comprehension comes. Men rise from the ground and stand, heads bared to the sky. . . ." The reaction was immediate. No cheering: they had lived at too intense a pitch, and even that day had been under fire since dawn. "The men lie down, wherever they may be, and rest. Sleep overpowers many." Just to the rear in Beaumont, at a church turned into a hospital, some of the newly wounded would rise painfully from stretchers among the blanket-covered dead and listen to the stillness.

As on the day before, General Bullard was satisfied with the performance of Major General George Bell's 33rd Division near Marchéville. "The others accomplished little. But the fighting went on until the last minute. I went early, with an aide . . . near the front line to see the last of it, to hear the crack of the last guns. . . . I stayed until 11:00 A.M., when, all being over, I returned to my headquarters, thoughtful and feeling lost." Afterward, when an assistant issued a report on the Second Army's gains that day which Bullard felt was "too modest" and failed to indicate the "great zest" his men demonstrated "in striking the last blows at the enemy," he "blew up," he wrote, at his subordinates.

Years later, *Collier's Weekly* correspondent Alden Brooks confessed his outrage at Bullard. Although the General knew that the territory his men were fighting for would be surrendered little more than four hours later, "he not only let many of them go to their death in that attack, but went out there himself . . . to watch them. Notice there is no question here of forcing the enemy to sign the Armistice. . . . The Armistice had been signed; the General knows it; it is all over."

Major General Robert Alexander, commander of the 77th Division (draftees from New York City and nearby counties), would have raised Brooks's hackles even more. At dawn on the eleventh, at the Meuse near Mouzon, he had received the news of the effective hour of the cease-fire. But Alexander was determined not to be ordered to stop fighting any sooner. "To avoid further solicitation on the question of a premature withdrawal before the Armistice," as he put it, he took an aide with him and "early on the morning of the 11th, went up to the front of [Brigadier General Harrison J.] Price's [154th Infantry] brigade where we remained until after the historic hour had struck. From the heights on his left, above Pont Maugis, Sedan was plainly visible." The view may have been less satisfying below, where his men were engaged. (Similarly, Colonel "Court House" Lee recalled "the unrelenting, driving influence" of the Vth Corps commanding officer, Major General Charles Summerall, "who seemed reluctant to stop fighting and insisted that all his Divisions continue feverish activity in preparing to move forward when ordered again.")

Due to push off at 10:00 A.M. was the 104th Infantry Battalion of the 26th ("Yankee") Division, a New England outfit which had moved into the Argonne Forest beyond Beaumont. Brigadier General Frank E. Bamford had taken over only two weeks before, Pershing feeling that the division needed a "driving" commanding officer. On the eleventh, according to *Boston Herald* correspondent Frank P. Sibley, because the division's line "was concave and it was the desire of the commanding officer and the Corps to straighten out that concavity," Bamford ordered the exhausted doughboys to make "one final effort."

The 104th were told nothing of the Armistice. The 101st knew. Lieutenant Harry G. Rennagel wrote to his family:

> I left the hospital November 10th, reaching my outfit about ten o'clock the next morning, the fatal one; we were all talking, laughing and waiting for the gong to ring when orders came to go over the top. We thought it a joke—it was a grim one of Fate's, for we jumped off at 25 minutes to 11 and advanced but very slowly for we knew that there were many machine gun nests ahead of us. At 10:55 a *minenwerfer* fell among my men and I was told one wanted to see me. I hurried over and there lay my five best men. One fatally injured, hole near heart, two seriously injured and the other two badly hurt. . . . I knelt beside the lad whose eyes had such a look of sorrow that my eyes filled with tears. . . . A glance at my watch, 11:05 . . . and when I looked back—he had gone. . . . I can honestly tell you I cried and so did the rest.

Dawn came misty and cold where the 104th had been waiting, and the men were ordered to squat and rest but to remain on the alert. After an hour, as they waited for the mist to congeal into snow, Bamford's new orders arrived: "Over the top at twelve noon." French and American artillery were to lay down a barrage beginning at eight. The men knew nothing about an imminent Armistice.

War is often fought in a fog of ignorance and misinformation.

In the rain and fog on the morning of the eleventh, metaphor and reality meshed in many places on the line. When muzzle flashes began flickering in the bleak morning light, beginning the 104th's covering fire, an early lunch of canned corned beef and hardtack— there would be little chance later—went the rounds. It was barely consumed when, at 10:30, German return shells began exploding. At the base of their hill a machine gunner died of wounds while being carried to an aid station. A Catholic chaplain rushed over to utter a few ritual words over the body, Connell Albertine, an infantryman in the 104th (and a colonel in the next war) remembered, "and without any other ceremonies we began to dig a shallow grave with our bayonets so we could at least bury him. . . . The Boches were shelling this particular spot quite heavily [and] we just about had him covered when a shell came so close that the dirt and stones and pieces of shrapnel fell all around us. The Chaplain decided we had better move, so we ran back to the brow of the hill, leaving the dead soldier covered except for his toes, which were sticking up about four inches."

It was now 10:50. They filled their cartridge belts with thirty-caliber ammunition and squatted in a trench, passing from hand to hand cans of hot coffee sent forward to them, while Chaplain de Valles, "who looked like a walking corpse, was up and down . . . cheering his boys on. Many of us asked for his blessing . . . and we always felt safe when he was around."

The boom of artillery from both sides continued. "Between the cooties biting us as never before, the smell that still lingered in our long underwear, and the Boches shelling us," Albertine recalled, "we were very anxious to get going and get this war over with. . . . But all of a sudden our artillery stopped firing. . . . Had they run out of ammunition? Now that the Boches saw we were not coming after them they would probably come after us."

They looked at their watches. It was eleven o'clock. They wondered whether there was a mistake in the time they were supposed to advance, expecting the command, "Over and after them!" But the German shelling, they realized, had also stopped. To their rear they saw French artillerymen throwing their helmets in the air and thought they heard one shout, *"Fini la guerre!"* Then an officer from their own G Company came running down the trench shouting "The war is over—an Armistice has been signed!"

"All the boys with Chaplain de Valles got down on their knees and prayed and thanked Almighty God. We then, being very excited and forgetting everything else, started shouting and hugging and kissing each other. Some ran to the top of the hill, and there we could see the Boches packing their equipment, preparing to move back to the Fatherland. Some were waving their hands for us to come over, and it looked as if they were drinking beer. But orders were that there was to be no fraternizing with the enemy." Timidly, the Americans went halfway into no-man's-land, "and stood there, stunned by the quiet.... [It] seemed as though everything was dead." Private Orin Fye, with the 26th's 103rd Field Artillery, remembered his captain reminding them that an 11:00 cease-fire meant that they were to fire until 11:00. "Everything then went dead. Not a sound. It was the funniest feeling I ever had in my life." Suddenly they found themselves cheering and shouting, forgetting hunger, thirst, fear, exhaustion, and even the stinging lice, for whom there was no Armistice. They fired their guns into the air, shot flares skyward, laughed, and cried. And only yards away were the Germans, now packing to leave, and apparently "as happy as we were."

Most men near the line remembered the unearthly stillness after the last shots. William March's novel *Company K* (1933) put it succinctly in the recollection of Private Upson. "The first thing we noticed was the silence of the German artillery. Then our own artillery quit firing. We looked at each other, surprised at the sudden quietness, and wondered what was the matter. A runner came up, out of breath, with a message from Divisional. Lieutenant Bartelstone, in command of our company, read it slowly and called his platoon ser-

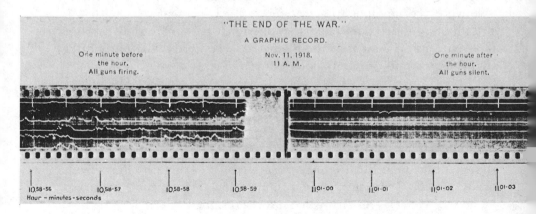

"THE END OF THE WAR."

A GRAPHIC RECORD.

One minute before the hour. All guns firing.

Nov. 11, 1918. 11 A. M.

One minute after the hour. All guns silent.

10.58-56   10.58-57   10.58-58   10.58-59   11.01-00   11.01-01   11.01-02   11.01-03
Hour – minutes - seconds

A sound recording of the stillness at eleven o'clock at the front.   U.S. ARMY SIGNAL CORP

geants together. 'Pass word to the men to cease firing, the war is over,' he said." A recording tape made by American sound apparatus near the Moselle shows the last six seconds of the war. The irregular sawtooth lines before eleven evidence considerable artillery activity. After eleven there is only one faint irregularity, at 11:01.01—very likely, according to the Army's Director of Munitions, "due to the exuberance of a doughboy firing his pistol twice close to one of the recording microphones . . . in celebration."

Among the many units along the Meuse in the final hours were the weary artillerymen of the 309th who had marched, the day before, for twenty-three hours up and down hills in the Argonne Forest and had spent the early hours of the morning sleeping in the rain in the ruins of a farm. Three miles from Bethencourt, on the edge of the woods near Verdun, they encountered a French soldier. His face glowed with joy and wine, and a half-empty bottle was in his hand. *"Fini la guerre!"* he shouted, running down the line of the trench. *"Fini la guerre!"*

Jumping down from a rations wagon, an American grabbed the Frenchman by the arm and haled him before an officer who could speak *poilu*. Excitedly, the Frenchman explained that the war was over. It had ended at eleven. "G'wan, Frog, you're a liar!" said the skeptical wagoneer. "How much does that stuff cost a bottle? I'd like to be Governor of Mississippi for a day." And they continued the march, leaving the *poilu* to his solo celebration. The soldiers, all draftees, talked as they slogged along about the possibility that the war would end soon, but agreed that if the only evidence were a drunk Frenchman, they had better remain alert.

At Bethencourt they settled down. The next morning, November 12, as they were breaking camp to move toward Verdun, a message arrived that they had missed the Armistice.

In a few American sectors news of the Armistice arrived so late that German forces attempting to stand down must have wondered whether the reports of an end to the war were premature. The U.S. 54th Infantry Regiment was still on the march at 11:00, passing lines of heavy artillery. At 2:00 P.M. the regiment slipped down over the hill at Chatel Chehery into the town. "A major was standing alongside as the men filed by," a recruit, Gregory Mabry, remembered. "It's all over, boys," he said. "The Armistice was signed at 11:00 o'clock." There was scarcely a cheer. The troops had stopped for water, wood, straw, and places to pitch pup tents and build fires before dark. They had heard rumors before. "It wasn't until after supper," Mabry wrote, "that one could begin to realize that the war was over. . . . Trucks ran with their headlights ablaze, fires were not doused at dusk, and the whole Argonne was alight." Even later that night, the 165th Infantry, having been released from assignment to the 40th French Division near Sedan, arrived at Buzancy to hear reports of an Armistice but "the men had no certainty that the rumors were true, and discounted them." On November 13, Father Duffy, the regimental chaplain, recalled, "We marched to Landres et St. Georges which we had striven vainly to enter from the other side five weeks before. The village was almost completely demolished and our troops with others of the [42nd] Division pitched their shelter-tents on all the hills surrounding the town. That night official information was given of the Armistice. The men raided the engineer and signal stores for rockets of all descriptions and the whole sky was filled with lights. . . ." Why they had not learned of the end of the war two days earlier, if only from the celebratory flares and rockets of other units, is unknown.

Captain Robert J. Casey, a battery commander in the 58th Field Artillery Brigade (once the Third Illinois Field Artillery), 33rd Division, near Pouilly, remembered getting the Armistice message by intercepting the Eiffel Tower transmitter's signals at 5:30 A.M. Although the 58th as well as the nearby 11th Field Artillery, detached from the 6th Division, had orders to lessen the rate of fire and cease firing by 9:45, heavy guns behind them kept "dumping everything they've got," and German return fire remained heavy. Casey's diary, later published anonymously as *The Cannoneers Have Hairy Ears,* records a busy morning for ambulances. Soldiers sheltering in an old sawmill are blown out of it by a shell, with twenty killed and thirty-five wounded. "The war has twenty-three minutes still to go," he writes. Another shell, at 10:38, hits an 11th Field Artillery soup kitchen, with fourteen dead and four wounded, and the "heavies" of the 11th open up again, "seeking pay for fourteen lives. There is quite a jamboree about the 155[mm] gun pits. Adjutants, majors, and volunteer workers of all ranks are howling, 'cease firing!' Nobody pays any attention to them."

At 10:59 Captain Casey's diary records, "The 11th has just fired its last shot. The guns are so hot that the paint is rising from them in blisters. The crews are sweating despite the autumn chill of the air. To them peace approaches as a regrettable interruption." A minute later he records, "The silence is oppressive. It weighs on one's eardrums."

Somewhere near Verdun, Sergeant Sol Cohen, whose 130th Infantry companions had grown uneasy at his fiddling and moved away, picked up his violin case and climbed farther up the hillside. The artillery still boomed, but it no longer worried him. On a slope he paused at the common grave of four German soldiers, read the marker identifying them as having been buried there since 1914, and ritually plucked a few blades of grass from the mound. He then moved gingerly around an overgrown barbed-wire entanglement which had protected long-abandoned dugouts and a decaying observation post. A sign, in faded French, warned that field-telephone conversations should be guarded, as the enemy might be listening. Descending the far slope, he took in the awesome landscape, realizing that in better times it was a beautiful sight. He looked at his watch. It was twelve minutes to eleven. "The guns were rattling away as if possessed; if anything, there was more confusion, more noise, than usual. . . ." He turned back, encountering a company of black soldiers digging trenches at the side of the road, as if the war were going to go on indefinitely. Cohen stopped to watch, then decided he had found his audience. Music, he understood, was a language they knew well.

"Oh, boy, kin you sit on dem BLUES?" asked one laborer when he realized what he was hearing. Cohen obliged. "The shovels stopped," he remembered; the black heads were lifted towards me; a smile of incredulity crept over each inky face; then, after a rebuke from their sergeant, in perfect rhythm the shovels started again." One after another the loads of clay were lifted in tempo and heaved over husky shoulders. "Oh, boy," said one black, "dat's just like home." And as Sergeant Cohen—who had been first violinist with the Cincinnati Symphony before the war—fiddled the blues, the kettle-drum accompaniment of cannon fire faded away. It was eleven o'clock.

Near the Meuse a corporal who had been in the line most of the previous fifty-two days, and who wore a bandage on one elbow and was sodden with rain and caked with mud, was aware of something extraordinary, which he identified as a ringing in his ears. And then he realized. The artillery had ceased. He listened in astonishment, wondering how they were supposed to take the ridge without artillery. Germans, with machine guns, held the high ground. Then a runner, apparently unworried at his exposure to fire, hurried past. "Hi!" he called out. "War's over! Armistice! Go down to the river and take a swim!"

Corporal Dudley was unbelieving. None of his men had seen a newspaper for weeks, and had discounted the gossip about peace. They moved on noiselessly up a bald, unwooded ridge from the riverbank, still worried about their lack of artillery protection. At the crest he peered cautiously into the enemy lines and saw Germans "running excitedly about. He saw them hurl away their rifles. He saw them join hands and dance a jig and fling their arms about. . . . For ten, twenty seconds, in tense, frowning absorption, [he] watched these grotesque figures, capering like lunatics, silhouetted afar against the lowering sky." And then he tossed aside the straw he had gathered as cover and made his way back to his men. His head rang in the stillness.

Somewhat to the south, in the St. Mihiel sector, Lieutenant Walter A. Davenport watched the war end in less well-organized fashion. The Germans had been quiet on their side of the Bois de Dommartin after about 9:30 that morning—until, Davenport thought, they had received orders to cease firing ninety minutes later. "Every Boche gun between Dommartin and Metz inclusive opened up on us. My God, how they strafed us. Everything from minenwerfers to 210's descended upon those woods. The soft ground billowed like the ocean." Fortunately, he realized, the heavy, resilient forest absorbed most of the impact, keeping casualties low. Behind his infantry unit the American answering barrage was just as intense, with geysers of earth rising as each shell struck.

"It was 10:60 precisely and—the roar stopped like a motor car hitting a wall. The resulting quiet was uncanny. . . ." In the sudden silence Germans began to emerge. "They clambered to the parapets and began to shout wildly. They threw their rifles, hats, bandoleers, bayonets and trench knives toward us. They began to sing. Came one bewhiskered Hun with a concertina and he began goose-stepping along the parapet followed in close file by fifty others—all goose-stepping. . . ." Orders forbidding fraternization were explicit, and American officers tried to keep their men under control, but the temptation to do more than look was too great. "A big Yank named Carter ran out into No Man's Land and planted the Stars and Stripes on a signal pole in the lip of a shell hole. Keasby, a bugler, got out in front and began playing 'The Star Spangled Banner' on a German trumpet he'd found in Thiancourt. And they sang—Gee, how they sang!"

Canadian novelist and magazine correspondent Herman Whitaker, fifty-two, ailing and lame, at 9:50 A.M. went over the top with

American infantrymen east of the Meuse armed only with his cane. A machine-gun bullet nicked the baggy droop of his breeches and, reportedly, officers were killed on both sides of him, a survivor commenting with awe, "Whitaker is some correspondent!" By eleven, Whitaker reported, "[We] had pushed the Boche back a kilometer and a half. Just before eleven the Boche took out their watches and fired until the second hands indicated the hour. Then they rushed forward crying 'Kamerad,' and tried to embrace us." The Americans spurned the gesture, content that they had seized a useless mile. (Whitaker would die two months later, of natural causes.)

The service newspaper *Stars and Stripes* described the end like a Hollywood extravaganza. The hardest fighting at the close, it reported, had been accomplished by the divisions of the Second Army, which

> launched a fire-eating attack above Vigneulles just at dawn. . . . It was no mild thing, that last flare of the battle, and the order to cease firing did not reach the men in the front line until the last moment, when runners sped with it from fox hole to fox hole. Then a quite startling thing occurred. The skyline of the crest ahead of them grew suddenly populous with dancing soldiers and down the slope, all the way to the barbed wire, straight for the Americans, came the German troops. They came with outstretched hands, ear-to-ear grins and souvenirs to swap for cigarettes, so well did they know the little weakness of their foe. They came to tell how glad they were [that] the fight had stopped, how glad they were [that] the Kaiser had departed for parts unknown, how fine it was to know that they would have a republic at last in Germany.

In other places, a *Saturday Evening Post* reporter wrote, "the Germans came down to fraternize and to ask for cigarettes. They were curtly commanded to 'get out!' American temper, at this stage . . . with the enemy guns not yet cold and their own dead not yet buried, was not of the sloppy, sentimental kind that embraces a recent foe." Instant *Brüderschaft* was an unpredictable thing.

The *Stars and Stripes* also wrote of the draftee who had finally arrived at the front as a replacement only to hear the news that the war had just ended. "Hell," Private George W. Legion said, "I just got here."

One *Stars and Stripes* correspondent, Sergeant Alexander Woollcott, wrote a friend at a military hospital that he had been at the front ("Isn't it a wonderful place?") until the last shot was fired. From another hospital, at Petit Mountjoy, corpsman Frederick Pottle wrote a friend:

> I suppose you would like to know how the war ended. . . . I went to the operating room and found the receiving ward choked with wounded waiting operations. It didn't look like the end of the war. We started in, all the tables full, everybody working at top speed. About nine o'clock we got the rumor that Germany had signed, hostilities to cease at eleven o'clock. But meanwhile the barrage was getting fiercer. We hardly believed the news. Besides we were too busy to think anyway. I forgot all about it. At eleven o'clock I was writing down a [postoperative report]. . . . I was about half-way through when it suddenly seemed strangely quiet and still—almost uncomfortable. It took me a moment to realize that the guns whose roar and concussion had kept the operating room shivering like a leaf in the wind almost without interruption for two months had ceased firing forever.

Captain Harold Horne of the Royal Marines, with the 63rd Division, had moved his unit to the village of Bougnies, five miles south of Mons, to be ready to push off on the morning of the eleventh, passing through the site of the 1709 Battle of Malplaquet. On the tenth, resistance had been spirited, as if the war were far from over. At 7:00 A.M., less than an hour after they had learned of the Armistice, they were ordered to advance to the northeast toward "objectives previously assigned." Their reaction lacked enthusiasm. "You can imagine our feelings—four hours, and then peace." Gingerly, they went forward through villages from which the Germans were just withdrawing, with enemy rear guards firing intermittently to slow the advance. By 10:30 they had reached Villiers-St. Ghislain, where the villagers gave them an emotional welcome. Then, strung out in open order to cover as much territory as possible, they moved out into the fields beyond the village. At the edge of a wood about a half mile away, German troops sent up warning flares. The Marines looked at their watches. "A few seconds later we blew the whistle and stopped—in the middle of a turnip field. Shortly afterwards the Germans came out of the wood onto a side road, formed up and moved off toward Germany."

Within half an hour streams of Belgians, pushing barrows or pulling carts—the Germans had commandeered all the horses—with their belongings and their children aboard, and waving magically materialized Belgian flags and streamers, began moving west along the roads the Germans had evacuated. Once the Marines set up roadblocks, the turnip field became a soup-kitchen area to feed the returning refugees before they went on to seek what was left of their homes and farms.

According to the Mons diary of Lieutenant J. W. Muirhead, "We now had hardly any ammunition left, and we should have liked to fire the guns at 11:00, but we were told not to do this, as there was no knowing where our infantry had got to." On the approach to a bridge into the city they saw the bodies of three men of the London Rifle Brigade, "each wearing the medal ribbon of the 1914 Mons Star. They had been killed by machine gun fire that morning. As we got into Mons there were the bodies of many of the enemy lying in the streets, also killed that day. . . . Boys were kicking them in the gutter. . . . The bells in the belfry were playing 'Tipperary.' "

Victor Senez, then eight, remembered walking from Flenus to Mons and seeing an explosion ahead of him. "Five small bodies were lying in many pieces; five boys my own age had been blown up by one of the many mines that were located everywhere." When he came home he found English soldiers "chopping up our bed so they could make a wood fire in the kitchen." In other cases it was vital for civilians caught in the tide of war to cross, whatever the danger, lines which might not be so flexible in the legalism of an Armistice. French infantry sergeant Desiré Bontelle, in a village in the Ardennes, near Sedan, recalled, "I will never forget the expression of a trapped animal on a miserable woman whom we passed. She was pushing a wheelbarrow in which her two babies were asleep. She was being helped by two boys between ten and twelve years old, her husband's sons who were helping to take away the German's sons." Sedan was still held by the enemy, and under fire. It was crucial for the woman to get there if she were to stay alive; in French territory her life would be of small value.

The Germans had relinquished Mons grudgingly, and Canadian General Sir Arthur Currie refused to wait to occupy the city quietly on the twelfth. "The reason Mons was taken," he explained, "was that we obeyed the orders of Marshal Foch that we should go on until we were ordered to stop. That is a thing that means much for Canada. It was a proud thing . . . that we were able to finish the war where we began it, and that we, the young whelps of the old lion, were able to take the ground lost in 1914." The city was declared cleared of the enemy by 6:00 A.M. Fighting on the tenth and eleventh had cost the Canadian 2nd and 3rd Divisions, according to their reports, thirty-one officers and 450 other ranks killed, wounded, and missing; but according to Currie later, only one of the dead and fifteen of the wounded could be attributed to November 11. Still, according to Will Bird's account of the 42nd (Black Watch) Battalion, it was already "full day" when a comrade pointed out another soldier, confiding, "He says he's going to shoot whoever arranged to have his brother killed for nothing. He really means it. He's hoping Currie comes here today. If he doesn't, he's going to shoot the next higher-up. He says his brother was murdered." Howard Vincent O'Brien's diary talks of the rivalry between Canadian and British troops for the distinction of taking Mons and alleges that "Imperials . . . actually laid down [a] barrage to prevent Colonials from getting there first. Must have been bum barrage. Sad incidents—loss of 5 officers, 60 men from Canadian battalion in last hour of war. Things droll—British R. R. gun kept firing all day at 10-minute intervals, despite frantic flashes from German wireless, first in German, then in French and English, that war was over. Great to-do. Phones between corps, division and brigade all humming before gun located. Many isolated detachments like that— kept going hours after time was called."

Even given hyperbole and rumor, it was obvious that Mons was a less glorious affair than its legend, and perhaps even an unnecessary one, which may be the reason Currie was sensitive to allegations that he had overdone his duty. In 1928 Currie—by then president of McGill University—sued for libel two Canadian journalists who claimed that "to glorify" the Canadian officer corps he had conceived the "mad idea that it would be a fine thing to capture Mons" and to be able to say that "the Canadians had fired the last shot in the war." Witnesses recalled seeing (after overlapping testimony was reconciled) only thirty-nine Allied soldiers' bodies in Mons and confirmed that the town authorities buried all bodies found in the streets in a public ceremony. The official report, Mr. Justice Rose noted, was that only four Canadian officers and ninety-one other ranks wounded, and one dead, were all that could be attributed to the last day of the war—that the other dead had to have been there from the previous day. The only announced casualty after Mons was officially declared captured had been that of Private George Price of Port William, killed by a sniper at three minutes to eleven, at a point between Havre and the Canal du Centre, between seven hundred and eight hundred yards east of Mons. When at the trial a telegram from Price's father to Currie was read, hoping that Sir Arthur would win his case and regretting controversy which "simply renews old wounds that are better forgotten," the trial was as good as over.*

The actual facts may never be known, but Private Price was not alone in meeting death on that last morning in Mons. And not all Allied losses were Canadians. Private Arthur W. Boyd, who served with an ambulance unit attached to the 56th London Division, remembered being in a village just west of Mons when the Armistice notice was posted. Although troops of the 56th had been marching in columns of four, unopposed, they reacted skeptically, anticipating that "things would flare up again," and were surprised "when eleven o'clock arrived and gradually all those infernal noises of gunfire we had got used to began to subside. . . ." Even then, the last mindless shots had not yet been fired. "At about half-past eleven one member of our own Field Ambulance, Lance Corporal E. J. Hield, a stretcher bearer, was brought in dead. It seemed inexpressibly sad to have survived the war up to the morning of the Armistice—indeed to the very hour of the Armistice—and then to die." Even a Canadian history refers to an officer in the 5th Lancers, "now attached to the Canadian Corps," who fought at Mons in 1914 "and then was killed [at Mons] an hour and a half before the Armistice." The "last round" fired by Canadian artillery, the account goes on, "shot off the arm of a German staff officer in a Headquarters Chateau by Hill 85 east of Mons."

Headquarters of General Sir Herbert Plumer's Second Army, which had crossed the Schelde in force several days earlier, had issued orders on the evening of the tenth that its 29th and 30th Divisions were to push forward at 8:00 A.M. and attempt to reach the Dendre. At 9:00 A.M., despite the 8:10 receipt of word of the imminent Armistice, the 7th Dragoon Guards were ordered to capture the

---

* Despite vindication, the publicity embittered Currie's last years and resulted, a generation later, in a CBC television play by Mavor Moore, "The Man Who Caught Bullets" (originally "Names'll Never Hurt Me"). In the play the libel trial results from a Korean war episode in which a Canadian battalion commander known as a tough disciplinarian is accused of sending troops into battle after the cease-fire is signed "from motives of personal glory." Moore's Brigadier General George Hyman wins his case but then shoots himself.

bridges across the Dendre just above Lessines. The XIX Corps' three divisions (31st, 35th, and 41st) were told of the Armistice but exhorted to make every effort to reach the Dendre by 11:00. "The essential problem," Captain Harold Parker, who was in charge of transport for his brigade, remembered, "was mud, plus a river with a pontoon bridge. Early morning was lovely and some time after 9:00 A.M. we passed some infantry. One shouted out 'Eleven o'clock finished!' This was the first thing I had heard about an Armistice." They were at the village of Nederbrakel, just west of the Dendre, and halted there without meeting any resistance. The 35th, despite poor country roads, also succeeded, but the strategic value of the effort was insignificant. A unit of the 29th, commanded by Major W. F. Chappell, hearing from its advance posts that the enemy was withdrawing, raced along the main road to Lessines to hold the crossing of the Dendre there. At 9:00, Brigadier General Bernard Freyberg, the much-decorated hero of Gallipoli then commanding the 88th Brigade (29th Division), arrived in Chappell's area, informed him of the Armistice, and ordered the major to advance quickly with his troops as Freyberg "particularly wanted to seize Lessines before 11 A.M. struck." At 10:45, just west of the village, the 88th encountered a nest of five machine guns and isolated pockets of snipers. At 10:45 Chappell sent forces around the strong point on both sides, rushed Lessines, captured twenty-four Germans and a machine gun on the western edge of the village and 106 others in Lessines itself, and secured the bridges at the Dendre which had been prepared for demolition. On the high ground above them the 7th Dragoons captured another forty-one men. The action had to have taken more than the twelve minutes which had remained before the Armistice, leaving questionable the likelihood of the actual blowing up of the Lessines bridges. "As it was by now after 11 A.M.," the *Official History of the War* confesses, "these prisoners were released, but, at the earnest request of the senior officers, were escorted to their own lines in order to protect them from the fury of the inhabitants." To Winston Churchill, describing the unnecessary exploit, Freyberg wrote, "I had the most wonderful finish to my war. . . . I thought this would amuse you."

To the north another much-decorated veteran of the Dardanelles expedition, Lieutenant Colonel Sherwood Kelly ("Mad Kelly of Gallipoli"), commanding a battalion of the Norfolk Regiment, had brought his men to the Schelde, under desultory fire, when an RAF biplane appeared, flying dangerously low over the course of the river. The observer was standing up in his cockpit firing bursts from his Very pistol. It was the first that the Norfolks knew of the cease-fire. But the enemy already knew, as at the same time, on a road along the opposite bank, an open German staff car flying two white flags appeared. Using a megaphone, the German officers shouted across the river a warning not to attempt a crossing, as the bank had been mined. It was not quite eleven, and there was a chance that the British might have attempted to seize a bridgehead before the hour struck. "It was an honourable act on their part," Lieutenant E. J. S. Bonnett, the battalion medical officer, thought. The foolish attempt would have given him a lot of work.

In the Third Army sector, Rifleman Cyril Flin, 13th King's Royal Rifle Regiment, 111th Brigade (37th Division), was marching with his battalion, having pushed off along a very muddy road nearly two hours earlier, at 7:30 "when, quite suddenly, a cavalryman came past at a full gallop carrying a lance bearing a red-and-white pennant. He drew his horse to a stop at the head of the column and shouted to our Captain, 'Armistice has been signed!' " They had known of the Armistice negotiations only from German leaflets, suspecting them as a trick. Invariably they waited for orders to take their ten minutes' rest in each hour of marching. Now no one waited. "Off came our heavy loads and we danced a jig with each other at the roadside." The cavalryman out of King Arthur may have been the same fey figure whom Lieutenant Ralph Donaldson of the 40th Squadron had seen when he landed in a field west of Mons—an aide de camp carrying the distinguishing lance of his unit as evidence of his authenticity.

John Vincent, in a Royal Engineers cable section repairing communications breakages, ironically recalled a similarly colorful announcement. "Into the stagnant potholes and decomposition there intruded the unmistakeable jingle of many horses on the trot. A troop of cavalry was moving forward with all the precision of an Aldershot parade. The fools, I thought; Jerry, ever lynx-eyed for a target, will blow them to pieces. I searched hurriedly for cover. But they kept steadily on. So there must be a reason. Only then did that dreadful curtain of despair fall away. . . . I rushed to the dugout where the section was awaiting orders, shouting, 'The cavalry, it's the cavalry. It must be over.' " Vincent's men had not heard the news, but it was nearly eleven. One more shell would crash about fifty yards away, but it did no damage.

Underage at enlistment, Corporal D. O. Dixon, of the 111th

Company, Machine Gun Corps, was one of the youngest in his company, while the oldest veteran was Harry Bessborough, "a brave and fanatical member of a religious organization who claimed he was under angelic protection." Before dawn on the eleventh, Dixon's half section of Vickers guns had been set up in a sunken road and prepared for action. Just before ten a runner arrived with orders to "stand fast" until 11:00 A.M., but he had no further details. At ten, after they had gathered for a meal, still cautious about cooking fires, "a storm of random shell-fire descended over the area. One of the first missiles killed Harry and several more, and wounding others." The Germans were firing off their superfluous ammunition before withdrawing.

It was noon before limbers arrived with news and orders to pack up their guns. "We loaded Harry and the others on to the vehicles. They were buried at Caudry, a town we entered during the advance [which] still has a unique war memorial with an illustrated plaque depicting our M.G.C. companies on arrival handing over their three days' rations to the starving inhabitants." They set up their headquarters in "a dilapidated and insanitary chateau which had been a Prisoner of War cage, still bearing the graffiti of some unknown comrades captured in the debacle of March 1918." Because of the unexpected casualties their rum ration was redivided, coming to eight double tots per man. Dixon went steadily through his share until the events of the morning had blurred out.

In the 38th Division, where the 33rd Battalion, Machine Gun Corps, had held a one-franc sweepstakes on the exact minute of the Armistice, at eleven o'clock 1,500 francs were solemnly handed in several helmets to Private Diamond of Company A.

Lance Corporal Alfred Billequez of the South Staffordshires had bedded down with his platoon the night before on the stone floor of an old church near Villiers Pol, well to the west of the action, with no thought but to move up the next morning. At 8:00 A.M., walking through the village, he saw a less colorful cavalry messenger than had Flin or Vincent. "A private soldier came galloping through on a heavy farm horse and shouted, 'Armistice at 11:00 A.M.!' We hardly knew what this meant, but supposed it meant some sort of lull in the fighting, and it wasn't until eleven that we noticed how quiet the guns were. They seemed to fade away until they ceased. We still did not know what all this meant. . . ."

Action was minimal in much of the Third Army's area, the

Germans having pulled back first from the Forest of Mormal and then, on the tenth, beyond Maubeuge to a line on the banks of the Thure. Except for advance units, most British and Commonwealth troops were still slogging far behind. Emerging from Mormal at Berliamont was Captain William O. Duncan, transport officer with the 244th Siege Battery in the 90th Brigade (Royal Garrison Artillery). With New Zealand infantrymen, the battery had to fight its way past entrenched machine gunners to the Sambre, where the only bridge which could take its guns and tractors was blown. Duncan's battery could not fire from where it was because it did not know how far ahead the infantry had gone. "This was very frustrating as the officers had drawn lots for the order of firing the last shots. We knew the war was coming to an end as the Germans were surrendering in large numbers. In one case I saw a complete battalion with colonel and band. The prisoners we were taking were mostly youths in their teens or elderly men."

Unable to cross, Duncan returned on his motorcycle to temporary Brigade headquarters. It was noon, and no one was there. Finally he found Colonel A. H. Thorpe, "an old Regular," sitting hunched over a little stove. "Good morning, Sir," he began, saluting.

The Colonel did not stir. "Good morning, Duncan," he said. "I suppose you know the war is over. Have a bottle of beer."

Quickly downing his beer, Duncan rode back to his silent howitzers and asked the sergeant major to have the men fall in. "I have to inform you," Duncan told them, "that the war is over. The Armistice was signed at 11:00 A.M. today."

The men "looked blankly at me with their mouths open and did not cheer or utter a word." Also unable yet to take in the stunning implications, Duncan closed the matter with a curt "Dismiss!" Twice wounded, he was the only survivor of four officers standing together when a shell landed nearby in March 1916. "It was a tremendous shock to realise that the war was really over, that we were alive, and that we had the prospect of a future."

Although Brigade Major Oliver Lyttleton, with the 2nd Grenadier Guards, heard of the Armistice sooner, his reaction was equally unemotional. On the tenth Brigadier General B. N. Sergison-Brooke, with Lyttleton (a War Cabinet member in the 1940s and later Viscount Chandos), had taken an advance guard along the Route Nationale into Maubeuge. "After a mile or two we felt very lonely; there was not a soul in sight. We could hear a battle going on a mile behind us, on our left flank, and one or two spent bullets . . .

fell harmlessly on the road. At last we came on a reserve company of the Grenadiers, and shortly afterwards rode into Maubeuge. The inhabitants surged out of every cellar and house: the enthusiasm was indescribable. We were smothered with flowers. . . ."

Before daylight he was awakened in the house in which they had set up divisional headquarters by news of the eleven o'clock cease-fire. "I did not wake the brigadier. I went off to sleep again and was first in to breakfast and, forgetting that he did not know the news, a minute or two passed before he said, 'Anything from the Division?' "

"Yes, Sir," said Lyttleton, "this: the war is over."

About 10:00 A.M. one formidable shell roared overhead and landed about five hundred yards away, "and frightened the life out of us. Then silence: silence, that is, except for the clucking of chickens, the creaking of cart wheels, mooing of cows and other sounds of a country town on market day. We rode round the troops; everywhere the reaction was the same, flat dullness and depression. . . . This readjustment to peace-time anxieties is depressing, and we all felt flat and dispirited." They had already begun to wonder "what England would be like."

At Petit Maubeuge, where the 16th Battalion of the King's Royal Rifle Corps (60th Rifles) had bedded down on the night of the tenth, news of the Armistice had come on time. Yet at eleven, when they expected the shelling to stop, six-inch howitzers of their own nearby opened up again and fired for another hour, leaving Rifleman L. W. Lee wondering whether the announcement he had seen was a hoax. At noon, however, "an uncanny silence" settled on the area, after which the battalion discovered that when one of its battery commanders had been killed by an enemy shell *after eleven*, his second-in-command had ordered his men to set their watches back an hour and keep firing.

Some Third Army units were moving away from the fighting, their battle done. Through a blanket of fog which covered the countryside, Guy Chapman's Royal Fusiliers battalion, having buried their mutilated dead at Ghissingnies, marched, on the eleventh, the fifteen miles back toward Bethencourt. At eleven o'clock, with packs on their backs, they tramped along the muddy *pavé,* their band playing in honor of the occasion, but few of them singing. "Before a man comes to be wise," Chapman quoted, "he is half dead with Cattarrhes and aches, with sore eyes, and a worn-out body." They were, he felt, prematurely old, "very tired, and now very wise."

One element of that wisdom which would be brought home

across the Channel was that Britain could never again permit itself to be drawn into an exhausting land war on the Continent. *Never Again* would become the watchword of the middle 1930s, even as Germany under Hitler began dominating Europe by intimidation when possible, by force when necessary. The idea of a large land army remained abhorrent, as if its very existence might be a provocation or a temptation. Britain could have no credibility in Europe otherwise, but the memories of mass slaughter would march back with the survivors and become reinforced each Armistice Day with the sale of replicas of Flanders poppies already growing on the graves of the dead. Nevertheless, Englishmen would be forced into another land war on the soil of France and Flanders.

Word had already gone to German pilots that all combat aircraft were to be surrendered to the victors. There would be no more German Air Force. At Tellancourt a pilot in the Richthofen *Geschwader* strode to the blackboard where orders for each day were chalked, and which was now blank, and wrote the epitaph *"Im Krieg geboren, im Krieg gestorben."* Born in war, died in war.

At Wavre, southeast of Brussels, Lieutenant Hans Schröder's aerodrome was in the center of the German Seventeenth Army area, where, when November 11 dawned, the streets were crowded with "endless processions of cars, all of which carried red flags." The troops—who had fought hard at Mons—had caught the contagion from the Sixth Army, which had started east even before the Armistice was to take effect. "As our officers don't want to go with us," said one driver, "we're going home by ourselves. The war's over." Not far away the Bavarian Crown Prince, Rupprecht, had abandoned his troops and headed for the German frontier in a red-flagged car helpfully furnished him by the Brussels Soldiers' Council.

The Seventeenth Army had its own council, which possessed a rubber stamp impressed with a star and the words *Wavre Soldatenrat.* Its authority emanated from the insistence upon its official seal upon all documents, and it went to work zealously. In the Wavre officers' mess airmen listened to Lieutenant Colonel von Klüber report the conditions of the Armistice which would separate them from their aircraft and furnish them with new duties. "So it is our task," he concluded, tears choking his voice, "to lead our valiant army back to its poor suffering country." Few now shared his sentimental patriotism.

Schröder was lacking in eagerness to lead troops. He had a girl in Brussels he wanted to take home to Westphalia to marry and had to find her before the wave of withdrawals engulfed them. He hailed a German truck traveling with six motorcycles in convoy, the driver—a corporal—stopping because he wanted to make contact with a Soldiers' Council. The lieutenant directed him. Soon the group was back, with red flags on the handlebars of the cycles and a red flag on a broomstick fluttering from the truck. "Here you are, Herr Leutnant," said the corporal. "We've got the right of way!" He held out a paper stamped with the now-familiar star which declared the truck "is in the service of the Soldiers' Council and must have free passage." Schröder laughed. "We've got to swim with the current," said the corporal. "It doesn't hurt anyone and helps us." Then Schröder and his batman, Joseph, climbed in and they drove off to secure the lieutenant's Belgian bride-to-be from the certain wrath of the imminent liberators of Brussels.

Another German airman in Belgium who much later wrote a memoir as "Hauptmann [Captain] Hermann,"* had just changed aerodromes again on the tenth as the one he had been taking off from for night bombing had been overrun. It was cold, and the burned-out house had little left in it but its enormous fireplace, which the new occupants fed with the remaining chairs to get warm enough to sleep. Soon machine-gun fire awakened them, and Hermann's chief mechanic rushed in to warn him to take off immediately if he wanted to avoid capture. Prudently, the ground crew had already warmed up the twin engines. Once both mechanics squeezed into the rear gunner's seat, Hermann gunned the engines and managed to get into the air seconds, he thought, before coming into range of the troops below, who he saw were wearing "British battle bowlers." Heading toward Liege, trying to save his plane, he struggled with an overheated port engine at a dangerously low altitude, his mechanics and spare parts and tools weighing them down. After about fifty miles the engine stalled. He found a field near a little village and landed, discovering that a bullet had pierced a cylinder. In the early light of morning a disorderly crowd of young German soldiers swarmed around the plane, shouting that the war would soon be over, that a revolution had broken out at home, and that soldier Soviets would lead the troops back. Hermann refused to believe any of it, and had one of his men fire a few rounds at soldiers

* Writing during the Hitler period, "Hermann" concealed his name to protect his relatives in Germany.

who tried to loot his plane for souvenirs. Finally an officer appeared, and his vehicle was put into service to find an aerodrome and new engine. Hermann's observer and chief mechanic quickly came back empty-handed. "There's no use exchanging the engine," one said. "We have to give up the plane." The Armistice had intervened.

At dawn on the last day Captain Erhard Milch, a stocky twenty-six-year-old former artillery lieutenant, paraded his *Jagdstaffel* 6, which he had commanded in eastern Belgium for five weeks. As a final test of discipline he inspected the doleful men rigidly, dressing down a puzzled flight officer for insolence and ordering them to form again properly. After they had stood at attention in silence for fifteen minutes he read out the Fourth Army's order for the election of Soldiers' Councils and directed that the squadron's motor transport be equipped with machine guns and that everything movable be hauled to the German border at Aachen. Their aircraft would remain. As a final favor he asked his men to fly the Kaiser's colors from their vehicles and, with heads held high, return to the Fatherland. (In Berlin his grandmother had lost all interest in life. "I don't want to live now that there is no King of Prussia any more," she had said, and promptly—and efficiently—began to fade.) In his diary for November 11 Milch would write of the Armistice, "The terms are the best possible cause for a future war." He would have a role in it, as Field Marshal and chief of the *Luftwaffe*.

At Lieutenant Rudolf Stark's *Jagdstaffel* 35, headquartered in a Belgian coach house north of Namur, November 11 dawned with thick swirls of fog and a five hundred-meter ceiling. Nevertheless, when Stark saw *Staffel* 34 begin to take off from the other side of the field, it moved him to action. Baggage for both squadrons was going east by truck, with mechanics inside guarding trunks and packing cases. Whatever could not be taken would be burned before Stark himself would take off at 11:30, Berlin time, half an hour before the Armistice was to take effect. Removing the aircraft was violating the cease-fire but Stark was unconcerned about that, looking down with satisfaction at the flames which would prevent the enemy from acquiring anything useful from the site. Crossing the Moselle, he landed in a meadow, asked directions from a farmer, then landed again at an airfield in Trier, on the Rhine just east of Luxembourg. He was in Germany.

Mechanics lounged outside a nearby shed. Stark asked for the duty officer. "There are no officers here," said a crewman. "There is a Soldiers' Council in charge now."

"To whom do I apply for petrol then?"

"There's no petrol to be had. The Soldiers' Council has stopped its issue."

Once other aircraft from the *Staffel* landed, Stark led the pilots into Trier, which was festooned with red flags, and clogged by parades and by crowds listening to revolutionary speakers. At council headquarters their appeal for petrol was turned down.

Returning to the Trier airfield, they transferred all their remaining fuel into two planes and took off for Munich after rendering the other machines unserviceable. In Munich, taking the control stick of his own aircraft as a souvenir, Stark and the others walked to the nearest tram stop. He was still wearing his epaulets, despite warnings from the mechanics that street mobs were looking for such provocation. On the way they found good reason to be cautious—an older officer on the ground, bleeding from a head wound. They took him to a nearby hotel. Carrying their own luggage and wearing coats with turned-up fur collars, they escaped seizure for their insignia, checked into a hotel near the railway station for a meal and a bed, and left word with the manager to be awakened in time to catch the 4:30 to Saarbrucken. The train left on time. Some order still survived.

"*Jagdstaffel* 356,"* led now by Lieutenant Hamann, who had joined the Air Force earlier that year at seventeen, had flown back to Krefeld with the body of their commander, who had shot himself. Defiantly, Hamann ordered that the Fokkers fly in battle formation, with black streamers attached to the plane carrying the coffin. But the flight from surrender of their machines would be useless. Allied planes would blanket German airfields and seize the aircraft, whether or not they were relinquished voluntarily. (Hamann would give up his eight Fokkers and one LVG to English and American forces on November 13.) Still, the pride in accomplishing the flight to the Fatherland seemed to outweigh the hazards and the final futility of the gesture.

Before the Armistice conditions were known at the Tellancourt aerodrome, the Richthofen *Geschwader* had been under orders to fly all machines to Darmstadt. Now they had to be surrendered, and a new order was issued:

FIFTH ARMY HEADQUARTERS TO KOMMANDEUR J. G. FREIHERR VON RICHTHOFEN NO. 1. YOU WILL DISARM YOUR PLANES AT

---

* See "Armistice Eve," pp. 108–10.

ONCE AND FLY THEM TO FRENCH AIR HEADQUARTERS AT
STRASBOURG WHERE ARRANGEMENTS HAVE BEEN MADE FOR
YOU TO LAND WITHOUT HINDRANCE. ACKNOWLEDGE.

When Ernst Udet walked over to his machine he passed bonfires of materiel that would have to be left behind, but the red-tailed
Fokkers were still there in the lifting mist. At 11:30, Berlin time—the
war would be over at noon—a watery sun appeared, and through
rifts in the clouds he could see, through his binoculars, British Spads
stunting over the lines, zooming, rolling, looping, spraying tracer
bullets and red-and-white flares through the overcast. Udet felt bitter and helpless.

Hermann Goering, the unit's final commander, vowed that he
would never surrender. Neither his men nor his machines would fall
into the hands of the enemy, he told an assembly of airmen. "We
cannot stay here and fight on, but we can make sure that when the
end comes, we will be in Germany."

Soon Goering had ordered the planes still able to fly withdrawn
to Darmstadt. Crews would truck separately whatever equipment
and records could be carried. Everything else would be burned. But
one airman cautioned that they might be wrecking the Armistice,
with broader consequences which no one could foresee. A Solomonic
solution was found to salvage honor. Five pilots to be chosen by lot
would fly their machines to Strasbourg. The others would fly into
Germany. As for the pilots surrendering planes, Goering declared
that he would not censure any who made rough landings—so rough,
indeed, as to render the aircraft useless.

In the poor flying weather some of the aircraft heading for
Darmstadt landed instead at Mannheim, only to find a *Soldatenrat* in
command. Revolutionaries disarmed the officers and stripped the
planes of their weapons. Then they supplied a truck to take the men
to Darmstadt, where Goering, hearing what had happened, was furious. "They must be taught a lesson!" he shouted, and ordered a
flight of nine planes to take off for Mannheim, two of them flown by
officers insulted there. While the other seven planes circled overhead, banking and rolling in obvious warning moves, the two pilots
forced to abandon planes at Mannheim landed and made for the
red-flagged administration building. Arms were to be restored at
once, or the planes above would move in and shoot up everything
that moved.

"We will wait four minutes and no longer," said one, brandishing a Very flare pistol. "I am to fire this if you agree to terms."

"Then fire, fire!" said the Council leader. "Of course we agree."

The nine aircraft returned to Darmstadt, Goering leading the way. Approaching the runway, he angled sharply, in order to smash the undercarriage. The other pilots took the hint and left nothing for the Allies to salvage. That night Goering put the final entry into *J.G.* 1's log himself: "11 November. Armistice. Squadron flight in bad weather to Darmstadt. Mist. Since its establishment the *Geschwader* has shot down 644 enemy planes. Death by enemy action came to 56 officers and non-commissioned pilots, six men. Hermann Goering, Lieutenant O[fficer in] C[ommand] *Geschwader.*"

A few days later the unit would disband, its remnants gathering in a local tavern to mark its passing. "Our time will come again," vowed Goering. His defiance of the Armistice had been impulsive bravado, but he was also beginning to see himself now as a figure to lead the Fatherland out of humiliation. He would look for the right circumstances.

Ben Simpson's section in the East Surrey Regiment's 8th Battalion had tumbled, exhausted and filthy, into an abandoned house on the edge of Landrednes. Having donned, as nightshirts, the ladies' chemises and drawers they found, they had gone promptly to sleep. Discarded were the "lousy garments we either dropped into the water-butt outside, hoping to drown the lice, or hung on pegs to freeze them to death." Into the water butt, too, had gone Simpson's tattered boots, as he was "lucky enough to find a pair of ladies' button-up boots that fitted." But the next morning "there was a sudden call to turn out on parade in the road outside"—to be informed, they would discover, that the war was over. Haig, however, had made it very clear in his cease-fire orders that morning that all commanders were "to pay the strictest attention to [the] discipline, smartness and well-being of their troops, so as to ensure [the] highest state of efficiency being maintained throughout [the] British forces."

Hurriedly, Simpson and his men pulled on their rancid uniforms over the frilly women's things and appeared on parade, lace around their necks and popping out at waists and sleeves from under the khaki. "Since I and all the others," he remembered, "were wearing our button-up boots, there was a skirmish to be in the rear rank to avoid detection. . . . We were spotted and the whole ghastly truth was out. We were severely reprimanded and told this looked suspiciously like looting. Since we had thrown all our lousy underwear into the water-butts we had to get them out and get them as dry as possible, so as to replace the ladies' underwear from whence it came." It was quite a life at ten shillings and sixpence a week, Simpson thought. And quite a way to spend one's twentieth birthday.

The British Fourth Army held positions below the Third, in a wooded, thinly populated sector. John Ventham of the 168th Brigade, Royal Field Artillery, taken in by stories of an Armistice on the seventh, was determined to be more skeptical on the eleventh, but the Germans were withdrawing so rapidly that it looked to him like the end. Rain had begun falling as they entered Avesnes, where civilians were already putting up flags. The Germans were gone. Returning to headquarters for instructions, the brigade encountered advancing British cavalry and asked where the squadron was going. "To take Avesnes," they said.

"We've just taken it," said Ventham, "but you can have it if you like."

To the east of Avesnes the Germans retired more reluctantly, putting up intense resistance at the village of Sars-Poteries before withdrawing yard by yard. The noise, Gunner James Davidson recalled, was deafening, as his 50th Divisional Trench Mortar Battery fired salvos of six-inch shells over the village to the other side while, from the dull, gray sky, scattered flakes of snow fell softly and melted away. Then at 11:00 A.M.—they knew nothing of date and time of an Armistice—they were suddenly ordered to cease firing. "When we did, the sudden quietness made us all feel dazed—almost stunned—and it was some time before anyone spoke. We who were left just stood gazing into space. It was rather like one feels in regaining consciousness after an anaesthetic. The Germans were at the other end of the village and we could see them. They, too, were standing and looked numbed and speechless."

A mobile force organized from elements of the 66th Division under Major General H. K. Bethell had been pushing through the small fields and woods between the villages of Sivry and Hestrud despite information received at 7:00 A.M. that the war would end four hours later. Orders from Fourth Army headquarters were to press forward, and the Germans held out stubbornly near Hestrud on a ten-mile front. The shelling on both sides intensified, divisional artillery of the 66th recording 1,800 rounds fired during the morning, the equivalent of a round of explosives for every ten yards of turf. The South African Brigade was already beyond Hestrud, at Grandrieu, when at 10:15 it learned that the last shot was to be fired at 11:00. But the final gesture in that sector, John Buchan wrote, fell to the enemy. "At two minutes to eleven a machine gun opened up about two hundred yards from our leading troops at Grandrieu, and fired off a whole belt without a pause. A German machine gunner was then seen to stand up beside his weapon, take off his helmet, bow, and walk slowly to the rear."

East of Mons, as the seconds ticked toward eleven, the forward companies of the 31st (Alberta) Battalion saw a German officer rise to his feet a few hundred yards away from the Canadian outposts. He fired a white Very flare into the morning gloom, the signal for his men to rise calmly from their dugouts, and begin methodically to dismantle their machine guns, pouring the water out of their coolant jackets. When they had packed up their equipment, like mechanics at the end of a day's work, they formed a column and marched off toward Boissoit—and home. A man could now stand up.

The Fifth Army's orders were to get to the line formed by the Blaton Canal and the River Dendre and take the bridgeheads. During the night of the tenth the Germans eased the task by withdrawing beyond Ath, but the British did not know it until after they began moving ahead. Dispatch rider Arthur Wrench of the Seaforth Highlanders received the message at eight and pedaled around the narrow streets of Cambrai, now a rear area. The news was different for troops not on the line. "Hostilities will cease at 11 hours," was Wrench's message; "today will be observed as a holiday." Now and then he bawled out the news to Belgian civilians, some of whom first doubted it until Wrench dismounted and repeated the information. "Then . . . they started to shout and dance out of pure joy and I had a hard time escaping their embraces." In his diary he drew himself cycling the news past the graves and the clamoring ghosts of his fallen Scot buddies, kilted in death as in life.

At Ath, Major Frederick Nicolson, eldest brother of a young Foreign Office expert on the peace treaty process, Harold Nicolson, took time to scrawl a few lines in his diary. "Entered ATH, extraordinary scenes. Hun prisoners nearly lynched in the square. The people hysterical, formed up in a field at Maffle, & were told hostilities ceased at 11. We had outbursts but 10th Hussars continued firing for some time. Huns hit back. Billeted at Maffle, very comfortable. Thank God." Few units had gone farther in the direction of Germany, but one of those was Lieutenant Vivian de Sola Pinto's company of the Royal Welch Fusiliers, which had the tiny village of Perquise, on the Tournai-Brussels road, as its objective. Shelled and machine-gunned occasionally as they advanced, they lost a captain to a direct hit on an improvised latrine. "That morning, as we were on the march, the elegant Captain Lord Chevington (once more arrayed in beautiful white breeches) galloped along the column shouting, 'No firing after eleven o'clock.' We halted at eleven o'clock outside Perquise on that misty November morning and at midday some German officers came to show us where the road had been mined. Soon after, as we approached the outskirts of the village, we were met by a little hunchback with an accordion who led us in triumph into Perquise, playing the *Marseillaise.*"

Also on the road east from Tournai was Captain Leslie Walkinton, adjutant of the 47th Battalion, Machine Gun Corps (47th Division), who had enlisted at seventeen as a private, in 1914. It was his third tour of duty in France, and despite the signs he could not bring himself to believe that the war was going to end soon. "We may have peace by Xmas," he had written home on November 2, "but that isn't very probable. Easter should see the end of it all." By the night of the tenth, however, he knew it would be over the next day. On the eleventh the battalion crossed the Schelde over "a rather wobbly pontoon bridge" at which his horse, Darkie, shied, and as they proceeded a single shell arched over them and fell harmlessly in a field about two hundred yards away. It did not explode, and they waited for the blast in oppressive silence. The clock was moving inexorably toward the cease-fire hour, and as they became "pretty sure that we wouldn't see another shell" they began, spontaneously, to sing a song that had been the great hit of the month of May back home in Blighty:

> *Good-bye-ee! Don't-sigh-ee!*
> *Wipe the tear, baby dear,*
> *From your eye-ee.*
> *Though it's hard to part I know,*
> *I'll be tickled to death to go.*
> *Don't sigh-ee, don't cry-ee:*
> *There's a silver lining in the sky-ee.*
> Bon soir, *old thing,*
> *Cheerio, chin-chin.*
> *Na-poo! toodle-oo!*
> *Good-bye-ee!*

"And so we said good-bye to shell fire."

A JOYFUL NOISE

How ya' gonna keep 'em away from Broadway,
Jazzin' a-roun' and paintin' the town? . . .
They'll never want to see a rake or a plow,
And who the deuce can parley vous a cow?
How ya' gonna keep 'em down on the farm,
After they've seen Paree?

—FROM A POPULAR AMERICAN SONG IN 1919

For the perceptive the coming of peace had been signaled in Paris the night before. On the orders of the Prefect of Police, the blue shading which had made inhabitants feel safe from zeppelins and Gothas was beginning to be sponged from the streetlamps. In the Place de la Concorde the sky was already bright. Lights had just been installed to illuminate a vast outdoor museum of trophies— German guns, German airplanes, German vehicles— displayed to publicize the latest War Loan appeal—"The Loan of the Last Quarter of an Hour" as the posters described it. Elsewhere on the night of the tenth, towns in France remote from the war zone were busy mourning not only their war dead, but the thousands carried away each week by the influenza epidemic silently ravaging Europe. In Germany the fact could not be hidden, but neither could it be printed. In France only the death of Clemenceau's son-in-law in mid-October had pierced the press censorship; yet at midnight, while the streetlamps of Paris were being cleaned, corteges were still arriving at the crowded cemeteries, for burials could not wait for convenient times.

That the news of peace was, this time, certain was apparent as early as seven in the morning, when elderly, threadbare men began parading with little French flags for sale, ten-sous flags being offered at four francs. Taxis already flaunted small Tricolors but most Parisians superstitiously kept their flags rolled up tightly under their arms, waiting for the official hour and minute of peace. Will Irwin passed by the knots of smiling, frail men and weeping women on his way into the Bourse to file a dispatch with the censor. Once he was inside, the official he usually dealt with, Captain Puaux, took him aside and whispered, "It's signed! Goes into effect at eleven." This time Irwin knew it was no false alarm.

France had been so close to defeat several times—Paris had even been threatened again in the last German offensive only months before—that victory was even less important than that the shooting had stopped. It was, Marcel Proust wrote from his cork-lined bedroom to Princess Soutzo, "the miraculous and vertiginous Peace." Socialist novelist Michel Corday noted in his diary that the rejoicing did not wait for the guns to boom at eleven. "Bells are ringing. The air is full of their peals. Soldiers dance with ecstasy. They brandish flags. It is a pleasure to witness their delight. Tragedy was looming over them. The 1919 class. . . . They were just on draft for reinforcements. Within six months they would all have been killed."

The Mayor of Paris issued a proclamation (distributed on hastily printed posters) urging Paris to "throw off the noble reserve for which it has been admired by the whole world. Let us give free course to our joy and enthusiasm, and hold back our tears." The populace needed no urging. The Minister of the Interior had messages sent to prefects throughout France ordering them to make the news known. "Put the flags out immediately. Illuminate all public buildings this evening. Have all bells ring out in full peal and arrange with the military authorities to have guns fired. . . ."

The satirical *Canard enchaîné* headlined, simply, "OUF!"—the French sigh of relief. While church bells rang in the old rue St. Jacques, Lieutenant Jean Piot, like other soldiers in the streets, was loudly cheered by the gathering crowds. *"Vous faites une drôle de tête?"* ("What are you making that face for?") someone asked him. "Aren't you glad it's over?"

"C'est aujour'hui que ça commence!" said the future editor of *L'Oeuvre* and vice president of the Radical Party, thinking of the Armistice not as an end, but as an unpredictable beginning.

Clemenceau wanted the news to be held back as long as possible and the announcement to be kept as uninformative as possible, so that he could turn his appearance in the Chamber of Deputies into a piece of theater. *Le Matin* was unable to get the news into its last edition on Monday morning, having to hold until Tuesday its pair of headlines, *"L'Allemagne a Capitulé"* and *"L'Armistice est Signé."* But at its offices, as eleven o'clock approached, an employee held up a sign at an upper window: *"Ça y est!"* It had happened. Later papers, like *Le Temps,* would pick up the Armistice terms from Berlin sources via Switzerland, but the conditions were unimportant to the first crowds, many of them women in black, now with a fragment of Tricolor ribbon in their hair.

The Premier had ordered guns fired at eleven, and precisely then there was a salvo of five cannon from the Paris forts. "The Peace barrage," said a French colonel on one of the boulevards. After that came the sounds of whistles and guns from ships in the Seine, and people in the streets sang, wept, and shouted for joy. From church steeples and clock towers the usual eleven chords at that hour began extending indefinitely wherever human hands were able to interfere with the mechanism, and, faithful to orders, functionaries in public buildings began—at eleven—to carry armfuls of flags outdoors. The Bourse remained open for only half an hour further, closing when most of its employees had left for the streets, already preceded by *midinettes* thronging the rue de la Paix.

Clemenceau's guns surprised Marie Curie in her laboratory in the rue Pierre Curie. The Institute of Radium had no flags to fly, and Marie and her assistant, Marthe Klein, rushed out to nearby shops. There were only bits of colored cloth left, but Mme. Bardinet, her charwoman, nervously fashioned them into Tricolors. Then Marie and Marthe found an attendant to drive them about in the Institute's battered Renault, with its red cross and French flag. The scarred gray "Little Curie" had gone from hospital to hospital on the periphery of the front with portable dynamo and primitive X-ray apparatus. Soon it carried joyriders on its fenders and flat roof and was mired in traffic jams.

In the Place de la Concorde the monuments encased in sand-bags through the war were now further covered by German steel helmets—"as thick as peas," an American nurse thought. The exhibition of captured armament had been drawing great crowds, impromptu parties formed under the noses of smiling gendarmes, to replay the war. Clemenceau had commented about the cannons, howitzers, machine guns, and *minenwerfers* that the children of Paris could carry them off, for all he cared. Now, amid the noise of horns and sirens and people, "grown-up children," the English *Paris Mail* reported, "harnessed themselves to the largest pieces human motor power could shift and dragged them in triumph along the boulevards with scores of their companions perched, swaying and singing, on the long barrels. The school children, who had another full holiday, completed the dispersal of the Hun artillery."

Someone on the scene who appreciated such high jinks with an almost professional perspective was Major J. Scott Button of the 106th Infantry, who in earlier days had been New York amateur bicycling champion and once, on a dare, had ridden down the steps of the old Edison Hotel on his wheel. In Paris on medical leave, Button wrote a long letter to his wife vividly describing, on blue Hôtel de Crillon stationery, how the spontaneous celebration became a game which the Parisian population played. The initial "mania for marching" developed, he thought, some organized patterns. First there would be "solid masses of people . . . locked arm-in-arm, sometimes the full width of the street, . . . singing and *Vive-la*-ing everything but the Bosche." The ubiquitous German artillery pieces would be towed by columns locking hands; and on the largest cannon "men, soldiers, girls and grown-up women would run up and climb onto the cannon and sit there waving flags and cheering and singing" as they passed flags from hand to hand. Some celebrants would join hands and surround another group "and dance around it singing some doggerel in French that I could not make out." Soldiers, particularly Americans, were enthusiastic about "this game" because "it always ended up with the men in the group grabbing and raising the girls in the circle. . . . And it wasn't always the *men* who did the grabbing. As one of the papers expressed it, 'Germs were freely exchanged.' "* American-born but London-based playwright (*Kismet*) Edward Knoblock, an officer with British intelligence, rushed into Paris to be swept, as he intended, into the delirium. A toothless hag selling newspapers turned to him, shouting, *"Ils sont morts le cochons—embrassez moi!"* ("Kiss me, the pigs are dead!") While his companion, a captain from his unit, roared with laughter, Knoblock recalled, "I kissed the old creature most heartily."

What was most surprising about such behavior to Major Button was that drink had little to do with it—people were "literally intoxicated with joy." Further, "There was always an outside edge of every crowd I've ever seen or been in. Here there was nothing but crowd." But crowds also furnished both anonymity and a kind of immunity to do violence, as Sergeant John M. Shaw discovered when his Army ambulance, marked with red crosses, was halted in a sea of people in the Place de la Concorde. Souvenir hunters and merrymakers swarmed aboard, and Shaw "managed to escape into the crowd, which proceeded to dismantle the car until little more than its chassis was left. Every other vehicle in the square suffered the same fate, as masses of shouting, gesticulating and singing pedestrians moved down the Rue Madeleine and the Champs Élysées, as if some irresistible force were pulling them. . . ." When he got back to his GMC ambulance hours later he found only "a mass of mechanical wreckage," but he had enjoyed himself in the interim, as happy café proprietors had trundled out casks of wine and offered drinks to anyone in uniform, and Shaw had sampled them all.

Another who had been wounded was Marine Lieutenant J. Harrison Heckman, who had fought with the 2nd Division and was on a six-hour pass from a Paris hospital when all Paris erupted. Caught in the pandemonium, he hardly remembered the painful "ragged

* Among the games reported is one described by Kathleen, Lady Scott, widow of the Arctic explorer, then working in Paris: "Jimmy Barrie came at six and we played together [among the celebrants] until midnight. After dinner at Ciro's we went out together arm in arm to watch the delirious crowds playing 'kiss in the ring' on the Grands boulevards—mad, wild scenes, girls dressed as widows were dancing with the rest."

hole" in his bad leg. The crutches singled him out as a special sort of hero, procuring for him a table at the Café de Paris, where, he wrote home, "half the men and all the women insisted on kissing me. They decorated me with flowers and ribbons until I looked like a Christmas tree. They danced on the tables and sang. . . . We brought a taxi and loaded half of Paris into it and rode around watching the other half celebrate. . . . If you saw a pretty girl on the street you'd stop the taxi and literally kidnap her until you found a better one in some other part of town where you'd dump the first one. Everyone was good-natured and I didn't see a single fight. . . . We would have been shot at sunrise for half of what we pulled off if it had been in the States. But the lid was off here. . . ."

En route to a meeting the next morning with Foch, Brigadier General George van Horn Moseley, of AEF headquarters, walked about Paris for an hour to watch the crowds, including doughboys straddling the statuary ringing the roof of the Opéra. On one of the boulevards, he wrote in an unpublished memoir, "I saw a large group of Allied soldiers . . . perhaps a thousand in number, who had captured a pretty French girl and placed her on top of this mob, where she walked around, stepping first on this head and then on another. She would attempt to reach the edge of this human island but as she did so, the soldiers would flock to that point, and it was some time until she was allowed to return to the pavement."

It was the sort of hilarity which Heckman joined, on crutches and without leave. "How I ever got around in the mob on crutches beats me," he recalled. But he got around. Finally returning to the hospital, he was told that the commandant wanted to see him immediately, but "Old Battle-Axe," the head nurse, would not let him report "the way I looked." She helped him undress, as he could not remove his breeches or his shoe, and got him into clean clothes. Then, giving the Colonel his most military salute, he prepared for disciplinary action.

"Lieutenant, explain where you have been and what you have been doing for the past five days."

"Sir, you know that I am on crutches. . . ."

"I am not blind."

"Well, sir, I had a six-hour pass to leave the hospital at noon on Armistice Day. There were mobs in Paris, and when I wished to return on time it was not possible to get a taxi and I cannot make the subway stairs, so I went to a hotel for the night."

"O.K., what happened the rest of the time?"

"Sir, Paris is still a madhouse and I could not get a taxi until this morning."

"You were five days trying to get a taxi?"

"Yes, sir."

"That was indeed a long, hard wait. Dismissed."

Heckman's friend Bill Davis, an Army captain, returned soon after, and Heckman reported how understanding the Colonel had been. Davis went through a clean-up, reported, and was asked his explanation for absence without leave. "Well, sir," he began, "you know I'm on crutches. . . ."

"Yes," said the Colonel, "and you could not find a taxi for five days. Thirty days' restriction to quarters. Dismissed."

Everywhere about Paris, as the hazy autumn sun hung in the sky or under the unaccustomed glare of outdoor lights, the shouting and singing would inevitably coalesce about a song, which would register emotions without the strain of thinking of something to say. The "Brabaconne," the "Sambre et Meuse," and "Madelon" echoed through the streets and squares, and as a bow to the Allies sometimes one heard the little English the crowds knew in "God Save the King" or "Yankee Doodle," which most Parisians assumed was the American national anthem. Most of the people milling about the Place de la Concorde had been attracted not by the German guns but by cries of "To Strasbourg! To Strasbourg!" which often seemed to bridge the gaps between songs. Since 1871 a black veil had covered the statue symbolizing the city. It was now banked with floral offerings. Italian airplanes, rarely seen on the Western Front, swooped low overhead, dropping flowers, and people picking them up would turn toward the sky and blow kisses at the intrepid Italians.

New York socialite Mrs. J. Borden Harriman, working for the Red Cross in Paris, remembered that her "one idea" had been to go to the statue of Strasbourg. Crowds swept her there as she left her building, and she "came in time to see the crêpe pulled down and the laurel wreath placed on the head of the beloved city. . . . They started to sing the 'Marseillaise,' but people could not sing. Their faces were bathed in tears, voices would not come, the old men sobbed aloud." American writer Dorothy Canfield watched a French soldier in field uniform push his way through the throng to place "a little bouquet—white and red roses, and forget-me-nots"— at the foot of the statue. An old woman in black took his hand in hers and asked, "You are from Alsace?"

"I escaped from Strasbourg to join the French army," he said. "All my family are there."

The old woman clasped him and kissed him on both cheeks. "You are my son," she said. And the crowd, pushing close to their symbolic Alsatian soldier to try to touch his hand, cried, "And my brother!" "And mine!" "And mine!"

Not far from the statue, art dealer René Gimpel watched a dummy of the Kaiser, hanging from the end of a long pole, being carried by a crowd along the Champs Élysées. "He was dragged along and shoved onto a cannon which some workmen had set up on the edge of the pavement. The Kaiser was wearing black trousers, a cap, and a pimp's red sash. His conquering moustache was made of straw, and a white placard had been hung around his neck with the word *Assassin* in red. He was hauled before the statue of Strasbourg and there he was burnt, but the placard was not consumed and the word *Assassin* was not obliterated. . . . Cries, songs, hilarious processions down the Rue Royale and along all the main boulevards. . . ."

In the Place de l'Opéra thousands were led by the famous soprano Marthe Chenal, from an upper balcony, in yet another rendition of the *Marseillaise*. The director of the Opéra orchestra conducted, top hat in his hand. "I thought she would burst a blood-vessel," Edward Knoblock recalled, "but she seemed to go on and on with undiminishing volume and ardour. She sang magnificently—her emotion giving the song a meaning and fire which I have never heard equalled before or since." Among the spectators was General James G. Harbord, head of American Services of Supply, who had driven from Tours with three aides to see the end celebrated. "When the last notes of the singers on the balcony . . . died away," he recalled, "a French bugler blew the *berloque*, the All Clear signal so many times sounded at the end of airplane raids. . . . And should I live a thousand years I should never forget it."

"I was curious to enter the Madeleine to see if this large outcry of national joy also carried with it a religious reaction," a young American lieutenant of French origin, Albert Leon Guerard, wrote (in French) in his diary. "There was none. The Rue Royale was swarming with people; but inside the immense hall of the Madeleine I could find only a few American officers, their noses in the air like good tourists. Oh! a soldier, also an American, is buying a 30-centime candle." Later his son, Albert J. Guerard, at twenty-one would write a novel, *The Past Must Alter* (1937), about which he confided later, "My chapter on Armistice Day 1918 was praised for its audaciously imaginative realism. But I was depending, for many details, on my father's very long diary entry for that day." In the novel the teen-aged Jim and Barbara push through the flag sellers and school-boy crowds to the Madeleine. It is "strangely dark" and silent. "The immense church, with its twinkling candles, and its majestic climb-ing darkness, appeared much larger than ever before. They seemed quite alone, inside . . . though a few old women were praying near the front of the church, and the candle-vendors flitted ghost-like along the vacant walls. It surprised [Jim] . . . that the church should be empty, on this day of thanksgiving—yet he was somehow glad."

Restaurants and cafés had been granted permission to remain open two extra hours—until eleven. Few had enough food or drink to warrant keeping the doors open and the lights on until then, but celebrants would not leave. A novel by an American pilot (twelve kills) who would become wealthy as a textile manufacturer, Captain Elliott White Springs, describes the frenzied scene in the famous New York Bar, which bulged with aviators. One "was just inventing a new drink called *L'Armistice*. It contained champagne for France, gin for Britain, whiskey for America, port for Portugal, chianti for Italy, saki for Japan, arrack for Greece, and rum for Liberia." The officer explains "that the secret of the drink was in the proportions, but he never got the right proportions."

Theaters and clubs overflowed. Maurice Chevalier, who had been a prisoner of war until his release in 1917 in an exchange of medical personnel (he was the POW camp pharmacist), sang with conviction at the Casino de Paris. The brassy Mistinguett, of the fa-mous legs and so-so voice, sang in *Phi-Phi* at the Theatre des Bouffés Parisiens, wearing a cape which appeared to be an enlargement of the field of stars in the American flag. And at the Folies Bergére General Charles G. Dawes, later Calvin Coolidge's Vice President, engaged a box to see *Zig-Zag* for the sixth time—"a fine, clean show," his guest General Harbord described it, in which the star, the American actress Shirley Kellogg, sang "Scotland Forever!" to the accompaniment of dozens of drum and pipe-playing Frenchmen in kilts and a plaided chorus which danced Highland flings. Several dozen British soldiers, unable to contain themselves, stormed the stage to join in. (The next night Harbord would return, this time bringing General Pershing with him, the staid "Black Jack" "shrinking back unseen behind the high partitions between the stage boxes, but enjoying it as much as any of us.")

After the show Dawes and Harbord tried to drive about Paris, but the throngs were too great. The guns from the Place de la Concorde were still being dragged about the streets and hundreds of *midinettes* on the rue de la Paix, unable or unwilling to go home, leaned out of Worth's and Pacquin's windows, pelting crowds below with torn paper, flowers, and anything else that would float down. General Billy Mitchell, also in Paris that evening, claimed that twenty-two people had climbed atop his staff car and ridden with him for blocks. Harbord and Dawes at least had managed to escape, but not before hearing, Harbord remembered, without apparent irony, two American soldiers caught up in the ecstasy of the event. It had been a "wonderful day," the doughboy with an empty right sleeve said. "Well, after all, this is worth losing an arm for." The other agreed—at least for *that* night. "Well, I don't mind leaving my leg over here so long as I can take the rest of my body home."

There were so many Americans in Paris on the eleventh that the celebration appeared in places to acquire an American flavor. Edith Wharton, writing as usual that morning in her apartment, heard the bells in nearby Ste. Clothilde and realized there was something unusual by the way they were answered by the bells of St. Thomas d'Aquin, St. Louis des Invalides, and other churches in the Faubourg. Everyone rushed to the balcony to listen to the surge of sound. "We had fared so long on the thin diet of hope deferred," Mrs. Wharton wrote, "that for a moment or two our hearts wavered and doubted. Then, like the bells, they swelled to bursting, and we knew that the war was over." She put aside her not-very-good novel *A Son at the Front*. It would not be completed until 1922.

Novelist Mary Roberts Rinehart, on her second writing assignment to France, had arrived in Paris only the day before, and could find a hotel room for the night only. The next morning, while looking for another place to stay, she happened to be on the street at eleven to hear the guns and bells. Looking up, she saw a captured German airplane "rolling and looping"—and realized that war correspondents would now have little to do. The gaiety, she thought, was tempered by "too many women shrouded in black, for whom the victory has come too late. I have a great thankfulness in my heart, of course. . . . Two boys are saved to us." Looking past the "mad processions of poilus and girls dancing, and kissing everyone they meet," she saw the legacy of war that was the underside of rejoicing. "The procession of the *mutilés* was too tragic, men with one leg stumping along and singing. It broke my heart." She would go off, two days later, on a tour of American battlefields. With the shooting hardly stopped, it was still an appalling and enormous rubbish heap. At one observation post she found a discarded notebook. Its last entry read, "11 A.M.: Guns cease firing." "Somehow," General Moseley wrote of his Paris experience, "I could not enter into the gay spirit of the occasion. Naturally I was happy over the signing of the Armistice, but it meant the disintegration of our Armies in France, upon which we had expended so much effort, would begin."

Crowds in front of the War Ministry roared "Clemenceau!" while in the solitude of the Élysée, Raymond Poincaré, the austere President of the Republic, was noting, succinctly, "Joy, fever, delirium of Paris." It was Clemenceau's day and Poincaré was going to be as small a part of it as the Premier could arrange. (Two days later, however, he entered Metz with Clemenceau and Pétain, and that evening wrote, "A day of sovereign beauty. Now I can die.")

At half-past two the stocky, seventy-seven-year-old Premier stumped into the tumultuous Chamber of Deputies and raised his hand to ask for silence. A cathedral hush fell. In tears he read, stolidly, the terms of the Armistice. Then, calling for gratitude to the soldiers of France he praised the example set for them by the revolutionaries of his youth.*

Then he added, "I remember that I entered the National Assembly . . . in 1871, and have been—I am the last of them—one of the signers of the protests against the [German] annexation of Alsace-Lorraine. . . ." History had come full circle. "One and indivisible," he concluded, Alsace-Lorraine was "at last returned to France."

The Deputies rose and burst into the *Marseillaise,* and the ceremonial guns boomed. In the Senate a proposal that "a statue should be erected to M. Clemenceau in his character as liberator of the country, and also one to Marshal Foch" was passed unanimously. But in the evening, after the tensions of the final, crowded days, the old man felt drained and depressed. "We have won the war," he told General Mordacq. "Now we have to win the peace, and it may be more difficult." (His remarks, especially to the Deputies, had

---

* At Farnborough Hill, near London, the widow of the man who had lost Alsace and Lorraine, Empress Eugénie, now ninety-two, would celebrate the victory although Clemenceau was still, to her, "that Communard."

suggested by omission that France had won the war alone. "No mention," Lord Derby would report to Balfour, "of Britain's share in it, nor, indeed, of America, Belgium, or any of the other Allies." That night at the Café de Paris, Derby would add, there was an uproar when an American got up and drank to the health of England, " 'who really won the war.' There is no doubt that the Americans are rather annoyed at the very little recognition that is given to our efforts.")

On leaving the Chamber, the Premier returned to his office in the rue Saint-Dominique, only to find crowds in the courtyard shouting, "Clemenceau! Clemenceau!" He opened the window, looked out quietly for a moment, and raised his arms, calling out, *"Vive la France!"* then he shut the window and sank into a small sofa, refusing to see any callers who had come to offer him their congratulations. As soon as he could get away, he returned to his home in the rue Franklin.

One of Clemenceau's oldest friends was the Impressionist painter Claude Monet, and it was to Monet's famous garden at Giverny to which the Premier had often gone in his darkest hours to restore his spirits. He is reported to have gone to Monet to tell him of the end of the war. "Yes," said the painter, single-mindedly, "now we have time to get on with the monument to Cézanne." His eyesight, retreated behind cataracts, left him little time, he felt, to finish the job.

"Dearest friend," Monet would write to Clemenceau the next day. "I am on the point of finishing two paintings to which I want to affix the date of the victory, and I should like you to act as intermediary in offering them to the State. It is a small thing but it is the only way I have of taking part in the victory."

Another painter in Paris found less cause for jubilation. The poet Guillaume Apollinaire, a one-time lieutenant, had just died at thirty-nine, of Spanish influenza. On hearing the news, Pablo Picasso, who had spent the evening of November 9 at his friend's bedside, had seen such grief in his own features—reportedly he was shaving—that he put down his razor, picked up a pencil, and drew his last self-portrait. *Mercure de France* editor Paul Léautaud, in his *Journal Littéraire*, recorded how Apollinaire's thin face, almost hidden by flowers on the tenth, had decomposed so rapidly that although he still lay the next day where he had died, "No one wants to remember him as he is now, and I could not look at him. . . ." But along the nearby streets an informal battalion of British soldiers, nearly a thousand of them, with a band at its head, was marching with an effigy of Wilhelm II and faggots to burn it, shouting execrations at the Kaiser (*Guillaume* II in French). Léautaud noted in his diary, "Crowds filled the Rue de Rennes, the Place Saint-Germain-des-Pres, and the Boulevard Saint-Germain. On the Boulevard, under the very windows of the small room where Apollinaire was lying rigid in death on his flower-banked bed, crowds were shouting, 'Down with Guillaume! Down with Guillaume!' " Léautaud found it ironic, and did not know the reason. Later a legend would arise that the cry of "*À bas Guillaume!*" was the last thing the stricken Apollinaire had heard, dying while believing in horror that the mob was referring to him.

In pacifist novelist Romain Rolland's 1920s novel cycle *The Soul Enchanted,* the Armistice arrives just in time. Nineteen-year-old Marc Riviére, about to be called up, goes into the streets to savor the peace. Caught up in the whirlpool of excited bodies, he is drawn to a frightened girl he picks out in the crowd. "Marc pounced upon her like a young hawk. . . . She fled up a steep side street, dark and narrow. He rushed after her and seized her. . . ." Later, guiltily unable to sleep between the icy sheets of his bed, he remembers how he had, in the piety of idealistic conversations with his mother, lashed out at "the wolves and foxes of the great War, who were tearing the world to pieces by force and trickery under the mask of right. . . ." Now "he had hastened to snatch for himself the more cowardly part. He saw once more the young girl kneeling on the pavement. . . ."

The febrile passions of Paris were duplicated on a smaller scale in cities and towns across the country. In the town of Belfort twenty-year-old Sergeant René Naegelen, twice wounded and home on sick leave, heard the bells of St. Christophe peal, and the sole venerable cannon of the local citadel fire a twenty-one-gun salute. "Why don't you pin on your Military Cross?" his mother asked. "You really should pin it on today." He walked with his parents through the central square, his mother and father stopping every few paces to hug and kiss him, weeping as they did. The women in the crowd "clapped their hands at this touching sight and kissed him in turn. . . . There was much kissing going around; indeed people no longer knew how else to give vent to their emotions. The boys put their arms around the girls' waists, and the girls did not object. I was carried away by the popular rejoicing as by a heady wine. I fancied myself bearing on my shoulders the awesome glory of the victors, the triumphant glory of those who survived."

Finally they returned home, to their accustomed chairs in the family dining room, where, on the mantelpiece in its gilded frame reposed a portrait of the son who would not come home. Joseph "stared at us with a frozen smile. He lay out there beneath his wooden cross. His comrades dug a bed for him and, to prevent the earth from hurting his eyes, put over his face the battered tin plate which was in his haversack. . . . We all turned our eyes toward the photograph that would turn yellow."

"I don't feel up to anything," Mme. Naegelen said, "but still I have to prepare your dinner." From the street there echoed the jaunty chorus of "Madelon." Naegelen got up and closed the shutters. A pastry cook before the war, he would become a Socialist journalist and a pacifist—until he joined the Resistance after the fall of France in 1940.

At the village of Docelles, in the Vosges, a soldier-priest who would later give the Jesuit hierarchy fits, Corporal Pierre Teilhard de Chardin, a stretcher-bearer, wrote a friend that the Armistice "pulled us up short" while moving toward Metz. But he now looked on his war service as "four and a half years of [spiritual] retreat" that were well over. "For some time I've been feeling that the war itself has lasted long enough for me . . .; it was time either for the war to finish or for me to change my circumstances. . . . Pray that I may take the right road in these opening hours of the new life that is soon to begin for me."

"Ah, General, what a lovely day!" bubbled the elderly lady in whose house near Nancy, taken over as headquarters, General Mangin had been preparing for the grand Lorraine offensive scheduled for November 14. "I don't think so," he said, sourly.

Soon to be in the vicinity was Gertrude Stein, who with her companion, Alice Toklas, was working far to the south, in Nimes, with a civilian relief agency. To a wounded French soldier, Gertrude said, "Well, here is peace." "At least for twenty years," said the soldier. Alice, overjoyed, wept with relief. Gertrude, in a lighter mood, warned her, "Compose yourself. You have no right to show a tearful countenance to the French whose sons will no longer be killed." There was a telegram from the relief committee: "If you speak German, close the depot immediately; return to process Alsace civilian relief." They secured a French-German dictionary, fur-lined aviators' jackets and gloves, and set on the road in "Auntie," their old automobile.

In Rouen, Edouard Vasseur de la Sostee, a twelve-year-old, was

waiting with his mother for a train to Calais. Until the summer of
1918 they had lived in the cellar of their house in Calais, cowering
from the ebb and flow of bombardment. Now, in Rouen, they were
waiting, with Edouard's aunt and cousin, for permission, as refugees,
to return. Bewildered, they walked the streets, until a man who
looked elderly and distinguished to the boy read the anxiety in their
faces and said, "Do not worry any more, ladies. The war is over. It
will be official at eleven o'clock." The women were puzzled, as they
saw nothing different around them.

"All of a sudden we heard an explosion, then another. Cannon
were being fired. We, people from the north of France, knew what
that meant. The anguish raised lumps in our throats. Sirens started
to sound. . . ." The streets filled with shouting people. Streetcars and
automobiles were clanging bells and honking horns. "An indescribable crowd which seemed to have emerged out of the paving stones
surrounded us. . . . Everybody was screaming and singing above the
noises of cannons, sirens and bells. . . . My cousin and I found ourselves holding flags in our hands, although I don't remember how
we got them. . . . We saw a woman wearing high-heeled shoes but
otherwise dressed like a soldier, her hair untidy, directing an impromptu military band and dancing while beating time with a stick.
A woman in such a situation, who looked like that, scandalized my
mother and aunt. I could sense the astonishment and moral repro-
bation on my aunt's face. But it was a day of happiness, and forgive-
ness was easy. . . ."

Suddenly in the midst of the delirium there was an island of silence. The victims of influenza were as insistent as had been the victims of war, and the funeral for a small boy had intruded into the
Armistice hysteria. The crowd opened up. "The little coffin was
lying on a hand-barrow which was the improvised hearse, and was
carried by four men dressed in black frock-coats and top hats; only
three or four people dressed in black followed. The tiny procession
went on. The crowd closed behind it, singing victory songs."

In Offranville portraitist Jacques-Émile Blanche heard "the
hooters of all the ships and factories . . . as clearly as if we were in
Dieppe." A mild rain was falling, but it kept no celebrants indoors.
From her hospital at Veules-les Roses, American expatriate painter
Nan ("Man") Hudson planned, with her friend Hilda Trevelyan, to
catch the next train for Paris, to celebrate at the Place de la Con-
corde, and stopped at Blanche's cottage to tell him they were going.
Blanche saw the rejoicing as premature. "An Armistice?—was that

all? Germany . . . would rise again, more arrogant, more ominous and more bellicose than ever."

Despite his dismissal of the Armistice, Blanche went off that afternoon to see what was happening nearby in Dieppe. "Tommies, their foreheads wreathed in green, sat astride barrels of beer, drunk and babbling, whilst lorries decked out with the French flag, the Union Jack, the Belgian and Italian colors, drove through the town. . . . Torrents of rain poured down from a menacing sky; there were no officers, no police to be seen. A quiet provincial town suddenly given over to madness, to primitive impulses. . . ."

At dinner the mayor of Offranville proposed a toast, and they raised their champagne glasses. The *Maire,* a Corsican named Casabianca, said, "Let us make hay while the sun shines. Tomorrow we shall have to think of how *they* are to be made to pay their ransom."

Boulogne had been even more chaotic than Dieppe. The huge convalescent camp overlooking the harbor was filled with ambulatory Australians awaiting recall to the line. After breaking into the stores of beer they broke loose into the rue de St. Pol, where from the brothel windows women and girls awakened before business hours looked out apprehensively.

"Boys, let's fuck 'em free," yelled a husky sergeant, waving his khaki sombrero with an ostrich feather in it. As he made a dash for one of the doors, the women inside quickly doused the glowing red light. Others followed, and Private Eric Hiscock, a homosexual to whom the affair was only of spectator interest, "could hear screams of the women, the hoarse cries of the tipsy men. Panic-filled tarts appeared at the windows shorn of their chemises, and were immediately pulled back from view to the accompaniment of even more strident cries. Then, out of one of the windows, was thrown a burning mattress, to be followed at most of the other windows by other pieces of past pleasure, all burning furiously. The Australians were purging their erstwhile pleasuredromes with any amount of vicious energy, and I, for an innocent one, couldn't help feeling sorry for the tarts." The gendarmes, Hiscock thought, arrived only "reluctantly," and after them the military police on their Triumph motorbikes; but no arrests were made. The burning beds were doused with fire hoses, and by noon the rue de St. Pol was quiet. "That," said an Aussie as they staggered back to camp, "was a fucking good end to hostilities."

At the port of St. Nazaire, eighteen-year-old Private John P. Troxell, destined for the American 91st Division if the war were to last a little longer, announced how relieved he was that the war was over. His older buddies scoffed. It was only an armistice, a truce. "This goddam war will start up again, and we'll get into it. You'll see." And sure enough, that afternoon they were loaded aboard railway carriages heading into the interior of France; but each village they passed through was crowded with reassuringly happy people waving flags and singing the *Marseillaise*. Also in St. Nazaire was John Dos Passos's fictional and more experienced sailor, Joe Williams. "The town was wild. Everybody ashore, all the doughboys out of their camps, all the frog soldiers out of their barracks, everybody clapping everybody else on the back, pulling corks, giving each other drinks, popping champagne bottles, kissing every pretty girl, being kissed by old women, kissed on both cheeks by French veterans with whiskers. The mates and the skipper and the chief and a couple of naval officers they'd never seen before all started to have a big feed in a café but that never got further than soup because everybody was dancing in the kitchen and they poured the cook so many drinks he passed out cold and they all sat there singing and drinking champagne out of tumblers and cheering the allied flags that girls kept carrying through." Joe would leave to look up Jeanette, "a girl he'd kinder taken up with whenever he was in St. Nazaire. He wanted to find her before he got to zigzag. She'd promised to couchay with him that night before it turned out to be Armistice Day. . . ." It would end badly, with the American pulling Jeannette away from a huge Senegalese officer in a cabaret and beginning a brawl. "Joe laid out a couple of frogs and was backing off towards the door, when he saw in a mirror that a big guy in a blouse was bringing down a bottle on his head. . . . He tried to swing around but didn't have time. The bottle crushed his skull. . . ."

Up the fog-shrouded river Gironde from St. Nazaire, the coaling vessel *Kermoor*, having steamed into the "False Armistice" frenzy of Brest on the seventh, docked at Bassens amid ships once again decked out in flags and sounding their screaming whistles. The American sailors had not known that the earlier celebration had been premature. Granted liberty, they crowded a "dinky trolley car, towing another just as small," and rushed to the bistros of Bordeaux. They were not too late after all.

At Brest, where the "False Armistice" bulletin had leaped off to America, the converted luxury liner *Aquitania*, a Royal Navy troopship, dropped anchor to disembark nine thousand doughboys from Camp Merritt, New Jersey. Private James Paxton Davis remembered coming down the gangplank in full battle gear, rifle on shoulder and pack on his back, to hear whistles and sirens going off everywhere in the harbor, and the crowds on shore cheering. It was exactly eleven o'clock on Armistice Day. By the time the ship's company made it ashore, Chief Warrant Officer John H. Nixon recalled, they discovered that the bands they had brought over from America as part of the replacement contingent were already in the victory parade through the streets of Brest, playing Sousa marches. With so many men in port to celebrate, Nixon thought, at eighty-eight, "Most of the girls in Brest will well remember that day. . . . All discipline went to the wall. . . ."

At Hondebecq on the Flemish border, R. H. Mottram wrote, ostensibly as fiction, there was a very different kind of celebration for the civilians displaced by war:

> No army this, and nothing victorious about it, though here and there a dirty old hat, or wonderfully made, decrepit wheelbarrow was decorated with the flags of the Allies, bought from Germans who had been selling them during their last weeks in the French industrial area. By one and two, here a family, there an individual with a dog, all those civilians who had been swept within the German lines in the offensives of 1914 or 1918, were walking home. Such a home-coming surely never was since misery began. . . .
>
> She left the veterans and the mules, busy in the fields, and stood, for a few moments, on the edge of the pavé, where the by-road to the farm left it, watching the melancholy processions. True, some were laughing, or greeted her with a cheer, but the general impression of those pinched faces and anxious eyes, above worn and filthy clothes, gave a better idea than any historian will ever do, of the rigours of the blockade. Madeleine gained from the sight just her first inkling of the irreparable loss that was to weigh upon the lifetime of her generation. . . .
>
> She returned to the farm, and now, finally convinced of the Armistice, yoked the mules to the strongest tackle she could find . . . and began to pull away the barbed wire that laced the farm about, fifty yards at a time.

To the north, at La Panne, in Belgium, Major Willy Coppens de Houthulst was in a military hospital, in agony with a postoperative infection which left him worse without his leg than he had been with it. Flying again seemed unimportant. He could dwell on nothing but the pain. Then "a huge clamor rose in the still air, shaking the whole hospital. It seemed to come from a thousand pairs of lungs, and sounded more like a death-rattle than a cry of victory. . . the Armistice. I should have felt a thrill of joy, and yet it was as if a cold hand had gripped my throat. An agony of doubt as to the future assailed me. . . . . A regret that I could not translate into words, at the passing of the days I had spent in the squadron, took possession of me. I saw the silhouette of our hangars and huts standing on the Plain of Les Moëres, bathed in sunlight and under snow, in the dawning and in the full light of day, and in the fading light of approaching night. The guns growled and grumbled in the east. . . . And as night fell and the wind died down, the bugles rang out with the crowing of cocks in the farmyards. The Armistice wrote *Finis* to this. . . ."

At another hospital nearby, where "a 70-year-old Scottish lady doctor" had put silver plates into the mangled knee and foot of a young Marine from Duluth, Frank R. Smith, six months earlier, he still lay crippled. His more mobile buddies slipped him out and carried him from one noisy *estaminet* to the next. It would be a year until he could walk, but he had his leg. Unlike Willy Coppens his memories were expendable. "It was so god-damn horrible I just didn't care to talk about it."

In Strasbourg, in German hands since 1870, mounted German police would stand by impassively as processions filed through the streets carrying banners inscribed "We Want to Be Reattached to France, Our Mother Country." Alsatian soldiers in German uniforms joined the demonstration while the mayor and local military commander appealed to the people to avoid any excesses. Four more years of annexation to Germany would come in 1940, when a new attempt to eradicate evidences of Frenchness would reach heights of absurdity unknown before 1918. Inscriptions would be removed from tombstones; labels would be changed on hot- and cold-water faucets, spice boxes, and flour and sugar containers; souvenir Eiffel Tower miniatures and French postcards were confiscated; and French-sounding family names were ordered Germanized. And the Place de Broglie in Strasbourg, focus of Armistice—and Liberation—raptures in 1918, would become Adolf Hitler Platz.

In Alsace, where Oscar Ludmann and other rebel sailors had returned home to confront the retreating *Reichswehr,* the ringing of the one remaining church bell in Andolsheim first suggested to them the marking of yet another German victory. While they worried about what would happen to outlaws and deserters, they began to sense that between peals there were no longer any cracks of artillery fire in the hills. Suddenly the lone bell, unbalanced in its belfry, overturned, and the frightened storks in the tower flew up and away. Above them a window opened and an elderly, gray-haired man called down, "What's the matter, boys? Are the French here at last, or did the Kaiser die?"

Hearing the sounds of many running feet on the cobblestones, they crouched in a deep doorway, hoping not to offer a good target; but rather than armed Germans, they soon saw a crowd of civilians and soldiers singing and shouting, "Armistice! Armistice!" A girl threw her arms around Ludmann's neck and kissed him. A burly Bavarian soldier grabbed him and began to whirl him around in a wild dance, but terrified that the Bavarian was attempting to drag him off, Ludmann struck him in the face. The soldier only laughed, and Ludmann asked, puzzled, "Tell me, what is it?"

"Peace! Peace!" said the Bavarian, as the street filled with soldiers who were obviously released prisoners—Rumanians, Russians, English, French—many in dirty rags, but singing and laughing.

Ludmann tried to push his way through toward his house, passing a shop where Florence, the baker, stood by his door, sweaty and stripped to the waist, shouting, "Peace, boys, peace! Eat, boys, eat! Long enough only the war chiefs have had good things. Now, all humanity can take my bread!" And he tossed crisp loaves of warm white bread into the crowd. Ludmann could not remember how it tasted. He caught a loaf and continued on, passing, near his own doorway, an unkempt beggar who pulled him by the sleeve. His filthy hair was shoulder length, and as he grinned two rows of yellow teeth showed through the straggly reddish beard. "Don't you know me?" he asked.

The sailor jumped back with a shudder. It looked like his former neighbor, who had been reported killed in the first months of the war. "For four years," the man croaked, "I lived in the attic under the tiles, while the dirty Boches paid a pension to my wife."

Across the street at the clothing store, old Isaac, the proprietor, stood wringing his hands helplessly while German soldiers pressed inside to help themselves to caps, jackets—anything to look out of uniform. On the sidewalk discarded *Gott mit uns* buckles, military caps, and other paraphernalia piled up. In the town church where the bell had rung itself out, an impromptu thanksgiving service began, while in the public park Germans complained that the statue of Napoleonic General Jean Rapp had already been draped with the forbidden Tricolor. Shouts of *"Merde la Prusse! Vive la France!"* echoed through the crowd.

"Damned Alsatians!" muttered a Prussian guard. "Can't you wait for your Frenchmen?"

The town was a confusion of loyalties. With authority broken down, the night of the Armistice would be without real peace. At home, as Ludmann fell asleep on the couch, he was awakened by the fire bugle. Some of the departing Germans were setting the torch to buildings on their way out of Andolsheim.

Across France in Angers, far from the last vestiges of combat, was an aircraft factory run by the firm of Potez, Coroller and Bloch. A twenty-six-year-old engineer, Marcel Bloch, was happily watching his first plane come off the assembly line. It would never fire a shot. A message would arrive, instead, that the ending of the war meant that no one would have any further use for airplanes. He would go into the furniture business with his father-in-law in the Faubourg St.-Antoine. After surviving Buchenwald, and changing his name to Marcel Dassault, he would design and build the *Mirage*.

HAVING A KNEES-UP

Knees up, Mother Brown!
Knees up, Mother Brown!
Under the table you must go,
Ee—eye—ee—eye—ee—eye—o!
If I catch you bending,
I'll saw your legs right off.
Knees up, knees up,
Don't let the breeze up,
Knees up, Mother Brown!

—HEARD IN TRAFALGAR SQUARE
AND MOST OF THE PUBS IN
ENGLAND ON ARMISTICE DAY, 1918

Just after six on the morning of the eleventh, as soon as the signatures were dry on the Armistice documents, Admiral Wemyss telephoned King George V and David Lloyd George. Like Clemenceau, the Prime Minister had hoped the news could be kept secret until he could announce the signing in the House of Commons. The King, however, spread the happy tidings in Buckingham Palace as soon as he put down his telephone, and the news began seeping across London.

Little preparation had been made to contain the expected repeat of Mafeking night—the chaos of May 17, 1900, which had followed the relief of a beleaguered garrison in the Boer War. But that Monday morning, while Parisian authorities expunged the blue from streetlamps, mechanics from Dent and Company of Cockspur were rushed to the Tower of Parliament to reactivate the mechanism by which Big Ben had struck the hours until August 1914.

Business was going on as usual in government departments, although the business generally had something to do with the winding down of the war. At the Foreign Office, Arthur Balfour worked on a memorandum to George V's confidential secretary. The King had warned that a rump Austria too weakened by defeat and peace conditions to survive independently might drift into a dangerous union with Germany. To assist in keeping the reduced nation viable, he wanted to see Austria retain a port on the Adriatic. Balfour agreed that an "economic outlet . . . on the Adriatic" was necessary, but downplayed the hazards of a union with Germany. It might even have its advantages, he added, for Prussian influence would be lessened. The peace treaty would leave Austria landlocked—and an Austrian-born corporal living in Bavaria would use a Prussian-led army to arrange the *Anschluss* which the King had feared.

In the basement of the Foreign Office, in an area painted green and violet to call attention to its use as an air-raid shelter, Harold Nicolson was working on Peace Conference preparations, in particular the "problem of the Strumnitza enclave"—an area of Macedonia with multiple claims upon it.* Soon he realized that he needed more details and started upstairs toward the map room. On the way he stopped at the chief clerk's office, where the window looked out on Number 10 Downing Street. Kept a safe distance from the front door by half a dozen policemen, a burgeoning throng stood in the street. Nicolson looked at his watch. It was 10:55 A.M. (His brother Fred, although Harold did not know it, had just halted at Ath, in

---

* Now in southern Yugoslavia.

Belgium, his unit's advance stopped by the clock.) Suddenly the door of Number 10 opened, and the Prime Minister, his leonine mane of graying yellow hair fluttering in the wind, emerged. Nicolson flung open the window to hear Lloyd George. "At eleven o'clock this war will be over. We have won a great victory, and we are entitled to a bit of shouting." Nicolson returned to the basement and the challenges of the Strumnitza enclave.

Elsewhere in Whitehall, Winston Churchill had already met with the heads of departments at the Ministry of Munitions to discuss the sale of unused materials and the conversion of munitions factories, with their three million soon-to-be-unemployed workers, to peacetime production. No decisions were made, as Churchill had been eager to return to his office before eleven.

As the hour was about to strike, Eddie Marsh, Churchill's private secretary, was with him at the window. "When the jubilant bells rang out," Christopher Hassall, Marsh's biographer, wrote, "Mrs. Churchill ran in, radiant, to share this moment with her husband, and the pigeons rose in a gyre around and above the Column." Churchill described the moments of waiting for Big Ben, long mute, to signal the end of the war—how his mind "strayed back across the scarring years" to the night when the tolling of the great clock signaled the beginning of the war. And then the eleven strokes began:

> Streams of people poured out of all the buildings. The bells of London began to clash. Northumberland Avenue was now crowded with people in hundreds, nay, thousands, rushing hither and thither in a frantic manner, shouting and screaming with joy. I could see that Trafalgar Square was already swarming. Around me in our very headquarters, in the Hotel Metropole, disorder had broken out. Doors banged. Feet clattered down corridors. Everyone rose from the desk and cast aside pen and paper. . . . The street was now a seething mass of humanity. Flags appeared as if by magic. Streams of men and women flowed from the Embankment. . . . Almost before the last stroke of the clock had died away, the strict, war-straitened, regulated streets of London had become a triumphant pandemonium. At any rate it was clear that no more work would be done that day. . . .

At the Accounts Branch of the Office of Works, Mary Veronica Wauchope asked if she might leave to see the excitement. She needed Treasury permission, the office manager said. Treasury was duly rung up, but no one answered. By that time everyone else in the Accounts office had left, and Mary and her sister rushed to Whitehall in time to see Admiral Beatty drive up, people "clinging like a swarm of bees to his car." Grace Emily Brightman remembered how personnel in the War Trade Department "erupted into Whitehall" when the hour struck, her group picking up additional strength from the Intelligence Division, which maintained the blacklist of firms trading with the enemy and worked in huts in the hollow of St. James's Park, where the lake had been drained to secure space.

Lloyd George's secretary to the Supreme Command, Colonel Maurice Hankey, had been in bed in London with influenza. His office telephoned the news shortly before eleven, and his wife, Adeline, "threw open the window for a few minutes so that, lying in bed, I might hear the joy bells." Listening to the tumult, the Churchills decided, although Clemmie was imminently expecting their fourth child, to hurry to Downing Street to offer their congratulations. Most of the Cabinet was struggling to do the same thing. Jan Christian Smuts, Arthur Balfour, Bonar Law, and Lord Milner had already managed the trick. Churchill's car was immediately swamped by a cheering crowd, which blanketed the vehicle as it crept forward.

Lloyd George had little time for each well-wisher. Parliament was to sit that afternoon, and before that he had a luncheon guest coming. When British Zionist—and wartime scientist hero—Chaim Weizmann had returned from Palestine after the Turkish surrender late in October, Lloyd George had invited him to lunch—on November 11.

The streets were already nearly impassable when he set out from his house on Addison Road. By 1:30 he had reached the iron gate that led into Downing Street, and timidly approached one of the policemen holding back the crowds. "I have an appointment with the Prime Minister for lunch," he said. So claim a lot of others, said the policeman. Weizmann asked that his visiting card be taken to the front door. Skeptically, the policeman carried it to the porter, and the future first President of Israel was escorted inside.

In his study the wily Lloyd George let himself be discovered reading the Psalms, "moved to the depths of his soul and . . . near to tears." His first words to Weizmann were, "We have just sent off seven trains full of bread and other essential food, to be distributed by Plumer in Cologne." It was not true.

After a hurried lunch, during which they discussed Palestine, the Prime Minister was off to the Commons for his report to the House, after which there was to be a thanksgiving service improvised that morning by the Archbishop of Canterbury. At a quarter to three Weizmann watched Lloyd George "emerge from the door of Number Ten, to be overwhelmed immediately by a cheering crowd and borne, shoulder high, from view."

Had Herbert Asquith not been ousted in mid-war to be replaced by the more aggressive and charismatic Welshman, who had made his reputation by turning around a floundering munitions program, it would have been his own personal triumph. Instead, Asquith heard the news at his house via a telephone call. His wife, Margot, quickly dispatched the servants "for as many flags as could be bought" for the house and the automobile, and sent a congratulatory telegram to the King. Then, after breakfast, the Asquiths left for the Golders Green crematorium for the committal service for H. H.'s brother, W. W. Asquith, a retired master at Clifton College.

They returned to Cavendish Square through a changed London, to Margot "more like a foreign carnival," with huge flags flying everywhere, the men putting them up "waving their caps . . . from the tops of high ladders," and pedestrians dancing on the sidewalks. A servant handed them a return telegram from George V: "I look back with gratitude to your wise counsel and calm resolve in the days when great issues had to be decided resulting in our entry into the war, which now, thank God, has been brought to an end."

Commons was crowded when Lloyd George and Balfour entered, members rising to wave their papers and cheer. The usual list of questions was dispensed with, the Speaker, immediately after opening prayers, calling on the Prime Minister. Lloyd George was unusually laconic. He read the clauses word for word, warning that last-minute emendations he had not yet received might change the final text. "I hope we may say," he concluded, "that thus, this fateful morning, came to an end all wars." Then he moved that the House adjourn and proceed to the Church of St. Margaret "to give humble and reverent thanks for the deliverance of the world from its great peril."

As the former wartime leader, Asquith seconded the motion, adding that it seemed clear to him from the Armistice conditions "not only that the War is at an end, but that the War cannot be resumed," and he hoped "that now we have entered upon a new chapter of international history, in which war will be recognised as an absolute anachronism. . . ."

The session had taken thirty-two minutes. At 3:17 the House adjourned, and joined by the Lords, who had heard a similar reading, walked across Parliament Square to St. Margaret's. Police cleared a path through the thousands who had gathered outside. No longer an influential person, Margot Asquith had to fight her way alone to the visitors' section, getting into the church only because a policeman recognized her. Future Conservative Prime Minister Stanley Baldwin noted in his diary after returning from St. Margaret's, "I think a good many people are nearer tears than shouting today. Old Bill Crooks [a Labour M.P.] came up to me today and taking one of my hands in his big paws said tremulously, 'This is a great day,' to which I replied, 'Yes, but I feel like crying myself,' to which he replied, 'I've had my cry this morning.'" But feisty former First Sea Lord "Jacky" Fisher, seventy-two and unwillingly retired, complained to Viscount Lee of Fareham (who would soon be Minister of Agriculture) that the Kaiser should have been hanged and Berlin sacked. "I am damned if *I* will give thanks to God for this ignominious and disgraceful surrender of all we have fought for!" But he had not been in the trenches as had Henry Williamson, who set his stolid Private John Bullock, in *The Patriot's Progress* (1930), out in hospital blue, waiting for the maroons to sound. Bullock, "with trouser turned up to show six inches of white lining," had swung himself on his crutches into the park when "an old toff stopped him and asked him how he lost his leg. John Bullock told him. A five-nine, as we were going over. The toff soon lost interest, and when the flags were waving, he said: 'Well, I suppose it's a good thing that it's over, but in my opinion the Government is weak. We ought to have driven the Huns back into Berlin, and given their country a taste of what they gave to France.' . . . At this moment a very little boy ran up, waving a flag. . . . 'Look, daddy, look!' cried the little boy. 'The poor man hasn't got only one boot on!' 'Ssh! You mustn't notice such things!' said the toff. 'This good man is a hero. Yes,' he went on, 'we'll see that England doesn't forget you fellows.'"

For children the Armistice was a kaleidoscope of confusing impressions. A *Punch* cartoon showed a small child excitedly returning home to tell her mother, "They've given us a whole holiday today in aid of the War." David Kneebone, at a charity boarding school for boys west of London, recalled getting cake with his tea ("It had no icing but not a crumb was wasted."), and Charles Percy Snow remembered a half-holiday at Leicester and playing football on "that pleasant misty autumn day," with fish-and-chips as a special treat for dinner. Turnips were plentiful, potatoes almost a luxury. At Holy Trinity Junior School, at Selhurst, near Croydon, seven-year-old Alan Elphick's teacher, Miss Freeman, told her students to take out their notebooks "and write down the following, which you will remember the rest of your lives." Then she dictated the numerals "11-11-11," and explained their significance.

Long before, all the boys in the class had decided what they would do to celebrate the end of the war. The twins Horace and Neville Barker would tear down the bell tower; Willie Chester would hide the bell; the rest would carry off the piano, chalks, pencils, and other implements required for learning. They went home in uproarious spirits, but after fervid celebrating into the night with everyone else, all parental rules suspended, they heard the school bell ringing as usual the next morning at 8:40. They had substituted the wish for the impossible deed. "But there isn't any more school—the War's over," said Alan to his big sister of eleven. "Don't be daft," she said. "That was a one-day holiday. Hurry, or we'll be late."

At St. Dunstan's, on the southern outskirts of London, Stephen Usherwood's class heard maroons go off "with a noise like gunfire and we all rushed to one side of the playground overlooking the playing fields and, staring up into the dark sky, made yellow-green by smog from a million coal fires, began to cheer." When the bell rang they were all summoned to the assembly hall, where the normally dour and emotionless headmaster, tears streaming down his cheeks, told them the news. At a council school in southwest London, A. J. A. Lunghi's master, a wizened old man who would have been retired had younger men not gone off, explained to his class that the firing of the maroons, normally an air-raid warning, would signal the end of the war. When that happened the boys were to file quietly into the assembly hall for prayers of thanksgiving, after which they would be sent home. As the clock ticked toward eleven the tension became unbearable. "And then the unnatural silence . . . was shattered by the first dull thud of a maroon, followed by others. Our pent-up emotions exploded, and with a yell the whole class leapt up and rushed for the door, sweeping the little master aside as he vainly tried to stop us. We clattered into the street, and I remember running all the way home, past weeping women and jubilant men, the wives, mothers and fathers of boys at the front."

West of London, at Southall Country School, fifteen-year-old Victoria Smith remembered happily shrieking boys and girls running along the corridors en route home. "As we rushed along I happened to glance through the open door of the geography room. There, amidst the empty desks, sat the geography mistress, head in hands, quietly but copiously crying. She had been widowed by the war. I remember that I hesitated. Should I turn back and speak to her? Youthful fear of adult grief stopped me and I went my way."

Edward C. Doughty's form master at a school in Clapham was unable to concentrate, surreptitiously checking and rechecking his watch. The class was used to his nervousness, a result of war wounds from Royal Flying Corps service, but after one puzzling pause they heard a distant booming. The master peered out of the window and said, "That will be the signal—the War is over." The students looked at each other unbelievingly. Rushing from school, Doughty made his way to Clapham Junction station, where he watched the unloading from a hospital train of dozens of stretcher-borne casualties to be taken by ambulance to the 3rd London General Hospital—a huge converted orphanage. Then he went home.

"Dad," Edward announced, "the war's over."

"I know, son," he said.

Then, remembered Doughty, "We both broke down and cried."

At Valentine Wannop's fashionable school in Ford Madox Ford's *Parade's End,* the girls had disgraced decorum on the day of the False Armistice, bursting into an unladylike anti-Kaiser ditty. On the morning of the eleventh a telephone call to Miss Wannop, who had been ordered to keep the girls at calisthenics to exhaust their enthusiasm, would inform her that her shell-shocked fiancé was back and that "the thing, out there, miles and miles away, must have been signed . . ."—something she vaguely realized from the insistent factory hooters. "Well, it's a great day," Lady Macmaster purred into the telephone, "I suppose you're bothered by the cheering, like me." Putting down the receiver, finally, Valentine is about to ask for leave to rush into London to find her Captain Tietjens when Miss Wanostrocht makes the request unnecessary. "I had to let the girls go . . ." she says unhappily. "The Governors—I had an express from Lord Boulnois—ordered them to be given a holiday. . . . It's very inconsistent."

Fourteen-year-old Lily Shiel, an immigrant child in a London orphanage, was learning how to make a school-leaving "trousseau" of two pairs of thick, ugly, mottle-green knickers (bloomers to Americans), two long calico nightgowns, and two cotton undervests. "Lily was turning the handle of a sewing-machine," she later wrote in the third person, "when the news flashed through the school that the Germans had surrendered. . . . It was incredible. The war had become a way of life. It would last for ever. It was hard to grasp that there would no longer be lists of dead and wounded in the *Telegraph.*" All activities were suspended and everyone summoned to the assembly hall, where the headmaster called for three cheers for the Allies and announced that they could soon expect a visit from his brave son, who would appear wearing all his medals. "It was hard to sleep that night. There was excited talking in all the dormitories, and for once the teachers did not appear to demand silence. They were celebrating in the staff sitting room." The bright new world to come would see Lily first as maid, the role for which she was being prepared, then as musical comedy actress for Cochran and Coward, finally as Scott Fitzgerald inamorata and Hollywood gossip columnist, Lily Shiel having metamorphosed into Sheilah Graham.

Home from school, Malcolm Muggeridge recalled watching, from the upper deck of a Woolwich bus, "the crowds singing, shouting, dancing, embracing, vomiting, climbing onto the tops of taxis, grabbing one another and making off to the parks." Victor Sawdon Pritchett saw nothing of it. "Some in Bermondsey didn't believe it and took their mattresses up to the tube or the arches, just in case. There was a bonfire in the yard at Guy's Hospital and a fireman's helmet was stuck on top of the statue there. . . . Father was late home too. He had celebrated . . . at the Albert Hall, singing 'Land of Hope and Glory,' and he had his wallet stolen. He was rather pleased, as if he had done an extra something for his country."

Traveling at holidays between the Sherborne School and his home in Dublin, Louis MacNeice had learned about the war on railway carriages, sitting in the crowded corridors "wedged between kitbags and rifles, half-choked with the smell of sweat, brass-polish, beer . . . and words I did not know but knew were bad." His family had two kittens, named *Mons* and *Flu.* Young MacNeice had no idea how well, in 1918, they symbolized the times. When news of peace came, the fourth-form boys pounced upon "a little painted man made with a fretsaw"—the sole work of art by a student nicknamed *Flounder.* They rechristened the wooden figure *Kaiser* and "burned him in a hole in the wall," not knowing that adults were doing similar things.

From France, James Barrie wrote a friend that he had heard that at Eton students had marched "with their bath-tubs as drums and [that] the night ended with Michael [Davies] getting 500 lines (for standing on his head on a roof when he should have been in bed!)." Michael, Barrie's foster son, had been due to enlist on November 12. Brian Howard, a first-year Etonian, confirmed the method of celebration in a letter to his mother, describing how "all the school rushed up and down the streets yelling and screaming, one person was beating a bathtub, another a tea tray, and you never *heard* such a noise . . . and then we carried a maid up and down the house and sang songs until nearly ten o'clock. Japanese lanterns were hung outside the houses, and the place is covered in flags. I have a Union Jack out of my window and a Belgian flag inside the room. Oh, it was great fun. . . ."*

When the Armistice hour arrived in Lancing, Evelyn Waugh, whose brother Alec was a prisoner of war somewhere in Germany, remembered he was

> idling in the Classical Middle Fifth under a exceeding dull form master. The event was boisterously celebrated. There was a cancellation of all impending punishments, a *Te Deum* in chapel, a bonfire, spontaneous processions, cheering, ringing of bells. Certain unidentified revellers went too far, I forget in what direction. I think they did violence to the fire-engine or threw something on the bonfire that should not have been burnt; perhaps they did both by putting the fire-engine to the flames. I cannot remember; but I do vividly remember the rhetorical performance of Mr Bowlby, who, addressing us in Hall, denounced "a dingy trick. I repeat a dingy trick." At that moment his eye alighted on an uncouth youth who was smirking at a table near him. "But Barnes laughs. Thank you, Barnes. Now we know Barnes's ideals." He then expatiated on the ignominy of the outrage introducing as the refrain of each reprobation: "But Barnes laughs."

---

* One risks charges of condescension by noting that some of the other schoolboys mentioned in these pages would later stake a claim to fame. C. P. Snow was later Lord Snow, novelist, savant, and public servant. Malcolm Muggeridge is the future journalist and literary curmudgeon, and Sir Victor Pritchett is the critic as well as one of the major short-story writers in his time. Louis MacNeice was the future poet and radio dramatist. Brian Howard became a literary figure of considerable but unfulfilled promise. Evelyn Waugh would become a major novelist, Christopher Fry a playwright, Rupert Hart-Davis a biographer, editor, and publisher, Lord Clark the art critic, Sir Francis Chichester the circumnavigator.

At the Modern School, Bedford, Christopher Fry, restless in the fifth form of the junior school, was being taught by an undersized clergyman known to the boys as "Smuts" when the bells of St. Paul's Church began to peal massively, a maroon went off, and other church bells joined in the noise. "We cheered and thumped our desks, bouncing up and down in our seats, quite prepared to run out of the building and into the street. We could hardly believe that Shepherd-Smith meant us to go on with our work, as though the world had not been completely transformed. The world was at peace, a state of affairs I could hardly remember, and at peace perhaps for ever. There would be bonfires, and flags, and fireworks, and no more death until the time for death. . . ."

Rupert Hart-Davis remembered a far less euphoric November 11 at school than most of his contemporaries. "Armistice Day at Stanmore was a lugubrious affair. After singing 'God Save the King' in the gymnasium we mooched round the sodden playing-fields in a damp mist, while maroons and church-bells boomed and rang all round us." Kenneth Clark, home on sick leave from Winchester, missed it altogether. At the moment the Armistice was to take effect, the train to Bath, in which Kenneth and his mother were seated, puffed out of Paddington Station. "How fortunate," his mother observed; "we shall miss the worst of the celebrations." She was correct. In undemonstrative Bath, the fervor had evaporated before their train arrived.

At Doon House School, temporarily at Yeovil in Somerset because of German air raids along the East Coast, ten-year-old John Straker participated in one of the few constructive ways in which the day was marked. Students gathered around the flag to sing "God Save the King," after which they planted an oak, which one of the masters had kept in the paddock for that purpose. There were only thirty-two students in the small school, close to its normal enrollment. Twenty-nine Old Boys of Doon House had died in action—an index to the way in which the war had drained England.

At Marlborough School the influenza victims lay in rows on the infirmary floor, as there were not enough beds, and Francis Chichester could not even raise himself on an elbow when he heard the cheering outside. "Only a few died," he remembered. Many more had already died in uniform.

At the fictional Bamfylde public school in Devon (R. F. Delderfield's actual source was the West Buckland School) in *To Serve Them All Our Days* (1972), the stupendous news arrives, prematurely, the day before, from an Old Boy with an uncle in Fleet Street. It offers time for the masters' wives "to perform a prodigy of baking for a communal supper and sing-song in Big Hall," and David Powell-Jones, the young master invalided, from the Somme, into teaching, is cheered, "although he could feel no personal achievement in survival when nearly a hundred Old Boys had died." When the school band strikes up "Long, Long Trail" and "Tipperary" he finds the setting incongruous and unbearable, and slips away through the sculleries, unashamedly weeping. "For Christ's sake . . . what is there to sing about?" he asks himself desperately. "Why does it have to be a celebration when it ought to be a wake?"

In Andrew Davies's television adaptation (1981) the headmaster vainly suggests that the gaiety is understandable. The students "all have brothers or fathers out there." It is small consolation, as an elder colleague, Ian Howarth, perceives. He suggests to Powell-Jones that they retire to drink gin "at a slow and steady rate until [they] lapse into unconsciousness." Yet, however bitter to Powell-Jones and his like, the raucousness had its point. The living would come home, and the students who were the next "class" of cannon fodder would not have to go.

On his way home from school young Robert Johnstone, passing the entrance to the Royal Military College at Sandhurst, had to leap aside for a crowd of wildly cheering cadets, a number of them jumping onto an old four-wheeled coach, drawn by two horses, which plied for customers at the gates. "The ancient vehicle collapsed under the weight and the old cabbie was left, clay pipe in hand, surveying the wreck whilst cadets rushed along the Great South West Road. . . ." It was almost a metaphor for what had happened to the Old Order in Europe.

At both ends of the Mall, along which, as in Paris, captured German weapons had been displayed, London's celebration gathered momentum. Where the Mall ended to the west, the tide of people washed against the railings of Buckingham Palace. Royal pages had draped the center balcony with a valance of red and gold. The King would appear there, and crowds chanted "We want the King!" until he did, after which they sang "God Save the King," listened to the Brigade of Guards band, and cheered and sang again and again until it was certain that there would be no more appearances—at least for a while. Even then they remained, singing "Rule, Britannia," "Auld Lang Syne," "Tipperary," and "Keep the Home Fires

Burning," although the morning mist had become a drizzle which would turn into a downpour by evening. Despite the weather, the King and Queen had gone off in an open carriage, driven at a slow pace along the Mall, through the Strand and Fleet Street to Ludgate Hill, and via Queen Victoria Street to the Mansion House, where the Lord Mayor, wearing his black-and-gold robes, and the Lady Mayoress, with the City Sheriffs, were on the balcony to salute their sovereign.

Only a fortnight earlier Arthur Conan Doyle, who had briefly reported the war from the French, British, and Italian fronts, had heard of the death of his son. Still weak from his wounds on the Somme, Kingsley Conan Doyle had been unable to fight off influenza. Sitting in the foyer of the Grosvenor Hotel at eleven on the morning of the eleventh, the creator of Sherlock Holmes watched a well-dressed woman of mature years push through the revolving doors to waltz with a Union Jack in each hand, then waltz out again. Realizing what had happened, he rushed out in the direction of Buckingham Palace. Outside he saw "a slim, young girl . . . elevated on to some high vehicle . . . leading and conducting the singing as if she were some angel in tweeds just dropped from a cloud." Then he saw "an open motor stop with four middle-aged men, one of them a hard-faced civilian, the others officers. I saw this civilian hack at the neck of a whisky bottle and drink it raw. I wish the crowd had lynched him. It was the moment for prayer, and this beast was a blot on the landscape." Conan Doyle decided to go home to Windlesham, as far away from the tumult as possible. "I lost my hat," he remembered, "or I got somebody else's."

There were relatively few private vehicles in London, but all of them seemed to have been flung into the streets by the bells and sirens of eleven o'clock. Buses, Captain H. W. Yoxall of the King's Royal Rifle Corps remembered, "forsook their proper routes and drove up and down . . . with 40 people on their roofs, 10 on their running-boards and 5 on the bonnet. Taxis with 10 to 15 people staggered around with flat tyres and breaking springs. Informal dances broke out in the streets." Caught up in the enthusiasm was American citizen Ezra Pound. A Londoner since 1907, and increasingly cranky because of real and imagined literary affronts and frustrations, he surprised himself. Roused at his Kensington flat by Stella Bowen, Ford Madox Ford's current mistress, he had hopped on an open-topped bus to central London with her, "Ezra with his hair on end, smacking the bus-front with his stick and shouting to

the other people packed on the tops of other buses jammed alongside ours." Pound would remain out in the rain so long that he acquired a cold; but he found himself once within a few feet of the
King's carriage, which was without escort except for a few policemen. To his friend John Quinn in New York he wrote, attempting to
appear more cynical than he had felt at the moment, "Poor devil
was looking happy, I should think, for the first time in his life."
Forty years later he recalled the experience in a *Canto:*

> *George Fifth under the drizzle,*
> *as in one November*
> *a man who had willed no wrong.*

On the way back the carriage, perhaps the only vehicle in London that day for which crowds parted to permit its passage, traveled
through Holborn, Oxford Street, Shaftesbury Avenue, Trafalgar
Square, and the Mall. Throngs were still ringing the Palace in the
rain. "Nine miles," George V wrote in his diary, "through waves of
cheering crowds. The demonstrations of the people are indeed
touching." Since his pledge to abstain from liquor for the duration
had now been fulfilled, he ordered the royal cellars to be unlocked
and broached a bottle of brandy laid down by the Prince Regent to
celebrate the victory at Waterloo. It tasted "very musty."

That evening the King and Queen sat on their balcony exposed
to the rain and staring into two floodlights which illuminated the
Palace. According to Captain Yoxall, who had watched the excitement, "at first no bigger than a man's hand, develop into a storm of
delirious thanksgiving," people attempting to see their sovereigns
"perched upon every vantage point, even to sitting in the arms of
Queen Victoria on her Memorial." Rising regularly to acknowledge
the enthusiasm, King George and Queen Mary, although rain-sod-
den, remained in view until midnight. Then, in the darkness, the
dampened throng turned east to join the celebrants still whooping it
up in Trafalgar Square and the Strand. Under the streetlights,
turned up for the first time in four years, their heads and upturned
faces, in Osbert Sitwell's description, "were like a field of golden
corn moving in a dark wind." The last time he had seen such a
crowd—before his own Army service in France—"was when it
cheered for its own death outside Buckingham Palace on the evening of August 4, 1914; most of the men who composed it were now
dead. Their heirs were dancing because life had been given back to

them. . . . A long nightmare was over. . . ." To Sitwell "the dread
God of Herds" had taken charge as people, "sometimes joining up,
sometimes linking hands, dashed like the waves of the sea against
the sides of the Square, against the railings of the National Gallery,
sweeping up so far even as the shallow stone steps of St. Martin's in
the Fields. The succeeding waves flowed back, gathered impetus and
broke again. The northern character of the revelers . . . was plain in
the way they moved, in the manner, for example, in which the knees
were lifted, as in a kermess* painted by Breughel the elder. . . ." As
the song went,

> *Knees up, knees up,*
> *Don't let the breeze up. . . .*

A *Punch* cartoon with a background of a mob of merrymakers
had the "First Pessimist" sigh, "I'm glad it's over; it's been a terrible
time. But think what the next war will be like!"

"Yes," says the "Second Pessimist," looking back at the crowds,
"—and the next Peace!"

When the guns saluted the end at eleven, Dora Carrington
wrote her brother Noel, she was on her way to meet a friend. "It was
interesting seeing how the different stratas of people took it. Travel-
ling from Hampstead, seeing first the slum girls, and coster people
dancing, pathetic scenes of an elderly plumber nailing up a single
small flag over the door. Then the scenes became wilder as one
reached Camden Town and more and more frantic as one [ap-
proached] Trafalgar Square. . . . In the Strand the uproar was appalling."

The revelry in Trafalgar Square, to go on without letup for
three days, would become legendary. There were echoes of the event
in another *Punch* cartoon caption, which would quote the testimony
of a scruffy, mustached defendant answering the charge that he
kissed the burly, mustached policeman who glares at him from the
witness stand. "Well, Sir, there was a lot of larkin' goin' on, celebra-
tin' the Harmistice, but I don't think as I so far forgot myself as to
kiss 'im. If I did, Your Washup, I deserves six months." (On the
other hand, artists Cedric Morris, twenty-nine, and Arthur Lett-
Haines, twenty-four, met on Armistice Night in London, immediately fell in love, and continued to live and work together for the rest

---

* kermess: a Dutch outdoor fair.

of their long lives.) Kingsley Martin, who would become editor of *The New Statesman,* recalled returning from France "to witness the glorification in Trafalgar Square. We danced round and round all night long, singing 'Knees Up, Mother Brown,' and other fragments from English folklore. Whooping, the crowd seized omnibuses and . . . played catch with policeman's helmets. . . ."

To Robert Emmet Sherwood, a Canadian "Black Watch" enlisted man, it was "a hazy, incredible blur." A gassed and wounded "walking case" in the Canadian hospital at Bushey Park, near Hampton Court, Sherwood was in the stable yard waiting for mail call when a sergeant blew a whistle and instructed the men wandering about in regulation hospital bright blue to report to the YMCA hut. There an elderly chaplain appealed for a prayer of thanks that the war had ended. Listlessly, they recited the prayer, sang "God Save the King," and cheered Haig and Currie. Then some of the patients, including Sherwood, conspicuous at six-foot-six in hospital pajamas, slipped through the fence, hailed a Hammersmith bus, and "rode into the insane bewilderment of London's celebration," absent without leave. (Afterward he could not remember whether he was gone for a week or only four days.) They passed a field where German prisoners were working and shouted, "Hey, Heinie—the war's over!" The PWs grinned and waved, "not understanding, or not caring."

"The well-known British phlegm went west," Sherwood would write his mother. "There was a wild conglomeration of Tommies, Jocks, Australians, Yanks, sailors, wounded men, Italians, Belgians, Indians, French, Portuguese, Land-girls, 'Waacs,' 'Wrens,' Munition Girls, and everyone else in uniform parading and howling and hooting and dancing through the streets and breaking things, and hurting each other. It was much worse than New Year's Eve in New York." A 1928 novel, *The Sons of Cain,* describing the violence, pictured

> half a dozen men in uniform . . . straddling the lions while half a dozen other men were trying desperately to pull them off and climb on in their places. The whole Square was packed with stalled motors. There was a taxicab not twenty feet away and on top was a general officer as drunk as only a general officer may be. Upon his head was a battered bowler hat, and packed in and around and over him were a dozen or so buxom munition girls. The taxi top had buckled under them and collapsed,

sinking the whole party up to their armpits and the backs of their knees in the splintered ruin and they were all struggling and laughing and shouting. . . . A sailor on the step of a motor 'bus that was jammed crosswise beside the taxi, reached up and flipped the slipper from the foot of one of the girls and then with a diabolical grin, proceeded to un-garter and strip the stocking from her fat, pink leg, and wrap it around his hat for an ensign. His mate grabbed the hat and scaled it across the Square toward the Monument.

'Wot price the Adm'ral?' he yelled at Nelson. ' 'Ow's yer elbow fer this?' He climbed up the steps of the motor 'bus and caught the girl's other leg in both his hairy hands and pulled. The girl screamed and took hold of the general's belt. Together the two sailors tugged until the girl came free of the struggling mob on the taxi top and slammed into the side of the omnibus, head downward. Then they hauled her up hand over hand, kissed her and dropped her into the street below.

The note of cruelty seemed even to run through the joyous cockney song—an abandoned invitation to the dance—which seemed to capture the spirit of Armistice Day in London:

If I catch you bending,
I'll saw your legs right off. . . .

Some of the violence was to the Square itself. The "battle of vegetables," in which Australian and Canadian soldiers seized a truckload of Brussels sprouts from the Covent Garden market and heaved them at each other and anyone else in the way, was relatively good, clean fun. But there had been rows of captured cannon along the Mall, and these, Robert Sherwood wrote, "had been seized by wild Australians* and Canadians, who were always the riffraff of the British army, and [their wooden carriages] formed into a bonfire at the base of the Nelson monument. This fire was kept going for hours—perhaps for days. . . . The flames enveloped the column of the monument and seriously threatened to cremate Lord

---

* Among British Commonwealth nations, the most boisterous celebrations were in Australia, where the *Sydney Bulletin* would title a cartoon " 'Armistice, A Brief Suspension of Hostilities': Noah Webster." Among other acts of violence it portrayed the day as "the occasion for tearing up tramcars by the roots."

Nelson himself. The London fire department fought manfully to check this destructive enthusiasm, but the hilarious Colonials captured the hose and turned it on the firemen." The first fuel for the fire had been the billboard erected at the base of Nelson's column on which such patriotic slogans as "Buy War Bonds" were displayed. Added to the flames were the destination boards from stranded buses. The heat generated damaged the granite facing at the base of the column. Those unrepaired scars remain the only physical reminder of Armistice Day in London.

That night, helping the rowdy mob to stoke the fire, Sherwood found himself jammed against a short, pretty young woman in a blue tailored suit with a silk American flag pinned across her blouse. "Why?" he asked, pointing to it. "Because it belongs to me, you big Limey." They were both Americans, Sherwood having enlisted with the "Black Watch" when his own country seemed unlikely to fight the Germans, the young woman having come over in the chorus of *The Pink Lady* and taken other theater jobs since. "She also told me that she had a nice little flat near Leicester Square, and why not come up some time soon? Unfortunately, I forgot the address in the heat of the moment, so I never saw her again." From the episode Sherwood would weave his play (and film) *Waterloo Bridge* (1930).

Also evading hospital guards was a young officer, Charles Rainier, a victim of shell shock and amnesia, who slipped out of his hospital blue and wandered dramatically through the pages of James Hilton's novel (and film) *Random Harvest* (1941), until another Armistice Day years later would set him on course:

> The crowd were still singing 'Knees Up, Mother Brown' in the bars below. It sounded new to him, both words and tune, and he wondered if it were something else he had forgotten. He did not know that no one anywhere had heard it before—that in some curious telepathic way it sprang up all over London on Armistice Night, in countless squares and streets and pubs; the living improvisation of a race to whom victory had come, not with the trumpet notes of a Siegfried, but as a common earth touch—a warm bawdy link with the mobs of the past, the other victorious Englands. . . .

Edward Doughty, who was taken to Trafalgar Square after school, remembered that the crush "became unbearable. I found myself clutching my father's arm and being pressed mercilessly against a lamp-post which refused to yield. I was frightened far more than when the Zepps were overhead. A movie cameraman struggled to get pictures from the roof of a van. Along with my father and the crowd I waved to him. Some forty-odd years later I saw myself and my father when that film flashed on Television."

In the City the Stock Exchange and the Bank of England closed soon after eleven, after employees sang "The Old Hundredth" ("Praise God from whom all blessings flow") and the National Anthem. Employees dropped everything and took to the streets. One courtroom proceeding closed after approval was granted for artist Herbert Gustave Schmalz to change his name to Herbert Carmichael. Cecil Rolph Hewitt, seventeen and in the "rag trade" warehouse of Spreckley, White and Lewis, Cannon Street, swept out of the building with everyone else, work having ended "by informal mass resolution. . . . Frock-coated men and shirt-sleeved juniors and immaculate saleswomen and beautiful models, all calling out incoherently and twittering and (incredible in those austere premises) actually embracing and kissing." The Royal Exchange, nearby, was already black with people. A No. 11 bus, C. H. Rolph (as he would be later known) noted, was lettered in chalk FREE TO BERLIN and was cheered madly, and both men and women had taken off their boots and shoes so they could bang them against the metal advertisement sheets on the sides of buses to make a noise. At Mappin and Webb's Corner, tens of thousands of rain-soaked revelers took up "The Old Hundredth," which to Rolph was "a colossal sound, frightening, isolating."

At the corner of Princes Street he saw Grace Jessett, the pretty, red-haired telephonist at Spreckleys. Like everyone else, she was weeping with emotion, and he seized the opportunity to put his arm around her waist to comfort her. Although he was ten years younger, she did not push him away. Instead, she said she wanted to go to St. Paul's. It was, according to a policeman outside, "packed to the doors" for the second service since one o'clock, but they squeezed in and flattened against the wall. This time it was the silence of the vast, lofty space that was shattering.

At Simpson and Company, Manufacturer's of Ladies' & Gentlemen's Gaiters, where she was a forewoman, Hettie Bundock was elbowing her way to the Red Lion Court exit, off Fleet Street, when, glancing through the workroom door, she noticed one woman not joining the rush to celebrate. "With her head on her table, she sat sobbing alone. I went back to offer her small comfort; she had, that morning, official notification that her husband had been killed in action." Mrs. Bundock's own husband, Frederick, as far as she knew, was safe. She pressed her way to the Mansion House steps to join in "The Old Hundredth."

Sergeant Noel Wisdom, with four overseas stripes on his sleeve, and on leave from the 56th London Division, was on a bus picking its way through Fleet Street as the bells rang and boat whistles in the Thames hooted. An older man sitting next to Wisdom turned to him and said, "I expect you are glad you won't have to go out now." A soldier himself, and headed back to France, Private Arthur Warren of the Queen's Westminster Rifles found himself in the opposite situation as his bus stopped outside the Law Courts and he saw a young woman looking up at him. "War finished!" he shouted, as she seemed not to be aware of the joyous news. Then he noticed her "sad look" and her black dress. "I have always remembered that sad expression." (Fiction seems full of similarly sad-eyed women. Miss Jean Brodie's fiancé, Hugh, for example, is killed a week before the Armistice.)

Survivors in fact and fiction were Ford Madox Ford (still surnamed Hueffer, but he would de-Germanize himself) and his creation, the lumbering, autobiographical Christopher Tietjens. Separated from his wife as well as from his notorious mistress, Violet Hunt, Ford had spent three years away from marital discord as an officer in France, appreciating what Bernard Shaw (in *O'Flaherty, V.C.*) had called ironically the "rest and quiet" of the trenches. From Easton he would write to Stella Bowen, his current mistress, on Armistice Day, "Peace has come, and for some reason I feel inexpressibly sad. I suppose it is the breaking down after the old strain." While Miss Bowen would push through the crowds with their friend Erza Pound, Ford, although not in London himself, would put more of the surreality of Armistice Day into his novels than can be found in any other major fiction. Not only is Mark Tietjens felled with a stroke on Armistice Day; his younger brother, Christopher, newly returned from France, spends the last part of *A Man Could Stand Up*—the third novel in the *Parade's End* tetralogy—living through it.

His wife having taken all his money, Captain Tietjens starts out on the morning of November 11 from his house in Gray's Inn to try to sell the only piece of furniture Sylvia has left in it, an eighteenth-century cabinet, so that he can celebrate with his thus-far-platonic mistress, Valentine Wannop. He is not offered more than five pounds, and by noon is at Mark Tietjens's estate, where Marie Leonie lends him forty pounds. Tietjens's damaged comrades from the trenches invade his reunion with Valentine. One officer who earlier showed signs of madness finally cracks; and another, Christopher's commanding officer, turns out to be melodramatically dying from his wounds. To complete the surreal celebration, the other officers run away, leaving Tietjens and Valentine with the madman and the dying colonel. As Marie Leonie remembers,

> It appeared that they had secured a four-wheel cab in which with the madman and the other they had driven to . . . an obscure suburb, with sixteen celebrants hanging all over the outside of the cab and two on the horse's back—at any rate for a couple of miles from Trafalgar Square. . . . Valentine and Christopher had got rid of the madman somewhere in Chelsea at an asylum for shell-shock cases. . . . But the authorities would not take the colonel so they had driven on to Balham, the colonel making dying speeches about the late war, his achievements, the money he owed Christopher. . . . Valentine had appeared to find that extremely trying. The man died in the cab.
>
> They had had to walk back into Town because the driver of the four-wheeler was so upset . . . that he could not drive. Moreover the horse was foundered. It had been twelve, midnight, before they reached Trafalgar Square. They had had to struggle through packed crowds nearly all the way. . . . They stood on the top step of St. Martin's [in the Fields] Church, dominating the square that was all illuminated and packed and roaring, with bonfires made of the paving wood and omnibuses and the Nelson Column going up and the fountain-basins full of drunkards, and orators and bands. . . . They stood on the top step, drew deep breaths and fell into each other's arms. . . .

With a new husband, and marriage clearly not working, young Agatha Christie had begun classes at a business school. Although Archibald Christie had an office job with the Air Force, his wife had no idea that the war was ending until her teacher announced that classes were suspended for the day. "I walked into the street quite dazed. . . . Everywhere there were women dancing in the street. English women are not given to dancing in public; it was a reaction more suitable to Paris and the French. But there they were, laugh-

ing, shouting, shuffling, leaping, even, in a sort of wild orgy of pleasure: an almost brutal enjoyment. It was frightening. One felt that if
there had been any Germans around, the women would have advanced upon them and torn them to pieces. . . ." Walking out of her
school in the Strand was Aileen McKenna, a first-year medical student at King's College. "The sight of middle-aged and elderly City
Gents riding on the bonnets of London Red Buses clad in black
coats and striped trousers beating the bus direction boards like
drums" was a memory she would never forget.

With his work over, perhaps for good, historian Charles Petrie,
then a twenty-two-year-old civil servant in the War Cabinet Office,
was in the Strand area when he saw a girl "being sick in the gutter in
Savoy Court. . . . Nobody minded or appeared to think it odd. Inside
a number of young officers were trying to burn a German flag in
spite of the protests of the management." In a novel, *Europa in Limbo*
(1937), Robert Briffault described a similar scene, in which a party
of subalterns drags Laurence Foster, still recovering from his
wounds, to join them at the Carlton, "where they held an orgy in the
palm court. The ringleader . . . from a city battalion of the Middlesex, smashed a magnum of Mumm over the spike of a German Pickelhaube, lit cigarettes with Bradburies,* and scattered round a
bundle of five-pound notes. . . ." That the fiction was very close to
fact is evident from Arnold Bennett's diary, where he reported "that
the scene at the Carlton on Monday night was remarkable. Any
quantity of broken glasses, tables overturned, and people standing
on tables, and fashionable females with their hair down."

As Petrie was going home on the District Railway, escaping the
rowdyism, a "rather drunken workman" in his carriage kept mum-
bling, *in vino veritas,* "We've won the bloody war, but we'll lose the
bloody peace: you see if we don't."

Returning from Piccadilly, Arnold Bennett's valet, Brayley, reported, "You wondered where the people came from. You could
walk on their heads at Charing Cross, and you couldn't cross Piccadilly Circus at all." James Warner Bellah in *The Sons of Cain* wrote of
soldiers "carrying a legless man who had lost his chair and his pals.
They were watching the human pyramid form up the fountain in
Piccadilly Circus, only to tumble down into the basin and onto the
pavement below." Enlisted men would also break into the officers-
only Leicester Lounge, "out of bounds for all ranks" since 1914.

---

* Bradbury: a pound note.

At the Savoy was Noel Coward, listening to Alice Delysia, who early in the war had made famous Paul Rubens's recruiting song, "We don't want to lose you, but we think you ought to go." Now she sang the *"Marseillaise"* over and over again. His only war service had been in a Labour Corps in Hounslow, and with the Artists' Rifles in Essex, but he could put the most melodramatic home front aspect of war into his long-running pageant of English life, *Cavalcade* (1931), where the social unwisdom of a marriage between two young people is settled for their mothers by the arrival of the dreaded telegram on Armistice Day:

> JANE (*takes telegram*) Excuse me, will you. (*She opens it and reads it, and then says in a dead voice*) There's no answer, Gladys.
> GLADYS (*excitedly*). It's all over, milady—it's eleven o'clock—the maroons are going off.
> JANE. Thank you, Gladys, that will do.
> GLADYS. Yes, milady.
> (GLADYS *goes out.* JANE *stands holding the telegram. She sways slightly.*)
> ELLEN. What is it? What's happened? Oh, my God!
> JANE. You needn't worry about Fanny and Joe any more, Ellen. He won't be able to come back after all because he's dead. (*She crumples up and falls to the ground. Maroons can be heard in the distance and people cheering. The lights fade.*)

One of the dreaded War Office telegrams came to fashionable Bayswater, to the parents of Lieutenant Stephen Burroughs, King's Royal Rifle Corps. He had been gunned down by a sniper seven days earlier. Meanwhile, at Crichel House, Wimborne, his old school friend, Captain the Honourable Gerard Philip Montagu Napier Sturt, Coldstream Guards, eldest son of Lord Alington, heard the bells of ancient Wimborne Abbey. Slumped in his wheelchair, he was paralyzed from the waist down from wounds suffered in France. He had been "so romantically good-looking" in a "Pre-Raphaelite" manner, his friend Sonia Keppel remembered (she was the daughter of Edward VII's last mistress), that "he could have posed as a knight in armour to Burne-Jones." As the Armistice bells faded away, he died in the arms of his valet.

Unaware what had happened to either friend, Sonia and her sister Violet were pressing on gaily from Grosvenor Square to Nelson's Column, and that evening would be hoarse-voiced with cheering in the rain outside Buckingham Palace. Happily extricating herself from the rain-drenched crowds, Adela Hill discovered that her handbag, "a saucy affair of black silk," had been scissored from her arm, leaving her with a set of handles. Patrick Ludlow, a teenage actor in *The Luck of the Navy,* left the Queen's Theatre with his mother and uncle to find that many Piccadilly restaurants, "owing to the excess of exuberance—broken glasses, bottles, and even furniture—" had already closed. But still open was Rectors, a new club in Tottenham Court Road, where two bands were beating out "The Wild, Wild Women" and "I Don't Want to Get Well" ("for I'm in love with a beautiful nurse"). When they left at four "the rain was still pouring and the crowds were still cheering."

"Tom" Mosley remembered that the first time he saw Cimmie, Lord Curzon's daughter, was Armistice Night, when she was at the Ritz Hotel, draped in a Union Jack and singing patriotic songs; later that night (in her sister Irene's description) "she tore round Trafalgar Square with the great crowd setting fire to old cars and trucks to the horror of my father." Cynthia was twenty, and her future husband—the future Sir Oswald Mosley—was a wounded officer demobilized to work at the Ministry of Munitions. He had not followed Cimmie. Most of the merrymakers were "smooth, smug people who had never fought or suffered . . . laughing on the graves of our companions. I stood aside from the delirious throng, silent and alone, ravaged by memory. Driving purpose had begun; there must be no more war. I dedicated myself to politics. . . ."

In Bloomsbury Square sexologist Havelock Ellis "felt sad" about the "shouting and gesticulating crowds," he wrote Margaret Sanger, "for Peace does not bring back what War took away. . . ." Future novelist Vera Brittain, then a VAD, would have understood. Working in Queen Alexandra's Hospital in Millbank, she heard the maroons crash and went on cleaning dressing bowls, thinking, with her fiancé dead, "It's come too late for me." In *Testament of Youth* she would graphically recall the horror and the heartbreak.

In The Vale, Chelsea, just above King's Road, artist Charles Ricketts heard the first hooters sounding. "I am crying like a pig. . . . I go downstairs, bring up the Jeanne d'Arc banner painted months ago; this . . . is put on the balcony— [Charles] Shannon like a schoolboy, pleased with flag." (It would see service again in Shaw's *Saint Joan,* which Ricketts designed a few years later.) As one traveled farther from the pulsating center of London, outbursts of Armistice joy were in much lower key. Julia Starling, returning to the suburbs in F. Tennyson Jesse's *A Pin to See the Peepshow* (1934) after being caught up in the commotion, would find that "at Hammersmith the world was still boiling and seething like stew in a pot, but it was comparatively quiet once Stamford Brook station was reached."

Not fed by continuous reserves of the curious, outbursts in the suburbs were more modest. To her sister Vanessa Bell, pregnant with Duncan Grant's child, Virginia Woolf wrote from Richmond, after the guns and whistles had been sounding for half an hour, "I suppose we are at peace, and I can't help being glad that your precious imp will be born into a moderately reasonable world." In her diary she noted that "the rooks wheeled round," reacting to the booming of the guns, a housepainter gave "one look at the sky" and went on with his job, and another man, "toddling along the street carrying a bag out [of] which a large loaf protruded," was closely followed by a mongrel dog. Out of that came an Armistice Day scene in her novel *The Years* (1937) in which the old servant, Crosby, drags herself across Richmond Green to shop, unaware of the implications of the day. " 'Them guns again,' " she mutters, "looking up at the pale-grey sky with peevish irritation. The rooks, scared by gun-fire, rose and wheeled round the tree-tops. Then there was another dull boom. A man on a ladder who was painting . . . paused with his brush in his hand and looked round. A woman who was walking along carrying a loaf of bread that stuck half out of its paper wrapping stopped too. . . . The guns boomed again."

Virginia found the sounds of celebration "unsettling" (as did the rooks), telling Vanessa that she felt "immensely melancholy," despite the shouting schoolchildren. "There is certainly the atmosphere of the death bed. . . . At this moment a harmonium is playing a hymn, and a large Union Jack has been hoisted onto a pole." According to Leonard Woolf they "celebrated the death of a civilization and the beginning of peace by sitting in the lovely, panelled [drawing] room . . . and eating, almost sacramentally, some small bars of chocolate cream. . . ." But they had to go into London briefly, which only accentuated Virginia's disillusionment, already reinforced by the rain. "A fat slovenly woman in black velvet & feathers with the bad teeth of the poor insisted on shaking hands with two soldiers: 'It's thanks to you boys &c. &c.' She was half drunk already, & soon produced a large bottle of beer which she made them drink of; & then she kissed them, & the last we saw of her was as she ran alongside the train waving her hand to the two stolid soldiers. But she & her like possessed London, & alone celebrated peace in their sordid way, staggering up the muddy pavements in the rain, decked with flags. . . . The Heavens disapproved & did their utmost to extinguish, but only succeeded in making feathers flop & flags languish." She would have been no more pleased by the way in which East Enders kept their enthusiasm unextinguished. Upper North Street, which connected Poplar with Bow, was zealously mined for its tarred wooden paving blocks, which made a glorious bonfire, impervious to the gloomy rain.

In London as elsewhere in Britain, pub keepers were pulling pints as rapidly as they could, happily slogging behind their counters in a sludge of suds. The usual closing hours were widely ignored. Yet the sirens, hooters, and bells had done more than compel people into the pubs and the streets: by declaring a finality to the war, they declared an end, too, to the working through sorrow, to the stiff upper lip, that the pressures of war had exacted. In the small town of Redcar, Rachel Taylor listened to the sirens wind down and said, with tears in her eyes, "Too late for Harry." Her widowed sister-in-law fell to the ground and writhed in anguish. Harry's mother, with another son missing, and two others in France, "stood by helpless and sad."

Buried by a shell at Ypres in 1917, wounded by another 5.9 at the Somme the next year, Dan Walker was in a military hospital in the country, a collection of huts on the edge of a wood, when the matron, trailed by a doctor, entered to make an announcement to the ward. "The War is over," she said. "This is not a rumor. This is official. An Armistice has been signed. *The War is over!*" Almost any announcement in the past had been greeted with practical joking and handicaps ignored—"tippling each other out of bed, bashing at each other with pillows, pushing ourselves along the floor on our bottoms, stumps waving. . . ." But what Walker remembered most sixty-one years later was the "uncanny silence," akin to the eerie quiet on the line when the shooting stopped. "Our world, a bloody world, a world of suffering . . . at times close to the ultimate, also a world of laughter, excitement and comradeship beyond description. Our world, and now it was gone—ended—Napoo fini. . . . Now we were just some of the wreckage left behind."

Writer and artist Wyndham Lewis remembered what he called "the Post-war" beginning for him in a military hospital where he struggled with double pneumonia. "Enormous Anzacs, the flower of colonial England," he recalled, "were dying like flies [of influenza], having escaped all the hazards of war. Our hospital was full of them." Major Clement Attlee, his back injured when heavy timber in a trench, dislodged by a shell, collapsed on him, was in a hospital on Wandsworth Common when the hooters sounded; and Lady Astor heard the sirens in her covered tennis court at Cliveden, temporarily a hospital. At Devonport Military Hospital, John Brooks, a corporal in the Royal Engineers, broke out of the hospital with others in his influenza ward and commandeered a tram in Fore Street. "Loaded with chaps in hospital blue, that tram was driven over the Half-penny Bridge into and around Plymouth amidst crowds beyond description. . . . Our hospital blue got us lots of free beer."

At the Royal Naval College, Devonport, cadets had been disappointed the day before when sirens in the harbor sounded. It meant they might never get to sea. Happily it had turned out to be a false alarm, but the next morning the noise began all over again, and many ships had now hoisted a white ensign at the mainmast, with the German naval ensign half-mast, upside down. Back at the college the sick berth steward greeted them, blinking through his steel-rimmed spectacles, "Gentlemen, you've all joined too bloody late!" At Dover, the commandant of the Women's Royal Naval Service, Dame Katherine Furse (a daughter of John Addington Symonds), was inspecting a woman's unit at the secret experimental base when vessels "set their hooters going" and the "experimental" rockets and guns joined the din. The test ordnance was frighteningly real, and everyone ran for shelter, worried "that the whole place might blow up." And at English aerodromes pilots went wild, some with frustration at missing the show, others with glee at having beaten the odds. To keep them from celebrating in their aircraft, leaves were hastily issued wholesale. H. H. Balfour remembered ruefully, "I jumped into a Sopwith 'pup' and proceeded to go about as near killing myself in as stupid and senseless way by low stunting as I have ever done." Two days later he and his cronies were in Trafalgar Square, checking on tales of goings-on there. None seemed exaggerated. Still wearing his major's gold-peaked cap, Balfour— later Lord Balfour of Incrye, Undersecretary for Air—was arrested in Piccadilly Circus, on the Eros statue, for conduct unbecoming to an officer and gentleman. His group was sequestered overnight in Vine Street Police Station next to a cell crowded with drunken prostitutes.

Machines such as his "Pup" had waggled their wings all over

Britain (and all in violation of grounding orders), but only one flight was memorable. A Handley-Page V-1500 from No. 27 Group went aloft with forty-one on board, ten women and thirty-one men. The Berlin bomber would fly only over London.

At a camp where newly arrived Canadian troops were in training, recruits ran amok, firing rifles into the air, and had to be herded into quarters by English cadres. At Larkhill Camp, on Salisbury Plain, near Stonehenge, Private Percy Hubbard's company of the Royal Warwickshire Regiment was on parade when the officer in charge called his men to attention. "Men," he said, "you will be glad to know that an Armistice was signed today with Germany and the fighting has ended. Sergeant, that man over there smiled whilst at attention on parade. Take his name and number and have him brought up for Company Orders in the morning." There would be no celebrations bursting out of control at Larkhill.

In Newtownards, near Belfast in Northern Ireland, a lieutenant who had served in the Salonika campaign was training a unit of the Royal Dublin Fusiliers when his colonel paraded the troops at midday to announce the Armistice. The men were given a few pounds in advance pay and told to report to camp the next morning. Five hundred emptied their barracks and "most of the lads were by sundown well and truly sozzled. I myself with two other subalterns and a Scots captain of the Cameron Highlanders complete with kilt safely reached the local railway station where we took the train to Belfast, all of us in fine fettle. We were met by hordes of Mill girls, who lay in wait for the train. They laid hands on us and produced a motor car of sorts, crammed three of us inside, placing the Scotsman astride the bonnet with his kilt pinned under his chin. The car was then pushed by these harridans to the local Unionist Club where we were decanted, being welcomed by such members as could still stand up." The next morning he found himself awakened "by a *very* majestic and disapproving butler who revived me sufficiently to go downstairs to breakfast with my host, who I didn't know from Adam. He and his good lady treated me as one of their family."

Some soldiers had elected not to celebrate. In England after years in the trenches, Robert Graves, a young captain who had become an officer right out of public school, was at a training camp. The hysteria, he wrote in *Good-Bye to All That* (1929), "did not touch our camp much, though some of the Canadians stationed there went down to Rhyl to celebrate in true overseas style. The news sent me out walking alone along the dyke above the marshes of Rhuddlan (an ancient battlefield, the Flodden of Wales), cursing and sobbing and thinking of the dead." Siegfried Sassoon's poem, he added,

> Everybody suddenly burst out singing,
>   And I was filled with such delight
> As prisoned birds must find in freedom . . .

did not represent his own mood. Nor did it represent Sassoon's. "Walking in the water meadows by the river below Garsington on the quiet grey morning of November 11th," he wrote, "I listened to a sudden peal of bells from the village church and saw little flags being fluttered out from the windows of the thatched houses on the hill . . . . It wasn't easy to absorb the idea of the War being over. . . . I just stood still with a blank mind, listening to the bells which announced our deliverance." A bemedaled and wounded veteran who had nevertheless protested against the war, he had little interest in joining the orgy of celebration in London. Still, he had the instinctively curious bent of the writer, and took to Paddington Station, arriving in the evening rain to walk to a friend's flat for the night. Walking through the crowds, Sassoon remembered, "I felt no wish to shake hands with anyone." He had already written a surreal poem, "Fight to a Finish," in which, the war over, the Army is marching through London in a victory parade, cheered on by the jingo journalists who had egged on the war hysteria. Suddenly the soldiers fix bayonets and turn on the grunting and squealing crowd.

One of the best young poets his country had produced, who had already written some of the most vivid war poetry in English, had returned to the line in September after recovering from his wounds. In October, Wilfred Owen won a Military Cross in Flanders. In trying to fight his way across the Sambre on November 4 he was cut down by machine-gun fire. At noon on November 11 the Armistice bells in Shrewsbury had been pealing for an hour when the dreaded telegram arrived at his parents' home. He was twenty-five.

Convalescing from his wounds at his parents' home in Canterbury, one young writer-to-be, Gerald Brenan, had been considering "faking my symptoms at the medical board in order to avoid being sent back to France. I felt that after surviving for so long, it would be just my luck to be killed on the last day of the fighting." To avoid France he had already made an attempt to join the force which was being sent to Archangel in the Russian Arctic to support the counter-revolutionaries. "Then on November 11 the armistice came and I danced in the High Street with a policeman."

"When the sirens and church bells proclaimed the Armistice," conscientious objector Herbert Morrison, later a Labour Party cabinet minister, wrote, "I was digging for winter planting at Letchworth. I stopped digging, put my foot on my spade and experienced a quiet and profound emotion; relief that the carnage was over; sorrow for the fallen. It was my own two minutes' silence. . . ." From his home in Kent, Joseph Conrad saw less cause for rejoicing. Only the month before his elder son, Borys, had been gassed and shell-shocked in France. "I cannot confess to an easy mind," he wrote to Hugh Walpole. "Great and blind forces are set catastrophically all over the world." Rider Haggard was also less than jubilant. He had seen his career sputter and fade as a changing public turned from his fiction, and he had felt less than fulfilled by his wartime work. In his diary he prophesied, as he heard the guns firing, that the Germans "will neither forgive nor forget." England, he felt, "will never have a more deadly enemy than the new Germany. My dread is that in future years the easy-going, self-centered English will forget that just across the sea is a mighty, cold-hearted and remorseless people waiting to strike. . . . For strike they will one day, I am sure."

At Southwold, a coastal town only eighty miles from the front in Belgium, the Town Clerk, Ernest Cooper, had already noted the outbreak of Spanish flu and the November 9 decision of the vicar, who had renounced the habit for the duration, to take up cigar smoking again as a result of the Armistice negotiations. On the eleventh he noted the guns firing and bells ringing at Ipswich, whereupon "a few of us adjourned to the Mayor's house and cracked some bottles of Fizz. An impromptu Meeting was called and the Mayor read the Official Telegram from the Swan balcony, some soldiers came up on a waggon with the Kaiser in effigy, which they tied to the Town Pump and burnt amidst cheers. At 12.45 we went to a short thanksgiving service at the Church and nearly all work was knocked off for the day. . . ." Very likely the day resembled the experience of most small towns. Cities seemed to have more emotional pressure to release, as a Canadian artilleryman found in Sunderland when buying a civilian raincoat at Southridge's. "I just got my coat and payed for it when the sirens started to blow. The store girl pushed me out the door, saying, 'Get out! The war's over!' When I got outside everybody was celebrating. Girls were coming along with scissors and knives, cutting the buttons and badges off soldiers. I kept my badges in my pocket for safekeeping. Some men had lost every button they had. The girls were half drunk, carrying around champagne bottles. They got hold of the soldiers, threw them in the air and passed them from one crowd to another. Oh, they were just crazy. . . !''

In Liverpool telegraphists in the Central Post Office rose en masse as the clock struck eleven to sing "God Save the King," while elsewhere in the city most workers emptied offices and factories to repeat, on a smaller scale, the enthusiasm of London. In the Censorship Section of the Post Office, J. C. Silber suddenly felt very tired. He told his staff to go home for the day and to leave all mail not yet examined for tomorrow. The streets were black with people cheering, singing, dancing, while ships in the docks contributed their sirens and whistles to the din. And above it, "as a canopy of sounds," he recalled, "one heard the majestic tolling of the church bells. I was glad to get away from it all." Silber was a German spy who had to retain his cover until he could leave England. "It seemed impossible," he wrote in a memoir from Germany years later, "to go on playing for another minute the part that I had played for the last four years." He carried on. The next day he would attend a victory dinner at his club.

At Cambridge, where the ratio of women to men had climbed higher and higher as the war depleted the supply of male students, Phyllis Taylor waited, at eleven, for her geology lecturer, Mr. Thomas, to stride in, the tattered skirts of his MA gown dragging on the floor. He arrived at 11:05, ceremoniously extracted his watch, and announced, ignoring the sexual balance of the classroom, "Gentlemen, the Armistice has just been signed. There will be no further lectures in this University today. Good morning." Then he strode out. Outside, students smashed the offices of the *Cambridge Magazine*, the only college periodical that had been pacifist in policy. Annette Kennedy-Cooke, at Oxford, recalled the frustrations of female students in Lady Margaret Hall, when all work was abandoned and the male students, either too young or too frail to fight or demobilized wounded veterans, went off to celebrate. "We were forbidden to go into the town centre a few hundred yards away, and had to watch with envy the bonfires and fireworks and only listen to the rejoicing of the unrestricted males and the citizens of Oxford as they crowded the streets. It was like a dream. . . ." As a result she missed the episode in the Cornmarket, where a presumably drunk woman paraded up and down the street waving a flag, her skirts tucked up to her naked middle, cheered on (according to one report) "as a sort of presiding Venus" by the Army and Air Force cadets quartered in the colleges.

Elinor Pike had changed trains at Sheffield, traveling from one farm to another as part of the Women's Land Army. In her compartment was an Australian soldier, as she assumed from his bush hat. As the train sat in its siding, the soldier asked about her uniform and confided that his sweetheart in Mildura was going to marry him as soon as the war was over. Then it *was* over. The railway carriage throbbed with the sounds of hooters and bells. "We both jumped up," she recalled, "and shook hands very solemnly, vowing that we would remember that day, even though it was a very chance encounter." The train went on through Yorkshire, and eventually they alighted in a gentle rain. As they began to move shyly apart, the soldier turned to ask if she would mind giving him her name and address. "When I am married, if my wife has a daughter, I hope she will allow her to have your name." Although embarrassed by the suggestion, Elinor agreed "and watched him as he laboriously wrote with a pencil stump on a small piece of paper as we stood on the cold damp platform." A few years later she was astonished to receive a letter from Australia announcing the birth of her namesake, christened in advance on Armistice Day 1918.

In Birmingham, Labour stalwart Sidney Webb wrote to his wife that the city was "Mafeking," and that he assumed London was in a similar condition. The streets were "crowded with shouting people," his hotel was "full and uncomfortable," and there was "perpetual noise in his bedroom," where he had fled from the tumult. "Some strange things are going to happen in the nation," he prophesied, "what I don't know. . . ." In London, Beatrice Webb noted in her diary that London was a pandemonium, "soldiers and flappers being most in evidence." Paris, she imagined, "will be more spontaneous and magnificent in its rejoicing." And she wondered, "How soon will the tide of revolution catch up with the tide of victory?" Men of property, she predicted hopefully, "are everywhere secretly trembling."

In the Yorkshire seaport town of Whitby, Storm Jameson, having all but finished her first novel, was living with her family temporarily, her sea-captain father, whose ship had been torpedoed, having been returned from prison camp. With a son dead in the war, and his life at sea closed, he was worn and withdrawn. And her mother had become harsh and hard. With the Armistice expected,

Jameson listened daily for the signal—a gun fired from the cliff battery. It might free her to return to her husband in Canterbury: the marriage had been difficult, but family life worse. Finally she heard the sirens from the harbor and the bells from the town, the original signal somehow having escaped her. She went back into the house, trembling, scarcely able to speak. "It's the peace," she said.

"What is the good of it to *me?*" her mother answered in tears. Storm felt ashamed of her excitement and joy, but could not contain it. With a changed world, perhaps she had a chance to make something of herself—certainly not in Yorkshire.

In Lincoln, Stanley Downing remembered, he ran home to the sound of pealing bells, past the cathedral. "Two of the Cathedral dignitaries—one with a long white beard and both in cassocks, gowns and mortarboards—met in the middle of the Cathedral lawn, joined hands and performed a little jig of jubilation. In those days the Cathedral clergy were almost as stately as God Himself, and the sight of those two elderly dancers is my strongest memory of the day." *Knees up, Knees up, don't let the breeze up.*

Punch published a cartoon, "Armistice Day in the North," suggesting how the news was received in locales where dourness was the norm. Two stooped elderly men, hands plunged into the pockets of their coats, passed on the unpaved road. "The news is no sae baad the day," says Dagal. "Ay," says Donal, "—it's improvin'."

In the north of Ireland, in County Tyrone, Maria Marks, the youngest of thirteen children, was gathering the potatoes that her father and brother were digging when the church bells began to ring. They paused to thank God, then took the potatoes already dug and went home, to be with her mum. Maria's brother James, a machine gunner whose post had been overrun, had been killed only six weeks earlier. He had been attached to a Canadian unit, and the family kept his medals on a cross with a maple-leaf insignia—no solace at the moment. For Maria there would be no more sessions at school to knit socks for the soldiers, tucking names and addresses into the toes in hopes of getting a reply; and no more writing of names and addresses on hard-boiled eggs to be sent to the soldiers either. It had been a happy and exciting time for an eleven-year-old. Things would get worse with a peace that in Ireland would be no peace.

In Dublin the rejoicing was limited largely to soldiers, who drank too much and paraded in mobs, breaking windows and blocking traffic. "So ended the peace carnival," Joseph Holloway wrote in his diary, "in useless destruction of property." In Ballydon-

nal, in Lennox Robinson's play *The Big House* (1926), the inevitable
telegram arrives just before eleven, as the family readies itself to celebrate: "His Majesty deeply regrets. . . ." Ulick Alcock, heir to the
property now that his brother Reggie had been killed in action, has
died of wounds on the eighth of November. As previously instructed,
Paddy O'Reilly pulls on the big bell in the yard, and the elder Alcock insists that it was all "for King, for Empire. That's what matters."

"Damn King and Empire," says his daughter Kate. "They
don't matter, not to us."

Scotland, too, was more subdued—by nature, as the *Punch* cartoon had suggested. Students at the University of Edinburgh had
poured into the streets, jangling handbells and clogging the con-
course of the Central Station for a march, with flags, to George
Square. But, as the *Glasgow Herald* reported, "while the air was reso-
nant with the note of rejoicing, there was among the more staid . . . a
marked restraint—an inclination, while expressing heartfelt gratitude, to remember the days of suffering and loss through which the
way to victory had led." Yet in Glasgow's teeming tenement district
of Townhead, Jean Pithie remembered, every window seemed to
have a Union Jack or other pennant flying from it, although the
crowds in the streets at eleven were smaller than they might have
been because curmudgeonly employers refused to let workers loose
"until the usual evening time."

Winifred Deans, a student at the University of Aberdeen, remembered the Scot restraint giving way to jubilation, which first
arose from church bells and ships in the harbor. Then came the students, who tied up Union Street with an impromptu, piper-led procession, "ignoring tramcars and other vehicles. There was
tremendous excitement; newsboys were shouting, apprentices from
the shipyards were dashing about, all sorts of people had abandoned
their work and were out on the pavements shouting and hurrahing.
I never expected to see such a stir in Aberdeen, where people are on
the whole staid and undemonstrative. . . . In the days that followed I
often thought of Wordsworth's lines, written in the early days of the
French Revolution: 'Bliss it was in that dawn to be alive. . . .' "

In Penicuik, just south of Edinburgh, where newspapers had
published the premature Armistice news on the seventh, Gunner
John Thomson's dream in the trenches that the war would end on
the eleventh day of the eleventh month was being validated by
church bells. According to Robert M. Black's town chronicle (which

had recorded Thomson's dream), "There was no inclination to be boisterous—there were too many stricken homes for that. The Seaforths, however, held a dance at the Guild Hut, in celebration. . . . The Institute clock was lighted that night after many months, and the Parish Church clock was allowed to strike again."

On the evening of the Armistice Winston Churchill dined at Downing Street "in the large room from whose walls the portraits of Pitt and Fox, of Nelson and Wellington, and—perhaps somewhat incongruously—of Washington then looked down." The venerable walls still reverberated with the sounds of celebration in the streets while F. E. Smith, Sir Henry Wilson, and Churchill talked earnestly with Lloyd George about "the great qualities of the German people, on the tremendous fight they had made against three-quarters of the world, on the impossibility of rebuilding Europe without their help."

In the quiet of tiny, narrow Swan Walk, just across from the Apothecary Garden in Chelsea, between Cheyne Walk and the Embankment, Osbert Sitwell presided over a small dinner party. Invitations had gone out a week before. A captain in the Grenadier Guards with service in France, he was now home for good. In the confusion there was no way to call the dinner off. The guests were few. There was Chelsea painter Ethel Sands, recently returned from the hospital at Veules-les-Roses which she had financed and which she and "Man" Hudson had run. Horse-faced but vivacious, she was little like her mother, a wealthy American beauty admired by Henry James and painted by J. S. Sargent. There was also Lalla Vandervelde, art-patron English wife of a Belgian Socialist politician. The exotics, however, were the men—bearlike ballet impresario Serge Diaghilev, whose Ballets Russes had been the rage of London for two months, and his lithe principal dancer, Leonide Massine.

In the tiny, narrow dining room they talked of Nijinsky, reportedly just released from a prison camp in Austria; of the Bolshevik revolutionaries who had made Russia inhospitable to émigré ballet companies; of the possibility, suggested by Lalla Vandervelde, that all Europe might go Red; and finally of English friends. Little reference was made to the pandemonium only a few minutes away until Sitwell remembered that they had all been invited, days before, to a party at Monty Shearman's. Barrister and art patron (and later judge) Montague Shearman lived in the posh Adelphi, just below the Savoy, the upper portion of which abutted the Strand.

In the rain they found a taxi, all five squeezing in, Diaghilev in a huge fur coat; and they crawled through the Mall, the cab covered with revelers, and around Trafalgar Square into the Strand. The delays while they sat stranded gave Sitwell, who had survived the trenches, time to meditate about the crowds dancing in the streets, and he would begin a poem. "How Shall We Rise to Greet the Dawn?" was published a week later in *The Nation*—an appeal for meaningful change in the aftermath of war, in which the "Old Gods" and "idols" whose worship had made the war inevitable would be crushed

> Beneath the dancing rhythm of our feet.
> Oh! let us dance. . . .
> We must create and fashion a new God.

Sitwell would title another poem, sardonically, "The Next War (November 1918)," and dedicate it to his brother Sacheverell, a fellow officer in France. In it, with the war long over and its miseries faded, the old men who had "converted blood into gold" meet to consider a memorial to the "brave lads / Who were so willingly burnt, / Or blinded, / Or maimed, / Who lost all likeness to a living thing, / Or were blown to bleeding patches of flesh / For our sakes." But the richest of them points out that the cause they had fought for was again endangered, and the "kindly old gentlemen" rush out into the streets to urge the children of the maimed and the dead to again make the world "safe for the young." And, Sitwell closes, "the children / Went."

Eventually the party from Swan Walk reached the Adelphi, and the crush in the Adam room, "covered with decoration as fine as a cobweb" and hung with paintings by Bloomsburyites. "I remember the tall, flagging figure of . . . Lytton Strachey," Sitwell wrote, "with his rather narrow, angular beard, long, inquisitive nose, and air of someone pleasantly awakening from a trance, jigging about with an amiable debility."

Almost as striking as the gaunt Strachey was Augustus John, who made his appearance amid cheers for his officer's uniform. The thoroughly unmilitary John, as an official War Artist, had earned service regalia by his work in France painting British and Commonwealth troops in action. Seldom without the swish of skirts at his side, John happily brought several Land Girls in leggings and breeches with him, apparently picked up in the Strand. They were quickly drawn into the whirlpool of the party but the celebrating proved exhausting for John. "Thank the Lord that's over," he would write a friend later, ". . . we have to face the perils of Peace now."

David Garnett and Duncan Grant had already begun work for the day (as conscientious objector laborers) on Ottoline Morrell's farm when they heard of the Armistice. Dropping their tools, they bicycled hard to catch the next train to London, where they found the streets already packed with people "dazed with happiness." There were "lorry loads of girls—munitions workers in their working overalls, straight from Woolwich Arsenal, or the factories, their young faces stained bright yellow with the fumes of picric acid. . . . Some of them exchanged catcalls and badinage with passing soldiers, but most of them seemed to be in a religious trance." Eventually the pair found their way to the Adelphi, and Monty Shearman's flat. It was only afternoon, but the rooms were already packed with people.

"In a rush of pleasure," Garnett went over to speak to D. H. Lawrence, whom he had not seen for three years. Lawrence had kept away from London, harassed by police and conscription authorities, first because he was married to the cousin of Baron von Richthofen, the German air hero, second—despite his clear unfitness for service—because of his outspoken distaste for the war. It had helped not at all that his novels were thought of as obscene, the stock of one of them—*The Rainbow*—seized and confiscated. He looked ill and unhappy. "So you're here," he said, and went on talking to someone else. Frieda gave Garnett "a squeeze and a look of pleased astonishment," and he moved away to dance with Carrington while Henry Mond played the piano. "I suppose you think the war is over," Lawrence challenged them, "and that we shall go back to the kind of world you lived in before it. . . . It makes me sick to see you rejoicing like a butterfly in the last rays of the sun before the winter. The crowd outside thinks that Germany is crushed forever. But the Germans will soon rise again. Europe is done for; England most of all. . . ."

Garnett tried to change the subject. "Let's go out to Trafalgar Square," said someone. He had just time to say good-bye to Frieda before he found himself pulled outside, where a group from Shearman's party joined a crowd dancing in a ring, young Garnett with Henry Mond's mother, a fiftyish blonde. When he returned, hours later, with Lady Mond, his last memory of the party was "of seeing Henry Mond banging on the keyboard of the piano with a tumbler of whiskey clenched in each of his fists." Garnett went back to Trafalgar Square.

The Lawrences left not only the party, but London. An apparently autobiographical passage in the highly personal novel *Kangaroo* (1923) suggests that they fled the revelry and returned via St. Pancras Station to Chapel Farm Cottage, the Berkshire retreat near Newbury where they had been living in near-seclusion. Somers and Harriet in the novel "sat and sang German songs, in the cottage, that strange night of the Armistice, away there in the country: and she cried—and he wondered what now, now [that] the walls would come no nearer. It had been like Edgar Allan Poe's story of the Pit and the Pendulum. . . . So the black walls of the war—and he had been trapped, and very nearly squeezed into the pit where the rats were. So nearly! So very nearly. And now the black walls had stopped. . . ."

No party like Monty Shearman's endless one, with its revolving-door guests, could be without its sour side. A rumor young Aldous Huxley had heard appealed to the reflex anti-Semitism of his class and time. "My enthusiasm for peace demonstrations," he wrote his future wife, Juliette Baillot, "was a little damped by the fact that one fireman was killed outright with a hatchet while attempting to quench the bonfire in Trafalgar Square, and three policemen were thrown into the river—while the chief instigator of the outrages was that repulsive German Jew, Henry Mond." He, Carrington, and others had "celebrated peace" earlier, with Mond ("an admirable shekel-producing machine") paying the bills for the dinner at "the accursed Eiffel [Tower]"—a posh eating place in Percy Street. Yet he resented Mond, who would inherit his industrialist father's later title of Lord Melchett; and he resented Mond's money. "Late that night," Osbert Sitwell wrote, as if it were true, "a young man who had been at Monty Shearman's party set fire to the plinth of the Nelson column." It may be the story Huxley told; however, it is generally accepted that the blame belonged to the Commonwealth troops who, long before, had gone wild in the Square. Henry Mond had fought in the trenches, and was wounded while in command of a trench mortar battery of the South Wales Borderers when he was only eighteen. Brought up in the Church of England, he became a convert to the Judaism of his forefathers in 1933 and died after a long illness at the age of fifty. When he was allegedly committing the acts Huxley attributed to him, Mond was pounding the piano for the dancers in Monty Shearman's Adam flat, whiskey in hand, grateful to be alive.

When the party began to wind to a close, Osbert Sitwell wrote, he left the Adelphi alone, on foot. "In the street and square the tumult born of joy still continued."

* * *

In *The Aftermath,* eleven years later, Churchill recalled, and explained, the emotions which exploded on the first day of peace. "Who shall grudge or mock these overpowering entrancements?" he challenged. "Every Allied nation shared them. Every victorious capital or city in the five continents reproduced in its own fashion the scenes and sounds of London. These hours were brief, their memory fleeting; they passed as suddenly as they began. Too much blood had been spilt. . . . The gaps in every home were wide and empty. The shock of an awakening and the sense of disillusion followed swiftly upon the poor rejoicings with which hundreds of millions saluted the achievement of their hearts' desire." The ritual dance of the victor had its origins in prehistory. Even so, the dance was as much one of survivors as of victors. The work of the world had to go on, and the ache for those who would never come home could not be danced away.

THE REAL THING

Give my regards to Broadway,
Remember me to Herald Square;
Tell all the gang at 42nd Street
That I will soon be there. . . .

—GEORGE M. COHAN

America awakened to the Armistice. When news of the signing began to trickle out of the forest, it was nearly six in the morning, French time—one o'clock, New York time. Before three, both Associated Press and United Press had transmitted flashes on their wires, the delay representing new caution after the events of November 7. Ships in the mid-Atlantic intercepted the wireless message, one of them the troopship *Nansemond*, loaded with 1,200 horses, 165 enlisted men, and four officers. It was a prank, the men decided. Then they sighted a German submarine plowing peaceably along off the port side, just out of gun range. A few hours later they sighted another, behaving like a performing duck and evidencing no signs of hostility. Then a British Admiralty wireless was picked up, advising ships to cease zigzagging and blackout precautions. Soldiers crowded the decks singing and cheering. There was chicken and plum pudding for dinner, and the men lolled on deck smoking cigarettes into the night while the vessel kept a straight line to St. Nazaire, with all portholes resembling searchlights. "Why don't you make some noise?" a docker would ask later when they disembarked to news of the Armistice. "We left our voices on the ocean back there," a soldier said. "We've celebrated every inch of the way in."

The British S.S. *Mentor*, which took fourteen days of zigzag steaming to cross the Atlantic, was near Liverpool with a shipload of draftees, mostly from Kansas, and most of whom had never seen New York or the sea before embarking. When they were twenty-four hours at sea, according to T. Newton Jackson, the ship's wireless operator, the Kansans were "one sick mass of humanity," but then came the False Armistice report and after that the real thing. To maintain discipline no news was given the troops, but somehow word leaked out and "pandemonium was let loose. On disembarking everybody went wild. These boys in Liverpool with a girl on one arm and a goose on the other, is a memory I shall never forget."

In New York it took only a few minutes after the message was received for air-raid sirens built to warn against improbable German attacks to scream happily for the second time in five days. Munitions factories on the New Jersey bank of the Hudson, working night shifts, took up the cry until it could be echoed by ships in the harbor and newsboys in the streets.

An hour before dawn the war-darkened Statue of Liberty was illuminated to the accompaniment of ferry and tugboat whistles in the lower harbor, the final symbol that the news, this time, was authentic. And this time inhabitants of New York's five boroughs were prepared. Long before the usual rush hour, people snatched quick breakfasts and hurried forth to celebrate, armed with horns, bells, whistles, and anything else which might make a noise while the sun began rising on what would be a perfect autumn day. There was just enough breeze to float streamers and ripple flags, and many in the crowds had prudently preserved equipment used prematurely the Thursday before. What was missing—to the joy of the city's "white wings," the street sweepers—was the snowfall of paper and other flying debris, as the supply had been nearly exhausted five days before. The Fire Commissioner had warned, besides, of heavy penalties. Citizens with an impulse to throw things from windows used money instead of wastepaper. Handfuls of coins as well as paper dollars showered onto the sidewalks while mobs below set out to retrieve the largesse. Some civilians even stood aside and applauded while servicemen in the crowds stuffed pockets and hats with coins and bills.

Much of the money would go to enterprising bootleggers who were already working the streets by early morning. November 11, 1918, would be the last day until late in 1933 when liquor would be sold widely—if unlawfully—and imbibed freely across the forty-eight states. A "temporary" Wartime Prohibition Act, allegedly to conserve grain for food, had been a concession to the political power of evangelical Protestant forces which had succeeded in legislating temperance in half the states and which had pushed through Congress a sweeping constitutional amendment to make the nation officially "dry" on January 16, 1919.* It was already against the law to sell intoxicating beverages to men in military uniform, and bartenders who had widely ignored that regulation on the day of the False Armistice were more cautious if not more law-abiding on the day of the real thing. After leaders of the militant state Anti-Saloon Leagues had protested vigorously to President Wilson, he had ordered enforcement officials to be more watchful, although that injunction seemed not to apply in New York City, where bootleggers operated brazenly all day under the benign gaze of policemen. From sea to sea an ocean of alcohol would flow openly, usually until supplies were exhausted, and for days afterward hysterical letters would pour into the editorial offices of American newspapers decrying the abandonment of vigilance.

On the teeming East Side the shrill, wavering notes of shofars,

---

* The amendment would become fully effective a year from the date, following ratification by the requisite number of states.

ram's horn trumpets which in biblical times sounded from the hill-tops of Israel to summon the people to festivals and holy days, roused dwellers in the tenements at dawn. Blown by ghetto patri-archs from rooftops, chimneys, and fire-escape stairs, they pierced the din of sirens and bells, sending elderly people to their windows and young people to dancing in the streets.

Most children marched off unwillingly to school, then flung themselves into the thronged streets as soon as they were released— usually after the singing of hymns of thanksgiving and patriotic songs. Factories emptied of the night shift were seldom able to put a morning shift together, so great was the absenteeism and so numer-ous the spontaneous parades. On Long Island there was a curious turnabout. At Camp Mills the two thousand carpenters constructing winter barracks at wages which reached an awesome twelve dollars a day, threw down their tools at nine o'clock, hopped into their Fords, and headed to Manhattan to celebrate. No pleas by the camp quar-termaster, Colonel C. H. Smith, that troops would be hard-pressed for winter accommodations, availed. But the troops themselves, quarantined by rampant influenza, discovered two thousand former carpenters among themselves who quickly picked up the abandoned tools and began hammering and sawing with a vigor which sug-gested their enthusiasm about returning to civilian work and their frustration over not celebrating in the world outside. The faithful would be rewarded with the first passes to be issued when the flu quarantine was lifted.

At Camp Mills was a troublesome and unmilitary lieutenant, Francis Scott Fitzgerald, who had writing aspirations but had bus-ied himself in New York, partying in the King Cole Bar, with its Maxfield Parrish decor, in the St. Regis Hotel on Fifth Avenue. (As a Princeton playboy he had learned the right places in which to get very drunk in style.) His unit had entrained for Quebec, where it was to board a troopship going to France, but it was recalled to unglamorous quarantine at Mills when the Armistice came. Fitz-gerald liked to remember marching onto a troop transport, steel helmet slung at his side, but that was among his earliest fictions. His Jay Gatsby would go to France to win medals and rise to major, making amends for Scott. Those who are certain that on Armistice Day Fitzgerald swaggered into the Café Continental in Paris, "where Ross, Woollcott, Winterich and the rest of the S & S'ers*

---

* The U.S. Army newspaper *Stars and Stripes,* with Harold Ross, later of *The New Yorker,* future critics Alexander Woollcott and John T. Winterich.

were supposed to be throwing a memorable brawl," recall, rather, Budd Schulberg's fictional version of the novelist's life in *The Disenchanted* (1950). (Zelda Fitzgerald, still Zelda Sayre, remembered how the Armistice was announced in Montgomery, Alabama, "with the flash of a message across the vaudeville curtain. There had been a war, but now there were two more acts of the show." Her alter ego, Alabama Beggs, in *Save Me the Waltz,* would think about the war "all night long. . . . Things would disintegrate to new excitements.")

Another future American writer would get as far as Canada, having been accepted at the Royal Flying Corps New York office on Fifth Avenue for recruit training as a pilot. William Falkner (as he still then spelled his name) was nearly twenty-one and filled with frustrated dreams of glory. The American army's pilot training program had rejected him—he was too short. In Toronto, visions of glorious fatality were cut short by the flu epidemic, which interrupted training. And then the war was over. He may have never gone up in a "Flying Jenny," the cheap, slow, American-made aircraft used for pilot lessons, but the Armistice would prove no block to his fantasies as he had already begun creating a personal myth of Faulkner the flyer, beribboned, wounded, daring. He wrote home of his reckless flying and returned to Mississippi in fancy officer's uniform, complete to swagger stick, even getting off the train in his home town of Oxford limping with a mythical wound; but he had been discharged ingloriously as a cadet. Several published stories about combat flying later, he had fixed upon a wartime record for public consumption. In 1946, after another war, Malcolm Cowley, writing an introduction to the *Portable Faulkner,* sent to the author, for verification, copy which noted that the novelist had seen action as a pilot and had crashed. At first Faulkner offered no correction. Then, hoping to avoid embarrassment, he wrote Cowley, "If you mention military experiences at all . . . say [only] 'belonged to RAF 1918.' " Later, even more worried, he suggested that Cowley seek no additional details. "The only point a war reference or anecdote could serve would be to reveal me a hero, or . . . to account for the whereabouts of a male of my age on Nov. 11, 1918."

John Dos Passos would place one of his heroes in *U.S.A.* as having his fill of wine and women in tumultuous St. Nazaire on Armistice Day, but he could do it realistically, having been a volunteer ambulance driver in France (as had Cowley, E. E. Cummings, and Ernest Hemingway) in 1916, when he was eighteen. Now he had been waiting to fight and would write from Camp Merritt, New

Jersey, the week before the Armistice that he was "still about to sail for France; nearly crazy with waiting and with the fear that we won't go." On Armistice Night—actually two hours into the morning of the twelfth—his unit finally left to board the U.S.S. *Cedric,* carrying replacement troops for quiescent Europe. He had seen nothing of the revelry either, but would put fragments from purported newspaper accounts in his "Newsreel XXIX" in the first *U.S.A.* novel, *1919.* One would record in New York

[J.P.] MORGAN ON WINDOWLEDGE
    KICKS HEELS AS HE SHOWERS
        CROWD WITH TICKERTAPE.

Mayor Hylan's canceled Manhattan parade of the Thursday before became a Monday fact, but crowds around City Hall prevented it from beginning as planned. The Mayor and Mrs. Hylan threaded their way to Canal and Lafayette Streets with police lieutenants and large flags to begin the march up Fifth Avenue and Broadway to Columbus Circle. There Hylan rested his weary feet and reviewed the rest of the parade, which, as it moved north, picked up participants, including a previously scheduled United War Charities parade. It featured six elephants from the Hippodrome who proved the only marchers able to clear a path for themselves. Ten thousand Boy Scouts formed at the Sheep Meadow in Central Park and marched down Broadway and Fifth Avenue to Washington Square, where they disbanded, but not before, a young Scout, Milton Loewenthal, recalled, the twenty-five-by-forty-foot flag they carried, taut, was laden with coins thrown into it by onlookers along the march route. The Scouts closest to "Old Glory" pocketed the bonanza and gorged themselves with ice-cream sodas.

Their elders in uniform—or partial uniform, since servicemen and young women seemed to be exchanging hats and coats through the day and into the evening—found more mature joys. As newspapers reported, one feature of the celebration was "the promiscuous kissing of soldiers and sailors by good-looking girls ... evident on every street of the city. The soldier or sailor, whether of the United States or the Allies, who got through inosculate, had only his fleet-footedness to thank for it, for enthusiastic and comely young women were everywhere and displayed a vivacity which was the envy and despair of disregarded civilians." After-dark inhibitions would loosen even further than a family newspaper could report.

Effigies of the Kaiser materialized everywhere, but their pervasiveness suggested something in the national psyche. One motor truck carried an oversized tin can with the head of William Hohenzollern thrust out of its mouth and the inscription, "We've got the Kaiser canned this time." At Fifth Avenue and Thirty-sixth Street a sidewalk artist had scratched a sketch of the Kaiser which people were encouraged to stamp upon. Another appeared, complete to bristling, upturned mustache, at Broadway and Seventieth Street. Near City Hall a young man trundled a wheelbarrow in which an effigy of the Kaiser rested uncomfortably, while another young man walked alongside belaboring Wilhelm II with a policeman's nightstick. At Battery Park an effigy was delivered in a wagon painted to resemble a country hearse. Scaffolding was erected on which the bundle was then hung, after which someone made a speech in which the Kaiser was consigned to hell. The dummy was then taken down and fastened to a stake on the Battery wall. A match was set to it, and while it burned briskly in the bay breezes, soldiers and sailors executed an Indian war dance around the flames to the cheers of several thousand spectators.

On lower Fifth Avenue a delighted throng watched while men tossed a dummy of the Kaiser from the top floor of a tall building. A rope not quite long enough to reach the outstretched hands of watchers below was attached to the figure, so that the screams of women as the figure plummeted down ceased abruptly when the plunge was arrested just above their heads. (The effigy would be dropped over and over again until it fell apart.)

An alleged facsimile of the Kaiser was carried down Fifth Avenue in a coffin by a group of boys. Made from two soap boxes nailed together, the coffin was draped in black and at the end hung a large "iron cross" with the lettering "Resting in Pieces." Another boy dressed in black, head framed by a high pasteboard collar, marched solemnly before the coffin, eyes fixed on a large "Bible" which he kept open before him. Beside him tramped another boy who tolled a knell with wooden spoon and large frying pan.

In the heavily German Yorkville section, residents escorted an effigy of the Kaiser, in a coffin made from staves of a mackerel barrel, to the Men's Night Court on East Fifty-seventh Street near Third Avenue. In front of the Court House a band played "The Star-Spangled Banner" while the procession moved into the large hall below the courtroom with "the remains of Bill." After a funeral oration over the body, the celebrants decided to go to court "to bring justice to civilization." The coffin was then borne upstairs by five men followed by a mob of yelling people, only to be stopped at the door by a court attendant. They were in the wrong place, he said. The trial should be held in Brooklyn.

"We want to give the Kaiser fifty years," shouted one of the pallbearers through the door.

"I am sorry, gentlemen," Magistrate Frothingham called out from the bench, "I cannot accommodate you. All I can do is to sentence your prisoner to the workhouse for six months. That is the severest penalty that can be meted out by this court. But that will not satisfy you men according to your present state of mind."

"You bet it won't," said a voice from the crowd.

"You can leave him to us," said a young woman. "We'll take him to the street and attend to him." And to the accompaniment of a helpful dirge from the band outside, the throng proceeded slowly down the stairs and into the middle of Fifty-seventh Street, where several gallons of kerosene were poured over the Kaiser. As he was loudly consigned to the lower regions, a torch was applied. While the flames flickered, the crowd, augmented now by thousands more, marched around, then away, singing, "There'll Be a Hot Time in the Old Town Tonight." Inside, the court resumed.

Effigies seemed everywhere. Another was suspended on a wire running from a building at Eighth Avenue and 125th Street to the trolley wires, and thousands cheered when a match was applied, cheering again when soldiers halted and climbed atop a trolley car to apply another match to the Kaiser's feet. In Grand Central Station railway porters marched single file carrying a flag with two gold stars marking their war dead. The last porter pushed an invalid chair in which reclined a figure of the Kaiser, with a sign declaring, "Gone to Perdition." In Wall Street, crowds were diverted by a dummy of the Kaiser washed down the curbing by a fire hose.

Even the upper classes had their Bill, as a crowded house at the Metropolitan Opera heard Louise Homer and Enrico Caruso, with a vast chorus, sing the anthems of the Allies between acts of Saint-Saëns' *Samson and Delilah*. A *coup de theatre* had been arranged by a stage technician who exhumed the dummy Siegfried used in Wagner's music-drama after the hero has been slain by Hagen. It was transformed into a mock Kaiser during rehearsal, and with a helmet on its head it was carried on a gibbet via the backstage exit to Thirty-ninth and Broadway, the day's "supers" stabbing at the Imperial corpse with stage swords while conductor Pierre Monteux led his singers and instrumentalists (excluding the unwieldy string basses) up to Forty-second Street and back to strains of Charles

Gounod's *"Marche Funèbre d'un Marionette."* How many understood Monteux's commentary in choice of selection is unknown, but the crowds loved it.

To Sigmund Sameth, watching the tumult from his father's shoulders at 110th Street where the elevated tracks (since dismantled) made a bend, the sight of the first tanks—never to cross to France—was unforgettable. "To see these vast clanking machines pressing their tread impressions into the street surface as if it were soft clay like the clay in kindergarten verged on the miraculous." Charles Baldwin, then a boy living in more posh surroundings, remembered abandoning his favorite dessert, "Floating Island," to dash from his Fifty-eighth Street flat to see the crowds and the effigies. The family chauffeur, Ezra Lufkin, was already at the curb in the elegant Pierce-Arrow, pumping hard at the accelerator to make explosions backfire, while crowds led by soldiers were singing,

> *Late last night in pale moonlight*
> *We saw you, we saw you.*
> *You were cutting our barbed wire*
> *When we opened rapid fire.*
> *If you want to see your father in the Fatherland,*
> *Put your head down, Fritzie boy!*

Without further ado, we all rushed over to Fifth Avenue, I still with bib, lunch forgotten. . . . Fifth Avenue had been renamed The Avenue of the Allies. That day it was a mass of flags of all Allied nations. . . . Up and down the Avenue, people were shouting and hugging, and, yes, hanging effigies of the Kaiser to lampposts. A few of these were dragged down and burned in the middle of the road. As if out of the concrete or from manholes small brass bands appeared. Many persons began to sing along with them. "Pack Up Your Troubles," "Long, Long Trail," "Over There." . . . Men in uniform were hugged and kissed. In one of the side streets, people had dragged out all sorts of burnable objects into the middle of the roadway, piled them up and had a large, dangerous-looking bonfire going. The scene, looking back, was reminiscent of the French Revolution. To a small boy it was frightening.

Some in New York stuck to business. Young publisher Alfred Knopf was lunching with novelist Joseph Hergesheimer in the bar of the Claridge Hotel. They stood to exchange greetings about what a wonderful day it was, and then got down to contracts and books. Attached to Camp Upton on Long Island, where his service musical *Yip! Yip! Yaphank!* had played through September, but now out of uniform awaiting discharge, Sergeant Irving Berlin was making the rounds of music publishers. He was seeking donations of sheet music for Army camps when the streets became impassable and offices closed. He would now turn out songs of demobilization like "I've Got My Captain Working for Me Now." Even one of his discarded *Yaphank* songs would come in handy later on, although it had seemed too sentimental for soldiers to sing, and clearly was inappropriate for the deflation of peacetime. It was called "God Bless America."

The normal business of the day—those things which could not be put off—also remained, from births to funerals. Some babies unscheduled to be born at home took their first breaths there anyway because it proved so difficult to press through the teeming streets to a hospital; and on 129th Street in Harlem, where David Langdon's dying had been interrupted by the revelry of the seventh, his burial was delayed on the eleventh by the difficulty of getting the hearse through the parades and the stalled traffic to St. Raymond's Cemetery in the Bronx.

Among the groups arranging impromptu parades on Armistice Day were the Socialists, who had scheduled a Carnegie Hall rally to celebrate the German revolution. Just beyond Thirty-fourth Street a group of soldiers and sailors waded into the procession, tearing down red flags and assaulting men and women in the line of march. The next day some newspapers would praise the way the pacifist radicals had been roughed.

The night in Manhattan was as brilliant as it was noisy. Fuel administrator Mercer Mosely had announced at noon that the city authorities wanted New York, long dark, and for weeks before the premature armistice shorn of crowds because of concerns about influenza contagion, illuminated that night as never before. "Let us give the Kaiser," he urged, "a wake so bright and gorgeous that for the moment the memory of all the fires his armies started and all the guns his armies fired will be smothered and obscured." The night was even memorable for its low incidence of serious crime, only one death by shooting reported. Acts of vandalism were another matter but—given the occasion—attributed to high spirits rather than criminal intent.

At the Garrick Theatre, in its second season of imported productions by Jacques Coupeau's Parisian *Théâtre de Vieux Colombier,* a new play opened on November 11. The policy of the repertory company was to present a new play each week, beginning on Monday, and the coincidence of scheduling resulted in the opening of a play by Georges Clemenceau, *La Voile du Bonheur.* "Play by 'Tiger of France' Comes at Fitting Time," the New York *World* headlined its review the next day. What the performance proved was that Clemenceau had been a better journalist than dramatist, but a crowded house cheered Coupeau's speech, before the curtain rose, about his pride in presenting the Premier's play "on the day of France's salvation." When the curtain came down, the audience streamed out into Thirty-fifth Street to join the other celebrants.

"A great many statesmen made speeches during the day," the *Evening World* would observe, "but nobody listened to them." Just to the south, in Menlo Park, New Jersey, one speech, made privately was a product of the day which can still be listened to. Thomas Edison, inventor of the phonograph, had been so moved by the occasion as to break his vow never to permit his voice to be recorded for the public and made a "peace record," a plea for a nonchauvinistic approach to victory. "This is Edison speaking," he began. "Our boys made good in France. The word 'American' has a new meaning in Europe. . . . [But] I hope that while we do reverence to the memory of our brave boys, some [who will remain] in France, we shall not forget their brothers in arms who wore the uniform of our allies."

In Livingston, New Jersey, Lieutenant Arch Whitehouse, a flier home on leave from England for family reasons (he had orders to go on to the Italian front) had been taken by his father to the big city—Newark—to see the victory celebrated. The extra sheen he had put on his belt and boots, he quickly realized, was out of place. "Mobs and gangs roared through the streets, dragging stuffed effigies of the Kaiser and [Crown Prince] Little Willie. Flivvers rattled along the highways, daubed with the crudest vulgarities of triumph. . . . Metal chamber pots were most prominent, and continued references to human excreta were swung aloft. . . . A few men in khaki or blue were to be seen amid the howling mobs, but most of the frenzied commotion seemed to be promoted by bedraggled women, screeching girls, and middle-aged gaffers who were stupidly drunk." And when his father retreated to local saloons in Livingston to celebrate less riotously, the pair learned that no man in uniform could legally be served beer or liquor. "Let's be sensible," suggested Arch, hiding his disappointment. "Let's celebrate at home, away from all this rag-tag."

In Hartford, Connecticut, the noisiest celebrants in the two-hour-long parade rode in a truck labeled "Maxim Silencer Company," and a butcher's van bore a stuck pig labeled "Kaiser." In small towns across New Jersey, jubilation was more restrained. Church sextons climbed to their belfries to peal the news, schools again emptied, and impromptu processions materialized. In tiny Berlin, in a large coffin trundled by a hearse, the Kaiser was buried with elaborate ceremony for the second time in five days. In most places where William Hohenzollern was hanged, burned, pummeled, poked, dragged, dropped, or quartered, his presence furnished a safety valve for strong emotions. Wreaking vengeance upon his stuffed likeness, crowds were strangely satisfied that they had contributed something to the victory.

In Philadelphia the Kaiser rode perched on milk wagons, trailed tied to the tailboards of garbage wagons, was the central figure in dozens of happy "funeral corteges," was strung by his neck in the window of a department store on Market Street before a hooting crowd. One burlap Kaiser Bill was thrown from person to person in the way a football would have been heaved in a forward-pass play, each time to tumultuous applause. Meanwhile, from three o'clock in the morning through the twenty-one hours to midnight, citizens marched and shouted and sang. Even eighty-year-old merchant king John Wanamaker, who had marched in parades after the Civil War and again after the Spanish-American War, trudged a two-hour stint, and then announced, "This day, and this celebration of it, shows us that God still reigns."

As early as 4:30 A.M. crowds had begun gathering at Philadelphia's Independence Hall to pay homage to the long-cracked and long-silent Liberty Bell. Most cities across the nation had no such symbol as Liberty Bell or Statue of Liberty, but Washington, rich in public landmarks, was different. Once the State Department announced the official news at 2:45 A.M., people began to gather around the White House, the Capitol, the Washington Monument, and other locations appropriate for the release of patriotic fervor. A hurried meeting was scheduled by Secretaries of War and Navy Newton Baker and Josephus Daniels, and War Shipping Board Director Edward N. Hurley, who issued joint orders to halt all overtime and Sunday work on government war contracts. But not yet production itself. Cancellation telegrams would go out the next day, the government eventually unburdening itself of its purchase obligations for about thirteen cents on the dollar.

Congress met in traditional joint session at one o'clock to hear the President, and thousands of government workers already released for the day flocked to Capitol Hill to see what they could of the show. Many Senators and Representatives had not yet returned from their home districts, where their campaigns for reelection had only concluded the Tuesday before, and there were scores of vacant benches on the floor. Two or three Congressmen had donned frock coats for the great moment in history, but most arrived without fanfare or formality, the greatest cheers reserved for Representative Fiorello LaGuardia (later mayor of New York), who arrived in his Army aviator's uniform. When President Wilson arrived, one Senator stubbornly sat out the standing ovation. Robert La Follette of Wisconsin had opposed the war.

Wilson's high-pitched, academic voice contained no hint of jubilation. He read the terms of the Armistice, which everyone already knew, and then added, much as had his counterparts in Britain and France, "The war thus comes to an end; for, having accepted these terms of armistice, it will be impossible for the German command to renew it." The arbitrary power of the German military caste, he declared, was destroyed; but even more gratifying to him was the likelihood that the victorious nations would now unite to secure "disinterested justice, embodied in settlements which are based on something much better and more lasting than the selfish competitive interests of powerful states."

At 1:35 P.M. the session ended, Wilson returning to the White House to the accompaniment of cheering crowds. He had managed only two hours' sleep, working (with his wife, Edith) on long, coded cablegrams, including one from Clemenceau, until one in the morning. Two hours later he was awakened by news of the signing. Twelve hours later he was reviewing parades passing the White House, and that evening he and Mrs. Wilson went out to see the crowds and watch the lighting of campfires on the White House ellipse, forty-eight huge fires, one for each state. Scheduled earlier to inaugurate War Charities Week, the fires blazed into new symbolism as part of the celebration of peace. Delegations bearing placards for the states gave the President, who was unexpected, a rousing ovation over the constant din, while overhead an Army flier circled, his path traced by searchlights and by varicolored rockets. Swarms of celebrants enveloped the presidential car as it proceeded through the city, overwhelming its token Secret Service protection. Only when soldiers locked arms and formed a ring around the car could it slowly make its way back.

Wilson's elation seemed to have no peak. It was not presidential custom to go to foreign embassies, but November 11 was the birthday of the King of Italy, and the prearranged occasion for a ball. Uninvited, Wilson, in white tie and tails, and Edith, in a resplendent gown, turned up unannounced at eleven at the Italian Embassy, where officials were happily flabbergasted. He toasted the King, remained an hour, and left, but as Edith Wilson put it, "The day had been so crowded with emotion that we were too excited to sleep when we got back to the White House. So kindling up the fire in my room we sat on a big couch and talked until the early hours of the morning. Then my husband read a chapter in the Bible and went to bed."

Franklin and Eleanor Roosevelt awoke at 2121 R Street on November 11 to the sounds of jubilation, hastily dressed, and were in the streets themselves, joining the impromptu processions as if Roosevelt were not the Assistant Secretary of the Navy—and as if she had not recently confirmed her worst fears about her husband and Lucy Mercer. "The feeling of relief and thanksgiving," Eleanor remembered long afterward, suppressing the strains in their relationship, "was beyond description." (It was not the same for her uncle, Theodore, for whom the noise of screaming sirens and automobile horns meant an ambulance ride from Oyster Bay on Long Island through traffic jams to a hospital in Manhattan. A colonel in the Spanish-American War, he had wanted to fight again but had been turned down by Woodrow Wilson. A hospital spokesman downplayed the former President's ailment as a flare-up of lumbago, concealing, for a time, his last illness.)

At the American Federation of Labor offices, where Samuel Gompers had viewed the months since April 1917 as the greatest opportunity that organized workers had ever had, the AFL president was reportedly overheard, according to Socialist leader Norman Thomas, expressing regret that the war had ended so soon, before the gains he had envisioned, such as a nationwide eight-hour day, could be realized. The end of war production, and with it the end of Labor's political clout, along with the flood of returned soldiers into the labor market, were gloomy prospects. For many of the government employees celebrating in the streets, it was the end of a Washington adventure. They would no longer be needed or wanted. Women at the War Department sang of the men they encountered, and the lively times they had:

> *We fought no battles stern and hot*
> *In No-Man's-Land by dark. . . .*

The nearest to a front-line experience they encountered, they confessed happily, was to fight off amorous soldiers in nearby parks. Now women would have a new fight on their hands—to find any job at all back home, in competition with the returning men.

The False Armistice having exhausted emotions, the authentic end on Monday lacked much of the spontaneity of Thursday. Not, however, in the Atlantic seaport of Newport News, Virginia, southeast of Washington, which erupted violently. Outrage had long simmered about the gouging of men in uniform in what was largely a military base under civilian administration. Now it exploded in what was no outburst of wrath against a stuffed Kaiser Bill. Thousands of soldiers and sailors rampaged, wrecking streetcars, raiding restaurants, and smashing plate-glass windows, and setting bonfires in the streets with anything that could be burned, including wrecked delivery wagons. Civil and military police, who had watched the riot begin as an orderly parade of holidayed workmen, schoolchildren, and sevicemen, stood by, too thin in numbers to interfere.

Tales of men about to leave for France, or who were about to be inducted into the Army, were legion. Ships only a few hours or even days out were turned back and draft notices canceled. In officer training at the Pennsylvania State College, Fred Waring, who already had a student band, was in a unit set to leave the next morning. "A friend of mine was in the contingent before mine," Waring recalled, "and he was already in Siberia. He stayed for three years!" That night Penn State students had a wild celebration which began as a parade through town and cut a wide swath of destruction. "I was disgusted and ashamed of myself," said Waring, "and I didn't think too much of my fellow students. For instance, we walked through the big candy store and just took everything there was, great huge bars of chocolate. We just *destroyed* the movie house. We did everything you're not supposed to do . . . because the war was over and you were supposed to make an idiot of yourself."

In the small western Pennsylvania town of McKeesport, William Walk was due to report to his draft board at 10:00 A.M. to be sworn into the Army. He reported on time and was given an armband marked "U.S.A." to wear over his civilian suit, after which the local Mothers of Democracy chapter presented each inductee with a khaki knitted vest. Then the new soldiers marched to the Baltimore and Ohio depot to entrain for Camp Meade. "At 11:00, all Hell broke loose! Whistles were blowing, bells ringing, people screaming. We were told the war was over and we were discharged right there." Walk had spent one hour in the Army. Several weeks later a representative of the Mothers of Democracy came to his house to reclaim the sweater. On March 18, 1919, he would receive a check for $1.00 from the United States Government for his military services.

Walter Morgan, of the nearby town of Bellevue, served slightly longer—until 4:00 P.M. on the eleventh. His one-dollar check came earlier, on December 19—from Camp Greenleaf, North Carolina. John Earl McKeever of Pittsburgh was not due to report for induction until 6:30 P.M. At the Pennsylvania Station he and others were sent home—the pattern undoubtedly one repeated all over the nation.

To the north, in the normally quiet Pennsylvania town of Port Allegany, the Reverend Loyal Adams again celebrated the Armistice. This time he had not even begun painting at the Roys house. The whistles had begun to blow before he was out of bed. There were two parades that day, but little William was in neither. He had the flu.

No city across the country remained subdued, but the farther west in the United States, the earlier the news arrived, four time zones banding the land from the Atlantic to the Pacific. In the second, Chicago appeared to set the pace for rowdiness, turning Armistice Day into a carnival, a gigantic costume party which began in darkness and continued into the darkness of the following night. Disheveled girls snatched caps from soldiers and hats from civilians, and were kissed and embraced in return, some quickly disappearing together in the night. According to the *Tribune,* "Harlequins danced beneath the street lamps in the arms of pretty girls dressed as men. Uncle Sam strode with dignity beside an uproarious Charlie Chaplin. Girls wore short trousers of boys, long ones of men, and one was seen in the full regalia of an army officer. Men jammed their way through the crowds with inverted waste baskets over their heads to protect their hats from the sticks and stones of the men and women revelers who lined the walls of buildings. Hundreds of overloaded men reeled along the streets beside women reeling with hysteria." A million people, the newspaper estimated, jammed the Loop, and a "world's record" for car thefts in a twenty-four-hour period (sixty) was set as well as a probable record for multiple drunkenness, as Mayor "Big Bill" Thompson refused to order the saloons closed. "Guests indulged in fantastic dancing. . . . The signing of the Armistice seemed to render inoperative the regulation against serving men in uniform with liquor."

Animals, too—if such a law existed. Ernest Erber remembered seeing, at a saloon near the corner of Hoyne Avenue and Iowa Street, a horse unhitched from a milk wagon and led up to the bar to be offered a celebratory bucket of beer. And in front of his house, at 909 Hoyne Avenue, he saw one of the rare cases in which a Kaiser Bill effigy led to violence, when an automobile careened by, dragging an effigy of the Kaiser, rope around its neck. "An excited bystander, intent upon demonstrating his patriotic hatred of our country's enemy (and killer of Belgian babies), leaped upon the effigy, only to tumble off and fall to his death beneath the wheels of a following vehicle." Hundreds of effigies decorated the radiators of automobiles, one with a spiked helmet made from a large, inverted oil can, and real hearses drove through the Loop advertising that the Kaiser was within.

There were few arrests, Police Chief John H. Alcock having advised, "The people of Chicago are fittingly celebrating the victory of the Allies in Europe, for which we are proud. I ask every man of the department to use his best judgment and not to interfere more than necessary with the amusement of the people." When a taxi disgorged two greased pigs in front of the Brevoort Hotel, police looked the other way while the animals headed east on Madison Street. When a woman wearing a soldier's cap began directing traffic at State and Monroe streets, police let her go on doing so, especially since traffic paid little heed anyway. When male revelers carried off female celebrants whose screams appeared to be those of joy, Chief Alcock's men did their duty. When an elegantly appareled woman danced with soldiers and sailors on Wabash Avenue, and a dignified gentleman somewhat the worse from drink hung uncertainly to a light standard on Adams Street, police kept their distance. When a parade of bluejackets escorting an effigy of Kaiser Bill on a bier preceded by a brass band was joined by three uninvited men thumping washtubs with trowels, and clearly off-key, they observed the scene with satisfaction. "Leniency," Alcock announced later, "stopped at one o'clock [on November 12]. The entire department will be on its toes today to enforce the laws and ordinances. . . ."

"Thursday's celebration," the *Tribune* concluded on the twelfth, "was to yesterday's titanic revel as a summer's thunderstorm is to a hurricane." Only seven people were reported killed, a modest total for twenty-four hours in Chicago.

Elsewhere in the Midwest one might see smaller celebrations, but little different than in other cities and towns across the country. At Milwaukee the hanging of a Wilhelm Hohenzollern effigy and a mammoth bonfire on the lake front crowned the festivities. In a small town in Iowa little Johnny Harrison was pressed into the parade in an Uncle Sam hat made from a cylinder of cardboard, and was tormented by bigger boys, who tossed marbles into the open top. And in another Iowa town, the future chronicler of the rise and fall of the Third Reich, William L. Shirer, in a high school ROTC unit, was bitterly disappointed as he watched Cedar Rapids go wild in celebration. "Gold stars hung in the windows of several homes, and some of the wounded were [already] back, hobbling the streets, a leg gone, an arm missing, a patch over one eye. A young doctor who had married a cousin of ours and then gone off to France had just returned, his lungs burned out by poison gas, slowly dying. Nevertheless, I found it hard to swallow the fact that I would never fight in the war to make, as President Wilson said, and I believed, the world safe for democracy."

In a village in Illinois where Elburt Osborn's father was Methodist minister, the seven-year-old was permitted, for the first time, to tug at the bell rope. Eleven-year-old John Ferguson, in tiny Elm Creek, Nebraska, climbed to the church steeple and pulled on the bell ropes until his hands were raw. ("It was the only noise in town other than the railroad.") Then he climbed down to watch townspeople drive away the undertaker's hearse—he was a German of suspect loyalty—after stuffing a Kaiser effigy inside. At the edge of town they threw it in the air and shot at it with rifles; then they burned the effigy and the hearse. In Caldwell, Kansas, where young Gordon Wallace had managed to get the flour-mill siren turned on prematurely four days earlier, the siren this time caught him in bed at four in the morning. Before long he saw careening vehicles, loaded beyond capacity with riders, churning up the dust on unpaved Main Street, occupants firing rifles, shotguns, and revolvers into the dawn until the air was blue and acrid. The commotion lasted twenty hours, climaxed by a huge bonfire in the middle of Main Street. "The town was turned inside out in a search for wood: boxes, crates, discarded lumber, dead tree limbs, anything that would burn." The final contribution was an effigy of Kaiser Bill. But in the small Dakota town where Edna La Moore was a new teacher, not even church bells rang. Schools, theaters, and churches were shut down by influenza, and wooden boxes of bodies—there was a shortage of real coffins—had piled up on the railway station platform until funerals could be held. There was no Armistice celebration.

In a small town in Kansas, Kenneth Wiggins Porter, who had dressed up as the Kaiser, with lightning rod tied to tin pot as spiked helmet, was warned out of the local parade by his school principal, who worried that an overenthusiastic patriot might get carried away and do violence to the lad. The little episode, like others around the country on November 7 and again on November 11, suggested something of the warped zeal of the superloyalist which had made life miserable for many German-Americans during the war. A corps of *kaiserlich* propagandists had worked hard until 1917 to woo the millions of ethnic Germans, heightening suspicions. Insistent patriots had even caused German language instruction to be dropped from many schools, and Beethoven from concert programs. Sauerkraut had been renamed "Liberty cabbage" and hamburger "Salisbury steak." Cartoons pictured Germans waving a tiny American flag from a window with the left hand and raising a stein in the right, with a whispered *"Hoch der Kaiser!"* And there were some Germans who obstinately flew German flags from farmhouses, displayed portraits of Wilhelm II on walls, or supported ethnic societies which looked at Germany through nostalgic lenses.

The end of the war suggested to vigilant domestic patriots a last lick at the allegedly disloyal spies, saboteurs, and conspirators. One victim was John Schrag, a Mennonite farmer in Kansas whose religious principles forbade him to support war in any way. When the Armistice bells began to peal in Kansas, superloyalists who remembered that Schrag had once refused to buy Liberty Bonds crowded into five automobiles and rushed to his farm. There they seized him, took him to the town of Burrton, eleven miles away, and demanded that he buy bonds, salute the flag, and march at the head of a victory parade with "Old Glory" in his hand. When he offered to contribute $200 to the Red Cross or the Salvation Army rather than perform acts against his conscience, someone forced a flag into his hand anyway, and in the scuffle it fell to the ground and was trampled underfoot.

Enraged by the dishonor to the flag (for which they were responsible in any case), the mob beat the defenseless farmer, doused him with yellow paint, put him in the town jail, and began making plans to hang him. Only then did the sheriff intervene, carrying Schrag off to Newton, the county seat, where he was charged under the Espionage Act for desecrating the flag of the United States.

In Michigan, Henry Ford calmly told his plant supervisors to cease war work and begin making tractors. "You call Washington and get permission to stop." He would lose a million dollars on the contracts, he was told. "Peace will be worth it," he said. And it would be, as he became first to retool. In one-time automobile plants across the state, employees left their assembly lines, crowded with unfinished—and suddenly obsolete—airplanes and tanks. In Detroit, hub of the industry, crowds of celebrating factory workers were thrilled by several Army airplanes—very likely their own recent manufacture—which swooped low overhead until one of them became entangled in a huge American flag unfurled atop an office building. Lieutenant Clifford Morrow, from the small town of Punxsutawney, Pennsylvania, was perhaps the last aviator to die in war-related fashion—while Charles Veil, once of the same town, who flew with the Lafayette Escadrille, and had even been up on the final day, had survived. The official Army report would claim that Morrow "was killed . . . while discharging his duty as a tester at the aviation field at Detroit."*

At a small Minnesota farm sale in Morrison County, a lanky sixteen-year-old standing in for his father was bidding for cattle when someone handed the auctioneer a note, which he read excitedly to the knot of bidders. "Gentlemen, I have good news. The war is over!" Charles Lindbergh would now be able to buy a war-surplus "Flying Jenny" and leave the cows to someone else. Less pleased was Major Omar Bradley, who with his wife, Mary, heard the whistles blowing in Des Moines, Iowa, near his base at Camp Dodge. While people surged wildly into streets all he could think of was that he

---

* Claims have been made—even a book, *Hurrah for the Next Man Who Dies* (1985)—that prewar Princeton athlete and socialite Hobey Baker was "the last man to die in World War I." A football hero and fighter pilot, Baker died six weeks *after* the Armistice when he lost control of his plane—a Spad painted in Princeton orange-and-black—in a rainstorm.

would soon be reduced to captain. "Having missed the war, I was professionally ruined. I could only look forward to a career of dull routine assignments and would be lucky to retire after thirty years as a lieutenant colonel."

To the South the lessons of the False Armistice in Louisville were not lost on the commanding officer of Camp Taylor, Kentucky. The gates were ordered locked, and no one was permitted to leave. The camp, Sergeant Harry Onken remembered, "was very still all day and that night." It was even more quiet in Camp Wheeler, Georgia, where Private Emanuel Gebauer remembered an announcement that any celebration of the Armistice would result in discipline for the offender.

In the West, peace celebrations were muted by the influenza epidemic. The tens of thousands of deaths would exceed the numbers of war casualties. Elliott Barker, supervisor of the Carson National Forest near Taos, New Mexico, remembered turning a schoolhouse and a church into makeshift hospitals, and watching 10 percent (1,250) of the county's population die. Stricken with grief, the able townspeople gathered in churches on Armistice Day to pray that the flu would subside before the boys came home.

In the first light of dawn, a French colonel lay awake in a lower berth of the crack *Overland* as it jolted along a valley in Nevada. Suddenly he realized that on a road paralleling the track a man wearing a ten-gallon hat was racing the train in a Model T Ford. He appeared to be shouting and waving, and an increasingly dilapidated zinc boiler, once part of a water heater, hitched to the Ford's rear axle by a rope, was banging against every rock and rut in the road. Soon the train outdistanced the madman, but the colonel lay awake trying to figure out the bizarre behavior. Then it came to him. He leaped into the aisle in his pajamas and began shouting, *"L'Armistice! L'Armistice est signe!"*

In most places in the West the celebrations began, eerily, in the dark of midnight. Revelers in the California foothills town of Sierra Madre, with pistols, rifles, whistles, and other noisemakers, lethal and nonlethal, welcomed peace in frontier fashion, led by Colonel John Boyd on a pack burro firing a .44-caliber revolver along the winding streets and trails. In San Bernardino, the official morning parade began at the unusual hour of 3:00 A.M. Complete to rifle-and-drum corps, Boy Scouts in uniform, Red Cross volunteers, and schoolchildren banging washtubs, tins, and pots, it was a delirious demonstration, as people had been cooped up in their homes except for essential business by an influenza quarantine for four weeks. In Long Beach thousands of shipyard workers abandoned their night shift to march through the night, the Los Angeles *Times* reporting, "All city ordinances regulating traffic and the use of firearms were ignored, and influenza precautions tossed to the winds." In Los Angeles the greatest celebration in the burgeoning city's history erupted, with hundreds injured although only one death was reported, but in the more sedate suburb of Pasadena people held a prearranged post-midnight victory parade with a recess declared at two o'clock so that merrymakers could go back to bed. By eight crowds were back on the streets. Future D. H. Lawrence biographer Harry T. Moore, then ten, remembered his Los Angeles neighborhood festooned with toilet paper bearing the Kaiser's mustached visage on each sheet. It was available to any patriot at the corner drugstore.

Up and down California there were mock funeral services for Kaiser Bill—complete to coffins—and in San Francisco there were dances through the streets to City Hall led by shipyard workers in soiled overalls and civilians in gauze masks to ward off flu bugs. The Fire Department itself set huge bonfires going on Twin Peaks, Scott's, and Telegraph Hill, an eerie sight at one in the morning, but no more eerie than celebrants in white face masks. By early morning the surgical masks had fallen away into the debris of confetti, whiskey bottles, and wastepaper which littered the city. And from Seattle to San Diego sailors in naval training stations broke influenza quarantine to pour into the streets. In San Diego's Balboa Park sailors "with quarts of talcum powder besprinkled the crowds until they looked as though in a stage snow scene."

Not everyone was as eager to celebrate. Young officers at home mourned the cutting off of promising careers—Lieutenant Jimmy Doolittle, the future bomber of Tokyo, was a frustrated flying instructor at Ream Field, down the bay from San Diego, near the Mexican border; future paratroop general and Korean War commander Matthew Ridgway was unhappily stuck at West Point as a young teacher of French, which he barely knew; and a young captain at Camp Colt, on the old Gettysburg battlefield, just jumped to temporary wartime rank of lieutenant colonel, realized that his orders to proceed on November 18 to Camp Dix, New Jersey, to command a tank unit in France would be canceled. Turning to another frustrated young officer he moaned, "I suppose we'll spend the rest of our lives explaining why we didn't get into this war. By God,

from now on I am cutting myself a swath and will make up for this."
It would be late in 1939 before Dwight Eisenhower would reach the
rank of lieutenant colonel again.

From sea to sea the Armistice tapped reservoirs of emotion which
seemed out of proportion to the American involvement and sacrifice. Even more so than in France or Britain, the Armistice in
America was celebrated with a remarkable atavism which only the
nearly exterminated American Indian might have recognized. The
primitive impulses which the event stirred suggested how thin the
veneer of civilization remained in years which had seen the development of radio, motorcar, airplane, and sophisticated weapons of
war. There was the irrepressible urge for dancing, abandoned and
en masse; and a sexual license which found men and women who
had never seen each other before embracing and kissing in public,
and indulging in even more wanton behavior in locations less than
private. There was a pyromania which harked back to the days of
signal fires, sacrificial pyres, and victory blazes, most notably in
Washington's symbolic forty-eight fires;* and the irresistible fash-
ioning, flaunting, and "punishing" of effigies, almost always of the
despised Kaiser, who was sometimes hanged or buried but more
often burned, a rite of repeatedly killing the enemy's god which
harked back many millenia.

With midnight the nearly twenty-four hours of celebration
began to wind down. Having been awakened to the world for eighteen months, America would try its best to go back to sleep.

---

* Dorothy Aspinwall recalled a huge crowd around an Armistice bonfire in the
darkness on a bare brown hill overlooking Calgary, Alberta. "Around the bonfire people were singing and hugging each other—a quite un-Canadian display
of emotion, although, naturally, I did not recognize this at the time."

AFTERMATH: THE FRONT LINES

When this bloody war is over,
Oh, how happy I shall be!
N.C.O.s will all be navvies,
Privates ride in motor cars;
N.C.O.s will smoke Woodbines,
Privates puff their big cigars.
No more standing-to in trenches,
Only one more church-parade;
No more shivering on the firestep,
No more Tickler's marmalade.

—SUNG BY BRITISH SOLDIERS TO THE
    TUNE OF "WHAT A FRIEND WE HAVE IN JESUS"

A *Punch* cartoon had a demobilized serviceman, an ex-footballer, boast to an admiring group at his pub, "We was just wipin' them off the face of the earth when Foch blows his whistle and shouts 'Temps!' " In most places from Flanders to Lorraine the feeling was very different. What seemed beyond price, as so many participants would insist, was that a man could stand up. The terror had vanished from a landscape in which every shattered tree or blasted bush, every shallow gully or rise in the ground, could be malign. According to American correspondent George Seldes, "Some of us who had been in the trenches [only] four weeks and not four years could imagine if not share the feeling. Millions of men had kept heads down for four years; no one could stand up without fear of the bullet bearing his name. Men stood up. . . . The British shouted, we have come through. The French shouted, we are alive. . . ." Only "the civilians back home," Seldes observed, "shouted Victory."

On the line, reactions to the end were much like those of actors in a demanding, long-running melodrama. Participants emotionally and physically drained each performance were now watching the curtain go down for the last time. As the fog lifted from the valley of the Meuse, the historians of the 103rd U.S. Field Artillery wrote, "Men talked in strange accents, like beings who had just come out of a long imprisonment." To British Private S. N. Preece, nineteen, with two years in the trenches and a Blighty behind him, life as a machine gunner was all the adult life he knew. "I still remember the lost feeling," he wrote sixty years later. "What do we do now? What has it been all about?" Captain A. C. Wilkinson, Coldstream Guards, remembered how his sergeant major, Oscar Warner, took the news when the shooting stopped just east of Mons. "I'm sorry it's all over, Sir," he said. "We'll never have times like these again!"

"I have a rather peculiar feeling," an American officer, Birge Clark, wrote. "Heaven knows I am enormously thankful the war is over, but nevertheless I feel as tho my occupation was entirely gone, and the idea of turning back to civilian life seems like an awful jump. I have really got accustomed to fighting, life in the open, running a balloon company with a lot of men, trucks, etc., and it is going to leave a rather gone feeling for a while."

"Boys, you've lost your jobs. The war's over and you can all go back to your billets," Harry Dadswell's brigade commander told an Anzac unit preparing once more to start up for the line. Of the original 1,100 men who had shipped out to France, only 180 were left. They stood quietly and looked at each other. Similarly, Thomas

Robbins recalled "a strange silence, no cheering and little visible ex-hiliration" in his 62nd (West Riding) Division. Finally several Yorkshiremen accepted the fact, concurring, "The war's over; the bloody duck's foot's down."

Conditions were different remote from the line, where brass buttons were still polished and warehouses bulged with supplies. "I cannot speak for places in the rear," R. H. Mottram wrote, "but, on what had been the battle-line, there was no glory, no jubilation. There was very little material for any festivity, and that was hard to get, so bare and worn was everything and everybody." The one hope was "some sort of artificial stimulant," and many are the stories of the solitary bottle of wine dug up by a farmer who had hid it for just such an occasion. "I don't know if being buried is bad for cham-pagne, but I recollect that it didn't seem very good to me." Since rank has always had its privileges, things were better for Brigadier General F. P. Crozier of the Royal Irish Rifles (mostly London drafts by 1918). "We dine with Belgian nobility, in whose chateau we sleep," he wrote that night. "We provide the food, since they have none, while the *grand seigneur* departs to the woods to dig up some priceless old wine, which has lain hidden under the leaves and mould for over four long years. 'The family silver plate is in the pond,' he says, 'please excuse us.' "

When the shooting stopped, Dudley Meneaud-Lissenburg re-membered, "it was dispiriting to find we had nothing but tea and biscuits with which to celebrate. The rum we should have had issued to us must have fallen off the lorry en route and into the billet of the conveyors." The men of the 21st Division Medium Trench Mortars returned to Maubeuge to scrounge. "But in this grim town, just re-lieved from four years of German occupation, all that remained were a few pregnant young girls, children and bemused old folks sit-ting dejectedly in the cellars of partially damaged houses." All the wine, they were told, was taken by the "dirty Boches." In the American 33rd Division, Sergeant Will Judy wrote in his diary, "We can now come out of our holes in the ground and breathe the air like free men. . . . And tonight we would drain dry the wine cellars of France except that there are no cellars, no houses, no drinking places on the battlefield. It rains, the chill deadens us, and we crawl away early into our beds."

At Souilly, Colonel George C. Marshall watched an aviator give "a demonstration of stunt flying over the village, and ap-parently the wings on one side of his plane collapsed, because he fell in a crash which ended his life." Some hours later another American flier, far off in Detroit, would make a similar mistake. A lieutenant colonel who would be one of Marshall's generals in France in the next war wrote in his diary, "Peace was signed and Langres was very ex[c]ited. Many flags. Got rid of my bandage. Wrote a poem on peace. Also one on Capt. English." George S. Patton, Jr., would not be known to fame as a poet, and his spelling and punctuation lacked perfection, but the end of the war set him musing over the fate which had preserved him, despite the risks he had taken, while claiming his closest friend. Captain Matthew L. English, 344th Battalion, Tank Corps, had been searching for a passage for his tanks through a mine field. "In Memoriam" failed to foreshadow the feisty later Patton, but it did suggest the way Patton aspired to live—and die:

> *Should some future war exact,*
> *Of me the final debt,*
> *My fondest hope would be to tread,*
> *The path which he has set. . . .*

Other Allied soldiers found themselves, on November 11, 1918, in locations where the atmosphere precluded high spirits, and supplies of the spirits one drank were nonexistent. The London Rifle Brigade found itself in the village of Erquennes, near Mons. "To think of being stuck here," wailed one rifleman. "No champagne, no vin blanc—only about ten widows and a cow." But they were welcomed into the cottages, where cups of something approaching coffee were offered, and tales of suffering and hardship told. A thanksgiving service in the village school was led by the local padre, and afterward there were roofs to sleep under—if only floors to sleep upon. There was only one subject the man talked about, Private Aubrey Smith remembered, as, one by one, they dropped off to sleep—demobilization. But that itself was a change. The last thought each night had been "When will my turn come?" Now it was "When shall I be in civvies again?" C. E. Montague, a prewar novelist and *Manchester Guardian* drama critic, wrote with relief to H. G. Wells, "Oh to be back at my beloved work, now that this job is over! It is frightful to have lost 4 years." In 1914, when he was forty-seven, he had dyed his hair and enlisted enthusiastically as a private. In November 1918 he was an intelligence officer. *Disenchantment* (1922), his bitter memoir, would record the soldier's progress from such early dreams of patriotic sacrifice.

At the least there was the sense of danger passed, but even that was sometimes premature. East of Mons, Robert Airey and his mates in the 8th London Regiment found a billet in a school, "which was lucky for us as the Church blew up a few hours later." Flanders was full of unexploded—and unlocated—mines, and undetonated shells. American Captain William A. Percy, remembering "that day when war stopped" somewhere between the Schelde and the Lys, wrote of "the tender aimless sunshine" and "incredible silence" in which he and his men "roamed the little town [of Olsene] singly, like drifting shades. The physical relief, the absence of apprehension, brimmed us with ease and thanksgiving, but for each of us our bliss and our serenity were only the superstructure over a hidden tide of desolation and despair. Each of us was repeating to himself in his own words something I heard crying out in me: It's over, the only great thing you were ever part of. It's over, the only heroic thing we all did together. What can you do now? Nothing, nothing. You can't go back to the old petty things without purpose . . . defending the railroad for killing a cow, drawing deeds of trust, suing someone. . . . You can't go on with that sort of thing till you die." Somerset Maugham's Howard Bartlett in the play *For Services Rendered* (1932) viewed the end of glory differently. "Those were the days," says the former officer, again a farmer. ". . . I had the time of my life in the war. No responsibility and plenty of money. More than I've ever had before or ever since. All the girls you wanted and all the whiskey. Excitement. A roughish time in the trenches, but a grand lark afterward. I tell you it was a bitter day for me when they signed the Armistice. What have I got now? Just the same old thing day after day, working my guts out to keep body and soul together."

For the temporary soldier, peace sometimes loomed as a worse horror than war. Even an officer out of the working class was—officially—a gentleman. But only for the duration. For many British civilian soldiers, however, what made the war so dreadful was that it had been fought against the background of liberal illusions that the lot of the average person had been getting better and better, and that scientific enlightenment and social progress would improve it even more. The war had made nonsense of both assumptions, and peace would undermine them further.

Lieutenant "Doc" Harrison, his platoon back in Beney after the canceled attack on Metz, set up housekeeping in an abandoned German billet, heated water in a five-gallon can, found a washtub, and luxuriated in his first bath in months. Fresh underwear was an additional luxury, after which he added the sweater a girl back home had knitted for him, his "frogskin" shirt, and his clean O.D. shirt. Yet in twenty minutes he was again crawling with lice. He stripped again and on examining his clothes, piece by piece, he found that his sweater was infested by thousands of bugs and larvae in the double-V neck. "Much as [I] hated to ditch the sweater for both sentimental and practical reasons, [I] pitched it in the stove and watched the bugs sizzle." Christopher Marsh, a subaltern with the Royal Garrison Artillery near the Schelde, with nothing to toast the victory, decided, with the Signals Officer, "that, as we had to purchase our own revolvers, we ought to have fired them; and, better late than never, we spent the afternoon firing off the ammunition which had been issued for them, using turnips in the surrounding fields as targets."

It was not an upbeat, romantic close. That was only posters and propaganda. The real ending was evident in the crossing of the front lines by the tide of civilian traffic—old men and boys carrying bundles, women pushing handcarts, each with real or makeshift flags tied to packs, carts, and caps. Returning to Lille, Valenciennes, and other towns from which they had been seized for forced labor, they were bedraggled and hungry but intent on home. One British account noted that not only was the Tricolor, carefully concealed until that day, displayed but also "a sprinkling of extemporised (and rather inaccurate) versions of the Union Jack and American and Belgian flags." Some sat down at the roadside in the drizzle and mud, too weak to go farther; others trudged gamely on. When soldiers passed, going the other way, refugees would shout a wan *"Vivent les Anglais!"*

In the Belgian town of Thielt, on the extreme left flank of the American Army, Bernard Bergman, regimental sergeant major at 37th Division (Ohio National Guard) headquarters, searched for a billet. With his friend Corporal Gus Edwards, Bergman—a future editor at Mencken's *American Mercury* and Ross's *New Yorker*—surveyed the possibilities. "Passed two pretty girls," he wrote when he was eighty-four. "Put on a long face, told them how desperately we needed to find a room and rest. Of course they took us to their home where alas we met Mama and Papa. . . . Came the Armistice and there was much singing and dancing and drinking in all the houses. One neighbor brought his violin and played while we danced. Since I was somewhat of a fiddler I too played . . . but that's all there was. Couldn't even get the girls into a closet. The only kissing was a kiss to Victory; and hell, we shot the works and kissed everybody—male and female." At Bruges the enthusiasm was slightly less decorous. Correspondents W. Beach Thomas and Philip Gibbs, the first men to enter Bruges after the Germans withdrew, were mobbed by Belgians who wanted British shoulder straps and buttons as souvenirs. They were barely able to keep their clothes together. "With the utmost difficulty we managed to get our cars to the gates of a nunnery where Gibbs had friends."

In Mons, Gibbs novelized later, women in doorways offered wine to passing troops, who "drank the wine and kissed the women, and lurched laughing down the streets. There would be no strict discipline in Mons that night." In some ways it would be no different than under the German occupation. "Come here, lassie," Gibbs had one soldier say. "None of your French tricks for me. I'm Canadian. It's a kiss or a clout from me." And he grabbed the girl by the arm and drew her into a barn.

Billeted in Mons, Canadian Will Bird, his head swimming from lack of sleep, mumbled to an elderly Belgian couple that he was too dirty for the bed they had offered. Then he lost consciousness. When he came to, Bird found himself in a tin tub, the old man supporting him, his wife washing him with a big cloth. Exhausted beyond argument, he let himself be led into a small room where he was helped between the sheets. The old woman even kissed him before going out and closing the door. Although sounds of celebration filtered into the room from outside, he was too tired to care. Dusk was turning into darkness, but there was enough moonlight for him to sense the closet door move slightly. Instinctively he leaped from bed and flung the door open. Crouched among a pile of clothing was a young German soldier. "He came out and cringed abjectly. He was no more than eighteen years old, a boy with a cloth cap on his head. His face was twisted with apprehension. . . . The moonlight showed a postman's rig on hooks in the closet, and I recalled the old couple telling me that they had lost their son and he had been a postman. I took the postman's cap and handed it to the German. He slipped it on, putting his own in his pocket. Then I handed him the postman's cloak and he threw it over his shoulders. I opened the door into the hall softly and let him out the front door. He squeezed my hand warmly, and was gone."

The story echoes Joseph Conrad's Malayan tale, "The Secret Sharer" (1909), but Bird's account in all verifiable details is persuasive. If it did not happen, it should have.

Near Mons, Lieutenant Stuart Whibley, attached with his battery to a Canadian battalion, awaited instructions from his Canadian major, who asked his men what they wanted to do. "A short service of Thanksgiving," the major reported, "and then a football match, Drivers versus Gunners." He located a prayer book, Whibley recalled, "and we admired the way in which he managed the Service as we stood around our now silent guns."

Celebrations ranged the spectrum of enthusiasm. The 47th (London) Division's *History* noted that the news "hardly raised a cheer." But at least the news had arrived in time, its young (thirty-one) chief of staff, Colonel Bernard Montgomery, having devised a system by which officers with ponderous but portable wireless sets at advanced battalions could send and receive messages. Unreliable and limited in range, the primitive devices were the prototypes of the jeep-radio units, which would bring efficiency to his 1940–45 operations. By the end of the war, "Monty" remembered, he had never seen Haig, and although a divisional chief of staff had only twice even seen an Army commander. Out of touch with the troops and in comfort in villas well behind the lines, the top brass had little realization of the exhaustion of their front-line men, who often stared blankly at the concept of peace, and had little way to respond to it. But where the shooting had only been distant noise, if that, the reaction was very different.

The Royal Irish Fusiliers recorded that its officers "played 12th Irish Rifles at Rugby." Sergeant Edmund Wilson at American headquarters in Chaumont took a walk with correspondent George Wood of the New York *Evening Sun*. It was damp; a few soldiers were messily drunk; life had suddenly become boring. "Well, b'gosh," said Wood, excited by Saturday's football scores from the States, which had just come in, "We beat Purdue!"

As British Sergeant B. A. Lewis put it, "After the awful and countless experiences of years of filth and slaughter and the knowledge before our eyes that it was coming to an end, the actual reading of the final words on the Divisional, Brigade, Company or Section notice board was an anti-climax and we just breathed a sigh of relief and thought about how soon we could get back home. By mid-day it was a question of routine carry-on. What else could we do? Doubtless, down in the back areas . . . there was plenty of booze and celebration but forward areas remained under strict control and there was no booze available in any case. The officers probably had their whiskey but other ranks just inwardly rejoiced that they no longer were in fear of death."

Once eleven o'clock came, according to Edmund Wilson, a Regular Army colonel in the area called his staff together and announced, "Now that we have finished with this war, it is time to begin to think about the next." At a hospital near Etaples a Scottish RAMC officer signed an order to be posted in the wards: "To celebrate the conclusion of hostilities every patient will be allowed an extra piece of bread and jam with his tea." Discipline, some officers felt, could not be revived at its former pitch if it were relaxed. Private Frank Richards, Royal Welch Fusiliers, described in *Old Soldiers Never Die* how, after the Armistice took effect, an officer with a peerage took temporary command, summoning the noncommissioned officers for a lecture. "He told them that while the War was on it was a case of every man for himself when in action, and discipline had become a little lax. They must remember that they belonged to a Line Battalion and discipline must revert back to a pre-War standard. He said that if any N.C.O. was brought up in front of him for walking out with a private he would reduce him to the ranks." Most were former civilians used to a brotherly camaraderie with the "other ranks" and did not care a damn whether they were reduced, since their only thought now was demobilization. It was "a lot of bally rot," an NCO told Richards. Harry Day, a veteran of Mons in 1914 and in the vicinity again at the Armistice, remembered his cavalry unit being paraded by the commanding officer, who warned of possible dangers still to come. After stable duties had been detailed, he announced, troops could celebrate until "evening stables," with everyone on his honor to return on time. "And this they did."

At some aerodromes the message was the same. W. R. Read paraded his men after the Berlin-Prague show had been canceled "and told them that they were expected to carry on as usual and keep up the reputation of the old squadron, no falling off of discipline. . . ." Then he added in his diary, "This afternoon the squadron's 1st eleven played the second XI at soccer and we got up an officers' team to play the NCOs at medicine ball. I played. We beat them three sets love." That was all the celebration there would be.

In French sectors there was far more enthusiasm among civilians than soldiers. One weary soldier recalled "no screaming, no singing among the riflemen, [only] a grave joy and some humid eyes." Another—the future Sorbonne historian Marc Bloch—had a one-word notation in his journal for the eleventh: "Armistice." One Frenchman to be caught up in the revelry, André Maurois, found himself celebrating because he was a liaison officer with a British unit, which gave him a dinner on Armistice Day. "At the end . . . they rose, forced me to remain seated and sang with great seriousness *For he's a jolly good fellow, and so say all of us.* . . . I felt myself very far removed. . . . My cousin Pierre Herzog, after being wounded ten times and being cited ten times, had been killed . . . a few days before the Armistice." Future French fascist intellectual Drieu la Rochelle was unready to exult, "haunted by the fear that the world to which he would return . . . would not be worthy of the sacrifices which his generation had been called upon to make. . . ." Future Nazi collaborator Jean Darlan (an admiral in 1940) was depressed about missing his promotion. Volunteering to put his knowledge of naval artillery to work where it was needed, he had helped arrange the transport of battleship cannon to Verdun, where their precise fire helped halt the Germans. Of all the naval officers to rush to Verdun, he was the only survivor. But not having been at sea, he was still a lieutenant on November 11. More successful was a twenty-nine-year-old cavalry officer, Jean Marie Gabriel de Lattre de Tassigny, who had been riddled with wounds, bemedaled, and promoted from *Chevalier* to *Officier* of the Legion of Honour. At the Armistice his 21st Division was advancing between Rethel on the Aisne and Mézières. In 1940 he would be with the 14th Infantry Division in the same area, retreating from the Germans. He would join the Free French and be on opposing sides from Darlan.

Another young officer, Jean de Pierrefeu, had received instructions to prepare an evening communiqué for headquarters in which he was to announce the close of operations and the cease-fire. He had to find someone to approve his text, and hurried through village after village, and continual merrymaking, but could not locate his commander in chief, who was probably in Paris. He then searched for his major general, who, "typically enough, . . . was at the theatre, where the soldiers and enthusiastic citizens had improvised a performance. The Provins theatre, tiny and shabby, bare and cold, was full of people. General Buat and the other G.H.Q. generals were watching . . . from a box, and there he read the victory *communiqué*, while a soldier from the *Conservatoire* declaimed heroic poetry from the stage."

The most frenzied celebrations were behind the lines. As Joyce Cary wrote in his novel *A Prisoner of Grace*, in the persona of his Lloyd George character, Chester Nimmo, "The soldiers were so wild to get out of the army that some regiments almost demobilized themselves.

They were tired of discipline, and it would have been dangerous for the officers to try to keep them in order." Totally beyond discipline were the Chinese laborers imported to maintain rail lines and do heavy porterage. Recovered from his wounds and on the way to rejoin the 1st North Staffordshires, Henry Waite watched the Chinese go berserk on hearing the news. "We were glad to get back on the train for shelter as the Chinese started throwing live hand grenades all over the place."

His squadron in Flanders "cut off in this little village miles from anywhere," Cecil Lewis and his fellow fliers searched for some way to celebrate. "There was nothing to drink . . . and nowhere to go. All we could find was a dump of Hun Very lights, of all colors, left behind in their retreat. With the help of the Chinese we made a bonfire of them." It was an idea that occurred to thousands at the front. After the silence at eleven, Corporal Horatio Rogers, with the American 26th Division, could hear, faintly, the church bells in Verdun. "We decided that if there was anything to celebrate [with] we would do our share, so we dug out all the Very pistol cartridges we had and fired them off. None of them would work."

Everywhere along the line, as twilight came early in the November mist and rain, campfires began to smoke and glow, and rations arrived swiftly, sometimes via vehicles with headlamps glowing down the rough roads. "Commanding officers came up to inspect," Frank Sibley wrote of the 26th, "and the majors, red-eyed with fatigue, dirty, unshaven for many days, and so hoarse with gas that they could not speak aloud, reported [the demarcation of] their lines. Here and there a dull explosion would sound, and the Germans sent out a piteous wireless, asking that the fire cease. But it was only the indefatigable engineers, blasting rock for a road."

There was the ever-present danger that an Armistice violation would renew the conflict, and both sides were at first cautious in the extreme. In the area of the American 33rd Division, a lieutenant in the 124th Machine Gun Battalion asked his men, in violation of orders, if any of them wanted to go over to see the Germans. Private Clayton Slack and a German-speaking soldier volunteered and crossed safely through no-man's-land. After an exchange of souvenirs, Slack and his buddy started back, flushing out, en route, a jackrabbit. Pulling out his revolver, Slack began firing at the bounding rabbit while men on both sides watched with anxiety. If misunderstood, Slack admitted later, "I could have started the war [again] all by myself."

"From our line," George Seldes would remember, "I saw helmeted heads of German soldiers appearing over the parapets. The Germans came into No Man's Land shyly, awkwardly, still frightened, but the Americans, followed by the French, rushed into the field and extended their hands in welcome. The Americans gave away food and cigarettes." Despite the rules, a large part of Armistice Day on the line was spent in swapping souvenirs. The French had a saying, said Seldes, "The Germans fight for the Kaiser, the French for glory, and the Americans for souvenirs." For the Germans, guns were now useless, the Lugers were being swapped for a five-cent chocolate bar.

"Thank the good God that the war is finished," said a middle-aged *Landsturmer.* "My only wish is to get back to Germany." And there was talk of what was happening there, one young soldier insisting, "There will be no revolution in Germany. A new Emperor will succeed." An uproar of disagreement drowned his words, suggesting what would come at home, if not en route back.

There was still another kind of dissent, not voiced loudly, and not even taken seriously amid the *Bruderschaft* of the moment. Sam Van Tries, an American Balloon Corps forward observer, was one of the first to cross into the German lines, swapping cigarettes for a razor of Ruhr-forged steel. "You didn't lick us," Van Tries was told. "We knew when to quit. We'll be back in twenty years."

The British were quick, too, to fraternize, before higher commands insisted that too much brotherhood was a bad thing when one operated under an Armistice that technically was not a real peace. R. F. Delderfield's stolid Henry Pitts, oblivious to international law, would discover subtleties in the German interest in him and his English cigarettes which would escape diplomats and cabinet ministers for decades more. In *A Horseman Riding By* cigarette-starved men from a Saxon regiment come forward on the run at the cease-fire signal, pressing badges and emblems on the Tommies in exchange for Woodbines. Henry Pitts acquires a match-box holder emblazoned with a double eagle and the motto *Gott mit uns* which he recognizes, from having seen dead Germans, had begun life as a belt buckle. A German officer, joining the group, is breathing hard, a sick young man, probably tubercular. His face is cavernous and pinched, his helmet now several sizes too big for him. But he is essential as he knows English. With a pale smile he translates woodenly for one of his men. "The sergeant asks if you will shake the hand," he says. Henry puts out his hand.

He had always respected the German front-line troops and, like most of the infantry, dismissed most of the atrocity stories as newspaper twaddle. Then the sergeant said something else and the officer, after a spluttering cough, again translated, telling Henry that the sergeant said he looked as though he was a farmer. Henry was so delighted at this that he seized the Saxon's hand again and shouted, "Youm right first time, Jerry! Now for Chrissake 'ow did 'ee work that one out?" . . . The officer said Henry's hands had given him away.

After a no-fraternization order from his lieutenant ends the fumbling barter as well as the dialogue, Pitts, ignoring the fireworks overhead, continues

to dwell on the bovine, broad-shouldered Saxon who had instantly recognised him as a fellow farmer. Somehow it never occurred to him that the men he had been fighting all this time . . . in better times, plodded about tending pigs, herding cows, ploughing up land and banking swedes for winter cattle feed. He had thought of them, if at all, as a race of efficient robots whose trade—if they had one—was war, who had never lived anywhere but in holes in the ground and whose tools included mustard gas and shrapnel. The encounter in no-man's-land undermined his entire philosophy of war and now, looking back, it seemed to him a very stupid, profitless business and he wanted nothing so much as to be done with it and go home.

Near the Meuse, the commander of Otto Brautigam's battalion, knowing Brautigam's knowledge of English, asked him if he were willing to cross to the American side to inquire about the fate of their missing men. "Of course I said yes, and I rode out together with a cavalry sergeant. It was a strange feeling to cross the front line with head erect. . . . We could hardly believe that we were not shot at. . . . I had taken along a white 'flag' in the form of a towel, but we did not [need to] show it. When we came into the village which we had lost the night before, we met an American officer, who was very friendly and wanted to know what I thought of his President Wilson, but he assured us that he did not know anything of the battery and its men." After consulting a map they located the four guns which had been overrun, still intact. Nearby was an unopened first-aid packet, which reassured him that his men had not been wounded. "I noticed horses in the village, which a German unit obviously had left behind, and asked the American a little impudently if I might not [use the horses to] take the guns back with me. He personally did not seem to have any objections, but he said that his orders read that 'nothing shall be moved.' "

His troops, the American told Brautigam, had not been informed of the approaching Armistice. "Otherwise they certainly would not have crossed the Maas last night and would have spared themselves the heavy losses." After he left, Brautigam confessed, "my companion and I removed the breeches and sights from the guns to make them useless, because it was a point of honor not to let the enemy gain control of still useful guns. . . . On our way to regimental headquarters we ran into American soldiers several times who looked covetously at the Iron Crosses on our chests. With a whistle that showed admiration they said, 'Oh, Iron Cross,' and they would have liked to take them as souvenirs. They offered food and cigarettes to the sergeant walking behind me. He repeatedly and furiously rapped the knuckles of the hands which were grabbing at his chest."

Worried that they might lose their way after dark and become prisoners, they turned back and relocated their horses. At their quarters in Carignan, just west of the Luxembourg frontier, they found the missing men had returned, slipping through the heavily wooded Argonne. Only the cannoneer had been slightly wounded.

Brautigam's exploit, and the return of the missing men, seemed almost a victory to the troops readying themselves for the long march home. In the gathering darkness the Germans, from Flanders to Lorraine, would ignite what seemed to be their entire pyrotechnic supply. Rockets and flares in red, blue, green, and white sputtered and sizzled in the twilight sky. From the Allied side the defeated enemy's cheering and singing of patriotic songs seemed inexplicably strange, but the Germans were as relieved as were their adversaries that the shooting had ended. Yet the fireworks of explosions that indicated the setting off of German ammunition stores had no festive meaning. Rather than surrender usable war materiel, the Germans were destroying what they could not take back. From a distance it seemed like celebration.

On the Allied side a band from the Black 92nd Division played ragtime to the bewildered French. A few years later they would be devoted to the music. In the 42nd Division area soldiers spent the evening firing the captured German rocket stores, and each man,

Colonel George Leach noted, built his own little fire for himself out of the wealth of local debris. If anything was as important to a soldier as to be able to stand up, it was to have a fire. As the 7th Field Artillery's history put it, "The artillery camp was illuminated by hundreds of little campfires around which the men tried to realize that the war was really over."

In the 54th Infantry's sector of the Argonne groups gathered around the fires and began singing. Then, Gregory Mabry, a recruit in the division, wrote, "some demoniac genius started working on his automatic. In an instant, bedlam broke loose—rifles, machine guns, grenades, artillery, rockets—a perfect horror of noise. The wiser ones donned their helmets on the principle that everything that goes up is bound to come down. Finally, after what appeared to be an interminable time, a bugle sounded 'Cease firing' and the pandemonium ceased as suddenly as it began." In the 101st Machine Gun Battalion's area, Wainwright Philips reported, the sky was aglow for miles with rockets and flares. "Even whole boxes of gunpowder are set off and go up with a roar. . . . We are ordered back to Marre, and the flivvers line up the road to receive us with all headlights streaming out into the night . . . the first time we have seen such a thing all through the war."

In the Verdun area, where the French had nearly bled the nation away, there was a resurgence of patriotism which seemed to belie the mutinies of 1917, and even a celebration which outlasted supplies of Very flares. "I went to bed about ten P.M.," Captain Harry Truman remembered, "but the members of the French Battery [to the rear of the 129th] insisted on marching around my cot and shaking hands. They'd shout 'Vive le Captain Américain, vive President Wilson,' take another swig from their wine bottles and do it over. It was 2 A.M. before I could sleep at all." For the most part, the exhausted French were less demonstrative, British Colonel Richard Meinertzhagen observing that to go from the French sector to the supposedly phlegmatic British zone was to go from Frenchmen "yelling with delight and all displaying small tricolor flags" to "unrestricted licence." Corporal Stanley Butcher, who had been in "Kitchener's Army" since early in the war, wrote to his parents, "Tonight I think the Army is going mad. There is one huge Brock's Benefit in coloured signals, flares and 'Very' lights. . . . What I would give to be home tonight!" Brock, a fireworks manufacturer, had been known for its profitable pyrotechnic displays, especially in the vicinity of the Crystal Palace in Sydenham, south of London, and had given its name to such shows. On the evening of the eleventh, the Western Front saw history's largest Brock's Benefit.

Few newly liberated towns, however close to the line, were without some incendiary ceremony. In the town of Aulnoye the brass band of the British 33rd Battalion, Machine Gun Corps, marched in a twilight procession illuminated more primitively than by Brock, with forty torches on twelve-foot poles. The *Maire* presented a bouquet to the bandmaster and a garland to the commander. Then volleys of Very lights were fired into the night. At Cuerne, Brigadier General J. L. Jack, commander of the 28th Infantry Brigade, was entertained with his staff by the mayor and his town council. "The town band," he wrote in his diary, "having hurriedly disinterred and cleaned their blue, silver-laced uniforms and instruments after four years' burial, is in grand form. . . . The healths of King George and King Albert are drunk. A few speeches are made in spite of linguistic difficulties—what does that matter on an occasion like this? . . . At last I lie down tired and very happy, but sleep is elusive." How far away, he mused, was August 1914, when he was a platoon leader at Valenciennes, about to confront the Germans. "Incidents flashed through the memory: the battles of the first four months: the awful winters in waterlogged trenches, cold and miserable: the terrible trench-war assaults and shell fire of the next three years: loss of friends, exhaustion and wounds: the stupendous victories of the last few months: our enemies all beaten to their knees. Thank God!"

Despite the fireworks in the night sky, below there were thousands of wounded in hospitals near the front, some of whom would not survive. Otto Brautigam had observed, on his trek into the American sector of the Argonne, "endless rows of graves," newly dug. And flu was killing more men on both sides in the last month of the war than shot and shell, and would soon take thousands who had come through the hazards of war. "I can never forget," Major Geoffrey Keynes, then an Army surgeon, wrote, "the sight of our mortuary tents with the pathetic rows of bodies of the men killed by one of the most lethal epidemics ever known. On Armistice Day . . . I was with a surgical team . . . near Cambrai. A close friend . . . George Leigh Mallory,* then in charge of a railway gun, was visiting me and shared my tent. . . . Together we witnessed that extraordinary scene, when the whole front in France seemed to be occupied

---

* Mallory would die in 1924 while trying to reach the summit of Mount Everest.

by maniacs, letting off flares, Very lights, and every other form of demonstration they could lay their hands on. . . . We thought we had seen the last of war."

Not far away, Leslie Walkinton's 47th Machine Gun Corps, which had sung "Na-poo, toodle-oo, Good-bye-ee" to the war, was being marched through Tournai "through welcoming collections of very happy people" to billets in a village called La Tombe. Their sergeant major could not resist a quip: "I always thought I should end up here!"

PRISONERS OF WAR

Brüder, zur Sonne, zur Freiheit,
  Brüder, zum Lichte empor!
Hell aus dem dunklen Vergangnen
  Leuchtet die Zukunft hervor!
Seht, wie der Zug von Millionen
  Endlos aus Nächtigem quillt,
Bis eurer Sehnsucht Verlangen
  Himmel und Nacht überschwillt,
Brüder, in eins nun die Hände,
  Brüder, das Sterben verlacht:
Ewig der Sklaverei ein Ende,
  Heilig die letzte Schlacht!

On to the sun and to freedom,
  Brothers, arise in your might,
No more the darkness of ages,
  Brothers, the morning is bright!
Onward the millions are marching,
  Bringing the future to birth,
See how your endless battalions
  Spill over heaven and earth.
Brothers, with hands joined together,
  Fearless in danger and strife,
Let's put an end to our slavery:
  Sacred the battle for life!

—*Brüder, zur Sonne, zur Freiheit,* ONCE A RUSSIAN REVOLUTIONARY
  SONG, WAS PICKED UP BY GERMAN PRISONERS
  OF WAR IN RUSSIA AND GERMANIZED
  BY SYMPHONY CONDUCTOR HERMANN SCHERCHEN,
  A PW HIMSELF IN 1917-1918

Between the Swiss border and the Belgian coast the fluid frontier between the armies was swarming with prisoners and potential prisoners on both sides. Neither side wanted to take any more mouths to feed; however, bouncing along east of the Meuse in a Ford truck, Sergeant William Hale and Corporal B. C. Warlick had outdistanced the insistent traffic of ammunition trucks, supply wagons, guns on caissons, rolling kitchens, ambulances, and staff cars. It was 10:30 A.M. when they jolted to a stop around a curve to avoid running down a group of men in field-gray uniforms. The pair were suddenly—in effect—prisoners of war.

German curiosity was aroused by the cargo in the back of the truck. With shortages in almost everything plaguing them, almost anything might be worth confiscating. Eager hands ripped open the bulky canvas sacks. Out fell several hundred copies of the November 8 issue of *Stars and Stripes* intended for the 90th Division. Uninterested in the booty and even less interested in having two more hungry men, the Germans sent Hale and Warlick wheeling back across the line.

In a reverse episode almost certainly with basis in fact, R. H. Mottram's Lieutenant Dormer in *The Spanish Farm* trilogy finds, soon after he announces the cease-fire to his men, that he has acquired 140 unwanted new prisoners. All along the opposite side of the street in the Flanders village, "faultlessly aligned and properly 'at ease,' were men in field grey." Addressing Dormer in perfect English, a tall man who gave his rank as *Feldwebel* and identified his regiment, adds, "I surrender to you, sir."

"We didn't capture 'em," Dormer's young subordinate says. "They just marched up the street. The post at the bridge let 'em through."

At Brigade headquarters the Colonel explains to Dormer and the *Feldwebel* his orders received for carrying out the Armistice: "Prisoners taken after 11.0 A.M. to be sent back to their own units, on the line of retreat." Courteously, the German sergeant major responds, "We refuse to obey the order, sir. Our regiment is twenty miles away. All the peasants have arms concealed. We shall just be shot down."

"How difficult War became," Dormer muses, "with the burden of civilization clogging its heels." Someone telephones for military police help. "In the meantime a French Liaison Officer made a speech, and Dormer grinned to hear him. Fancy apologizing for the War. . . . The crowd quieted, thinned, dispersed. The police arrived, and had a discussion with the Adjutant. . . . The *Feldwebel* strode up

and down in front of his men, master of the situation. At length . . .
six lorries rolled up in the dark, an interpreter was put on board, and
the party moved off in the November dusk." The twenty miles
would be no problem that way, and the Armistice conditions would
be carried out.

In Belgium, British troops would encounter thousands of released or escaped British and even Italian prisoners of war flooding
through their lines, the British ones marching back steadily in makeshift squads under a sergeant or the oldest soldier. Hundreds had
broken out of a prisoner compound in Brussels on hearing that the
Armistice had been signed. German officers watched their orders
disobeyed, as their soldiers would not fire. Others were set free by
mutinous guards in red armbands. Reports began to drift into the
American sector, Colonel George Marshall noted, "that the Germans had promptly withdrawn all along the line, and there was thus
left a zone in which there was no constituted authority to maintain
order. Released prisoners, Russians, Italians, Rumanians, etc., were
reported to be endangering the lives of the French inhabitants left in
this region. We were forbidden, however, from taking any action as
we could not go beyond the Armistice line."

When the mayor of a town in the Woëvre plain reached American lines with information that released Russian prisoners had
raided abandoned German supply dumps for arms and ammunition, and were terrorizing the villagers, Marshall decided to investigate. With his driver he motored to Stenay and passed beyond the
American lines, on the Montmedy road, into unoccupied ground.
Two kilometers to the east he found the road "filled from side to side
with long-bearded, filthy-looking Russians." When they saw the
ramrod-straight American colonel emerge "they instantly formed up
into a column of squads and stood rigid and motionless, looking
straight to the front."

Neither Marshall nor his driver spoke any Russian. "So I called
out to them, using the greeting that I understood they always received from their Czar, 'Good morning, my children.' To my embarrassment, not a child moved or spoke, and the chauffeur
indulged in some ribald laughter. I then pointed toward our own
lines and motioned them forward, and the column marched by like
a regiment in review." There were 1,800 of them, captured by Hindenburg's army in 1914 and worked like slaves by Germans ever
since, building fortifications near Verdun. "They were so cowed,"
Marshall remembered, "that at the least frown they jerked into a
rigid posture, from which it was hard to relax them."

Cecil Roberts, a young correspondent for provincial newspapers and later editor of the *Nottingham Journal,* encountered other abandoned Russian prisoners between Mons and Namur. A "pathetic clump" devastated by influenza, they struggled with coffins on a barrow to bury their dead, a bearded, bareheaded Orthodox priest walking with them, preceded by a prisoner bearing a large crucifix.

Prisoner-of-war camps for German and Austrian soldiers in France had been placed far to the west, to keep them remote from any possible shift in the battle lines. Prisoners were also shunted to Corsica, Algeria, Morocco, and Tunisia, German books of PW memoirs recalling French treatment bitterly as *"Todesurteil"* (death sentence) and *"französischer Sadismus."* One Hungarian writer, Aladar Kuncz, arrested in France at the start of the war although not a soldier, was put in a prison camp nevertheless, and offered his release if he joined the Foreign Legion. It was a dubious freedom tendered often but rarely accepted. In prison still in November 1918, on the Ile d'Yeu in the Bay of Biscay, with German and Austro-Hungarian companions ranging from seamen to tramps, he remained without news of the war except what was passed on by guards and new arrivals.

Two or three days before the Armistice they had been given a copy of *La France* which described the defeat "with indisputable exactitude. . . ." Despair gripped the Germans, who huddled together for comfort or drifted about from cellblock to cellblock like sleepwalkers. Kuncz's description sums up the motley "enemy" population the French had swept up:

> The Count, the flaxen-haired Baron, the gymnasts; Däumling, Nagel and their pupils, bearded Müller, who had had such an unshakable faith in the future of Germany, friendly Bohnen; . . . fat, oily Bürger, Däumler of the many letters, hook-nosed Hacke of the tail-coat, handsome Tienemann, Georges, Von Bergen; then Kaufmann the tennis-player, our own special friend Schuler, Levi the old owl of No. 51 who used to chew and read all day in his little den and only go out at night; the noisy, brawling seamen and workmen from Nos. 53 and 55; Biesenbach and Von der Hohe, the two business men; Klein and the cunning canteen waiter, the blond apprentice watchmaker, the drunkard Varvey . . . and all the commercial travellers and artisans whom we otherwise scarcely ever saw. . . . Sometimes

someone who had got hold of a copy of *La France* would read
out a couple of lines, loudly, slowly, like a funeral oration. . . .
Then the growl of talk swelled again, as though they were repeating it in German and explaining to each other what they
had just heard.

Announcing the Armistice, the prison authorities encouraged
its celebration by hoisting a large Tricolor to the highest point of the
citadel at Port Joinville. "And in the yard, in pouring rain, twenty
or thirty of the prisoners set off with a band and lanterns to celebrate
the end of the War. Their shadows were projected monstrously in
the light of the lanterns, and in the wet mist of rain their fiddles and
mandolins tinkled mockingly. They went round the yard once. No
one joined them. Even the French soldiers watched them from
under the gateway with some contempt. So the celebrators stopped,
looked round and slunk back underground."

In the camp in France where Hermann Reese had spent much
of the war, the prisoners were taunted on the morning of the eleventh by music and singing from the guards. Angrily, the Germans
sprang from their beds and rallied in front of the commandant's office. Despite the heavy rain they marched up and down singing
"Deutschland über alles" until the French tried to end the demonstration by announcing an inspection. No one obeyed, despite threats of
court-martial. Some prisoners loudly cursed the fluttering Tricolor
and cried "Down with France," making gestures as if to rip down
the offending flag. "The waves of bitterness," Reese wrote, "rose
higher and higher. In front of the gate a machine gun was set up, yet
it intimidated no one, even when a few shots flew harmlessly overhead. . . . The cannons are silent," Reese appealed in his diary.
"Why don't they let us go?"

Kurt Wilke's autobiographical *Prisonnier Halm* (1929) professed
to be the memoir of a bookbinder-draftee captured by the French at
St. Quentin, during the last retreat from the Somme. At one French
camp he nearly dies of hunger and exposure. At others he is sent off
on salvage jobs, encountering daily through the local population
and new prisoners the worsening news from the front. How far
would the retreat extend, Halm wonders—to the Meuse, to the
Rhine? One day he reads a word in heavy type which he does not
know—*"L'Armistice."* His comrades do not believe it. "The French
papers told monstrous lies. For example, the whole German army
would not account for the number of prisoners said to have been

captured in this last week." Still, even French children shout the word, and soon the Germans began believing that they would soon be home.

On November 11 the French were beside themselves with joy. The order was given to march east to Chauny, and each PW given a day's supply of food. But they would not be taken to the railhead of St. Quentin to entrain for Germany. Instead they would be put to work in reconstruction, in the very area in which Halm had been taken prisoner, now being reoccupied by the remnants of its former inhabitants. "There were placards on the walls depicting the German Emperor, bowed, humbled, surrounded by the twenty-two flags of his enemies. It was a picture that brought tears to the eyes of every patriotic German, but it was the least offensive of all the placards. The others were full of hate and calumny, displaying over and over again the Boche, reeking with the blood of children. It was incomprehensible that the French should be continuing the violent war propaganda. Were they not victorious? The German philosophy of life included consideration and sympathy for vanquished opponents." The French thought otherwise.

It would be January 1920 before Prisoner Halm was returned across the Rhine to Hildesheim.

An unnamed German flying officer is taken prisoner in France on the last day of the war in William Faulkner's short story "Ad Astra." Born into the lesser Prussian nobility, he had resisted assimilation into its ways, studying music at the university and marrying "the daughter of a musician who was a peasant." But one older brother dies "of a lady's husband" in 1912 and another, a General Staff officer, just after the Kaiser's fall "iss shot from his horse by German soldier in Berlin street." A letter arrives at his base addressed to him as *Baron.* "So I burn all my papers," he tells his English and American interrogators, "[even] the picture of my wife and my son that I haf not yet seen, destroy the identity disk and remove all insignia from my tunic. . . ."

Fleeing one's inheritance becomes a form of mind-suicide for the reluctant baron, who, his head wrapped in a turbanlike bandage, responds to the suggestion that his escape from Germany was an admission of being "whipped."

"Yes," he says. "It wass our time first, because we were the sickest. It will be your England's next. Then she too will be well."

"And what will you do now?" asks one of the Englishmen. The

prisoner does not answer, and the Englishman is asked, in turn, by one of his colleagues, "What will you do? What will any of us do? All this generation which fought in the war are dead tonight. But we do not yet know it."

German prisoners shipped to the United States were psychologically as well as geographically remote from the Armistice. Prisoners—all captured sailors—at Fort Oglethorpe, Georgia, prevented from publishing news or comment about the war in their *Orgelsdorfer Eulenspiegel*, were busy on the eleventh hand-printing essays on art and literature. Richard Goldschmidt, later director of one of the Kaiser Wilhelm Institutes in Berlin but then a sailor PW, remembered that the editor was "a kind of Bohemian named [Erich] Posselt. The contributors were men from all walks of life, only one professional writer, H[anns] H[einz] Ewers, being among them. For example, Kuhn was a banker . . . Schlimbach a sea captain. . . . The publishing met with the greatest difficulties. There was nothing but a small hand-press used for printing menu-cards on steamers and very little [type]. . . . As the prisoners were not permitted to have tools, all the illustrations were cut with ordinary pocket-knives into cigar-box lids or strips of linoleum." The issue dated November 15 would include a line engraving of a wooden barracks on stilts along a dirt street, the building's yellow boards beneath a green roof; and another showing a wooden *Wachtturm* looming above the huts. Future wars would demonstrate no advance in design of barracks and watchtowers or in handling of prisoners. The only concession the authorities would make to the Armistice—if they even recognized it as such— was to permit the printing (in German) of an "Im Memoriam" poem in which the writer noted that on this day, when the prison was quiet, they remembered those comrades who had died far from the Homeland. It was labeled a translation from Walt Whitman. Clearly the gullible censor in Georgia had never read Walt Whitman in any language.

Even more remote were the German sailors in *Kriegsgefangenen* in Japan. One camp newspaper, *Die Baracke,* in Bando, on Shikoku, north of Tokushima, like the American *Eulenspiegel* apparently forbidden to mention current events, settled for essays on billiards and Beethoven, and prints of local landscapes in the Japanese manner. Yet the *Kriegesgefangenen Zeitung*— a nearly daily newsletter on Ninoshima, a tiny island in the bay south of Hiroshima—kept up to date with material supplied by the Kokusai Agency from news services in London, New York, and Paris. On the ninth the Germans in Ninoshima learned of the Kaiser's abdication and on the eleventh of the Armistice.

Far different were circumstances in Siberia, where the shooting should have stopped much earlier but would not in fact cease for months and even years, as the Western Allies attempted to undo Lenin's revolution. Erich Edwin Dwinger's Siberian diary notes the increasing despondency of German prisoners in Siberia as the collapse in the West became clear. "All for nothing," a lieutenant kept muttering. "We dragged ourselves around," Dwinger recalled, "like criminals whose term of imprisonment had become a life-sentence. How could we return home now?" One German cavalry sergeant major in Dwinger's barracks would hang himself, and Dwinger's captors, followers of the anti-Bolshevik leader Admiral A. V. Kolchak, would urge that he join them. ("What about it? Your Emperor is in exile, and you are no longer bound by your oath of fealty. . . . I'll bring you the newspapers tomorrow. Then you'll come along with us. . . . A man like Kolchak . . . a hero—a gentleman!") It would be a long winter.

For many prisoners, German, Austrian, and Hungarian, months would pass before the news of the Armistice would arrive in Siberia via Japanese newspapers shipped through Vladivostock. Months more would pass, and American newspapers would arrive, before they would believe it. Despite armistice—theoretically—on every front, and revolutions across Europe, they were still prisoners, and to compound their desperation they were suffering from the cold and from lack of food. Of the thirty prison camps in Siberia, one would be taken over by the Americans and two by the Japanese. In the others, PW misery would be prolonged until the Russians took effective control of their land mass.

Louis Bourdon was a peasant's son, in the reserves since 1909 when at twenty his "class" was called up. With his broad blond mustache he had looked severe and military when his picture was taken as he went on active duty. A teacher, he knew German and English, which caused the Germans to appoint him *Dolmetscher* (interpreter) for his group of prisoners when they were captured early in the war. The *Gefangenenlager* near Münster in which he was housed with other Frenchmen was a stark, bare collection of one-storied barracks on the edge of a wood. From there the prisoners were marched out to mines in the Ruhr. But not on the day of *Waffenstillstand.*

Sergeant Bourdon had known it was coming. Miners worked side by side with German civilian foremen who had newspapers increasingly free from censorship. On the fifth the French read of English successes in Flanders along the Escaut. Then Red "Spartakists" quietly checked to see whether the Münster PWs would join the revolution when it happened. Bourdon's diary noted that the barracks were quiet. "The Spanish flu is raging. I am sick and stay inside as much as I can. Joseph brings me the newspapers. It is Armistice Day. I read in wonder but with skepticism at the conditions that it imposes. . . . I quickly translate the article and post it on the bulletin board. The uproar starts."

For officers, especially career men, waiting for the end was a humiliation. At Friedberg and then at Ingolstadt, Captain Charles de Gaulle, wounded and taken prisoner thirty-two months earlier at Verdun, was back in his compound after his fifth escape attempt. He had used enemy newspapers to perfect his German, but tunneling, stolen uniforms, fluent German, and other devices had been useless. His great height had given him away after a few miles of freedom. A punishment camp for officer escapees, Ingolstadt housed Americans, British, and even a stocky insolent young Russian named Mikhail Tukhachevsky, later a marshal of the Red Army who would be executed in one of Stalin's purges in the 1930s. But while in Ingolstadt de Gaulle had written notes for his first book on military tactics—which interested the postwar *Reichswehr* before the sluggish French Army. And he was a survivor. On the beaches of Dunkirk in May 1940, having been held back in promotion because of his captivity, he was an elderly colonel of fifty, named, in desperation, an acting brigadier general.

Americans had been on the line too brief a time to have populated German PW camps with many ground troops. Forty miles from Munich, on the grounds of Schloss Trausnitz, the prison at Landshut was a transient camp for airmen, most of them housed in a huge five-story stable of wood and stone, the top level a single-windowed attic in the inverted V of the roof, where James Norman Hall solaced his boredom by stretching out his reading of Chaucer to one Canterbury Tale per week.

In October a new contingent of captured pilots arrived, with stories of advances which suggested that the war would end soon. Early in November a *Feldwebel* back from a leave in Munich confided that he had seen violence in the streets. Americans who had dreamed of escape in the direction of the Swiss border, two hundred miles away, settled down to waiting. Still, no alteration in the camp routine was perceptible until the PWs noticed a guard throw his cap on the ground and stamp on it. Then another tore off his regimental insignia.

On the eleventh Herr Pastor, Bavarian inspector of prison camps, arrived for his regular visit, greeting the Americans in his usual urbane, bantering manner.

"Well, gentlemen," he began, "I hope you are enjoying your solitude these cool autumn days?"

"Herr Pastor," asked Henry Lewis, a flier from Philadelphia, "what has happened?"

The inspector, Hall recalled, toyed with them by pulling his pipe from his pocket and stuffing it in leisurely fashion with ersatz tobacco. Then he lit it and puffed deliberately, finally pausing to say, "Yes, you are right. Something *has* happened. I'm sure that you'll all be sorry to learn of it, but the fact is that the war is over. An Armistice was signed at eleven o'clock this morning."

For a moment the Americans only stared at him. Then Charles Codman broke the silence. "And so you've come to bid us farewell," he said. "We'll often think of you, Herr Pastor. You've been very decent to us, and in some ways we have enjoyed our stay here. . . . Well, good-bye. Shall we go out at the main gate or at the little one on the other side?"

"Herr Pastor, you're not joking, are you?" Hall asked.

"If there's any joke about it, it's on us, not you. No, the war's finished." But he cautioned them, "Now don't be in too great a hurry. I said that an Armistice had been signed, not that there is to be an immediate release of prisoners. It may be some weeks, even months. . . ."

The prisoners argued, pleaded, cajoled. All Pastor had to do was to leave a gate, inadvertently, open. "No," he said, between puffs, "it's quite impossible. I'm sorry, but you must stay here until you can be released in the proper way." But he would "think it over."

Just inside the high-arched stone doorway to the barn, Guy Brown Wiser and his cronies celebrated after a raid on the stocks of Rhine wine in the castle. Someone had a banjo, and inspired by alcohol and the prospects of freedom, they raised their voices in toasts and in song, one airman leaping up upon a large wooden crate to raise his right arm, bottle in hand, to represent the Statue of Liberty with her torch. Wiser (Cornell, 1917, and a future commercial artist) drew a picture of the scene in his notebook.

Toward noon the following day, Herr Pastor would reappear to authorize the disappearance into Switzerland of any who cared to make their way to Munich to entrain from there to Lindau and Lake Constance. "Remember," the inspector would warn, "this is an escape. . . ."

"Theoretically," said Hall, who would take his Chaucer with him, and later, with James Nordhoff, write a memorable tale of his own, *Mutiny on the Bounty.* And he would also write a story, "Falcons of France," about airmen PWs who would escape at great hazard, across the Swiss border, only to be awakened the next morning by church bells ringing the news of the Armistice. *"Ja, ja,"* says their Swiss host happily. *"Krieg fertig!"* Hall had taken an artist's license with history.

Herbert Empson, a prisoner at a camp near Cologne, remembered how quickly choruses of *"Hoch! Hoch!"* returned—how the revolutionaries floundered about and then elected their officers to their former positions. Red armbands often remained, but "rifles reappeared and soon the innate German discipline had triumphed and saluting was back in full rigor."

At Cassel the commandant ordered the mutinous guards back to their duties. Then, when they refused, he agreed to run the camp under their orders. The routine was almost unchanged, but a bulletin posted in the courtyard verified the Armistice and announced that one of its conditions was "immediate repatriation without reciprocity of all Allied and United States prisoners of war."

The prisoners in the camp, according to Norman Archibald, were more bitter than content. "Shall the vanquished [Germans] leave a demolished country and return to one intact? Shall they walk from barren, shell-blown fields into meadows fertile and green? . . . Shall they leave a desolate mass of filthy twisted ruins and return, submissively, to a country untouched? To a country where streets are clean, where cities loom in their old splendor and where in every town and hamlet their homes, still standing, await them?" (At a camp for British soldiers a *Postern* would tell J. A. Chester that Germany would now be looking forward to the next war. "We could have beaten France and yourselves, but America has been too much for us.")

From the military school across the road, uniformed students poured out past the red brick prison. Long forbidden to pass the building, they knew that the rules were as valid now as were their helmets emblazoned with *Mit Gott für König und Vaterland.* "You are free!" they yelled. *"Mit dem Kriege sind wir jetzt fertig. Der Krieg ist aus! Der Krieg ist alles fertig!* Comrades, go home!" *Comrades* was a new word to toy with.

As in the American sector, where Colonel Marshall had to enter the vacuum of authority between the lines to restore order, the British in Belgium found PWs of all nationalities. George W. Barrow, a private in the 20th Middlesex Regiment who had been captured the previous April, was technically an inmate of the camp at Friedrichsfelde, but actually had been kept, with thousands of others, for manual labor in the receding rear of the German lines. "Thanks to the efficiency of the [Royal] Navy," he thought, "food was indescribably in short supply." In the final days of the war they were re-formed each afternoon and marched until dusk to the next site of operations. West of Brussels he was billeted in a local hall, where he slept atop a billiard table. "The following day, November 11, dawned fine and clear and after our ersatz coffee (burnt acorns, some said) we marched off and reached the main road, Brussels to Mons. . . . I well remember seeing a signpost that Waterloo was 2 or 3 kilometers farther down that road. . . . There were no civilians about and only a few parties of German soldiers. . . . Some of these shouted as we passed *'Kreige ende'* but we took little notice as we had heard similar expressions before and the sound of distant gunfire soon contradicted them."

They continued on through the Soignies Forest, emerging in a light rain near the Brussels-Louvain road, where an electric tram line ran. Wet and tired, but under orders to keep marching, they continued until they found a building which in better times had been used for horse shows. There they improvised fires to cook "various items we had thieved or been given by Belgian civilians en route. . . . So far as I knew, no one concerned themselves with events; indeed the day's significance had never registered. Then the German officer in charge . . . told us that an Armistice had been signed and we were free to go back to the Allied lines. To his credit he gave us a map of the route we had come by. . . ." Forming ranks, the Germans marched off in the other direction, toward Louvain and then Germany. Left on their own after months of captivity, discipline disappeared. They began straggling back in small groups, Barrow and two others finding an *estaminet* and ordering their first beer in eight months. The bartender would not accept their few marks. Curiously, a lone *Feldwebel* was there drinking his beer and tried to explain the mysterious Armistice to the British. Then, as a parting gesture, he gave Barrow his Iron Cross medal ribbon, and the bartender offered Barrow a 1914 picture postcard of the hotel and *estaminet*. (In his mid-eighties Barrow still had both.)

"After a short interval a tram came from Brussels and, after reversing, took us into the City. No fare was charged." In Brussels "even smartly dressed women embraced us although [we were] dirty, our clothes in tatters and crawling with body lice. We must have presented a sorry picture of the British Army."

All over Belgium, British prisoners were abandoned only at the last moment, when they could be of no further use. It was, Thomas Johnston, of the 5th Seaforth Highlanders, remembered, "nine months of starvation." When the war ended for him he was taking wounded German horses to be treated. German soldiers wanting help in getting home offered him two cigarettes for them—a bargain he accepted. "The Germans piled their rifles in the centre of the town, poured petrol over them and set them on fire." Then they headed for home.

Wilfred Stevens, who had been a rifleman with the 8th Division until his capture that May, was employed destroying aerodromes and other military installations as the Germans retreated. Late on November 10, at the Luxembourg-Belgium border, his group of prisoners was told that the war was *"Alles kaput"* and that there would no longer be any restrictions on their movements. Quickly three of them set out for the first civilian houses they could find and, identifying themselves in French, asked for hospitality.

While eating their first substantial meal in months they learned about the Armistice. But then made the mistake of returning to their billets in order to have a place to sleep the night. "The next day, Armistice Day, our guards decided to leave for home. They packed their bags, loaded them onto a handcart and used us as human horses to drag it back to the Fatherland." For two days they were afraid to resist, but then slipped away into the Ardennes. In Paris they reported to a British major, "who was so delighted to see us that he gave me a hug. Something not to be forgotten by a mere rifleman."

Corporal Joseph Price of the 12th Middlesex Regiment had been in a PW working party in Belgium, learning how, from an exrailwayman in the group, to sabotage, with grit, the axle boxes of trains which stopped in the vicinity. They had no idea of the progress of the war until a captured airman was marched past them under escort. "Good luck, sir," they shouted, and he responded with a thumbs-up sign and the prediction that the British troops would be there shortly. Soon, indeed, the PWs were under shelling, and moved east of Cambrai, where Price escaped into a town whose name he never knew. There a Belgium railway worker offered a hiding place but his frightened wife refused. Price was recaptured, and it took another escape before his schoolboy French got him into a house in the Belgian village of Gemblouse which turned out to be the residence of the burgomaster.

Although there were eight German officers billeted in the house, he was offered refuge in the cellar, a mattress, and two blankets. "I was locked in, given some magazines and a pack of cards and the maid brought me such meals as could be spared. The [burgomaster] used to bring me up for fresh air anytime day or night when safe and convenient. This procedure went on from mid-October until on the morning of November 11 [he] came and took me under the house to a front cellar where through a grating that looked up on the street I saw . . . Belgian flags flying. I was amazed." Then the mayor unlocked a wine cellar, produced a bottle, and poured enough for a joint toast, and they shook hands and kissed. But the Germans had not yet left, and Price was again hidden away. Later, when the mayor "was fully satisfied the area was clear of Germans he took me to his garden & we dug up a trunk buried there. When we raised the lid & unwrapped his treasures he was delighted to see his antiques & rare silver again. He kissed various pieces, all in good condition, then shook hands with me which I took to mean a 'thank you' to the British Army."

As has been the convention in wars before and since, officer prisoners (who once came exclusively from the ranks of gentlemen or the aristocracy) did not have to work, while men in the lowest ranks, who came from the working classes anyway, were expected to perform useful labor. There was still another class of prisoners—civilian internees, mostly business and professional men who were trapped when the areas in which they were working suddenly became enemy territory. Nearly five thousand—Russian, French, and Belgian included, but mostly English—had been interned, many since the beginning of the war, at a racetrack in Ruhleben ("peaceful life"), two miles west of Berlin's 1914 boundaries, near Spandau. The flat, reclaimed marshland just south of the Spree, canalized at that point, was damp, dreary, and windswept in winter, dusty and dry in summer. The eleven stables became congested barracks in which the men lived, often out of the suitcases with which they arrived, since there were no hooks, shelves, or closets. Prisoners lay elbow to elbow at night, and when indoors vied for a beam of light by which to read or write. As horses did neither, there had existed little provision for electric lighting, and the chief activity—since it provided warmth, exercise, and something to do—was walking on the track in front of the empty grandstands, soon dubbed the *Promenade des Anglais.*

The only newspapers the prisoners were ever offered were German ones, which had purveyed a steady diet of victories, but every day in October the familiar places of August 1914 reappeared in the German press—St. Quentin, Valenciennes, Cambrai, Le Cateau, Lille. Also, the signs of collapse elsewhere—Turkey, Bulgaria, Austria—could not be hidden, and the Berlin press was reporting freely the exchanges with President Wilson. Soon there were red armbands among the sentries, and the prisoners began to form supervisory committees to take over functions which had to be performed regardless of the outcome of the internal struggles in Berlin. By November 11 they were virtually running the camp.

One of the younger internees was John Balfour, an Oxford student of twenty-four who had been in Freiburg to study German when the war broke out. Joseph Powell, he recalled, had been elected captain of the camp by the others, and in the vacuum of authority had gone off without German interference to consult the Dutch Legation in Berlin, whose *chargé d'affaires,* Chevalier Van Rappart, gave him a copy of the Armistice terms, just received.

> Returning to Ruhleben in the evening, Powell made straight for the camp theatre, underneath the grand stand, where he knew that several hundred prisoners would be gathered for the nightly theatre performance. On that evening the Theatrical Society were playing . . . [Edward Sheldon's] *Romance,* in which I had the part of the family butler. The first act had just finished, and standing in the center of the stage with the actors grouped around him (I felt foolish in my chop whiskers on such an occasion), Powell read out the sensational news that the once-invincible Germany army had laid down its arms and that the war was over. After the wild cheers of the audience had subsided, the producer of the play inquired whether those present would like to disperse or would prefer that the play should go on. The majority voted for the continuance of the play and it

was with a sense of ridiculous anticlimax that I began the second act—opening the door on to the stage and announcing, "Madame Cavallini!"*

Taken prisoner in the last German offensive had been 51st Division telegraphist George Waymark. He had been put to work loading wood and sand from barges on the Schelde onto railway cars, for fortifications in Flanders. But as the line moved east the prisoner work force was moved as well, Waymark finding himself in a camp at Worms, in the Rhineland, weak from poor food and exhausted from battling the "everlasting lice." In a camp for Russians and Frenchmen, the English were in a compound occupied by "Froggies" until the French escaped—another sign of deterioration. "Two water soups and 12 to a loaf a day. The only consolation is that we have no work to do." With everything caving in, the iron discipline which had found work even when there was none had disappeared. On the tenth Waymark wrote in his diary of the "glorious news" that the Armistice had been signed. It was premature by a day, but he could see the end coming. In his diary he wrote, "They don't seem to mind what we do. For example, we broke down the 10′ partition dividing us from the next camp and Jerry walked to the other end of the camp so that he should not see. When we got in the other camp I saw two men, or rather skeletons, because they were nothing more. They wore khaki clothes and looked ghastly. I asked them who they were and what regiment they belonged to, but they had lost all power of speech. I don't know whether they were British or not, but they must have been treated hellishly to be in that condition."

The prison camp for officers in the Rhenish city of Mainz was, by prison standards of comfort, a London club. Still, Alec Waugh wrote, "The entrance of the Citadel Mainz was calculated to inspire the most profound gloom. An enormous gate swung open, revealing a black and cavernous passage. As soon as we were all herded in, the gate shut behind us, and we were immersed in darkness. Then another gate at the end of the passage creaked back on unoiled hinges, and ushered us into our new home." A product of the military college at Sandhurst, and already the author of a widely discussed public school novel, *The Loom of Youth*, Waugh had become a *Gefan-*

---

* Sir John Balfour would later appear on a larger stage, as Minister in Lisbon, Moscow, and Washington, and Ambassador to Argentina and Spain.

genen at twenty, soon after his arrival in France. Block III in the spring of 1918 seemed like a dungeon to him, with its bad light; and the bland routine of miserable meals, three o'clock ersatz coffee, and eleven o'clock lights-out measured the days. There was, however, an alcove the PW educational committee reserved "for authors, architects and other students." "The Alcove" was Waugh's "equivalent for a University. It was there that I met for the first time adult minds upon equal terms."

Other captives were Hugh Lunn, who would write as Hugh Kingsmill; Gerard Hopkins, an author and translator; Milton Hayes, a writer and music-hall entertainer; and a brilliant young man, John Holms, "who came to nothing, who died young." In the Alcove, Kingsmill remembered, he wrote a novel which, not surprisingly, reflected "a mood of general disillusionment. . . . I did not expect the war to further my felicity [but] I felt no bitterness against it as it drew to its tired close." Trying to find out what was happening, Kingsmill volunteered to a sentry, cautiously, "It seems as if the war is nearing its end."

"Ja! Ja!" he laughed. *"Deutschland kaputt! Duetschland kaputt!"* He explained the situation to Kingsmill as he saw it. "Germany's one aim now was to please President Wilson and the *Entente.* How glad the good President would be when he heard that the Germans were no longer militaristic! He would raise the blockade at once. There would be butter and sugar again, oh, dear God! and tea and soup and white bread! and no more army, no more discipline, no more rich and poor! And all nations at peace and friendly. A new world, a new world!"

Rumors swept the *Gefangenenlager* that Mainz was under the red flag and that German officers could not walk the streets in uniform. For a day or two red-armbanded Germans assured the prisoners that revolution was breaking out in the West, that soldiers' councils were being formed in the armies of the *Entente,* even "that the terms of the Armistice would be cancelled by the English and French socialists, now about to take over the governments of their respective countries, and, finally, that the English fleet was sailing up the Kiel Canal under the red flag, to fraternise with their German comrades."

By November 11 the revolution had taken hold in Mainz and in the camp, and release, with Waugh taking his two thirds of a novel with him, was only a matter of time and transportation.

Enlisted men had no time as PWs to write novels. Since April

1918, Private E. C. Pattison, captured near Kemmel Hill, had been in a work gang digging coal at Golpa near Wittenberg. Twelve-hour days—or nights—on a diet of thin soup and potatoes guaranteed job inefficiency, which was compounded by the ineffectiveness of the civilian workers alongside them, all overage or medically deferred. What kept Pattison's group going were reports from new prisoners that the war was going well. Then civilian workers began to talk of the likely abdication of the Kaiser, and on November 9 they heard it had happened, and that a *Soldatenrat* had taken over the mining camp—men in uniforms without rank who were wearing red rosette badges. A copy of the *Berliner Tageblatt* confirmed the end was at hand, but November 11 found them "in rather a depressed mood," for they had been on very short rations for three weeks. That evening a Frenchman returning from work (and therefore in communication with civilians) told the Englishmen that the Armistice had been signed, and even had the terms, down to the number of railway cars and locomotives to be surrendered. But the prisoners "did not know if we ought to continue work until we were released; so, without wishing to stir up the anger of the Germans toward us, we continued [to dig coal] for eight or nine days afterwards."

Much of the same destiny awaited Thomas Williams of the King's Liverpool Regiment, who would spend Armistice Day digging poor-quality soft coal out of a German mine. Most of his fellow miners were Frenchmen, who tolerated less stoically than Williams the bleak diet which left them barely able to move about. At night they would remove the iron bars from the barrack windows and hunt in nearby fields for unharvested potatoes, risking blasts of shotgun pellets, even in darkness, from farmers on guard. (Many prisoners dug for coal with back and buttocks peppered with pellets rather than chance turning themselves in.) Conditions did not improve on November 11. When the prisoners declined to work they were informed that unless they brought the coal in there would be no food. The country was desperate for coal. Lacking any news about their repatriation rights, they agreed to work as paid laborers until, one morning in late December, they left the mines in force and trekked forty kilometers back to camp, where they awaited the long-promised trains.

Thousands of prisoners were scattered among mining sites. Private John Cummings of the Oxford and Bucks Light Infantry had been working in a salt mine at Volkenroda, north of Mulhausen (now in East Germany), and realized, from deserting soldiers and sailors, that the war had turned, when the elderly guards told him one day, *"Deutschland kaputt!"* Marched back to their camp, they were left without guards but also without any way to return. They would not reach Holland until December 17. Private W. H. Somerset, a prisoner since he had been wounded in March, had been working in a mine at Zerbst, in Saxony, with French and Russian PWs when, on the eleventh, guards were relieved of their weapons by cheering civilian revolutionaries. "Towards evening the [unarmed] sentries took us in relays to a local Beer Garden, and supplied German Lager." Private Tom Easton, Tyneside Scottish Brigade, had volunteered, as a prisoner, for the mines because it had been his occupation and he preferred facing what he knew to what might be worse. In a Westphalian mine near Münster he spent his working hours with two German civilians attacking a coal face, then his nights in a prisoner barracks. The routine changed only when an English-speaking German clergyman who conducted a weekly service confided in his sermon that the war would end in about ten days. "The people had had enough, and with the addition of the American forces in the field they could never win the war. The Kaiser would have to abdicate and a republic would have to be set up. . . . But we were to go on and say nothing. . . . A fortnight passed and when we went to the pit a big red flag flew at the pit head pulleys." The war had ended for Private Easton, and he would do the rest of his mining in Yorkshire. "Never at any time," he recalled more than sixty years later, "did we suffer any abuse. Only hunger at times, for they could hardly feed themselves."

In 1979 he returned to the pit he had left on November 11, 1918. It was still producing 16,000 tons a day. The authorities presented him with their traditional stamped miner's identification tally with his old number, 108: "So I have a passport if I want to go back."

After recovering in a German hospital from a "slight but lucky head wound" suffered at St. Quentin in March, when his brother Thomas was also captured, Corporal E. G. Williams of the King's Liverpool Regiment had found himself in a *Lager* at Marseburg, near Halle. He was still there on November 11. Bulging with ten thousand prisoners, mostly French and Russian, held since 1914, the camp had been built to house four thousand. At one corner was a large wooden barracks, no different from the others, which held five hundred British prisoners, half of them nonworking NCOs. (The British and Germans recognized the noncommissioned officer ranks as exempt from labor; the French recognized only sergeants as NCOs; thus the Germans put French corporals in the mines and on road crews.) Since Williams knew a little French and proved useful at sick call, he had wangled, by late October, a pass into town with a French friend. Hunger had gnawed at them all the time, and he remembered with bitterness, even in his eighty-seventh year, how the PW staple meal, vegetable soup, had been "defiled" with earth to give it the illusion of substance but served only to increase the incidence of diarrhea. In the town of Marseburg the smell of defeat hung heavily in the air. Reports of unattended wounded lying in railway cars all night at the station had come to them from new arrivals. The town seemed empty of people, and the shops were empty of merchandise. A butcher's window displayed "a mock joint of meat but nothing else."

The Frenchman on an earlier pass had met a local woman who invited him on his next opportunity to hear her daughter play Beethoven. He and Williams went and sat in a very small room hardly large enough for the upright piano. While waiting, the prisoners (almost the only men in Marseburg) made small talk in French, and the "good lady, large and middle-aged . . . on learning I was English, recoiled in horror and hatred and was pacified with difficulty. The hymn of hate was real." German patriotic posters had been blaming the British blockade for all domestic discomforts and privations. Beethoven went unperformed.

On November 9, Williams discovered that a "workers' committee" had taken over the camp. "The British showed their sang-froid and just told them to get on with their business and to remember that they had lost the war." On the eleventh "relief was overshadowed by anxiety. . . . Satisfaction was blunted by being still behind the barbed wire. Here in the drab conditions of imprisonment the sudden change of conditions was too shocking to be appreciated."

Even when Williams was free to leave he remained, waiting for his brother to be released from his mine. They had enlisted together on November 5, 1914, and gone to France together in 1915. Taken prisoner in the same action at St. Quentin, E. G. and Tom Williams would go home together.

To the east in Silesia, five hundred miles from the Western Front, in the town of Schweidnitz, near Breslau (now Wroclaw in Poland), a *Lager* housed three hundred British officers, mostly from the infantry, who had spent many of their waking hours planning escapes.

The daring escape of Captains J. H. Hardy and W. Loder-Symonds, who sent a taunting postcard to the German commandant from Holland to announce their safe arrival—they had not been missed as the others concealed their absence—had been the most notorious. The success had whetted the appetites for freedom of others, and a daring tunneling attempt, an engineering triumph requiring the construction of an air pump from makshift parts, had almost succeeded. Only the accidental presence of a German soldier and his girl making love in a field, when the earth opened and escaping prisoners appeared in the dark, had foiled the effort. But on Sunday afternoon, November 10, escape no longer seemed necessary as the vague rumors reaching *Lager* I appeared confirmed, Captain J. B. Sterndale Bennett remembered, "by the half-comic, half-pathetic spectacle of our German guard ripping the Imperial eagles from their helmets and helping each other to cut off the epaulettes from their tunics. I am afraid that we stood and laughed at them, which made them furious." All the sentry at the gate would tell the prisoners was that the Kaiser had fled. They could walk out of the prison if they pleased, but he advised prudence, "hinted darkly at an infuriated populace, and told us of the rumours . . . that bands of bloodthirsty sailors were expected hourly from Kiel."

None came, but that evening there appeared a deputation of the local *Soldatenrat* led, according to Sterndale Bennett, "by an unshaven, rat-like little man wearing a red armlet." Everything would continue as before, he announced, except that, for the protection of the prisoners, he was installing a few machine guns. There was no telling what the exasperated townspeople might do when they heard that the war was lost. "Furthermore, we had better not show a head at any window after sunset. We thought this all very considerate and kindly of him. But when the machine guns arrived, they were pointed at us instead of at the expected desperadoes. One was at the bottom of the stairs trained on the only exit from our dormitories; one was on a raised slope leveled at the only exit to the courtyard."

It dawned on the prisoners that the *Soldatenrat* was actually worried that the British might harbor counter-revolutionary sentiments, for after the Russian revolution in 1917 German officer-prisoners had sided with Russian officers. An additional month of days would pass before Allied forces found them. But they had the satisfaction of watching "the blustering ex-sugar-manufacturer who was our [camp] commandant . . . turned unceremoniously out of his Orderly Room by his own clerk." The junior officers disappeared, too, but in a few days, "after they had taken the oath to the new regime and abjured Kaiserdom for ever, they crept back with inconspicuous little [red] buttons in their caps, unsaluted by their own bewildered soldiers."

Another camp for officers at Schweidnitz, *Lager* II, had been opened to accommodate prisoners resulting from the last great German offensive in 1918. A five-storied former workhouse, with *"Gott und Arbeit"* carved over the forbidding, arched entrance, it was disorganized, dirty, and verminous, with many officers suffering from untreated wounds and all weak from near-starvation. The 150 men, including two winners of the Victoria Cross, had remained combative nevertheless, rioting when a young German officer ordered a roll call outside in the exercise yard during a heavy, cold rain.

As discipline among *Lager* II overseers deteriorated, Murray Lewis recalled, they watched a barracks set on fire accidentally by revolutionaries seeking food. Somewhere in the camp, they were sure, would be found parcels from England which the bureaucracy they replaced had never delivered and had kept for themselves. With no authentic news, the prisoners had to wonder about the boasts of their radical guards that they had been deprived of their commissions by the "Red British Army," which had taken over the government. King George V and the Prime Minister, they were told, had fled England.

It was, as the prisoners would soon realize, a widely prevalent wish-fulfillment fantasy based upon events in Germany.* With communications in chaos, there would be no news into the Breslau area for days. Meanwhile, with the machine guns capable of firing toward them or away from them, prisoners kept a low profile. According to Lieutenant Harold Gray the order from the Soldiers' Council that no one was even to look out was tested by a prisoner who put a hat up at one window and found it fired at. By the fourteenth they learned that the war had actually ended, and the senior British officer, Captain Barry Bingham, V.C., "more or less took over com-

---

* Yet it proved not to be a complete fantasy, as in December, when British military authorities attempted to "compulsory-draft" soldiers awaiting demobilization for service against the Communists in North Russia and Siberia, there were widespread demonstrations and refusals to obey orders. Military authorities feared an insurrectionary, even Bolshevik, tide surging through the armed forces, and Haig stubbornly put down one mutiny in Calais with infantrymen wielding fixed bayonets. The government finally solved the problem in the way the war-weary troops demanded—by demobilization.

mand." Yet it took until December 20 before they were extricated from Silesia and ferried home via Baltic ports.

There were also many men in the ranks in eastern prison camps. Private Cecil Bacon remembered being in a PW hospital in Czersk, now part of Poland, on Armistice Day, luckier than most men. ("We left behind . . . 75,000 Allied prisoners buried there.") He was, on Armistice Day, on a straw bed, with his heel, elbow, and buttock bones poking through his skin, debilitated with amoebic dysentery, when a British officer came through the hut which served as a hospital ward to tell the patients, many of whom would not survive until repatriation, that they would be home in thirty days. ("We did not believe him, as we were in rather bad shape and inclined to be rather light-headed.") Soon after, German officials arrived to check on which patients were in condition to be repatriated and announced that only those who could walk could leave the hospital. Those who could walk, many of them PWs since early in the war, "marched to the Commandant's office and threatened to burn the whole place down if they did not let us all leave.

"Two days later we were carried out on stretchers and taken to . . . railway box cars. It was not until hours later, when the door slid open, and I could see the Red Cross on the side of a white ship, that I believed I would ever see England again. . . . In the short distance from the box cars to the ship's gangway, someone put a large loaf of black bread on each stretcher and in many cases the bread fell off and went into the water 20 or 30 feet below. Many German civilians threw themselves into the water to recover the bread and had to be restrained by the guards, who used the flats of their swords to keep the populace back."

It was a Danish hospital ship, quickly pressed into service to attempt to save men whose chances were poor. Because the Baltic was heavily mined, progress would be slow, and there were many burials at sea before Copenhagen was reached and, eight days later, the port of Leith in Scotland. "I hope you will be all right soon, my boy," said Victoria's great-granddaughter, Princess Alice,* greeting the wan forms on the stretchers at the dock. "I have always remembered her," Bacon wrote sixty years later.

---

* She would be the mother of the Duke of Edinburgh, and thus mother-in-law of Elizabeth II.

THE OTHER FRONTS

It's a long way to Tipperary,
It's a long way to go;
It's a long way to Tipperary,
To the sweetest girl I know.
Goodbye, Piccadilly!
Farewell, Leicester Square!
It's a long, long way to Tipperary,
But my heart's right there!

—"TIPPERARY"

His armies retreating in Italy, in the Balkans, and in Poland, Emperor Karl I, at thirty-one, had reigned less than two years, having succeeded his eighty-six-year-old great uncle, Franz Josef I. Karl had not expected to be Emperor of Austria and King of Hungary, but in 1914 Archduke Franz Ferdinand, the old sovereign's heir, had been murdered at Sarajevo, a senseless political act which precipitated the dual monarchy's ultimatum to innocent Serbia—and fifty-one months of war.

By October 31, Karl's divisions had already disintegrated into bands of compatriots—"unredeemed nationalities" in the current euphemism—intent only on going home to help establish and protect their new states. At railheads Magyars, Czechs, Poles, and Slavs battled each other for weapons to take with them for their emerging national armies and for trains in which to go home. Unable even to conclude an armistice with efficiency, the Austro-Hungarian General Staff—more a geriatric staff—bungled its way to a cease-fire, while the Italians, eager to collect territory promised to them in secret agreements with Britain and France, dragged their feet about ending a war which was finally, after years of retreats and reverses, going their way.

When the armistice came on November 4, the Austrian Admiralty had already surrendered its fleet to the hated Yugoslavs rather than turn it over to the grasping Italians. The German U-boat flotilla based in the Adriatic, still harassing shipping, abandoned its only Mediterranean ports. Ten unserviceable submarines were scuttled, and sixteen that were still seaworthy assembled for the dismal voyage home, among them the UB 128, commanded by a young lieutenant, Wilhelm Canaris. On the way to Kiel he would receive alarming news of mutiny in the North Sea ports. The future admiral and Nazi intelligence chief was still at sea when he heard of the Armistice.

For the royal house in Vienna the end came on the evening of November 11 when the King and his family left by motorcar. Karl's last melancholy proclamation insisted, "Ever since my accession to the Throne, I have unceasingly tried to deliver my peoples from the tremendous war, for which I bear no responsibility. I have not retarded the re-establishment of constitutional life, and I have reopened to my people the way to solid national development. Filled with unalterable love for all my peoples, I will not in person be a hindrance to their free development. . . ." Then he left for his estate at Eckarteau and, from there, exile.

Discharged as a disabled veteran (a howitzer he was practice-firing had blown up), Lance Sergeant Benito Mussolini, again editing the Socialist *Il Popolo d'Italia* in Milan, exulted in the Austrian defeat, "This greatest joy is accorded to us: that of seeing an Empire annihilated. . . . This is the great hour!" The Vittorio Veneto campaign, which had begun north of Venice on October 24, had finally by the armistice driven the faltering Austrians and their few supporting German units back across the frontier. Unresisting, 275,000 prisoners had surrendered. Without British, French, and American help, and internal collapse in Austria, the Italians could not have won their own sideshow of a war, which had cost them 600,000 dead.

By November 9 the cease-fire on the Italian-Austrian front was in full execution. Austrian and Hungarian units were not only operating separately but permitting their Slav troops to wear a Yugoslav cockade. On the eleventh the American 332nd Regiment was one mile from Trieste, where Italians and Yugoslavs were squabbling over rights to the port. To keep U.S. troops out of trouble, Private Edward Sturm recalled, they were ordered back to their base at Treviso. The British XIV Corps command was more interested in moving north into Bavaria if the Germans refused to quit. Private John Clark, with a field ambulance unit of the 7th Division, complained to his diary on the day of the German armistice, "We are being messed about more now than ever. . . . All the Divisional troops and transport are en route to the Vicenza area." But the prospect of further fighting proved a false alarm, although tensions were rising between the Italians and Austrians, trying to hang on to their border areas, and between the Italians and the newly independent Yugoslavs.

Artist Alfred Kubin, an unmilitary-looking Austrian draftee, was appalled to learn that the armistice with Italy had granted the right of access across the border. He foresaw Allied troops pursuing the Germans across Austria into Bavaria. Then had come the German surrender, and he was astounded to encounter, on a country road near Linz, not the legendary *Reichswehr*, retiring, but

a ghostly caravan consisting of some ten wagons, pulled by tired, emaciated nags with manes and tails matted with filth. They were accompanied by some officers and soldiers from a German Bohemian regiment. I was asked about the nearest town, and I directed the fantastic troop to our wayside inn; it disappeared into the fog like a phantom left over from the

Thirty Years War. Later that evening, I went to the inn myself and chatted with the men, who had brought their wagon train up from Italy. Early next morning, the wagons and the horses—not to mention the lice and scabs—the harnesses and blankets, sugar and coffee, were auctioned off. Useful items were acquired at a laughably low price, and this resulted in a lively squabble. Immediately thereafter the warriors disappeared. It was rumored that they made their way across Bavaria to their homeland, Czechoslovakia, which no longer belonged to us. Two days later, the rural militia arrived and announced that it was forbidden to sell army goods, but they were too late; the peasants would not return a single item.

Arming its Czech prisoners of war in order to destabilize Austria as much as possible, Italy was sending them home with captured weapons and had seized ten thousand Austrian troops after the Armistice, setting them free only after confiscating their horses and mules. There was even tension between France and Italy because the Italians wanted all of Austria's warships. "Whether it is due only to the attitude of the French, or to their actual intrigues with the Yugo-Slavs," diplomat Guido Speranza wondered in his diary, "I don't know. Certainly it must be trying to France to see Italy sweeping along by herself and spoiling what was possibly France's plan of keeping Austria-Hungary on her feet." On the signing of the Armistice at Rethondes he added, "The Italians seem bent on making the most of this great opportunity. There is a sort of greediness in the air, very unpleasant after months of heroic daring and sacrifice."

On November 11, 1918, American nurse Agnes von Kurowsky returned to duty at the Red Cross hospital in Milan. *A Farewell to Arms*, with its Italian-front setting, would not be written for a decade, but Ernest Hemingway had conceived much of the novel at the hospital, with Agnes as Catherine Barkley. A *Kansas City Star* reporter seeking excitement, Hemingway at twenty had joined the Red Cross Ambulance Service and was seriously wounded during the fighting at the Piave in July. Full of shrapnel wounds, he needed two operations, but healing had been made easier by his falling in love. The Italian Army added to the glow of his convalescence, awarding him three medals, including the *Croce di Guerra*. In the cynicism of maturity he would know how cheap medals were, and how mean and grim war was, but even in his pain, war was then fun and games. He thought the Italian troops were, he wrote his family, "the bravest . . . in the Allied Armies," and on November 11 he illustrated, in a letter to his mother and father from the hospital, his "railroad track" of ribbons.

"Well, it's all over!" he had begun, "and I guess everybody is pretty joyous. I would have liked to see the celebration in the States but the Italian Army showed the wonderful stuff it is made of in that last offensive. They are great troops and I love them! . . . I did come very close to the big adventure in this last offensive and personally feel like every body else about the end of the war. Gee but it was great though to end it with such a victory!"

Restlessly, he had wondered what to do with himself after the war was over. Once he traveled in Italy and Austria (a plan which fell through), he told his family, he would return briefly to the States and then "not be back for several years. Because about next fall I am going to commence the real war again. The war to make the world safe for Ernie Hemingway and I plan to knock 'em through a loop and will be a busy man for several years. By that time my pension will have accumulated a couple of thousand lire and I'll bring my children over to view the battle fields." Armistice Day had forced him to formulate his goals. Oak Park, Illinois, was not part of them; nor was the *Kansas City Star*.

In Sardinia, at a cafe in Cagliari, remote from the war, Anthony Burgess's homosexual novelist Kenneth Toomey in *Earthly Powers* (1980) would rush to his hotel on the Largo Carlo-Felice, on hearing of the Kaiser's fall, to pontificate in his diary, "It has been right to hate the Germans: soon it will be right to love them." And on the eleventh he would add, as if he had taken part (he was a medical reject), "We wanted this war. If we had not wanted it we would not have had it." Then, while bells clanged, out he went, a *Britannico,* to celebrate with the locals. "I climbed a corkscrew street down which a lone loaded donkey slithered. . . . I entered a little wineshop and was welcomed, the Englishman, his war ended only a few days later than theirs. I drank too much of colorless spirit that smelt of old sheepdog." And though no one else knew the language, he sang, twisting the words of the parody closer to the truth,

> *You wore a tunic,*
> *A dirty khaki tunic,*
> *While I wore civilian clothes.*

He had come through, he knew, while better men had been slaughtered or maimed. His fellow drinkers in their bright stockings, bunched-up clout trunks, and stiff red jackets understood nothing of his confession, and Toomey switched to

Oh the moon shines bright on Charlie Chaplin,
His boots are cracking
For want of blacking. . . .

"They all knew Charlie Chaplin. . . . The last thing I clearly remember of that evening was a young man doing a very competent imitation of Charlie running from the cops and braking on one foot as he turned a corner. And then I was waking up in my hotel room at four in the morning, queasy and dry-mouthed, with a naked woman next to me. . . . A church bell told four. I began to retch. . . ."

The Balkan fronts had been stepchildren of the war since the catastrophe at Gallipoli in 1915. From his headquarters in the Greek port of Salonika, General Franchet d'Esperey was following up his last directive from Clemenceau—to complete the liberation of what had once been Serbia. It meant, since the Allied commander thought in broad terms, prying all subject peoples from Hungary and Turkey, in the process fatally weakening the Magyar nationalist Count Karolyi, who would soon have to confront the Bolshevik Bela Kun. But d'Esperey took such matters lightly: he wanted to advance into Germany from the east. Although putting such a *coup de grâce* to Germany would have been, he thought, the proper culmination for his little-publicized labors, he could do no more than enter angrily in his diary from Salonika on November 11, "A telegram from Paris announces the general armistice. Germany has capitulated. I hope the conditions are severe. I have not been consulted nor even notified of the conversations, notwithstanding that my troops were in Hungary, and that—unique action in this war—I have occupied two enemy capitals, Sofia and Constantinople."

Greek, Turk, and Bulgar had been clashing indecisively along the rocky northern reaches of Macedonia—"Muckydonia" to the British forces in the region. Half the 26th Division, Private William Mather estimated, was on the sick list with flu when a telephone message reached them, on the Turkish-Bulgarian border at Svilengrad (called Mustapha Pasha by the Turks), that the war was over. It was eleven in the evening on November 10. The next day came a second message canceling the first and furnishing the official date and time in writing. Between the two, Mather had celebrated in the only way possible: "We did get a rum issue and, wandering round at night, I came across one or two small groups shivering round a huge fire and doing their best to appear merry and bright. However it was all a dismal failure as we certainly did not feel in the mood to celebrate. After all, it was really only that which touched us personally that affected us and we felt so cut off from the rest of the world that Germany's surrender was too distant and nebulous for us to grasp."

The 8th South Wales Borderers (24th Regiment) had sailed from Greek Macedonian ports, ferried in French and British destroyers, to attack the Turks at Dedéagatch (now Alexandroupolis, in Thrace), only to find when they arrived in the harbor that the war with Turkey was over. "In fact, the first thing I saw at Dedéagatch," Transport Officer Gerald Evans remembered, "was a Red Cross flag, which must have come up by land. My job . . . was to get back to Salonika our transport of 130 mules, limbers, etc., which had arrived by land. It was hard work. We started back, while the main body of soldiers returned by sea. For us the journey was rough, muddy and very tiring. I thought how wonderful St. Paul had been to make that same journey—Ephesus, etc. My men were exhausted, when a message led me to announce: 'Information has been received that the war in the West has just ended, and there is peace in all areas.' So tired were my men that they showed little interest and made no response, until I added, 'In view of the good news, there will be an extra ration of rum tonight.' . . . After this we resumed our journey, [which] . . . had cost us some casualties, for malaria and pneumonia took their toll."

Another lieutenant taking his men back to Salonika was F. A. Baker, of the Royal Scots Regiment, which had been in the plains below Strumnitza. They were in the Rupel Pass to the south when, on the afternoon of the eleventh, word came that the war was over. "There we were, stuck out in the blue, living on bully beef and biscuits, with nothing to celebrate with whatsoever." Still, they found a way. "After nightfall, adjacent [Royal Scots] units in the area attacked each other's encampments with Very pistols, setting some bivouacs on fire."

In Salonika was Australian flier T. W. White, who had flown in Mesopotamia against the Turks until he was forced down and taken prisoner. He and his observer, Francis Yeats-Brown, had escaped, and after an epic trek were in Greece awaiting another chance at the enemy. In the garden of the British Command's rest house, White was relaxing in shabby "hand-me-down clothing and never-to-be-forgotten waistcoat" when "an elated Tommy batman" entered. Assuming the captain was a Greek laborer, the soldier slapped White on the shoulder and in the pidgin French then common in Salonika announced, *"La guerre est fini,* Johnnie!"

"And then it came," White recalled of the news, "—to the accompaniment of gunfire from warships in the harbor and rattling of musketry in the streets. . . . Selfishly we wished the end had not come quite so soon, for we had escaped to serve again. Our thousand-mile journey and months of thrills seemed now with the turn of events to have been almost in vain."

On the morning of the eleventh an Allied flotilla was poised to enter the Dardanelles en route to Constantinople, led by two British battleships, the *Temeraire* and the *Superb.* As they were getting up steam, word came of the signing in France. "Following astern of the battleships," E. G. Middlecote, then a signal boy on the *Temeraire,* remembered, "was a French cruiser complete with a haystack and cattle on the upper deck. Then came men of war of Greek, Italian and Roumanian nationality. . . . At 10:58 the 'still' sounded by the bugler brought us to attention for two minutes to indicate the cessation of war. . . . We gave three hearty cheers for His Majesty [and] . . . proceeded through the narrows with a sense of thanksgiving and relief."

When, after the Turkish armistice, General Liman von Sanders was ousted by the Turks as their Army commander, Franz von Papen, his deputy, consulted him to arrange for the transport of German troops to internment in Constantinople. Von Papen had been military attaché in Washington, recalled hurriedly in 1915 when implicated in espionage and sabotage. A monarchist to the end, he was staggered first by the Kaiser's abdication and then by General von Sanders's bland suggestion when he heard of Soldiers' Councils being formed in Germany that "similar institutions could properly be organized by troops under his command." The Armistice had just come into effect in the West, and von Papen, after hurriedly consulting other German officers, told the General "that it would be better, in view of his ill health, if he were to give up command of the German troops and return to Germany." Sanders understood the language and offered to furnish a decision within the hour. It came quickly. Once free of his OHL spy, he ordered von Papen's arrest on the charge of insubordination and an immediate court-martial. Finding out in time, von Papen bought civilian clothes in a nearby bazaar and fled to Germany, where he entered politics on the extreme Right. In 1932 he would be, briefly, Chancellor, and after Hitler's takeover would serve him in a variety of posts. His last appointment (1939–44) would be as German ambassador to Turkey.

For the Turks the major prize falling from their grasp in a time when the ocean of petroleum under the Arabian sands was unknown was Palestine, magnet of the major religions in the West. There in Ramleh, Anthony Brand, an English private attached as signaler to an Australian mounted corps, listened to the steam whistles blasting their announcement of the far-off Armistice. Since he was ineligible for the Sergeants' Mess, where a bottle of whiskey (or a dozen pints of beer) was six shillings, "My buddy and I, to celebrate, went into an *estaminet* nearby. There was a small orchestra, all Austrian—a pianist, a cornet, a trumpet, a clarionet, a violin and a cello. . . . We ordered a small pot of wine but when we had disposed of it there were dead flies left in it." The East was an incongruous place to toast the victory of the West, which seemed to have happened in a different world at a different time.

In Jerusalem the military governor, Sir Ronald Storrs, noted in his diary how the city celebrated while rain came down in torrents. At three in the afternoon General Edmund Allenby's office telephoned that the Armistice had been signed, and Storrs set his staff to informing units in the area. Then, he wrote, "I went out imparting it to any soldiers I met, to the Patriarchates, the Custodia, the 'American' Colony and the Mufti. As I drove up to the Mufti's house some R[oyal] A[rtillery] unit sent up Very Lights, which came down so slowly that I thought for an instant that they must be [shooting] stars. The Mufti, rising finely to the moment, dwelt on those who had given their lives to bring about all this glory. . . ."

In his home city of Rochester the bells were pealing as, in a later time zone, Storrs heard the news. "My mother was thanking God," he recalled, "that all her four sons had come safely through the War, when the Admiral of the Nore called to tell her that her second [son], Francis, had died last evening. The next day I [also] heard. . . ." In the cradle of religions Storrs thought of his brother's "true religion streaked with classical paganism." The "good Franciscans," he added, "celebrated Mass for my heretic before the Holy Sepulchre."

In Egypt, the staging area for operations in the eastern Mediterranean, the Armistice meant one thing to troops being pulled back into the base camps at Cairo and Alexandria: they would not be shipped to the Western Front for a winter of war. According to Leonard Francke, who was in Alexandria, the report "was tardy in arriving, no wireless then, and it was not until evening that the news arrived." War-weary troops, exasperated by the return to severe "peacetime" discipline, broke loose. "From the camps at Sidi Bisha and Mustapha, soldiers poured into the town rioting. Windows were broken, shops raided and drunkenness rampant. The whole of that night, the men rampaged, the Military Police wisely keeping out of the way." According to a Cairo account, the ceremonial parade "was followed by a *Walpurgisnacht* of riotous military celebration from which the military police were conspicuously absent. Besotted troops roamed the streets wielding entrenching-tool handles, while their officers, among other feats of strength, rolled up the great hall-carpet of Shepheard's Hotel, with the German-Swiss manager inside it."

"Actually, the situation was restored by the troops themselves," Francke recalled. "With the coming of daylight they returned to the camps themselves, chastened, I feel, by their own excesses. From that day, discipline fell away. Men did not trouble to salute officers in the streets and surly acquiescence to orders was a common feature in infantry regiments." Instinctively, soldiers seemed eager to demonstrate that their units were poor choices for occupation duty. The War Diary of the Australian Remount Depot in Cairo suggests the level of celebration there in cautious officialese: "On the definite news of the signing of the Armistice by Germany there was great gratification and relief shown by all ranks in the Camp."

For his four-day crossing from Italy to Egypt on board the *Cosmao,* English diplomat Mark Sykes was guest of the French National Marine, as was only appropriate for the coauthor of the secret Sykes-Picot agreement. What they had initialed had divided the mostly Arab colonial Turkish empire into French and British dependencies—while T. E. Lawrence was innocently promising Arab sheikhs independence.

Early on November 11 the *Cosmao* arrived at Port Said, Sykes spending part of the day inspecting an Armenian refugee camp on the east bank of the Suez Canal. In the evening his dinner with the British commander at Kantara was interrupted by the happy detonating of flares and fog signals, and the drone of the RAF planes celebrating the Armistice. He would catch the last train that night, en route to Allenby's headquarters.

One of the least attractive assignments of many unappealing ones in the Middle East was Mesopotamia. The climate was hostile and British troops were low in morale. The Turks were often less of a problem than marauding tribesmen, and disease, along with the marauders, remained unaffected by the Turkish surrender. With other patients, mostly suffering from malaria and dysentery, Artillery Gunner Alex Booth was on a flat-bottomed hospital boat brought down the Tigris from Baghdad. In Basra, at six o'clock, the nursing sisters were preparing tea when other ships moored in the broad, shallow river shattered the silence with their whistles and sirens. "Patients, bed-ridden, seriously ill, some with temperatures up to 105°, lurched out of bed . . . shambled to the door [of the ward], and went out into a heavy downpour and a sea of warm mud, about a foot deep. A military band of sorts miraculously appeared and played all the popular, well-loved tunes—'It's a Long Way to Tipperary,' 'Good-bye Piccadilly, Farewell Leicester Square,' 'Keep the Home Fires Burning,' 'Dear Old Blighty,' and then finally 'God Save the King.' There we stood at attention as far as the mud would allow, with hearts full and visions of homeland ahead. Then we trudged back to the ward and bed, apparently none the worse. . . . Surely, if ever, a triumph of mind over matter. I was 22 years of age. . . ."

On dry land, Flying Officer Sydney Bull was at an RAF airfield at Ba'qubah, northeast of Baghdad, which had the only wireless receiving equipment in the area—Morse code only. It picked up a signal that there was a possibility of an armistice that day and that stations should tune that wavelength at 8:00 P.M. their time for further details, if any. At eight everyone who could get near the wireless listened for the dots and dashes and picked out the confirmation. Since they were the only ones who could have acquired the message, the airmen decided to take out their Crossley tender, which carried fifteen men, and a supply of Very flares, and spread what they had heard. "Naturally, before we departed, a celebration took place and whether by accident or that the driver had celebrated too well, our tender finished up in a *nullah*—a small ravine. . . . We were forced to continue our trek on foot. There were no roads, but at intervals sign posts were planted and some of our more hilarious colleagues considered it a good idea to switch them around—much to our consternation later!"

Northeast of Kirkuk, where the Russian, Persian, and Mesopo-
tamian frontiers were fuzzy, the Royal Warwickshire Regiment had
engaged the Turks, taking two thousand prisoners. Much of the regiment then turned northeast toward Mosul, while a smaller force
moved into Persia toward the Caspian Sea, where Russians were reported to be contesting the area. Returning, they were captured by
the Turks. Armenians and Russians with them, including women
and children, were summarily shot, and the Warwickshires were
stripped of everything but helmet, shirt, and shorts.

The survivors would endure hundreds of miles of moving
about—on foot, and in cattle trucks in which the manure and mos-
quitoes made life so difficult that the Russian-built prison in which
they were finally dumped appeared at first a relief. "There were
about 50 of us," Sergeant Wood wrote a dozen years later. "The
menu consisted of a buffalo head [for the group] each day and hot
water at 7 A.M. and 5 P.M. We never saw any [other] meat. . . . The
bread was . . . not enough to keep our strength going. It was wet and
full of straw. As time went on, things got worse. . . . Men could be
seen sitting by the dustbin gnawing at the bones from a buffalo's
head, just like dogs."

Although they had not come from the Caspian port of Baku,
across the border in Russia, the Turks insisted that Sergeants Wood
and Horton furnish information about the army there. Marched to
headquarters under heavy guard, although they were too weak to
need it, they were informed through an interpreter that they would
be shot if they failed to answer appropriately. "I said," Wood recalled, "we might as well be shot as go back to prison, where we were
dying a slow death. We said nothing more, but were allowed to
live."

Conditions changed abruptly on November 11, Wood wrote,
but the time-zone factor suggests that it may have been the next
morning. "The Turks came into our room about 5 A.M. with fixed
bayonets. They were shouting like madmen. We thought they had
come to carry out their threats, but they came to tell us, 'Alliman
finish.' They were mad with joy. I must say it was a relief to us."
Apparently the news of the earlier Turkish surrender had not caught
up with their captors, who had understood only that the Armistice
on the eleventh had ended whatever was left of their war. Although
the Warwickshires were permitted to leave the prison, there was nowhere to go, as "it was none too safe being in Turkish uniform with
three months' beard." Three weeks later they were escorted by the
Turks to Baku, where a Staffordshire regiment was deployed to keep

the Bolsheviks out. It was January 1919 before they could embark for home, surprising families who had assumed they were dead.

In Africa the war had touched much of the Mediterranean coast, for the sea was a British lifeline, and U-boats were ubiquitous. A. P. Herbert, later editor of *Punch* and an MP, but then a young naval officer who had served at Gallipoli and with the Royal Naval Division, was with a convoy which had discharged its cargo at Port Said and was gingerly hugging the coastline en route back. At Tunis the ships put in long enough to hear that Turkey had "thrown her hand in," exhilarating news for a veteran of the disastrous Dardanelles campaign. On November 11 his ship docked at Oran, where Herbert decided to sightsee by taking a train to Tlemcen, "which everyone assured me it was my duty to do. Curiously enough, exactly at 11.00 we heard that the Armistice had been signed." Soon flags were out, "nearly all French, numbers of American, but very few Union Jacks." Caught up in the excited crowd, he found himself next to the town mayor, who toasted Herbert with champagne. "I must have been the only Englishman for at least 80 miles." A self-appointed master of ceremonies talked him into singing "Tipperary," then "flung himself upon me and kissed me violently on both cheeks (he was extremely prickly)."

After listening to halfhearted public compliments to *Angleterre*, Herbert "rose in duty bound and spoke a few appropriate remarks in halting French, a feeble attempt." Bands played and processions pushed through the narrow streets, torchlit after dark. Suddenly "a Boche . . . approached me and asked if I spoke Allemand. I was amazed. He had a French wife, so I could not have slain him if I had felt like it." Although Herbert finished the evening "promenading with 2 amusing French officers, and was glad to get to bed," the encounter with the German was more disturbing that he realized. On November 17 he would note in his diary "a most unpleasant" war nightmare in which he faced a crowd of Germans in field gray, all armed menacingly with carving knives. "I realized that I had only a fish knife. This I stuck in his throat. It was sufficiently horrible but I did not make a good job of it. [Douglas] Jerrold [a naval officer comrade of earlier campaigns] appeared with a carving knife and finished the disgusting deed." At home Herbert would have further nightmares about the war, in which he would throw off his bedclothes and stumble about the room screaming. Finally, Gwen, his wife, tied his wrist to hers at bedtime to reduce his alarm.

*　　*　　*

When the news of the Armistice reached Nairobi, a great bonfire was lit in the Ngong hills and curious crowds poured out of the city to see it. Kenya was British, but not so one of its neighbors. In 1914 the Germans had a colonial empire in Africa, the largest segments known now as Namibia and Tanzania. Near Dar es Salaam in what was then Tanganyika, German East Africa, the trapped cruiser *Königsberg*, early in the war, had been deliberately beached upriver to prevent its capture in operational condition. Then, led by its wounded captain, Max Looff, who reported to the German Admiralty that they were "not beaten," the crew had managed to remove the ship's ten 105-mm cannon onto locally constructed mobile gun carriages. Guns in tow, they then rendezvoused with an outnumbered land force under Major General Paul von Lettow-Vorbeck and accomplished military feats which read more like fiction than fact. Indeed, novels have been written about the episode, one of them William Stevenson's melodramatic *The Ghosts of Africa* (1980). When the Armistice became effective in France four years later, only fourteen men and one workable gun remained from the *Königsberg*, but the crew and the small force it joined (at the end only 155 were Europeans) had tied up a quarter of a million British soldiers by crisscrossing mid-Africa as guerrillas and assault troops.

With Lettow-Vorbeck's undefeated little army furnishing a rare opportunity for pride in the gloomy final days of the war in Europe, Erzberger's armistice delegation could not merely surrender them. They pressed for a revision of Foch's African clause which would make the matter less distasteful at home. Meanwhile, the Germans had no intentions of giving up. On November 6 they had arrived at Kajambi, well inside Rhodesia, ready for a fight and well armed except for artillery. The further they advanced, the better supplied they became, as the British had abandoned warehouses and depots as they withdrew. Monica Wareham, whose father was a missionary doctor at Mbershi in Northern Rhodesia (now Zambia), remembered evacuating mission stations and the "tin trunk on the verandah packed ready for a quick getaway" in the final days. But Lettow-Vorbeck already knew from months-old English newspapers which told of the worsening of the war for the Germans that he could not go on indefinitely.

On November 11, 1918, the general bicycled with an advance party to Kasama and sent a unit farther south. On November 12 the main body of German troops, their numbers dwindling from fever, also reached Kasama, only to be attacked in the rear by the King's 4th African Rifles. The Germans drove them off easily. Confident further now that he could win any engagement, Lettow-Vorbeck hoped, beyond that, to resupply himself so completely from enemy dumps that he could move back into German East Africa and renew the war his government was about to lose elsewhere. Long without any direct contact with Europe, he had no idea what had been happening in Berlin, in Spa, or in the railway car in a French forest where Erzberger had finally signed an agreement which salvaged German honor in Africa, limiting Clause XVII to "Evacuation of all German forces operating in East Africa within a period specified by the Allies." On November 13, however, when the General was again bicycling ahead, an aide handed him a message, apparently from British sources, that Germany had agreed to the unconditional surrender of all troops in Africa. They were to release their prisoners, disarm their native troops, and march to Abercorn, the British headquarters at the foot of Lake Tanganyika, where they were to give up their own weapons. One piece had too much symbolic value for that. Lieutenant Richard Wenig, in charge of the remaining gun from the *Königsberg*, blew it up. On a hill near the Chambezi River, Lettow-Vorbeck handed over his sword to the British district commissioner. None of the arms and ammunition his troops surrendered was German: all of it had been acquired along the way. They had not lost a battle, but had lost the war.

Far to the south, on a warship in Table Bay, off Cape Town, Harold Owen heard the news of the cease-fire over his ship's loudspeaker and like other young officers accepted an invitation to the captain's cabin for champagne to mark the occasion. He was uneasy, and failed to drain his glass. "This did not go without comment and a few disapproving looks but I could not help myself." He worried about whether he should cable home for news of his brother Wilfred, who had recently returned to action in Flanders, but remembered the dread which telegrams had inspired in England since August 1914. "The sight of a red bicycle within a hundred yards of your own house could make your heart jump and miss a beat. At home, perhaps secure in the knowledge of Wilfred's safety, might not a cable from Africa mean only one thing? Slowly I tore up my telegram and threw it into the wastepaper basket. It *must* be all right. After all I had no cable from home and the war was over." But the red bicycle had already stopped at the Owen home in Shrewsbury.

* * *

Also in existence on November 11, 1918, was the burgeoning embarrassment of many small and futile Allied forces on Russian soil, trying to reverse the Communist revolution. In north Russia at Archangel and Murmansk the British (with Canadians and Americans) were there ostensibly to protect 212,000 tons of munitions and other war materiel which, if not kept from Bolshevik control, might fall into German hands. Besides, Murmansk was now precariously connected by rail to Petrograd (now Leningrad) and U-boats had been active in the icy Barents Sea. There was fear that a German foothold could lead into the heart of Russia.

To the south, Czarist armies which had faced the Turks had now melted away. Earlier in 1918 the British had feared that the Germans, through the Ukraine and Caucasus, might dominate the trans-Caspian area, from Baghdad to Tehran and even into India. To many in Britain, the Empire was India. Whether or not the threat was exaggerated as an excuse to intervene, small forces had gone north from Mesopotamia. In central Asia the British were helping local movements against the new Russian regime, hoping to encourage them into a national force. There was even a Czech legion in Siberia, a coalescing of Czech and Slovak former prisoners of war and civilian internees who were pushing west in hopes of recovering their independence as a nation, a move the Czar's government had encouraged earlier as a means of undermining Austro-Hungarian unity. And in maritime Siberia, far to the east, the excuse of protecting vast military stores intended for the former regime had led to a landing at Vladivostock. Its actual objective had been an advance along the route of the Trans-Siberian railway to further reverse the tide of revolution.

The Allied intervention had become more complicated and confused through the year, with troops at cross-purposes and sometimes with no ostensible purpose. In his first public appearance since an attempt on his life, Nikolai Lenin addressed cheering crowds from a balcony on the night of the eleventh, telling them of proletarian revolts in Germany, Austria, and Hungary, and of the Armistice in the West. Privately, however, he had misgivings. "I fear," he frankly told an English visitor, Philips Price, "that the revolution in central Europe is developing too slowly to provide us with any assistance from that quarter." Karl Radek noted his "excited but profoundly anxious look."

In frozen Archangel news of the Armistice was celebrated with solemn masses and Te Deums. Making extemporaneous and now-forgotten speeches were the remaining Allied ambassadors to the puppet Provisional Government of the Northern Region, theoretically an arm of Admiral Kolchak's hapless, British-financed "White" Russian Army, then stumbling through Siberia. None knew that at dawn that day a Bolshevik detachment that had circled around the supposedly impassable forest to the south had fallen suddenly upon the rear of the surprised Tommies and Yanks. (A battery of Canadian artillery would abort the assault.) Allied soldiers in the American base hospital had been awakened that morning when the Bolshevik leader, Melfochofski, had broken in and ordered the two riflemen with him to shoot every patient. The order was immediately countermanded by a beautiful woman in Russian battle gear who entered and declared that she would kill the first Communist who raised his rifle. (She was Melfochofski's mistress.) He shrugged and left the building just in time to be riddled by a burst of Canadian fire. In fascinated horror the bedridden Yanks then watched a tender love scene, as Melfochofski crawled back inside to die in her arms.

The Armistice had altered the Allied legal position in Russia. The fiction of a wartime ally was gone. There was nothing they could legally protect. German war prisoners in Russia were no longer a threat, and Austro-Hungarian prisoners had splintered into nationalistic factions eager to join independence movements. One was the Czech legion, deep in Siberia. The released and escaped prisoners of war were thousands of miles from Prague or Bratislava and had no way to get home except to fight their way or to depend upon the British on the southern flanks of Siberia. And they wanted the Czechs to remain to fight the Bolsheviks. The November cold was already intense, but units of the crack Middlesex Regiment, reinforcements just shipped into central Asia by train, came prepared. Czechs gazed enviously at the smart uniforms, complete to heavy boots. For them the most crucial part of their motley garb, as they shuttled west in their rickety, drafty railway carriages, had been their headgear. "We were smart little bastards," recalled a survivor, John Fenchak, sixty-three years later. "It got damn cold. We'd pry a board loose from the floor, and grab chunks of coal from the roadbed. We'd burn their coal in our helmets to keep warm."

The British had brought a band with them, Gustav Bevcar remembered, "and after still more welcoming ceremonies the detachment lined up behind our armoured train and the British National Anthem was struck up. Hardly had the final strains of 'God Save the King' died away than the enemy started vigorously to shell that part of the line from which the music had come. . . . The explosions thundered in the forest. Smartly, the British detachment marched back to the station, smartly they entrained, and as smartly the engine whistled and drew them out of the danger zone on their return journey to Omsk, leaving the Bolsheviks in a thoroughly nasty frame of mind which they proceeded to vent upon us. The demonstration was over. . . ."

The same evening the Czechs were relieved for "two days of complete rest" one station down the line only to be routed out of their warm railway carriages the next morning because "White" troops holding Ust-Kruky were in danger of being surrounded. The Czechs were in a bitter mood as they lined up in the fierce cold. "If a whole Siberian regiment can't hold a village like Ust-Kruky," one legionnaire complained, "they aren't worth bothering about. Let 'em sink, I say." At Ust-Kruky they could clearly see long skeins of enemy troops advancing over the snow-covered meadows. As they waited in reserve, shuffling about continually to keep the blood circulating, the Czechs were actually angry at the Bolsheviks for being so slow in their advance.

Suddenly a messenger from the village appeared and handed a piece of paper to the Siberian commanding officer, who looked at it, then turned to the Czechs. "Gentlemen," he said, "this message says that an Armistice has been signed in France." He crushed the slip of paper between his fingers and put it in his pocket. The Czechs went on shuffling to keep warm. The Armistice seemed utterly without meaning in their circumstances. Moving their battalion into a flanking position, they swept over the summit of their hill and poured fire into the enemy, who fled leaving many casualties, "dark spots on the white snow."

In the farthest east, at drab, treeless Vladivostock, American, British, and Japanese troops were without real duties except to stand fast. The Bolsheviks to the west were far too preoccupied on other fronts to be seriously interested in the terminus of the five-thousand-mile Trans-Siberian Railway. Polyglot writer William Gerhardie, promoted to captain on his arrival in Tokyo en route to Siberia, perhaps because he knew Russian, found himself in Vladivostock without his "inmost beliefs . . . being bound up with the re-establishing of an obsolete regime," but determined to resist being ousted from a comfortable Military Mission office by "senior new-comers from England." In his boredom be began a novel, *Futility* (1922), which would bring him recognition as a writer. "I have a re-curring dream," he wrote a dozen years later. "The war, though most people have forgotten about it, is still on. Everyone has agreed it should stop, since neither the Germans nor ourselves take any fur-ther interest in it. But the Government has other, more topical ques-tions on the schedule—Unemployment, Trade Disputes . . . and the war must wait its turn. So drafts are still being sent out from Vic-toria Station to the trenches of France, but nobody comes to see one off. The war, it is agreed by all, is a bore; and so the casualties are no longer reported. On one such draft I am going out, much against my will, fully equipped, with gas mask and hand grenades. . . ."

When Gerhardie applied to go home after the Armistice he was told that his services were "indispensable." He would remain, with nothing whatever to do, until August 1920.

In a novel by Archie Binns, *The Laurels Are Cut Down* (1937), two American soldiers in their "box car headquarters" in easternmost Siberia learn of the Armistice on the other side of the world when a troop train stops with the news. "They cheered like fools [and] went A.W.O.L. looking for something for all of them to get drunk on. . . . The boys didn't find anything to drink. But the lieutenant killed four black cocks, and they had a kind of Thanksgiving in the box car. They even made speeches. . . . After that many trains passed over the bridge. And much water passed underneath, until it froze and stood still. The trains kept on passing, but there was never one to start them on their way home. While they were up there, four thousand Canadian soldiers arrived in Siberia."

One of the Canadians was an artillery officer and future actor, Raymond Massey, who had been shell-shocked at Ypres in 1916, sent to an ROTC unit at Yale after hospitalization, then shipped out again with a combat unit in October 1918. There was nothing for him to do in Vladivostock. Even their barracks "were only par-tially completed and quite useless . . . without windows and only partly roofed." He asked a "White" Russian officer why the build-ings were in such a state. "Many rich people in Russia!" said the of-ficer.

Early in November, Massey had been ordered to take his gun-ners north of the city to Gornastai Bay to prepare a compound for two infantry battalions. With them were fifty Austrian prisoners as a labor force. The Armistice news was two days old when they received it there. A "peace parade" materialized—elements of all the Allied troops in the area, including the Japanese. "Many of the thousands who watched us pass," Massey remembered, "were refugees for whom peace was a meaningless word." Even for the Allied soldiers in the line of march, peace did not mean going home. They were not, technically, occupation troops on enemy soil, but in a confusion of purpose they would remain until it was more than clear that their presence would do nothing to turn the revolution from Red to White. Newton Baker, Wilson's Secretary of War, would write ten years later of the Russian intervention, "The expedition was nonsense from the beginning."

From England on November 11, Nellie Gray would write her young husband, Alf, serving in Siberia, that her heart was full at the news that the war was over. Flags were flying everywhere, she told him, and there were fireworks in the streets. With so many lives lost, she was thankful that he was—she hoped—safe. "How long do you think it will be till you return? I am afraid we shall get very impatient. I was thinking of you all day & wanting oh so much just a little snuggle with 'old Dad.' . . . do you think it possible to be home by Christmas?" Russia was very far away, and more than one Christmas would pass before some of the soldiers mired there on Armistice Day 1918 would return.

BEHIND THE RHINE

Es braust ein Ruf wie Donner hall,
Wie Schwertge klirr und Wogen prall:
Zum Rhein, zum Rhein, zum
    deutschen Rhein!
Wer will des Stromes Hüter sein?

A shout is heard like thunder peal.
'Mid surging waves and clash of steel:
The Rhine, the Rhine, the
    German Rhine!
Who guards today that stream of
mine?

So lang ein Tropfen Blut noch glüht,
Noch eine Faust den Degen zieht,
Und noch ein Arm die Buchse spannt,
Betritt kein Feind hier deinen Strand!

While still one drop of blood can flow,
Or still one fist a sword can show,
Or still a rifle spring to hand,
No enemy shall tread your strand!

Der Schwur erschallt, die Woge rinnt,
Die Fahnen flattern hoch im Wind:
Am Rhein, am Rhein, am
    deutschen Rhein,
Wir alle wollen Hüter sein!

The oath resounds, the waves run high,
The banners flutter in the sky:
The Rhine, the Rhine, the
    German Rhine,
We all will guard you, river mine!

Lieb Vaterland, magst ruhig sein!
Lieb Vaterland, magst ruhig sein:
Fest steht und treu die Wacht,
    die Wacht am Rhein!
Fest steht und treu die Wacht,
    die Wacht am Rhein!

Dear Fatherland, may peace be thine!
Dear Fatherland, may peace be thine!
Firm stands, and sure, the watch, the
    watch on the Rhine!
Firm stands, and sure, the watch, the
    watch on the Rhine!

—*Die Wacht am Rhein*, LYRICS BY KARL WILHELM,
  WRITTEN IN 1854, SPRANG TO FAME
  AS A NATIONAL HYMN OF GERMANY
  DURING THE FRANCO-PRUSSIAN WAR
  IN 1870 AND WAS SUNG ARDENTLY INTO
  THE GREAT WAR AND AFTER

Early on November 11 a British spy, Henry Landau, remembered, "I got up to watch the [Kaiser's] train go by at a crossing near Maastricht. All the blinds were drawn, as I thought they would be." Although pulled by a Dutch engine, there was no mistaking the Imperial train. At every station en route to Count Godard Bentinck's estate at Amerongen, according to Count Detlef von Moltke, Wilhelm's unhappy aide, "Thousands of people were gathered, greeting us with shouting, whistling, cursing. They threatened us, made signs of choking and hanging us. . . . In such manner was our poor Emperor received on Dutch soil."

That morning, too, Prince Friedrich Wilhelm addressed a letter untactfully to "Imperial Chancellor Ebert," which was rushed off to Berlin. "The Crown Prince urgently desires to remain at his post to do his duty like any other soldier. He will bring his army back home in a well-disciplined and orderly manner, and undertakes to do nothing whatever at this juncture against the present Government. What is the Government's attitude in this matter?"

In Berlin, Ebert would query his Minister of War and wire a refusal. There would be no way the Kaiser's heir could retire into private life in Germany—which was exactly why the generals in his Army group encouraged him in his efforts to remain. If he followed his father into exile, warned General von Einem, with whom Friedrich Wilhelm was staying in Roumont Castle, "Then the banner would be lacking to which we could cling and around which we would gather."

The Crown Prince, nevertheless, was a flawed banner. Arrogant and spoiled, he had been a less-than-effective commander fortunate in his generals. His public reputation was such that few were sorry to see him go. When Count Rantzau in the Ministry of the Royal House was consulted by Ebert's government about the possibility of permitting Friedrich Wilhelm to return to his estate (now Oelze in East Germany), the Count advised, "A return of the Crown Prince to Oels would be impossible; the farmers would beat him to death." He also was known to have woman problems, which made him less than a useful rallying point for monarchists. In the final days he had even sought the assistance of General Roeder von Diersburg "to free him from this woman"—apparently one who had lost favor—"and take him to a neutral country with a lady from Metz whom he admired."

Had the enchantress from Metz been available, the Crown Prince might have fled with her into Switzerland. He would escape

379

into Holland, insisting in a parting letter to Marshal Hindenburg, copies of which he sent to political and military leaders in Berlin, "It is repugnant to my whole nature not to be able to lead my brave troops home. . . . I was not only not heard, but was simply passed over as Crown Prince and heir to the throne. No renunciation was either demanded or made by me." He had wanted to "persevere" at some post, but to permit Friedrich Wilhelm to remain a rallying force for the old order would have made no sense to the new one. With what was in effect his farewell address to the people he had hoped someday to rule, he disappeared into history.*

At the little Dutch frontier station, the ex-Kaiser mourned to the German ambassador, "How can I begin life again? My prospects are hopeless. I have nothing left to believe in." In his numerous bags and trunks, the residue of a life at the top, were five handsome volumes in English. The eldest of Victoria and Albert's grandchildren and the only one the Prince Consort ever knew, he had been given a set of Albert's biography (by Sir Theodore Martin) inscribed "To darling Willy from Grandmama." Pages still uncut, it would remain unread.

Of his host, upon whom would descend a reduced Imperial entourage still too numerous to be housed, Wilhelm asked, "Who is this Bentinck? I don't think I know him." They would meet for the first time at Maarn Station, west of Utrecht. "Now," said the new exile as they drove across the bridge leading to the Count's seventeenth-century, moat-enclosed country house, "for a cup of good English tea!" Indoors over his tea he wrote his wife, "My reign is ended, my dog's life is over, and has been rewarded only with betrayal and ingratitude."

Nearby at Doorn Castle, the ex-Kaiser would live out his exile—with an imported second wife after his ailing Kaiserin, joining him in Holland, died. On June 17, 1940, after the capitulation of France, he would send from Doorn, then in Nazi-occupied Holland, a curious telegram to Hitler, whom he had privately scorned as a vulgar upstart. "I congratulate you and the whole German Wehrmacht," he wrote at eighty-one, "on the mighty victory granted by God, in the words of the Emperor Wilhelm the Great in 1870: 'What a turn of events brought about by divine dispensation.' " Hitler was

---

* The former Crown Prince would be permitted to return in 1923 on his promise not to engage in politics. His covert intrigues, including a flirtation with the Nazis, would be profitless.

not interested in divine dispensations or former German monarchs. Wilhelm's passing on June 4, 1941, would go almost unnoticed in Germany.

Hindenburg's Armistice message to his troops had closed with the injunction that its terms "oblige us to march back to the Homeland without delay. In view of existing conditions, this will be a difficult task which will require self-discipline and devotion to duty on the part of every one of you. . . ." The message, dated 5:38 P.M. on November 11, arrived when many units in the West were already on the move. Assuming even before Erzberger had left Spa (which would become the headquarters of the Allied Armistice Commission) that the minimum price of peace would be military withdrawal to the Rhine, the OHL had ordered the process begun even before the signing. Departure from Spa—now with its own Soldiers' Council—would not be without bitterness on the part of some officers who wore the wine-red stripe on their trousers. Shouting at a Belgian mob from the train that was taking him back to Germany, Lieutenant Colonel Hermann Kriebel warned, *"Auf wiedersehen* in a few years!"

Unwilling to wait that long, Admiral Adolf von Trotha, fleet chief of staff, went on the eleventh to see his cowed and quiet superior, Admiral Franz von Hipper. The head of the High Seas Fleet had been invisible since a red banner had been hoisted on his flagship and he had fled ashore. Brazenly, Trotha and Hipper approached Berhard Kuhnt, chairman of the sailors' revolutionary "Council of Twenty-One" in Wilhelmshaven, to seek assistance in getting steam up on all ships for a last patriotic hurrah. The British fleet, Trotha lied, was approaching the German coast; it was the duty of all German sailors to rally to their country's defense. Only when Kuhnt refused did the admirals concede that the war was over.

In the ranks the Armistice was accepted with relief rather than acrimony. No more grand gestures were needed. To be a survivor was to be able to go home. The brief parting exchanges with the enemy were an education to those able to accept the fact of defeat. "An unknown existence had suddenly revealed itself to us," an Italian soldier had written about his Austrian enemy. "These strongly defended trenches, which we had attacked so many times without success, had ended by seeming to us inanimate, like desolate buildings uninhabited by men, the refuge of mysterious and terrible beings of whom we knew nothing. Now they were showing themselves to us as they really were, men and soldiers like us, in uniform like us." The experience was a universal one in war. But among the German troops there were many, especially in the officer corps, who would not believe that defeat could have come after four years of victories, especially when they were still everywhere on enemy soil. At Bende, in Belgium, a farmer told a Scots Guards private how a German officer billeted on his farm received the news. He was sitting at his table with a bottle of cognac and a novel when a corporal came in with the cease-fire message. With a deep groan the officer rose from his chair and threw his helmet with a crash on the stone floor. Then he took a long drink, put the bottle down to pick up his helmet, and was lost in thought until the memory of defeat again broke through. Once more his helmet went crashing to the floor. But there was little sympathy from his men, who arrived after dark to turn him out of the farmhouse. "Up to now," one said, "you have slept in a bed and we in lousy straw. Now it is your turn to sleep in the straw."

Retirement to the Rhine would not be without lapses into chaos nor outbreaks of rebellion. A 1929 German novel described the scene the way it could not have been drawn a decade earlier. In Franz Schwauwecker's *The Fiery Way,* an officer in Brussels is still clinging to a Belgian woman in a last, greedy embrace when he hears a rumbling over the rough paving stones below. Rushing to the window, he watches columns on the march, "a gloomy swarm of rifles and packs." Suddenly he realizes that they are not reinforcements from the rear, and that they are going the wrong way:

> They've reached here. Defeated. Worn to pieces. Grey. . . . The company commanders ride at a walking pace. The horses hang their heads. Yes. . . . indeed . . . these are the front-line troops going back. . . . Strange, gloomy, horrible to watch here amongst palaces and wealth, like ghosts of earth and stone, as though the ploughed fields were to stamp suddenly over the causeway and squeeze themselves down the narrow gorges of the streets. A hurrying mush of clods and mud is shoving by. . . .
>
> Beside me a shout rings clearly, a taunt, a secret triumph. . . . French . . . I understand.
>
> Like nineteen-fourteen . . . only the other way about!

When his thinned-out company demobilizes across the Rhine he will parade it for a last inspection. "I don't need to walk far," he writes. "I'm soon past the three groups of twenty-four men. . . . Ten weeks ago there were two thousand."

Germans were not only withdrawing from lands their leaders had once talked ambitiously of annexing to a Greater Reich, but returning to a Germany they did not recognize. Prosperity was a memory. The Kaiser and the ambience of Empire were gone. Victory had turned sour. Comrades were left behind in mass graves if any graves at all. As an observer recalled of the decimated, expressionless ranks, "One platoon passed, the ranks close, a second, a third. Then a space. Could this be a whole company? Three platoons?" Yet in a report to a 1920s Reichstag committee investigating the causes of the German collapse in 1918, General von Kuhl, attempting to give credence to the "stab-in-the-back" myth, would exaggerate "the anarchy created by the revolution to the rear of the Army" and ignore the depleted condition of the Army itself. It was beaten, but it was retiring in order, little affected by the facade of *Soldatenraten* or by slogans of politicans far off in Berlin.

Had the spirit of rebellion taken hold very deeply, the withdrawal could not have been accomplished with the proverbial Teutonic efficiency which characterized it from beginning to end. "Even under normal conditions," Kuhl conceded, "it would have been a great feat suddenly to set this huge army in motion and feed it regularly on the march. . . . The intervention of Radical Soldiers' Councils added to our difficulties. They set up discharge offices where discharge papers were arbitrarily issued to the men, interfered with the forwarding of rations, seized stores and used their contents as they pleased, held up trains and disposed of them arbitrarily, issued warrants for the journey home, seized the automobiles of the staff . . . occupied the telephone offices and thus prevented the transmission of orders. Even the Commanders of Armies were stopped on the road. . . . I myself was held up and my car seized. . . ."

Anarchic and stupid behavior did occur in the guise of revolutionary zeal. Had it been as prevalent as maintained, the armies of Hindenburg might still be mired in Flanders. Some rebellious gestures were hardly more than token acts. In Spa a *Soldatenrat* posted sentries at the entrance to Kuhl's Army Group Headquarters and required him to secure a pass. Although acquiring it was as easy as it had been for Count Harry Kessler in Berlin to become a revolutionary policeman in order to carry safe-conduct papers, the extra layer of bureaucracy was exasperating. But "contrary to [Kuhl's] expectation," the retiring troops were kept in motion. "This was due," he suggested, "solely to the firm attitude of the officers and to the sound common sense which still imbued the greater part of the men from the front. Here and there a few Soldiers' Councils showed that they were anxious to exert a good influence, but good will without professional knowledge is no use and often does harm."

An example he offered was that of a noncommissioned officer in the Fourth Army who organized a *Soldatenrat* in order—he claimed—"to avoid a catastrophe." On the ninth Sergeant Ludwig Lewinsohn had set himself up as president of his council and issued an order that "Home is our watchword! Come what may, the farther we retire the sooner we shall have peace." On the eleventh his council announced measures to maintain order on the march home, warning the men "to be quiet and self-possessed," to address their officers in the third person plural (as equals), and to eschew marks of respect (as saluting) "except when on duty."

Lewinsohn reported lapses into behavior which he condemned as unrevolutionary in spirit—and which Kuhl took to be inevitable consequences of the breakdown in order. "On the way through Antwerp," the sergeant wrote, "we saw scenes which disgusted us. Drunken soldiers and sailors tore off the cockades and epaulets of the officers who passed by and presented them to Belgian prostitutes. We stopped near a crowd of about a thousand soldiers who had just knocked the cap off the head of an Army doctor of high rank. . . . The lowest instincts, which had been nourished by the war and which were held in check only by iron discipline, came into full view. To our shame it must be said that many German soldiers thought of nothing but enriching themselves. They endeavored . . . to get as much as possible for themselves out of the confusion of the revolution. . . ." One veteran of the trenches remembered bitterly the "very young boys, degenerate deserters, and prostitutes [who] tore the insignia off our best front line soldiers and spat on their field-grey uniforms. . . . That was the liberty these heroes from behind the lines were talking about. . . . For the first time a searing hatred rose in me against these subhumans who were stepping on everything pure and clean."

For a people—and especially a soldiery—used to discipline, and self-discipline, as a fact of everyday life, the breakdown of order would be a festering psychological wound. "In the streets of Harburg," one wrote, "the mutineers tore the uniform piece by piece off my back." Revolutionary mobs in particular singled out officers as a criminal class, an error of judgment on the part of the radical leadership—if there was any leadership involved in mob violence. There would be more order than chaos, but chaos and violence and bitterness would be disproportionate in the memories of the defeated. "It is a painful business," wrote Lieutenant Walter Kempowski, "slogging back through the countryside that has been wrenched from the enemy with sweat and blood; a sense of bitterness arises: all for nothing, all for nothing. . . . That's what rises in the soldiers' ears as they tramp wordlessly along, stupefied and dejected at the same time."

With the need for front-line altruism evaporated, self-preservation had replaced self-sacrifice. Everyone wanted to go home. No one wanted to be last to pick up the surviving fragments of his life. In a novel by the pseudonymous "Schlump," the withdrawal is so quickly in progress that Schlump's unit has to wait for hours before a break in the line permits them to join it. "They marched along the banks of the Maas, past wonderful castles which were reflected in the green waters of the proud wide river. But on both sides of the road lay the first victims of the retreat: dead men, abandoned cars, dying horses, which kicked out blindly with their hind legs. . . ." Finally his column reaches a rail line and marches along the tracks to the next station, where soldiers had already fallen in, twenty to a row, waiting, silent and motionless, for the unheated and dilapidated, but still efficient, express from Strasbourg which went on to Cologne.

> Schlump knew that there would be a terrific struggle for places. He was right. A drumming was heard on the rails. The column of soldiers waited, tense, rigid. . . . Two white lights came out of the night. . . . Schlump ran along with the rest. A fearful struggle took place round each window. They crawled into the engine, into the tender; the night rang with wild voices and the splintering of glass. And then it was silent. . . .
>
> A couple of hours later he went out again. An enormously long local train stood on the tracks. He went up to one of the cars; it was dark. Then he heard voices.
>
> "Any room in there?" asked Schlump.
>
> No one answered. Someone laughed. He knew that it was hopeless. He went forward towards the engine. There he saw a faint shimmer of light: it came out of the baggage car. Schlump took the fifty-mark note out of his pocket and waited. At last someone came out—a postal official. Schlump went up to him, thrust the fifty-mark note into his hand, and said, "Good

morning, comrade. Do you think you can find room for me?" The man took out a pocket-lamp, examined the fifty-mark note, and answered, "You come along."

Not all men in uniform were as happy to return. Friedrich Sieburg, a junior officer enjoying his elite status as well as the *frisson* of war, wrote, "I never again want to go home; I would like to live my life walking along this road, searching the sky, measuring the world by co-ordinate squares and division combat sectors, evaluating the daylight hours by the strength of the artillery fire. . . . My Germany begins where the flares go up and ends where the train for Cologne departs. I can't go home again and live the old life." (He would join an irregular unit fighting the Bolsheviks in the Baltic states.) Another, Friedrich Wilhelm Heinz, refused to accept defeat. "Those people told us the war was over," he said. "That was a laugh. We ourselves are the war: Its flame burns strongly in us. It envelopes our whole being and fascinates us with the enticing urge to destroy. We obeyed . . . and marched onto the battlefields of the post-war world just as we had gone to battle on the Western Front." He would look for Rightist military organizations to join, and eventually became a *Gruppenführer* with the Nazi S.A.

Despite the reluctance to believe, and the reluctance to behave, order and discipline largely prevailed. The triumph of organization, with Groener as its presiding genius, would be a psychological plus for the military. It would restore the confidence shaken by the last weeks of the war and leave the General Staff convinced of its power to command the loyalty of the ranks, and with that to be the maker and shaper of German governments. Groener's elite would co-opt the revolutionary apparatus with the same success by which it would then dominate, usually behind the scenes, the Weimar Republic of the 1920s. Managing the withdrawal, coping with the revolution and evading the restrictions of the Armistice would be the first tests of the army of the next war.

From Holland the American military attaché reported on the withdrawal from Belgium, "Most German columns of troops moving steadily eastward, discipline maintained; men marching calmly and silently. Officers are in proper place in columns and seem to have men in hand, but do not wear insignia of grade. Most troops are without arms. Not many red flags carried by troops but many on motor trucks. . . . German Army supplies available for whole population expected to prevent starvation but critical moment will not come until great mass of men from Western Front are distributed to their homes." The withdrawal of millions of men beyond the Rhine within the limits set by the Armistice meant marching troops day and night, moving for twelve hours (with a short break each hour), resting for twelve hours while other units passed by. And when the exhausted horses were unable to drag wagons uphill, soldiers did. When available, trucks pulled several wagons behind them. And men who, innocent of military logistics, had formed *Soldatenraten,* soon confined themselves to the distribution of rations and—according to Army surgeon Stephen Westman—"putting a stamp on any document, as nothing in Germany was recognized as valid without at least one stamp and several illegible signatures." The price of such disciplined *Heimkehr* (the return home) was a shutting off of all normal responses in order to focus on moving one foot after the other for fifty minutes each hour. Some reminiscences talk of singing bawdy songs about Hamburg whores or sentimental ones about home. In reality there was little to sing about. "Each step [back]," Werner Beumelburg wrote, "leads over fields of slaughter once seen by German victors. The yearning to return home and to see once again wife, children and parents overshadows the terrible conscience of the lost war. Everything is still like a heavy dream. Neither the past nor the future is clearly comprehensible. We sway about in a strange semi-trance. One day it will become clearer."

Haggard troops crossed the border into the *Heimat* often to enthusiastic receptions. Ludwig Renn's battalion, reaching Aachen at dusk, found the houses beflagged. "Our band played . . . in front of us, and the drums echoed from the houses, from which people were gazing. A crowd accompanied us as we marched." Insolent red flags also waved in some towns, but even there the civilian population greeted the weary columns with cheers of admiration as well as relief. For the most part the return brought a patriotic outpouring. "The Homeland does its duty," Werner Beumelburg would write. "Flags are swaying. Garlands decorate the streets. . . . On the joyous faces of those watching us, tears are falling. What a reunion! The Homeland receives its returning sons like victors."

The Armistice had made it possible. The German Army was permitted to march home in orderly fashion, in uniform, carrying personal arms, bands playing, and colors flying. Soldier and civilian alike would remember the contrast between the consummate skill of the disciplined withdrawal and the chaos of demobilization under the new democratic government. Once in the German interior, the

Imperial Army demobilized by simply falling apart, with unemployed, battle-tough veterans wandering the streets to add another destabilizing element to the shaky republic.

At a rally in the Berlin Philharmonic Hall, for example, a bemedaled Air Force officer who had flown back on the last day of the war and was damning the revolution at every opportunity, climbed to the platform to denounce the ragged demobilization and the inability of the government to support its war veterans. "We did our duty for four long years," Hermann Goering shouted, ". . . and we risked our bodies for the Fatherland. Now we come home—and how do they treat us? They spit on us. . . . And therefore I implore you to cherish hatred—a profound, abiding hatred of those animals who have outraged the German people. . . . But the day will come when we will drive them out of our Germany."

"After four and a half years of separation from the homeland," Sergeant Lewinsohn wrote, "many soldiers lacked any kind of political understanding. They had only one wish: peace and work. In contrast to them were the great mass of those brutalized on the battlefield, men who were dishabituated to any kind of work; especially the youthful soldier who came into the army from the school bench, or from his apprenticeship, was drawn into sloth by long periods of idleness [and] fantastic thoughts of distorted communism. . . ." The political distortions would take other directions as well.

Like Lewinsohn, many *Soldatenrat* leaders were non-Communists who seized the device to win over pliable soldiers who might otherwise have turned to more radical options. One was the future Weimar Chancellor Heinrich Brüning, who as a young officer with a unit withdrawing eastward through Eupen in Belgium helped form a "confidence council" on the evening of November 11 after a more radicalized battalion marching ahead awakened anxieties. A corporal from OHL in Spa had exhorted troops in the sector not to salute officers, and to act as a body by majority vote. He spoke with "revolutionary phrases mixed in with Wilsonian slogans" and closed by asking that the men sing the "Internationale." Brüning's men sang the hymn of international Bolshevism so enthusiastically that he worried that even those who had spoken of marching to Berlin to put down the revolution had succumbed to the OHL corporal. Then they confounded expectation by voting Brüning chairman unanimously, with experienced and bemedaled corporals and privates as council members.

Even mutinous sailors from Kiel, let loose from claustrophobic shipboard inactivity and filled with revolutionary slogans, were reputed, according to local jokes which must have had substance in fact, to have purchased platform tickets required by posted regulations, before taking over railway stations and stopping trains. Soldiers were long used to accepting orders from superiors, military or civilian. When General Sixt von Arnim reluctantly agreed to permit *Soldatenraten* in the Fourth Army, still on the line, one company reacted by electing its commanding officer, who then was further elected chairman of the regimental and divisional Soldiers' Councils. In that capacity he was rushed to a mutinous *Landwehr* unit from which officers had fled after losing their epaulets to revolutionaries and addressed the ranks with the familiar Groener line that discipline was needed to get everyone home as quickly as possible; otherwise the roads would be chaotic and bottlenecked. The men, he closed, should attempt to win back the confidence of their officers. "After ten minutes," Ernst Lemmer, later a minister in the post-Nazi Bonn government, remembered, "order in this unit was restored."

Even in occupied Poland and other sectors in the East, the *Soldatenraten* usually defused mutiny and helped assure an orderly withdrawal. The command of the Tenth Army could even telegraph to Berlin that the retreat was proceeding according to plan "because the soldiers' council is supporting the efforts to maintain discipline in a selfless and most devoted fashion."

Although Lemmer observed that discipline improved with each kilometer the troops moved closer to the German frontier, when it was crossed the red flags carried by many units were replaced by the familiar Imperial black, red, and white flags "which clearly enough indicated their views." For that reason, Brüning claimed, the streets were empty in Eupen when his troops entered the town. Window blinds were down, and Belgians who had watched a red-bannered unit come through earlier were hoping to escape any fratricidal terror. As Brüning's battalion marched through singing *O' Deutschland, hoch in Ehren,* relieved citizens emerged from hiding places "with flowers and the best wines they had." (It is possible that the offerings of goodwill were actually made because the battalion was *leaving* Belgium and inhabitants wanted no parting violence.)

Lammersdorf was just across the frontier in German territory, on the road to Bonn. There Brüning's men were preparing night quarters when

all of a sudden there came a corporal with a red cockade and a big engineer pistol. He demanded that the two privates I had with me hand over their weapons "in the name of the new government of Berlin." Drawing my own pistol from my pocket was enough to make him flee hastily. When the battalion approached, and I came to meet it, I saw the same corporal try to stop the troops, again "in the name of the Berlin government." I signalled to the corporals who were marching in front to attack him with their rifle butts. Leaping like a hare and crying loudly for mercy, he ran away. The local population was glad to be free of this man. They knew he had been sentenced as a deserter to many years of confinement . . . but was released at once by the soldier's council there. One of my later colleagues in the Reichstag who was from this region went to the effort to trace this man further. In 1923 he was a [Rhenish] separatist, in 1929 he was one of Hitler's S.A. men. There are revolutionaries who are indifferent to the goals of the revolution.

Moving onto German soil renewed spirits. Troops made extra efforts to appear soldierly and even proud. Bands played the old marches and patriotic hymns—the *"Hohenfriedberger,"* the *"Radetzky Marsch," "Fredericus Rex," "Die Wacht am Rhein,"* and *"Deutschland, Deutschland über Alles."* Soon the occupation commissioners in the Rhineland would forbid Imperial flags and decorations, but in the early days of the march home the commission was not yet in place, and some Rhenish towns were seas of flags and bunting. Troops crossing the Rhine bridges often found their oppression lifted and would enthusiastically sing *"Die Wacht am Rhein."* Railway stations in frontier areas, when not in the hands of revolutionaries, were decorated wth welcoming banners encouraging the exhausted soldiers. "UNCONQUERED IN THE FIELD" was one, and "YOU WERE VICTORIOUS NEVERTHELESS." *Prisonnier* Halm's train was barely come to a stop on German soil when a military band strikes up *"Was is da für ein Leid?"*—with lines which forebode much in the early postwar days:

> *Victorious we'll conquer France,*
> *Dying like heroes.*

That the words were not out of the ordinary is clear from a pamphlet, harmlessly titled *Deutschland als freie Volksrepublik* and issued by the executive committee of the Social Democratic Party in November 1918 to returning soldiers. "A new Germany greets you!"

it begins. "... Perhaps you do not return as victors who have completely crushed the enemy to the ground.... But neither do you return as the vanquished, for the war was stopped at the wishes of the leadership of the Reich [*Reichsleitung*].... So you can hold your heads high." Inevitably such phrases, offered to soldiers marching home, weapons proudly on shoulders, flags flying, would contribute mightily to the *Dolchstoss* myth and to Rightist allegations about "November criminals," which Hitler would seize upon.

The sense of an armistice which was only a lull for rearming, and a defeat that was only a deferral of the ultimate victory, arose quickly and not often by design. For the moment the returning soldiers of the November Army, desperation in their drawn faces, were victors if only that they had triumphed over death. If they had not beaten the French, the British, the Americans, they had beaten the odds. And they would be back. *Die Wacht am Rhein* would continue, but from the other bank.

In Cologne, Walter Kempowski wrote, the remnants of his 210th Regiment saw little flag-waving enthusiasm. Some times and places were inopportune. It was better not to provoke the radical elements where they appeared to be in temporary control of things. Rather, the regiment marched across the Rhine bridge "with baggage carts and steaming field kitchens, but mute. Outside the black, silent cathedral stands General von Larisch acknowledging the march-past, beside him a few revolutionary types who first keep their hands in their pockets and smoke but then refrain. Beside him also the band, but the instruments remain in their cases. Crunch-crunch-crunch, that is the only music. The populace lines the streets and silently watches. ..."

The new peace would not be an instant millenium. It began drably, an extension of wartime privations without the gloss of war propaganda to sustain them. Bertolt Brecht would satirize that world, in which he would mature as a playwright, in a scene from *Mother Courage* (1939). Ostensibly it is Europe in 1624; it could easily be Germany in 1918–19:

> SERGEANT: What they could use around here is a good war. What else can you expect with peace running wild all over the place? You know what the trouble with peace is? No organization. And when do you get organization? In a war. Peace is one big waste of equipment. Anything goes, no

one gives a damn. . . . It takes a war to fix that. In a war, everyone registers, everyone's name is on a list. Their shoes are stacked, their corn's in the bag, you can count it all up—cattle, men, *et cetera*—and you can take it away! That's the story: no organization, no war!

RECRUITING OFFICER: It's the God's truth.

SERGEANT: Course, a war's like every real good deal: hard to get going. But when it's on the road, it's a pisser. . . .

Corn, cattle, and shoes were in short supply, as was everything else. American agents who made their way into Holland from Germany just after the Armistice reported that "meat, milk, oil, candles, soap, shoes, [and] clothing" were "very scarce." The list covered most staples. "Children and young people," the survey went on, "appear underfed. In towns . . . agents could not buy a glass of milk. . . . Almost any peace acceptable to Germans if they are assured food by Allies. Great self-confidence on part of Germans that they will quickly make good . . . recovery from war shock." A civilian internee, Paul Cohen-Portheim, who had been waiting eagerly in Holland for entry after three years in England, found the streets filled with half-starved old men and war invalids, beggars, and gaunt children. "Endless queues of grey-looking women lined the pavements in front of the food stores," but the *Kriegs Bröt* they could buy was "some gritty stuff," the coffee made of acorns, the sugar only saccharine, and the cream something which looked and tasted like shaving lather.

In the old college town of Heidelberg red-armbanded sailors had invaded the university square to attack officers in uniform. Signed up for lectures was Gustav Regler, who had been gassed at Laon in 1917, then hospitalized and discharged as a hopeless case. "It was pointless," he would write, "to sit scribbling in notebooks, filling them with facts and dates from the past, while one knew nothing of this world in which Germans ripped away the shoulder-straps of other Germans as though they were a part of their bodies, and where hatred paraded in the neat dress of sailors, assailing the wrong people." But a girlfriend, Hanna, insisted that events were so momentous that Dr. Hermann Oncken, the professor of history, would have to refer to them. Oncken usually rejected recent history as not History.

The low-ceilinged room, dimly lit, was filled with students who were mostly discharged soldiers who had been declared unfit for further duty. One, Regler noticed, was a young officer he had seen degraded in the square. "If it is true," the professor was saying in his reedy voice, "that his Majesty today crossed the Dutch frontier without making any struggle, then all our sympathies must go to that handful of officers who have barricaded themselves in the royal palace in Berlin, resolved to resist the mob to the last and"—his voice sank in grief—"prepared to die at their posts than shamefully surrender." There was, in fact, no such last stand, but rumors suggested it, and it was what his embittered audience wanted to hear. There was a thunderous stamping of feet in applause.

"Idiotic!" said Hanna as she and Regler walked away. "Treating a few sentimental fools in a cellar as though they were heroes!"

Regler recalled intervening to keep a young pacifist speaker from being beaten by Rightist ex-officers, and names him Ernst Toller. Toller, however, was at his mother's house in Landsberg, ill with influenza, on November 9. A veteran on sick leave as *kriegsuntauglich*—unfit for warfare—he had been discharged in time to become a disciple of Kurt Eisner at his *Goldene Anker* coffee-house discussion group and revolutionary cell. In Munich he had already been elected deputy president to Eisner. There would be more years of revolution, repression, and imprisonment before Toller, gray at thirty, would become an exile—still a spokesman, as polemicist and playwright, for futile causes. Frustrated and depressed, he would commit suicide in a New York hotel in 1939.

On the day of the Armistice, with Oncken again scheduled to lecture, Regler returned, but mistook the time and found himself addressed by the Liberal economist Alfred Weber, brother of sociologist Max Weber. They must not let the Republic be suffocated by premature criticism, he warned. "It's very young. . . . Some talk as they do because nothing will satisfy them; others because they can never forget that the Kaiser locked them up—but is the Republic the Kaiser? Yet they would sooner go to the barricades with the scum of Berlin. And there are not enough young men to sweep them away!"

Regler went to Hanna and told her that he was going to leave Heidelberg for Berlin. "Of course you must go!" she said. With her money for his fare, he took the train to Frankfurt, where he stopped long enough to send Weber a picture postcard of Goethe House, on which he wrote, "I'm doing as you advised. It isn't a question of who is right. But there must be no more war, that is the first thing, and that is what the Republic means to me. And the second thing is that the young must again begin to believe in something."

Regler would take up Toller's causes, becoming a Loyalist

leader with the International Brigades in the Spanish Civil War
(where a good friend would be the American who on Armistice Day
in Milan was planning on "making the world safe for Ernie Hemingway"). After breaking with the Communists, Regler would become a war refugee in Mexico.

At Wurzburg University a student with a clubfoot and a limp
who had been rejected as unfit for military service in 1914 and again
in 1917 found keeping his mind on the writings of Johann Winckel-
mann difficult. Reading the works of the Catholic classicist and ar-
chaeologist seemed absurd to Joseph Goebbels amid the political
unrest and the news of the Armistice. There had been a huge meeting in the Auditorium Maximum, he wrote his friend, Fritz Prang.

> The question was raised as to how German students should face
> the new powers-that-be, and one of the older students
> (wounded in the war) had his say: "I think that for the time
> being the most decent line for us to take is to watch matters
> calmly. Just now the blind and raw masses seem to be on top.
> But maybe the time will come again when they feel the need for
> an intelligent lead, and then it will be for us to step in with all
> our strength." Don't you also feel that the time will come again
> when people will yearn for intellectual and spiritual values
> rather than brutal mass appeal? Let us also wait for that mo-
> ment, and meanwhile persevere in steeling our brains for the
> tasks then awaiting us. It is bitter enough to have lived through
> those dark hours of our Fatherland, but who knows if one day it
> might not profit us after all. The way I see it, Germany has cer-
> tainly lost the war, but our Fatherland may well turn out the
> winner.

The old order did not pass easily. The blasphemy—*Gottlosig-
keit*—of liberal-bourgeois government was decried as a "rottenness"
which had sullied the sacrifices of the dead in battle. The univer-
sities, with their masses of wounded veterans, would be seedbeds of
discontent.* The churches, represented by the *Gott mit uns* buckles on
millions of uniforms, were another, in the conservative, older breed
of clergy. Erna von Pustau, whose father was then manager of a linoleum business in Hamburg, remembered the sermon her family's

* The rector of the University of Berlin, Reinhold Seeberg, ordered the university war memorial to students killed in 1914–18 inscribed *Invictis victi victuri*—
  promising victory next time to the defeated but unconquered.

minister gave on the day the Armistice was signed. The setting was
the middle-class Uhlenhorst district, the church an unpretentious
neighborhood one. For his text the minister took "for when they say
peace and safety, then sudden destruction cometh upon them."

"The whole sermon," Fräulein von Pustau told American author Pearl Buck,

> was a militant speech against the enemies from without and the
> enemies from within. But he was much milder against the ene-
> mies from without than against the enemies from within; with-
> out his naming any names we knew, naturally, that the Reds
> were the enemies from within. But while he prayed to God to
> give wisdom to our enemies from without so that they might
> give us a fair and just peace, he said that the enemies from
> within were devils and were destroying our whole culture and
> civilization and Christianity, and that it was our duty to stand
> up against them. He ended his prayer by adding that as a
> nation we had abandoned our Kaiser in his days of danger. He
> ignored the fact that the Kaiser had abandoned his people—
> which was really a queer way of looking at things!

On their way home mother and daughters argued about the
sermon, with Frau von Pustau insisting that Germans had been "ungrateful" to the Kaiser. "I did not agree with her, nor, by the way,
did I agree with Miss Ritter, our school director. She just couldn't
make up her mind whether to take the Kaiser's picture off its place
of honor on the wall above the desk from which Miss Ritter used to
make her speeches and the minister used to pray. She made a very
touching speech about the Kaiser, saying, 'He was our Kaiser and
we followed him. It is too early to judge justly, and those who condemn him now are throwing stones upon themselves, too.' "

Erna had dared to remark in class that morning that it was
wrong to leave the Kaiser's portrait in place when the nation had
become a republic. Suddenly she found herself called a "Red." Returning home from church, she went to her diary and wrote,
"Everybody says that we are ungrateful to the Kaiser, but we are not
ungrateful to him. It is only that so many greater things are at stake
that the person as an individual doesn't count any longer. And if the
new world which is to come is what Schiller dreamed of, human
rights and equality and justice, it is better than the old, and we are
thus not unfaithful to the Kaiser but faithful to the greater ideals."

For her father, November 11 had been a working day. When he

came home that evening it was with a newspaper which spelled out the Armistice conditions, and the realization of defeat overwhelmed concerns about Kaiser and Republic. That the Rhineland was to be occupied excited the children more than any of the clauses which dealt with matters remote to them. "Now Grandmother is occupied," said Erna.

In Königsberg, East Prussia, Eva Ehrhardt felt little relief at the Armistice. "There was the shock—and, yes, the shame—of the revolution, and the obviously lost war. There were also the vague fears engendered by history lessons of the French terror and the Russian revolution next door. People in East Prussia could not know that it would take another revolution and war for these and worse horrors to come to pass." An armed, pro-Bolshevik *Volkswehr* roamed the back streets, and a rival, Rightist *Freikorps* was growing out of independent bands of ex-soldiers, mostly officers at first, who had fought the Czarist forces, and then their successors. The Baltic lowlands would be in ferment for many more months. After the next war Königsberg would disappear behind the Soviet frontier and become Kaliningrad.

Most Germans accepted with gratitude any signs and symbols of continuing normality. In Munich, poet Rainer Maria Rilke, whose conscript service had been brief and who had worked as a government clerk, watched the weird but peaceful Eisner revolution there with the hope, he wrote his wife, Clara, that "this unusual insurrection will engender sense in people's heads and not go beyond fatal intoxication." Bearded like an Old Testament patriarch, and a scholar and idealist without sufficient political cynicism for survival, Kurt Eisner operated amid amiable disorder in the halls of the Wittelsbachs. "Diplomatic acts, parchments, revolutionary proclamations, even telegrams," a visiting journalist wrote,

> cover tables and armchairs in a confusion suggestive of the backroom of a shop, and he hardly tries to conceal the most compromising documents from the indiscretion of the journalists who besiege him. On the contrary . . . Eisner himself offers to their curiosity the acts concerning his own politics. Would you like the telegram that was sent today to the government of Berlin? Here it is. . . . Would you like the order of the day for the coming council of ministers? Here it is. . . . Sometimes some hurried visitor, tired of waiting, bursts all at once into the first office, where several young men and women secretaries . . .

work, smoking cigarettes and eating sandwiches in a chaos of tables and chairs piled high with newspapers and proclamations. . . . For no method and no organization seems to prevail in the functioning of this odd ministry.

For Rilke, writing to a friend on November 11, the external world nevertheless suggested confidence. "The morning paper which brings the reassurance that most businesses are functioning and in order," he assured, "speaks for the fact that the hour now belongs not so much to words as to quiet confirmation through work." Never having identified with the war, he felt no sense of loss in defeat.

Recovering from the shock of the Armistice terms ("They go beyond all expectations.") and the Bavarian upheaval, Thomas Mann worried more about the "enormous arrogance" of "Republican America" than about the revengeful Clemenceau, "the fossil from Bordeaux," who represented the past. "Despair," he decided on the eleventh, "would be the enemy of law and order. What is going to happen? A man will cultivate his garden, prepare it for the winter, cover the flower beds—just like every year." Then at noon he went out into Munich to buy a rubber stamp and a shaving brush (an effort toward normality) and to examine the latest wires posted in newspaper office windows. But they made him worry further about the breakdown of order. "As soon as I lie down, images of a revolutionary tribunal and executions come to my mind. If things are driven to their extremes it is not at all impossible that I will be executed as a result of my attitude during the war." It was a passing fear. "After all," he concluded to his diary, "I believe that the Germans will somehow be able to master the situation even if all the [Armistice] terms have to be accomplished." Then he "wrote to a mother whose son once wrote an admiring letter to me and who had committed suicide during the war."

The surrender, Mann persuaded himself, "should not cause the Germans to commit abominable moral self-betrayal," but that was exactly what the outraged junior member of the two-man German observer team with the Austro-Hungarian Armistice Commission was certain he was seeing all around him on returning from Italy to Munich. Not only had Captain Heinz Guderian been ignored by the Austrians as they rushed to sign any sort of peace; on the way north to Bavaria afterward he had to pass withdrawing Austrian regiments singing happily and wearing red flowers. In the towns he traveled through, he wrote indignantly to his wife, Grete, from Munich, shops were being plundered and men in military uniform assaulted. "Our beautiful German Empire is no more. Bismarck's work lies in ruins. Villains have torn everything down to the ground. . . . All comprehension of justice and order, duty and decency, seems to have been destroyed." The revolutionary regime, he complained, "suffers from teething troubles . . . and makes ridiculous regulations. . . . I regret not having civilian clothing here in order not to expose to the jostling mob the clothes I have worn with honor for twelve years." Seething with bitterness, he would become a Rightist *Freikorps* officer in Berlin before rejoining the rebuilding *Reichswehr,* where he would mold the *Panzer* forces of 1939 and beyond.

In Berlin on November 11, Albert Einstein wrote to his mother in Switzerland, "The great event has happened." Not the news, which had trickled in from Holland, that British astronomers were planning to test his relativity theory during the next major eclipse, but the almost simultaneous birth of the Republic and the end of the war. Spreading his message over two postcards, he added, "I was afraid of a complete breakdown of law and order. Thus far, however, the movement has run its course in truly imposing fashion, the most tremendous experience conceivable. It is most curious to see how readily the people have accepted it. What a privilege to have lived through such an experience! No breakdown can be so severe that one would not willingly suffer it in return for so glorious a reward! Militarism and bureaucracy have been thoroughly abolished here."

A political innocent who would be forced to flee Germany in 1933, he had little idea how tenacious both militarism and bureaucracy, operating under physical laws he never studied, could be. "Do not worry," he added on the second card; "everything has gone smoothly—indeed, impressively—so far. The present leadership seems thoroughly equal to its task. I am very happy at the way things are developing. Only now do I begin to feel at ease. The defeat has worked wonders. . . ."

In the Berlin suburb of Potsdam, Hans Ludendorff, an astronomer very likely known to Einstein, found an unwelcome visitor at his door. False beard and blue-tinted spectacles concealed his more famous brother, General Erich Ludendorff, for whose arrest radicals were already clamoring. He would remain a few days, despite his brother's unsympathetic politics, then escape on a coastal steamer to Denmark. On arrival in Copenhagen a curious crowd watched him disembark: he had been recognized (under the beard and glasses) boarding the boat. On he would go to Sweden, where he wrote his wife, Margarethe, "To me it all seems like a bad dream. I do not know if I was right to go away. Things cannot go on like this forever. . . . For four years I have fought for my country and now when so much is hanging in the balance I must stand aside. . . . My nerves are too much on edge and sometimes my speech gets out of control. There is no help for it; my nerves have simply gone to pieces! . . . Tell everybody how my fate was like that of Hannibal. . . ."

For inhabitants of Berlin rumor took the place of news, and few had any idea what was happening in their own city, let alone in Munich or Frankfurt or Hamburg. Party newspapers and handbills printed what appeared useful, and with travel erratic, and travelers themselves misinformed, exaggerated reports of civil war spread and were often believed. Although there would be bloody violence in December and January as radical and Rightist groups in Berlin jockeyed for power, the period immediately following November 11 was relatively quiet and even euphoric for many Germans, who expected utopian results from the revolution, abdication, and Armistice. In the Baltic ports, where Gustav Noske, a minister of Prince Max's and in Ebert's government, had applied his charismatic personality and the mutinying sailors' leadership vacuum to co-opting the movement, quiet was returning. Many sailors, however, like the Alsatian Oscar Ludmann, had gone home by rail to spread the revolution, even as far inland as Bavaria. In Berlin on November 11 the band of sailors who had arrived in time to spearhead the revolution of the ninth decided—although they were the most unruly and quarrelsome of the revolutionaries—to form a unit to help maintain order. They marched to police headquarters and offered themselves to the new, self-appointed chief, Emil Eichhorn. Their help was unwelcome, and to get rid of them he assigned them quarters in the barracks of the Alexander Regiment of the Guards, a short walk from the police offices.

Marching along looking for the barracks, they passed a soldier who asked them curiously where they were going, as six hundred sailors on a Berlin street, even then, seemed unusual. When they explained he offered to escort them instead to the *Marstall,* the Imperial stables opposite the Palace. Quarters were more comfortable, he explained, and in such curious ways the process of containing the revolution began to operate. A Count Wolf Metternich received them warmly and permitted them to gather to elect a leadership council. Inevitably they made the Count a member, whereupon he saw to it that they were fed and housed well, probably utilizing money (although he had enough of his own) contributed by financial and industrial circles eager to see the sailors content.

The group would name itself the People's Marine Division, busy itself with leadership rivalries, and become a factor in the December agitation. Its appearance on the streets, armbanded and in Navy gear, would strike home the reality of revolution, although its impact had been temporarily defused. At her home in Berlin, where she was insulated by upper-class patriotism, Princess Blücher had noted in her diary on the tenth that she was shocked and surprised at the "universal rejoicing" which followed the abdication and exile of the Kaiser—almost universal, as the grief of the aristocracy "at the breakdown of their country, more than at the personal fall of the Kaiser, is heart-rending to see. I have seen some of our friends, strong men, sit down and sob at the news, whilst others seemed to shrink to half their size and were struck dumb with pain."

On the day of the Armistice she felt safer, despite the occasional crack of desultory shooting. "Our general impression is that the people are much too weak and starved to be really bloodthirsty unless goaded by fanatics like Liebknecht and Rosa Luxemburg, and one can't help admiring the disciplined and orderly way in which a revolution of such dimensions has been organized, with until now the least possible loss of life." Her nephew Ludwig Karl Strachwitz had telephoned from the General Staff offices in Berlin. "He said he was still at his old occupation, but in plain clothes, and there were several sailors and soldiers about him, apparently entrusted with the task of managing everything; but as they themselves admitted they understood nothing at all of what was to be done, they begged him to continue in authority and go on with the work. It is the same everywhere. . . ."

That it was indeed the same suggested the surface quality of the revolution. It had brought an end to the Kaiser and the war, but institutions and their bureaucracies were another matter. *Berliner Tageblatt* editor Theodor Wolff (who would flee Germany in 1933) realized this only later, writing of going on the afternoon of the eleventh, with Otto Nuschke, editor of the *Volkszeitung,* to the Chancellor's residence to discuss the political situation. "The same well-drilled, noiseless old attendants who had opened and closed the doors here in the time of Wilhelm II, took us to the room on the ground floor which had been Bethmann-Hollweg's ante-room."

The accommodation between the Ebert-Scheidemann Majority Socialists and the Hugo Haase-Wilhelm Dittmann radical wing was uneasy, and the men had arrived to mull over the alternatives. "I have no soldiers," said Scheidemann, throwing up his arms in perplexity; "what can I do?"

As the discussion proceeded, a gray-haired usher entered to announce in the same sepulchral tone he had once used to announce ambassadors, "The Supreme Soldier's Council." It was obviously unwelcome news to the politicians. Scheidemann bolted from his chair in annoyance—"That lot again!" But the newspapermen had to leave, and filing in from the vestibule were four men in insignia-less officer's uniform, with red armbands: a radical writer, two Socialist Reichstag members, and a curious General Staff captain with a *von* to his surname. The group encapsulated the revolution.

One of the rising politicians with whom Wolff had been negotiating in an attempt to create a party with "middle-class Left-wing" rather than Bolshevik sympathies was the forty-one-year-old manager of the National Bank, Dr. Hjalmar Schacht, who was reluctant to go so far as to endorse the Republic. He was prepared, according to Wolff, only "to countenance it." After learning of the Kaiser's flight into Holland, a group of seventeen Berlin industrial and business leaders had assembled—it was Sunday morning, the tenth—at the house of Theodor Vogelstein in the Kurfurstenstrasse. (Vogelstein had been the organizer of an earlier manifesto of Berliners petitioning Prince Max to press for a cease-fire before enemy armies crossed into Germany.) Total social and economic collapse, they realized, would only play into the hands of the extreme left.

Volgelstein, Schacht, and several others visited Wolff at his home, then telephoned him (phone service remained efficient) to ask that he put his paper at the service of the group. It had emerged untainted from the war because of its opposition to annexation and to unrestricted submarine war. "We finally decided to form the GDP (German Democratic Party) on November 11, the day the Armistice was signed," Schacht remembered. He helped write a manifesto intended to appeal to every possible constituency. "The peoples of Germany will be able to develop their special characteristics independently and freely," one line offered, and that Schacht had come aboard should have been warning enough. "The comment was made, not entirely without justice," Wolff recalled in his memoirs, "that among the signatories there were rather too many big capitalists." It was no surprise to Dr. Schacht, whose name brought confidence to the enterprise. In retirement in 1933, he would be returned to the *Reichsbank* by Hitler.

Although Theodor Wolff had editorialized in the *Tageblatt* that the Imperial regime had been overthrown "at first assault" and that of its "apparently invincible bureaucracy . . . nothing remained," he had judged too hastily. The rulers of the federal states which comprised Germany had quickly gone, but even the most radical of the revolutionaries exercising power could not use that power without the apparatus of the old order. Ebert, Scheidemann, and others of their persuasion were happy that this was so; the more radical leaders in the uneasy coalition were frustrated by the realization but not adept enough as administrators or manipulators to do much about it. In its innocence the Executive Council of the Workers' and Soldiers' Councils—which included the delegation which Wolff had seen at the Chancellor's office—published a proclamation on Armistice Day which verified that fact of political life. "All communal, state, federal and military authorities will continue to function," it began. "All decrees emanating from these authorities are approved by the Executive Committee and must be obeyed by all. All provisionally formed bodies in Greater Berlin dating back to the beginning of the revolution, including those called workers' and soldiers' councils, which had assumed certain administrative functions, are now defunct. All further measures and decrees will from now on be announced as fast as possible by the competent civilian and military offices. All proclamations and measures of the Executive Committee will be signed by the two chairmen, [Richard] Müller and v[on] Beerfelde."

Hans Georg von Beerfelde was the tall, bushy-browed one-time captain whom Wolff had seen in Ebert's anteroom, a wounded and decorated officer of Theosophical bent. "None," wrote Wolff, "was so ill-suited to our age than this Knight of the Grail and the child-minded Quixote, mystic and social idealist." Neither he nor the more professional radical, Müller, could run the affairs of the sprawling German bureaucracy, and had solved the problem by writing it a blank check. On the Monday after the revolution—the day the shooting stopped in the West—civil servants returned to their desks, policemen to their stations, town and country prefects and petty officials to their offices, some with councils ostensibly over them. The General Staff in Spa and Berlin continued to function, setting the stages of withdrawal from the Armistice lines; and the same officers commanded their military units as before (with the rare exceptions of some prison camp commandants). Even the major ministries were unchanged, except that instead of an Imperial Chancellor over them there was now a six-man committee of "People's Commissars," of whom one was the Chancellor, Friedrich Ebert. Unlike the situation in Russia, there had been no Bolshevik apparatus ready to become the instrument of power; and in the confusion and cross-purposes of the Left, from liberals to radicals, the old conservative bureaucracy and officer corps would survive, minus the monarchistic trappings.

In Saxony, Württemberg, Brunswick, and even Bavaria, where there were governments of People's Commissars, the actual machinery of government was largely unchanged although the rhetoric at the top was different. As Count Harry Kessler would notice in Berlin, the Palace guards continued to parade through the Brandenburg Gate with appropriate precision and to the accompaniment, as before, of the *"Hohenfriedberger Marsch."* Only now it was under a red flag.

Less than a week after the Armistice, with troops returning home, largely in good order, General Groener composed a blunt letter to Ebert for Hindenburg's signature. If the Army were to remain "a useful means of power in the hands of the government," it warned, Ebert would have to restore all powers of military command to "the legitimate authorities" and cause all soldiers' councils to "disappear from the units," retaining as facade only *Vertrauensleute* (trusted men who had been co-opted) limited to informing officers "of the mood of other ranks." Groener was insisting upon public recognition of what in fact had already been happening, although it was too soon for the Berlin government to be able to acknowledge it. Further, Groener added political demands—that Ebert prevent interference in the administration of governmental units by *Arbeiterraten.* The challenge was unnecessary and heavy-handed, for the Supreme Command knew that the councils, already being phased out, were relatively impotent anyway, and were needed by Berlin for window dressing to placate the radicals.

Although Ebert would be accused of betraying the revolution by cooperating with the military, he was hardly alone in acknowledging that necessity. The far more radical Wilhelm Dittmann, of the rival Independent Socialists, rationalized in his unpublished memoirs that if "the government of the People's Representatives" had unseated the Army command as well as the generals of the field armies, "there would have been a complete disorganization of the retreat, and the danger existed that large parts of the armies in the West would have been captured by the Entente troops which followed them closely. . . . This would have caused a justified storm of indignation in Germany against those responsible, and the right-wing circles behind the officers would have had a popular argument to make propaganda against the People's Representatives and the revolution. . . . Therefore my consent to the leading back of the army by the old command was a foregone conclusion."

While Ebert cautiously dragged his feet about the additional demands from Hindenburg's headquarters, realizing their political implications, several of Groener's colonels were drafting a plan to retain one division at the ready in each army by unobtrusively exchanging front-line troops with "undesirable elements" during rest periods on the line of march in the withdrawal process. The intent was obvious: to put down the revolution when it was safe to do so. Such divisions would sometimes declare revolutionary councils dissolved as they marched eastward and would tear down red flags. After all, hadn't the Armistice left them their weapons for just that? In Brunswick, members of the local *Soldatenrat* turned out to welcome the returning soldiers, only to be ridden down by mounted Hussars. In Lennep, the Council was scattered by loyal Sixth Army troops, the red flag removed from the city hall, and the Prussian emblem hoisted to the cheers of the burghers. There were clashes between returning soldiers and revolutionary groups in Aachen, Cologne, Essen, and other cities, and the uneasy accommodations with the Left in some locations only emphasized the impulsive heavy-handedness of the Right elsewhere.

Eventually more subtlety would be infused into the General Staff's subversion of the revolution, especially when it was realized how essentially conservative the Social Democratic leadership was. But the officer corps worried about the further radicalization of the Republic and intended to make an inescapably symbolic show when the troops marched back into Berlin. According to the Army's bold scenario, the best-disciplined divisions would parade through the Brandenburger Tor to be welcomed by Ebert in the name of the nation. In his reply the general in command would express concern over conditions in the country and demand that the Chancellor assume dictatorial powers and dissolve all workers' and soldiers' councils and other revolutionary apparatus.

The chief author, Colonel von Haeften, brought the plan to

Ebert's right-hand man, Dr. Walter Simons. Simons discussed it with Ebert, who cautiously refused to say yes or no. Haeften then sent for other colonels to apply pressure, including Groener's cagey deputy, Wilhelm Heye, who had been instrumental in the Kaiser's abdication. Yet a hitch remained: no one of sufficiently high rank was willing to expose himself to the risks of responding to Ebert at the Brandenburg Gate before masses of Germans who very likely had supported the revolution.

One month to the day after the shooting stopped in the West, on December 11, the returning regiments under General von Lequis marched up Unter den Linden, where their fathers and grandfathers had paraded after victories over Denmark and Austria and France. The sky was a typically leaden December gray, but the air was bright with banners and martial music, and the defeated troops bore their arms. One, an officer in the Imperial Guards, was the half-English son of the Princess von Pless. To his mother, Daisy, Hans von Pless wrote that most old veterans—*Kriegsverein*—along the march route wept aloud as they watched the return of men "who for four years have defended a proud country, and now find, instead of a home, a manure heap which one formerly called Germany." As a boy of sixteen, Ernst von Salomon watched raptly, with tens of thousands of other Berliners. The eyes of the soldiers, he remembered,

> were hidden in the shadows thrown by the peaks of the caps, sunk in dark hollows, grey and sharp. These eyes looked neither to the right nor to the left. . . . Those thin faces, impassive under their helmets, those bony limbs, those ragged clothes covered with dirt! They advanced step by step and around them grew the void of a great emptiness. . . . But here was their home, here warmth and fellowship awaited them—then why did they not cry out with joy? Why didn't they laugh and shout? . . . Why didn't they even look at us? . . . Somebody had lied to us. These were not our heroes, our defenders of the Homeland! These men did not belong to us at all. . . . These men had come from a totally different world! Suddenly I understood.
>
> These were not workers, farmers, students. . . . these were soldiers . . . united in the bonds of blood and sacrifice. Their home was the Front—that was their Homeland! Fatherland! *Volk!* Nation! . . . Yes, that is why they could never belong to us. That is the reason for this stolid, spectral return. . . . War

moved them; war dominated them; they could never abandon it. . . . They would always carry the front in their blood: the approaching death, the glorious suspense, the suffering, the smoke, the cold steel. . . .

And suddenly they were supposed to become peaceful citizens in a *bürgerlich* world! Oh, no! That was a . . . counterfeit which was bound to fail. . . . The war is ended but the warriors still march!

"I salute you," Friedrich Ebert declared, "who return unvanquished from the field of battle."

EPILOGUE:
A BEER HALL IN MUNICH

Die Fahne hoch, die Reihen dicht geschlossen!
S.A. marchiert mit ruhig festem Schritt.
Kam'raden die Rotfront und Reaktion
    erschossen,
Marschieren im Geist in unsern Reihen mit.

Die Strasse frei den braunen Battaillonen!
Die Strasse frei dem Sturmabteilungsmann!
Es schaun aufs Hakenkreuz voll Hoffnung
    schon Millionen,
Der Tag für Freiheit und für Brot bricht an.

Zum letzten Mal wird nun Appell geblasen!
Zum Kämpfe stehn wir alle schon bereit.
Bald flattern Hitlerfahnen über
    allen Strassen,
Die Knechtschaft dauert nur noch kurtze Zeit!

Hold the banner high! Close the ranks!
S.A. marches on with steadfast stride.
Comrades killed by Red Front and
    Reaction
March with us in spirit at our side.

Free the streets for the Brown battalions!
Free the streets for the Storm Troopers!
For the millions, the Swastika shines
    in hope,
Daybreak comes for bread and freedom.

For the last time will the trumpet blow!
We stand ready for the struggle.
Soon Hitler's banners will wave over
    every street,
The time of slavery is about to end!

—THE *Horst Wessel Lied,* THE OFFICIAL
    MARCHING SONG OF THE NAZI PARTY IN ITS HEYDAY

In 1923 the *Bürgerbräukeller* was one of the most popular eating places in Munich. A meeting hall as well as restaurant and beer "cellar," its main room could seat three thousand at traditional rough-hewn tables. It was often used for political gatherings, of which there were many in that troubled year. The young Republic had weathered coup attempts from both Left and Right, several of them bloody, and remained unstable. Preserving, within democratic forms, the economic order and militarist values of Imperial Germany had been far from easy. Versailles had shorn the nation of productive areas and demanded war reparations which the truncated, partially occupied, and prostrate country could not pay. A war guilt clause added to justify the settlement had only compounded German bitterness.* "If our army," said Social Democrat leader Konrad Haussmann, "and our workmen had known on the fifth and ninth of November that the peace would look like this, the army would not have laid down its arms and all would have held out to the end." The unreality of such claims, given the desperation of the High Command in the last days of the fighting, would be forgotten in the difficult postwar years, but such claims appealed to the German sense of lost honor.

By November 1923 inflation (some of it rigged to undermine reparations) had made the mark worthless, and unemployment, hunger, profiteering, and depravity added misery to the ongoing national humiliation. Yet Germany remained in fact what it had been before the Armistice—the leading power in Europe. Even defeat had not altered that, and the Germans knew it.

Extremist parties continued to profit from the situation. Communists had become urban guerrillas, while Rightists had put together their own private armies, exploiting the German love of uniforms and disciplined organizations. In Bavaria even *Land* (state) officials, seeking panaceas, were talking about reinstating the Wittelsbachs, as Crown Prince Rupprecht, who had led an army in France, remained popular. Among the political groups using the *Bügerbräukeller* was one which had expanded from a tiny German Workers Party after a demobilized corporal, who had briefly served the peacetime Army as an educational assistant, had been ordered

---

* One must wonder, however, what a German *Diktat* would have been like if victory had gone the other way, since 1914 ambitions included huge territorial acquisitions from Belgium, France, and Russia, an augmented colonial empire at the expense of Belgium, France, and Britain, and economic dominance in Europe.

to one of its meetings. It would become the National Socialist German Workers' Party—*Nazi* in its anagrammatic form. Corporal Adolf Hitler's duty had been to combat ideas which the military found threatening—pacifism, socialism, communism, even democracy. And, of course, Jews. The role had suited him. He was described as a *Volksredner,* "a born popular speaker." The war—the matrix of fascism—had been worth to him, he later wrote, thirty years of university study, and November 1918 had focused his thinking and furnished a cause. Despite officers and ex-officers among the membership, by 1923 his talents as *Volksredner* had propelled him into the leadership of the burgeoning Nazis, who fattened their ranks amid the misery of Munich.

A year before, in October 1922, with only a splinter political party, Benito Mussolini had ridden popular disaffection into power by marching on Rome with nationalist slogans and a small army of Blackshirts. Hitler's Brownshirts in 1923 had even more going for them—the weakness of the "Weimar" Republic in Berlin, administered by the "November criminals"; separatist feelings in Bavaria, fed by armed bands of Rightist extremists; and the realities of astronomical currency inflation, lingering economic depression, and national malaise. From Berlin had come an order from General Hans von Seekt to arrest the leaders of the three most notorious private armies in Bavaria. The State Commissioner, Gustav von Kahr, who had monarchist leanings, and Colonel Hans von Seisser, head of the State Police, ignored it. Seekt then fired General Otto von Lossow, *Reichswehr* commander in Bavaria, for failure to carry out his orders, but Kahr refused to recognize the dismissal. Hitler's SA (*Sturmabteilung*) Brownshirts were not considered by Berlin to be a serious enough threat to be included among the disloyal bands to be suppressed.

A *coup,* or *Putsch,* to take over Bavaria, and then the nation, had been thought of, and even planned, by a number of small Rightist groups in Munich. None had felt ready. Hitler was not sure he would still have the opportunity if he waited long enough to accrue more support from disaffected nationalists; and when his lieutenants, Alfred Rosenberg and the self-ennobled Max von Scheubner-Richter, suggested taking over the Memorial Day (*Totengedenkstag*) parade on November 4, seizing the reviewing stand and forcing Kahr, Seisser, and Lossow to join the rebellion at pistol point, and then proclaiming the new state, he thought the risk was worth taking. He knew his few hundred Brownshirts could not carry out a

Putsch alone, but if he could compel Kahr, Seisser, and Lossow to follow him, he might be able to seize the apparatus of state, police, and army.

The *Totengedenkstag* plot evaporated when Rosenberg's reconnaissance showed that well-armed police were protecting the *Feldherrnhalle*. Undeterred, Hitler decided on a Sunday morning *Putsch* the next weekend. Sunday would be November 11, the fifth anniversary of the unforgivable surrender in the forest. He would erase the memory and the shame by sending his S.A. troops behind the facade of a band playing martial music to take over the *Feldherrnhalle* and other strategic points (likely to be almost unoccupied on a Sunday) and run up the Imperial black, white, and red and the National Socialist hooked cross. It would be over before Kahr, Seisser, and Lossow were out of bed.

Then Hitler read in a local newspaper that at the request of business interests in Munich there would be on the evening of the eighth a mass meeting at the *Bürgerbräukeller* at which Kahr and his associates would outline the future economic and civic program of the Bavarian government. To Hitler it sounded suspiciously like a forum for the announcement of a royalist *coup*—that the state commissioner might have arranged the gathering in order to proclaim the restoration of the Wittelsbachs and the severance of links to Berlin. If so, it would leave the National Socialists on the sidelines. Yet the meeting beckoned as an even earlier opportunity to seize the Bavarian leadership—and government—at one blow. The march on Sunday might not be necessary.

Beer cellars of massive proportions were traditional meeting places in Germany, where exhortation and enthusiasm were lubricated with gallons of the local brew. In a similar Munich setting on November 7, 1918, Rainer Maria Rilke had written to his wife, Clara, that he had been "among the thousands" in the huge beer hall of the Hotel Wagner when Professor Max Weber of Heidelberg had spoken, along with students and men "who had been at the front for four years." It was all "so very simple and folksy," although "people were seated about the beer tables and between them in such a way that the barmaids could only work their way through the crush . . . like wood-worms." Yet it hadn't been "stifling or hard to breathe," he explained, caught up in the revolutionary fervor, and "you didn't mind at all the smell of beer and tobacco and people; in fact you hardly noticed it because the whole business was so important that things could now be said that were long overdue. . . . Moments like this are wonderful. . . ." It was a different moment in time. By 1923 that temporary republican euphoria long had waned.

In the early evening on Thursday the eighth, hundreds of SA men gulped down their dinners, donned uniforms of gray windbreaker with swastika armband, gray ski cap and revolver belt and assembled under the direction of ex-Lieutenant Colonel Wilhelm Kriebel, who had barked at Belgians from his train nearly five years before that he would be back. Some men would be sent to strategic locations in Munich; others would gather outside the beer hall.

Commissioner von Kahr had already been speaking for twenty minutes when Hitler, in a red Benz touring car recently acquired for him by the party, arrived with his bodyguard, Ulrich Graf, and two deputies. Wearing his familiar trench coat, he was recognized by ushers at the door and admitted with his group. Inside, Scheubner-Richter and Kriebel were waiting tensely. At 8:30, SA men were to surround the building. "Not even a man equipped with the greatest executive powers," Kahr was exhorting, as the knot of Nazis could hear in the hallway, "can rescue the *Volk*, without the nationalist spirit and energetic help of the people themselves. . . ."

Trucks could be heard pulling up to the building. Soon a squad of about fifteen men, led by ex-Captain Hermann Goering and armed with submachine guns, pushed into the lobby and burst open the doors of the hall, where they set up a heavy machine gun, pointed at the audience. Kahr bolted from the lectern, thinking that the Communists, whom he had been denouncing in his speech, were about to disrupt the meeting. Men leaped on chairs and tables to see what was happening. Women screamed.

Elbowing through the crowded aisles, and preceded by Goering and Graf, Hitler forced his way forward, a pistol in his hand. When they were blocked in the uproar altogether, he climbed on a chair and shouted, *"Ruhe! Ruhe!"* ("Silence! Silence!") Then, impatiently, he pointed his gun at the ceiling and fired.

"The National Revolution has begun!" he screamed into the hushed hall. "This hall is occupied by six hundred heavily armed men, and no one may leave. . . . The Bavarian and Reich governments have been removed and a provisional national government formed. The barracks of the *Reichswehr* and the State Police have been occupied. The Army and the Police are now marching on the city under the swastika."

Only the first statement had any truth to it, but no one in the hall knew how much was bluff. Certainly the revolver and the machine guns were genuine, but, having taken off his trench coat to reveal that, in deference to the occasion, he was wearing an ill-fitting cutaway, he looked, with his toothbrush mustache, more like Charlie Chaplin than the presumptive dictator of Germany. Retired Admiral Paul von Hintze, who had played a role in the abdication drama five years before, was sitting nearby and recalled, "When I saw [Hitler] jump on the chair in that ridiculous costume, I thought *armes Kellnerlein!*" ("poor little waiter!") But such belittlement was put to rest quickly, as Hitler climbed over a table onto the platform and—pistol in hand—forced the expressionless dignitaries into a room behind them. Someone in the audience shouted to the cowed police, "Don't be cowards as in 1918. Shoot!" But with Kahr, Seisser, and Lossow as hostages, no guard moved. The three thousand people in the hall, trapped and puzzled, began to murmur protests, which Goering quieted with another shot into the ceiling. Then he walked to the lectern and bellowed that no one was in any danger, and that the situation would soon be clarified. "Besides," he added, "you've got your beer. What are you worrying about?"

In an anteroom Hitler had been trying to coerce the three officials to join him in his revolution, with titles he would authorize: Regent of Bavaria, Minister of the National Army, Minister of the Reich Police. "I have four bullets in my pistol," he warned. "Three for my collaborators, if they abandon me. The last one for myself." With several armed Storm Troopers in the background, the threat seemed real enough, but Kahr answered, "Herr Hitler, you can have me shot or shoot me yourself. Whether I die or not is no matter." Then Seisser reproached Hitler for breaking his word of honor not to undertake a *Putsch* against the police.

"Forgive me," said Hitler, "but I had to for the sake of the Fatherland." Still, getting nowhere, and with the crowd growing more restless, he needed some further dramatic gesture. Throwing open the door, he strode to the podium. Kahr, Seisser, and Lossow, he announced, had decided to join him in forming a new government. The November criminals in Berlin were ousted, and General Ludendorff (whom Scheubner-Richter had brought to the hall in his car) would be the new commander of the National Army. "The mission of the provisional government," he declared, "is to begin the march on that sinful Babel, Berlin, and save the German people. . . . Tomorrow will find either a nationalist regime in Germany or us dead!"

Scheubner-Richter then produced the cranky war hero, who

had been rushed away from his villa still wearing an old tweed shooting jacket rather than dress uniform and spiked helmet he affected for grand occasions. Although annoyed that the one-time corporal and recent protégé had announced himself as dictator of Germany, and that the former Quartermaster General would only be an underling in the new order of things, Ludendorff had not forgotten how he had been ousted in 1918. He joined the Bavarian officials in the anteroom and urged that they work together with Hitler in a great national cause: to restore honor "to the old black-and-white cockade" that the revolution had disgraced. The three gave in, or at least appeared to, and all five returned to the platform to loud applause, compounded of relief and the feeling that perhaps all were witnessing a momentous event.

Leading the group to the rostrum, Hitler launched into a closing peroration which stirred the once-hostile audience to frenzy. "I want now to fulfill the vow which I made to myself five years ago when I was a blind cripple in the military hospital: to know neither rest nor peace until the November criminals had been overthrown, until from the ruins of the wretched Germany of today there shall arise once more a Germany of power and greatness, of freedom and splendor."

Spellbound, the three thousand in the *Bürgerbräu* forgot that they were there under duress, forgot that the speaker looked like an ungainly, mustached penguin, and gave Hitler a standing ovation, after which they burst into a roaring rendition of *"Deutschland, Deutschland über alles."* Many were so moved that they could not sing to the end, and broke down and wept. "There are many inexplicable things," Robert Musil wrote in *The Man Without Qualities*, "but people cease to feel them when they sing their national anthem."

Both inside and outside the hall a campaign of terror and intimidation had already been launched against Bavarian officials, some having been led from the building by Storm Troopers as prisoners. Others, as well as Communists, Social Democrats, and Jews were added during the night under the direction of ex-Lieutenant Rudolf Hess. Many of the victims rounded up had been chosen from the phone book only because their names looked Jewish.

Meanwhile the crowd streamed out of the beer hall into the starless night—except for the notables whom Hess and his henchmen had detained. But when Hitler heard that an SA unit was having trouble taking over a local barracks, he left abruptly to oversee the matter himself, assuming he could sway others in the manner he had moved the *Bürgerbräu* audience. It proved a mistake. Not only the *Reichswehr* battalion proved difficult; when Hitler returned to the hall he discovered that Lossow, Kahr, and Seisser had departed. He was indignant and suspicious of a double-cross, but Ludendorff cut him off sharply. "I forbid you," he warned, "to doubt the word of honor of a German officer."

Despite the hour Kahr quickly ordered placards printed and posted throughout Munich denouncing the "deception and perfidy of ambitious comrades" who had extorted pledges "at the point of a revolver." Further, Kahr declared, "The National Socialist German Workers Party, as well as the fighting leagues *Oberland* and *Reichskriegsflagge,* are dissolved." (In Nuremberg several months earlier, Hitler had organized a German Fighting Union [*Kampfbund*], which allied his Brownshirts with two even smaller paramilitary groups, the Overland League and Ernst Röhm's monarchist The German War Flag.)

At 11:30 that night in Berlin, Chancellor Gustav Stresemann was having a late dinner with Dr. Hjalmar Schacht to discuss the horrendous currency situation, as the nation could not survive if a wagonload of bank notes was needed to pay a workman's wages. When a telephone call apprised him of the *coup* attempt in Munich, he called an emergency cabinet session, driving to it with General von Seekt, who dismissed the events in Bavaria as "comical happenings." At the cabinet meeting Friedrich Ebert asked him whom the Army would obey. "Herr Reich President," said the general, "the Army obeys *me.*" Seekt was given virtual dictatorial powers to quell the disturbance and issued a proclamation that anyone supporting "this mad attempt in Munich" would be guilty of high treason.

With only 50,000 members in all, and many fewer in his fighting cadres, Hitler had to work quickly to save the situation. It was one in the morning. Other uniformed bands, as well as state police and *Reichswehr* troops, roamed the streets. (One of them, Röhm's *Reichskriegsflagge,* included a young, bespectacled fertilizer plant official, Heinrich Himmler, whom Hitler would get to know better.) At five o'clock word came that the three officials coerced in the beer hall had repudiated their pledges. It would take another bold stroke—or flight into hiding.

With the coming of daylight, the sleepy SA forces milling about the *Bürgerbräu* were served coffee, bread, and cheese. There were still no plans, but few went home. Playing soldier was more fun than working. Besides, they expected to be paid. Many Brownshirts were unemployed and had no work to go to anyway.

Early in the morning a detachment of Storm Troopers made

good on the expectation by invading the Parcus printing plant—it was Jewish-owned, which was another justification—and "in the name of the nationalist regime" looted several formidable stacks of freshly printed inflation money. It amounted to 14,605,000,000,000,000 marks—little more than seven thousand American dollars at the time. The Parcus brothers demanded a receipt. Lieutenant Heinz Pernet, Ludendorff's stepson, distributed some of the largesse at the beer hall—two trillion marks (about a dollar) per thug.

In a second-floor room, wavering from plan to plan, Hitler discussed the next move. He had already dispatched an emissary to Crown Prince Rupprecht to see whether mediation with Kahr was possible; however, the Brownshirt messenger, unable to find an automobile to go to Berchtesgaden, unhurriedly took the first train. He would arrive after the *Putsch* was over. At the *Bürgerbräu* the stocky former Quartermaster General, a vigorous although neurotic fifty-eight, wanted no repetition of Spa and 1918. In his strangely high voice he croaked eagerly to Hitler, *"Wir marschieren!"* They would march their way into the respect and the fear of the citizenry. Moved by the sense of their power, *Müncheners* would join the column and, Hitler later wrote, "Kahr, Lossow and Seisser . . . would hardly be foolish enough to use machine guns against a general uprising of the people."

A band had played through the morning but had left the *Bürgerbräu* after a halfhearted rendition of the "Badenweiler March," Hitler's favorite tune, having received neither breakfast nor pay. As noon approached, Colonel Kriebel ordered the detachments to form up, eight abreast. They marched off into flurries of wet snow. Some units were short in members, and the parade had a motley look about it. At the head was the *Stosstrupp Hitler,* eighty men in menacing green-gray uniforms, complete to steel helmets, two potato-masher grenades and carbine slung on shoulder. Behind the Shock Troop was the crack 6th SA Company, a veteran unit seasoned at rallies, street fights, and beer-hall brawls. Other groups followed—about two thousand in all. In the front rank, leading the *Strosstrup,* was Hitler, his trench coat covering his cutaway; Ludendorff, his face still recognizable after his wartime visibility; Goering, the SA commander; a half dozen other Nazi officials, and a color guard with the swastika banner and the black, white, and red flag of Imperial Germany.

A few hundred yards north of the *Bürgerbräu* they crossed the Ludwig Bridge over the Isar. The outnumbered police at the bridge were jeered at, pummeled, and disarmed. Spectators and supporters joined as the Nazis marched and sang through the Tal, the broad, ancient street leading into the Marienplatz, the heart of the city. It was already packed, as an SA unit had gone ahead to seize the ancient Rathaus, the town hall, where a *Hakenkreuz* flag was already flying. Blocked by the enthusiastic crowds, the parade halted, and Ludendorff, wondering what to do next, turned it toward the War Ministry. There, he knew, Ernst Röhm and his Rightist followers were barricaded. His *Reichskriegsflagge* had been trapped there by the Army during the night when they had attempted to support the *Putsch.*

To reach the Ministry and extricate Röhm, Hitler and Ludendorff led their columns into the narrow Residenzstrasse on their way to the Odeonsplatz. In his dark-brown overcoat and felt hat, Ludendorff, looking as unmilitary as Hitler, stubbornly led the way. Civilians mingled with the SA as the group pushed toward a thin line of police singing *O' Deutschland, hoch in Ehren* ("O Germany, high in honor"). As they moved closer the Nazis saw a platoon of police reinforcements on the run to join the cordon already there. They had carbines, pistols, and truncheons. "Don't shoot!" shouted the hulking Ulrich Graf. "His Excellency General Ludendorff is coming!" Hitler added another cry: "Surrender! Surrender!"

The column was eight abreast again. On the right was the *Residenz*—the Wittelsbach Palace. The marchers were approaching the *Feldherrnhalle*—the Hall of the Field Marshals. The police shout of *"Halt! Nicht weitergehen!"* was ignored, and a shot rang out. Hitler had locked his left arm with the right arm of Scheubner-Richter, perhaps evidence of the state of his nerves, since his companion was small and myopic. Ludendorff was trudging on, certain that no one would touch the First Quartermaster General. Other shots followed, from both sides. Scheubner-Richter fell, mortally wounded, pulling Hitler down with him. Goering went down with a wound in his thigh. For a few seconds more the shooting continued; then the Nazi column panicked. The front surged back, and people began running away over prostrate bodies. Sixteen Nazis and three police were dead, with more on both sides wounded.

Ludendorff, with his aide, Major Streck, calmly continued on between the police ranks, reaching the empty Odeonsplatz untouched. "Excellency," said a guard, "I must take you into protective custody."

Most witnesses saw Hitler go down, and assumed he was dead.

He had only dislocated his shoulder. Some of his men had fled for cover into a nearby pastry shop, hiding weapons in stoves, flour sacks, and coffee bins. Many more found a girls' school near the Odeon Square, where they discarded identifying gear and weapons and fled out the back. Two or three units reached the woods on the outskirts of the city and buried their weapons.

At the Military District Headquarters, Captain Röhm gave up when he heard about the debacle at the *Feldherrnhalle*. He and his men, including his aide Heinrich Himmler, were arrested and disarmed. At the *Bürgerbräu* police cleared out the remaining Nazis, ordering them to stack their weapons and go home. The prisoners held there were released.

Given first aid by the Jewish manager of a nearby bank into which he had been carried, Goering was then smuggled by his wife across the border into Austria. Rudolf Hess also fled into Austria. Not finding Hitler's body, police began a search. He had slipped into a waiting automobile and been hustled off to the country home of his friend Ernst ("Putzi") Hanfstaengl at Uffing, thirty-five miles from Munich, on the secluded Staffelsee. Two days later Hitler was located in an attic bedroom. Trapped, and handicapped by his sore shoulder, he seized the pistol he had fired into the *Bürgerbräu* ceiling and appeared to attempt suicide. But there was no shot.

With Hitler under arrest, his bungled political career seemed over. For the front page a European correspondent for *The New York Times* furnished what was already a consensus of press opinion: "The Munich Putsch definitely eliminates Hitler and his National Socialist followers."

Others before Hitler had managed, after being written off, to exploit courtrooms and prison cells. His philosophy of hate—some of which had emerged in his harangue in the beer hall—had long been festering. So had his strategy for power. Hitler remembered how and where he had learned of the abdication, revolution, and armistice. No one would be allowed to forget. The disenchanted who remained unwilling to accept the shame needed a bible and a blueprint. Prison would be a good place in which to write.

It was Sunday, November 11, 1923. Armistice Day.

SOURCES AND ACKNOWLEDGMENTS

I am grateful to the many who remembered the period November 7–11, 1918, so vividly and who shared their memories with me. Those whose recollections are quoted from are cited below. Where other credits or permissions are involved, such acknowledgments are made with the citation itself or in the narrative.

My appreciation must be noted, too, to the staffs of the BBC (especially Alan Haydock); the Imperial War Museum; the U.S.A. Military History Institute: the Hoover Institution on War, Revolution and Peace; the Library of Congress; and the Pattee Library of The Pennsylvania State University. For research leads I am especially grateful to Harry P. Clark, Charles Mann, Fred D. Crawford, Eileen Hanley-Browne, Capt. Alan Hanley-Browne, Kenyon Emrys-Roberts, and Richard Gidez. It must be added that *A Stillness Heard Round the World* could not have been written without the editorial assistance of Rodelle Weintraub and Warren Hassler, and the research and typing skills of Louise Goldschmidt and Shirley Rader. For research support I am further grateful to Penn State's Institute for the Arts and Humanistic Studies and to the American Council of Learned Societies.

For the use of future scholars and researchers I have given all correspondence received on the final days of the Great War to the United States Army Military History Institute in Carlisle, Pennsylvania, and to the Imperial War Museum in London.

SOURCE NOTES

PROLOGUE: ENDINGS

The sandbag story is from Ian Hay [Beith], *The Last Million* (Boston, 1919). General Nugent's remark is quoted by Dennis Wheatley in *Officer and Temporary Gentleman, 1914–1919* (London, 1977). The Very flare forecast is from Paul Fussell, *The Great War and Modern Memory* (New York and London, 1975) and is very likely a more artistic version of Stephen Southwold's recollection in "Rumours at the Front" in *Martial Medley*, ed. Eric Partridge (London, 1931) that "Peace, it was said, was to be signalled by green rockets along the whole length of the Front; a frequent variant was 'three dark-blue lights.' " Temporary truces, including the Christmas truce of 1914, are discussed in John Ellis, *Eye-Deep in Hell. Trench Warfare in World War I* (New York, 1976); the Verdun mutinies are detailed in Alistair Horne, *The Price of Glory, Verdun 1916* (New York, 1963). Otto Heinebach, killed September 14, 1916, is the former University of Berlin philosophy student quoted from *German Students' War Letters*, eds. Philipp Witkop and A. F. Wedd (London, 1929). Ernst Jünger's *Der Kampf als inneres Erleblis* is quoted in the translation by Hanna Hafkesbrink in her *Unknown Germany* (New Haven, 1948). The apocryphal story of the Pope is told by Pierre Van Paassen in *Days of Our Years* (New York, 1939), while the fictional "Peace" by F. Britten Austin appeared in *The Strand* (London) in September 1918. The no-man's-land legends are related by Ardern Beaman in *The Squadron* (London and New York, 1920) and Osbert Sitwell in *Laughter in the Next Room* (Boston, 1948), and were first brought to my attention by Matthew Bruccoli. The Penicuik chronicles were made available to me by W. W. Black of Silverburn, Penicuik, Scotland.

THE FALSE ARMISTICE

Sources for the preliminary armistice planning and negotiations are to be found in the notes to "The Dining Car in the Forest." Thomas Mann's diary entries, here and later, are from *Tagebucher 1918–1921* (Frankfurt, 1979), as translated for me by Waltraud Böhm. Foch's message to Pershing about the possibility of a German false armistice plant is in Thomas M. Johnson, *Without Censor* (Indianapolis, 1928). Arthur Hornblow's account is "The Amazing Armistice," *The Century Magazine*, November 1921, supplemented by Will Irwin's account in *American Reporters on the Western Front, 1914–1918* (New York, 1959) by Emmet Crozier, *The Wilson Era* (Chapel Hill, N.C., 1946) by Josephus Daniels, and memoranda from State Department Series, No. 65, in *Foreign Relations, 1918,* Supp. 1, Vol. 1. The American GHQ's investigation is summarized in GHQ/AEF Fldr. 1205, November 9, 1918, from the Assistant Chief of Staff, G-2, SOS to Commanding General, SOS signed by Lieutenant Colonel Cabot Ward.

"Dolly" Shepherd's account is no. 00579/12 in the oral history archives of the Keeper of Sound Records, Imperial War Museum, London (hereafter IWM). J. B. Priestley's recollection is in *Margin Released* (New York, 1962). John Ventham's account is from a 1968 letter to the BBC in London, while Will Judy's is from his *A Soldier's Diary* (Chicago, 1930) and Frederick Pottle's from *Stretchers* (New Haven, 1929). Joe Latta's letter to me is dated March 31, 1980, and George Crohn's is dated November 12, 1979. William M. Seuter's account of sailors celebrating at Brest is from his letter of November 16, 1979, while Ivor Lawrence's letter is dated October 12, 1979.

Eleanor Wilson McAdoo's reminiscences and those of her step-mother are from Edith Bolling Wilson's *My Memoir* (Indianapolis, 1939) and Ellen Slayden's from her journal, *Washington Wife* (New York, 1963). Evelyn Shipman's letter to me about the November 7 frenzy in Washington is dated August 9, 1981. Elizabeth Stuyvesant Howard's reaction is from Robert W. Kean's *Dear Marianne* (New York, 1969) and Lady Duff Gordon's from her *Discretions and Indiscretions* (New York, 1932). The death of David Langdon is described for me by his grandson, John C. Martin, in letters dated June 2 and June 12, 1980. Orville Wright's letter, dated from Dayton, Ohio, November 7, 1918, is in *The Papers of Wilbur and Orville Wright,* II, ed. Marvin McFarland (London and New York, 1953). Richard L. Strout's memory of Norwich comes from his still-incomplete ms. autobiography. Malcolm Cowley's letter to me is dated March 26, 1979. Thomas L. Stokes's reminiscence is from *Chip Off My Shoulder* (Princeton, 1940). For Henry Luce at Camp Taylor, see W. A. Swanberg, *Luce and His Empire* (New York, 1972).

The ledger/diary of the Reverend Loyal L. Adams of Port Allegany, Pennsylvania, is owned by his daughter, Mrs. Audrey Kiffer of Petersburg, Pennsylvania. The situation in Bridgeport, Indiana, is described in an unpublished manuscript by Homer Schnitzius, which he sent to me on April 6, 1980. Mary McCarthy's Minneapolis is described in her *Memories of a Catholic Girlhood* (New York, 1957).

Lee Hays wrote me November 13, 1979, about Newport, Arkansas, while Arnold Larsen's letter about "Bucktown" in Chicago is dated April 6, 1980. Beverley Nichols wrote about his Chicago experience in *The Unforgiving Minute* (London, 1978). John Toland's memory of La Crosse, Wisconsin (he was six), is from his *No Man's Land* (New York, 1980). Gordon Wallace wrote to me on December 3, 1980. The Kansas City story comes to me from Sara Saper Gauldin on December 3, 1979, from her unpublished manuscript, "Mama Said." Mrs. Barbara Crawford wrote to me on November 24, 1979, about Wilson's appearance in front of the White House, while the story of the minor RAF mutiny at Manston is told by E. E. Seeder in a letter dated March 8, 1978, to Alan Haydock of the BBC. Lieutenant Joseph Lawrence's account of hearing the news in a French village comes from his unpublished memoir in the U.S. Army Military History Institute, Carlisle, Pennsylvania. Darryl Zanuck's memory of the False Armistice at the front is from Leonard Mosley, *Zanuck* (Boston, 1984), while Gloria Swanson's recollection of the event in Hollywood is from her *Swanson on Swanson* (New York, 1980). Gene Fowler's observations on the aftermath of the False Armistice are from his *Skyline. A Reporter's Reminiscences of the 1920s* (New York, 1961).

Other details of the day come from the daily press across the nation, from New York to Los Angeles, and from *Stars and Stripes.*

THE DINING CAR IN THE FOREST

Basic sources for the armistice negotiations are Harry R. Rudin, *Armistice, 1918* (New Haven, 1944); Maxime Weygand, *Le 11 Novembre* (Paris, 1932); General Henri Mordacq, *L'Armistice du 11 Novembre 1918* (Paris, 1937); *Memoirs of Marshal Foch,* trans. T. Bentley Mott (New York, 1931); Prince Max von Baden, trans. W. M. Calder and C. W. H. Sutton, *Memoirs,* II (New York, 1928); Raymond Recouly, "What Foch Really Said," *Scribner's Magazine,* 67 (May 1920), 531–38; Klaus Epstein, *Matthias Erzberger and the Dilemma of German Democracy* (Princeton, 1959), which quotes substantially from Erzberger's diaries and journals; and Lady Wester Wemyss, *Life and Letters of Admiral of the Fleet Lord Wester Wemyss* (London, 1935). Military communiqués and radio intercepts are from *The Armistice Agreement and Related Documents,* Historical Division of the Department of the Army (Washington, 1948). The role of Baron von Lessner in the appointment of Erzberger is noted by Gerhard Ritter in *The Sword and the Scepter. The Problem of Militarism in Germany*, IV, trans. Heinz Norden (Coral Gables, Fla., 1973).

Bethmann Hollweg's smug observation about Hindenburg is quoted by Gordon A. Craig in his *Germany 1866–1945* (London, 1978), from Karl-Heinz Janssen's *Der Kanzler und der General* (Gottingen, 1967). Weygand's description of an armistice as a "vigil of arms" is from his report of a conversation with Pierre Laval on November 12, 1942, as quoted in Paul Reynaud, *In the Thick of the Fight* (New York, 1955). The quotation from Hermann Labude's letter of December 8, 1917, is from *German Students' War Letters*. Sir Basil Thomson's story of the reading of the Lille armistice conditions is from his memoir *The Scene Changes* (New York, 1937). Georges Clemenceau, trans. F. M. Atkinson, *Grandeur and Misery of Victory* (New York, 1930) quotes Poincaré's hostility to an armistice. Thomas Keneally's *Gossip from the Forest* is quoted from the American edition, in which Oberndorff is "Maiberling" because of objections from the Oberndorff family (New York, 1975), and the Granada television script (London, 1979).

General Winterfeldt's comment to Bourbon-Busset is reported by Joseph Paul Boncour in *Recollections of the Third Republic* (New York, 1957), to have been told to him by Major de Bourbon-Busset. Henri Deledicq reported his role on the Armistice train to me in a letter dated February 27, 1980. He was on that date the last person alive who had served on the train. A translation of Winterfeldt's wireless arranging for a courier to fly to Spa on November 9, 1918, is at the U.S. Army Military History Institute at Carlisle (Pa.) Barracks (hereafter USMHI). Princess Blücher's diary note is from Evelyn, Princess Blücher, *An English Wife in Berlin* (New York, 1920). Information about von Winterfeldt's father and Geyer's strategic contribution to the Spring 1918 offensive are from Basil Liddell Hart, *Foch* (London, 1931).

ARMISTICE EVE

Where otherwise unmentioned, data about individual units is taken from their official unit histories. Other American sources include Shipley Thomas's *The History of the A.E.F.* (New York, 1920); Lawrence Stallings' *The Doughboys: The Story of the A.E.F., 1917–1918* (New York, 1963); and General John J. Pershing's *My Experiences in the World War* (New York, 1931). Individual accounts include Douglas MacArthur's *Reminiscences* (New York, 1964); William Manchester's biography of MacArthur, *American Caesar* (New York, 1978); Forrest Pogue's *George C. Marshall: Education of a General* (New York, 1963); Marshall's own *Memoirs 1917–1918* (Boston, 1976); Roger Manvell's *Chaplin* (Boston, 1974); Martin Blumenson's edition of *The Patton Papers* (Boston, 1972); and *World War I Through My Sights,* by Horatio Rogers (San Rafael, Calif., 1976). References to General R. L. Bullard's diary are from his own quotations from them in his *Personalities and Reminiscences of the War* (New York, 1925). Lieutenant General John C. Lee's unpublished memoir, *Service Reminiscences* (1956), is at the Hoover Institution, Stanford. Lieutenant General (Major in 1918) Andrew D. Bruce's papers are in the USMHI, Carlisle Barracks, surveyed for me by Dr. Richard J. Sommers, Archivist-Historian there. Lance Corporal William Manchester's experience in the 5th Marines is told by his son, William Manchester, Jr., in *Goodbye Darkness* (Boston, 1980).

The use of *contemptibly little army* rather than the more common (and mistranslated) *contemptible little army* is deliberate. The Kaiser in 1914 had ordered General von Kluck to walk over the four divisions of General French's army, which was—accurately—*verachtlich klein* in relation to the German ninety-five divisions and the French sixty.

Published British accounts include Georges Licope, "The Double Miracle of Mons," in John Hammerton, ed., *The Great War;* Guy Chapman, "Nightmare Thoughts of the Ending Days," in Hammerton, and his memoir, *A Passionate Prodigality* (New York, 1966); R. H. Mottram, "Stand To!" in George Panichas, ed., *Promise of Greatness* (New York, 1968) and *Sixty-Four, Ninety-Four!,* the second volume of *The Spanish Farm* trilogy (London, 1925); and Albert Dunn, "On the Trail of the German Retreat," in Hammerton, *The Great War.* The sweepstakes at Aulnoye is reported in the (Anon.) *History and Memoir of the 33rd Battalion, Machine Gun Corps* (London, 1919). Will R. Bird's graphic Mons account is in *Ghosts Have Warm Hands* (Toronto, 1968). Vivian de Sola Pinto's memoir is *The City That Shone* (New York, 1969); Siegfried Sassoon's relevant novel in *The Memoirs of George Sherston* is *Sherston's Progress* (London, 1936). The German peace leaflet referred to by Pinto is in my possession.

More general British and Commonwealth accounts include H. Essame, *The Battle for Europe* (New York, 1972) on the rum ration; G. W. L. Nicholson, *Canadian Expeditionary Force 1914–1919* (Ottawa, 1962); James E. Edmonds and R. Maxwell-Hyslop, *Military Opera-*

tions in France and Belgium, 1918 (vol. 5 of The Committee of Imperial Defence's *History of the Great War* [London, 1947]); Gregory Blaxland, *Amiens: 1918* (London, 1968); and J. F. B. Livesay, *Canada's Hundred Days* (Toronto, 1919).

German field orders, reports, and messages are from the U.S. Army compilation, *Translations [of] War Diaries of German Units Opposed to the Second Division, 1918,* vol. 9, *Meuse-Argonne* (Washington, 1928). The report from a division in the Seventeeth Army of Crown Prince Rupprecht's group is quoted in Major General Sir Frederick Maurice, *The Last Four Months. How the War Was Won* (Boston, 1919). General von Kuhl's comments are from his typescript "The Execution and Collapse of the German Offensive in 1918," vol. 2, trans. Henry Hossfield, at the USMHI. Tank casualty statistics are from Len Deighton, *Blitzkreig* (New York and London, 1980). Third Army Corps Intelligence reports, including the story of General Hoeffer, are from its Intelligence Summary No. 57, November 10, 1918.

Allied field orders to attack as late as 2130 hours on November 10 are in the USMHI; the English wireless pickup of the last French troop movements on the tenth is in the IWM. The Sedan orders are from Pogue's *Marshall.* Desmond Young's recollection of the postwar Düsseldorf industrialist is from his *Rommel. The Desert Fox* (London, 1950). British daily rum usage is certified in Brigadier General Hubert Essame's *The Battle for Europe 1918* (London, 1972).

Werner Beumelburg's *Sperrfeuer um Deutschland* is translated from the Berlin/Oldenburg edition of 1929. Bertolt Brecht's "Legende von toten Soldaten" is quoted from the Eric Bentley translation/adaptation in the *Kenyon Review* (1958). Otto Brautigam's diary extracts are from his *So Hat Es Sich Zugetragen: Ein Leben als Soldat und Diplomat* (Wurzburg, 1968), while Heinrich Himmler's letter is quoted in *Heinrich Himmler: A Nazi in the Making,* by Bradley F. Smith (Stanford, 1979). Carl Zuckmayer's memoir is *A Part of Myself,* trans. Richard and Clara Winston (New York, 1970). Oscar Ludmann's is *Stepchild of the Rhine* (New York, 1931).

Firsthand British accounts of the war on the ground include letters to me from Stuart N. Whibley (November 7, 1979), A. F. Marshall (November 11, 1979), Arthur W. Boyd (October 13, 1979), Arthur Russell (from his letter of October 9, 1979, and proof of his book, *The Machine Gunner* [Kineton, 1977]), A. C. Wilkinson (October 15, 1979), H. A. F. Radley (November 5, 1979), and Arthur E. Wrench (letter, November 16, 1979, and unpublished diary). Also letters to Alan Haydock, BBC London, from Alfred Billequez (March 13, 1978), Ben P. Simpson (undated, 1978, followed up by a letter to me, June 12, 1980) and H. Horne (undated, 1978). Also, transcript of Harry Smith's reminiscences, 1974, Department of Sound Records, IWM, No. 000045/06. The XIX Corps intelligence summary was furnished to me by Sir Harold Parker, retired Permanent Secretary of the Ministry of Defence (1948–56). Sir Harold was a captain in the 187th Brigade of the 41st Division in Belgium at the Armistice. Brigadier (Ret.) Thomas Robbins wrote to me about the "Pelican" Division on November 11, 1979.

Unpublished American accounts include Lee Harrison's memoir and letter to me dated May 6, 1980, and Private Allan Neil's letter to his mother dated November 25, 1918, but recalling the last days of the war. My copy is from the Neil family, although most Neil letters are at the Hoover Institution.

Data on RAF matters comes from Christopher Cole, ed., *The Royal Air Force 1918*, (London, 1968), for the November 11, 1918, communiqué on the bombing of Louvain; and, for the abortive Berlin raid, from Anthony C. Kilburn's letters to me dated October 25, 1979, and November 25, 1979; from Maurice Baring's *Flying Corps Headquarters, 1914–1918*, (Edinburgh, 1968); S. F. Wise's *Canadian Airmen and the First World War* (Torondo, 1980); H. H. Balfour's *An Airman Marches* (London, 1933); Harald Penrose's *British Aviation: The Great War and Armistice* (New York, 1969); and Handley-Page, Ltd., *Forty Years On. 1909–1949* (London and Reading, 1949). Information on the Barlow-Martin "flying torpedo" comes from "Armistice Averted Bombing of Berlin," *The New York Times,* October 16, 1922, p. 31. The Belgian incident is described by Major Willy Copens in *Days on the Wing* (London, 1933). Reports of the 104th Squadron are from Captain Ewart Garland's diary in the IWM, his annotated typescript of the diary kindly lent to me by Captain Garland, and his letters to me dated December 12, 1979, and August 21, 1980. General Billy Mitchell's mock communiqué is quoted in his *Memoirs of World War I* (New York, 1960).

M. E. Kahnert's story of the last days of the air war is from his *Jadgstaffel 356*, trans. Claud W. Sykes (London, n.d.). The Poll Triplane details, quoted from Hadow and Grosz's *The German Giants* and from IWM files, are in Robert Davidson, "The New York Bomber," *Air Classics*, II (May 1975). Rudolf Stark's story is in his *Wings of War*, trans. Claud W. Sykes (London, 1933), while Ernst Udet's is told by H. Herlin in *Udet, A Man's Life* (London, 1960).

Hermann Goering's role is described in Leonard Moseley's *The Reich Marshal* (New York, 1974); Charles Bewley's *Hermann Göring and the Third Reich* (New York, 1962); and Quentin Reynolds's *They Fought for the Sky* (New York, 1957). Rudolf Hess's Air Force experience is chronicled in Wulf Schwarzwaller's *Rudolf Hess* (Wien/Munchen/Zurich, 1974).

Carl Zuckmayer's memoir is *A Part of Myself,* trans. Richard and Clara Winston (New York, 1970). Alfred Doeblin is quoted in his own translation by Frederic V. Grunfeld in *Prophets without Honour* (New York, 1979). Shaw's comment on American casualties is from his letter to Frank Harris, March 10, 1919, in S. Weintraub, ed., *The Playwright and the Pirate: Bernard Shaw and Frank Harris, A Correspondence* (University Park and London, 1982).

IMPERIAL SUNSET

The basic source for details of the long, drawn-out abdication drama at Spa is Maurice Baumont, *The Fall of the Kaiser,* trans. E. I. James (New York, 1931), which utilizes the memoirs of participants published through 1930. Details of the political aspects of the revolution, largely from the Berlin side, are from Rudolf Coper, *Failure of a Revolution* (Cambridge, 1955), and Sebastian Haffner, *Failure of a Revolution,* trans. Georg Rapp (New York, 1972). Princess Blücher's diary is quoted from her *An English Wife in Berlin,* Count Bernstorff's from his *Memoirs,* trans. Eric Sutton (New York, 1936), and Count Kessler's from *In the Twenties,* trans. Charles Kessler (New York, 1976).

The Kaiser's praise of then-Colonel Groener is quoted in Gordon Craig, *Germany 1866–1945* from Müller's *Regierte der Kaiser.* The Kaiser's speech at the Emperor Alexander Barracks is published in Christian Gauss, ed., *The German Emperor as Shown in His Public Utterances* (New York, 1915). Prince Max's version of events in Berlin on November 9 is from his *Memoirs.* The General Strike orders are published in *The Political Institutions of the German Revolution,* eds. C. B. Burdick and R. H. Lutz (Stanford, 1966). The Ebert-Groener telephone call is reconstructed from Groener's testimony at the Munich *Dolchstoss* Trial of November 1925 and reported in many places in varying detail, most fully in Erich Otto Volkman's *Revolution über Deutschland* (Oldenburg, 1930). Admiral Müller's diary references are from his *The Kaiser and His Court,* ed. Walter Gorlitz (London,

1959), while Hans Peter Hannsen's diary is published as *Diary of a Dying Empire* (Bloomington, Ind., 1955), trans. Oscar Osborn, eds. Ralph H. Lutz, Mary Schofield, and O. O. Winther, from the original published in Copenhagen in 1924. Caroline Ethel Cooper's letters to her sister from Leipzig are from Decie Denholm, ed., *Behind the Lines: One Woman's War 1914–18* (London, 1982). Arthur Schnabel on his concert is quoted from his *My Life and Music* (New York, 1961). The account of the Crown Princess and the Potsdam *Soldatenrat* is from Ernst Toller, *I Was a German* (London, 1934). Theodor Wolff's reminiscences are from his *Through Two Decades* (London, 1936). The Crown Prince's side of the story, from his papers, is found in Klaus W. Jonas, *The Life of Crown Prince William*, trans. Charles W. Bangert (Pittsburgh, 1961). The Kaiser's letters to his wife, here and later, and the story of the eviction of his daughter, Princess Viktoria Luise, Duchess of Brunswick, are from her *The Kaiser's Daughter*, trans., ed. Robert Vacha (London, 1977, from the 1965 German original).

The events at the Adlon Hotel in Berlin are reported both by Count von Bernstorff in his diary and by Hedda Adlon in *Hotel Adlon. The Life and Death of a Great Hotel*, trans. Norman Denny (New York, 1963). Theobald Tiger's cabaret song is quoted in Frederic V. Grunfeld's *Prophets Without Honor* (New York, 1979). Kurt Tucholsky's comment, from "Preussische Studenten," is quoted in Harold L. Poor, *Kurt Tucholsky* (New York, 1968). The anonymous "Red Year" (the translation is my own) appears in *Deutschland, Deutschland: Politische Gedichte* (Bremen, 1969).

"The Song of the Lost Troops" is translated in full in Robert G. L. Waite's *Vangard of Naziism: the Free Corps Movement in Postwar Germany* (Cambridge, Mass., 1952); Waite does not furnish a German source for his translation.

THE SIGNING

Basic sources for the armistice talks were noted in "The Dining Car in the Forest." Foch's rejoinder quoting Bismarck is from Richard Meinertzhagen, *Army Diary 1899–1926* (London, 1960). His remark about making war "only for results" is from C. R. M. F. Cruttwell, *The Great War* (Oxford, 1936), while his comparison of *Boches* and Austrians is quoted by Jean de Pierrefeu in *French Headquarters, 1915–1918*, trans. C. J. C. Street (London, 1924). Foch's final words to the German delegates are reported by Meinertzhagen. Hindenburg's pre-armistice order to the troops in the West is from a copy at the USMHI. Thomas Keneally's novel is *Gossip from the Forest.*

Walter Lippmann's letter to Colonel House is from Ronald Steel's *Walter Lippmann and the American Century* (New York, 1980). The Dreyfus letter to Clemenceau is from Jean Martet, *Georges Clemenceau* (London, 1930). Backgrounds of German officers who rose in the General Staff in Weimar years and under Hitler are from Gordon Craig, *Germany 1866–1945: Memoirs of Ernst von Weizsäcker*, trans. John Andrews (London, 1951); Telford Taylor, *Sword and Swastika* (London, 1952); and John Wheeler-Bennett, *Nemesis of Power: The German Army in Politics, 1918–1945* (New York, 1954).

Ebert's defense of Winterfeldt occurs in the notes of the December 20, 1918, cabinet meeting in E. Kolb, ed., *Der Zentralrat der Deutschen Sozialistischen Republik* (Leiden, 1968), quoted by F. L. Carsten in *Revolution in Central Europe, 1918–1919* (Berkeley, 1972).

Data on the little-known Ernst Vanselow is from biographical details furnished by Professor K. P. S. Jochum, Universität Bamberg, June 19 and June 26, 1980; Professor A. Harding Ganz, Ohio State University, in a letter dated June 16, 1980; Professor Holger H. Herwig, Vanderbilt University, in a letter dated June 23, 1980; Vanselow's doctoral dissertation (1921) at Albert Ludwigs Universität, Freiburg im Breisgau; and his books *Kriegs und Neutralitätsrecht* (with Dr. Eduard von Waldkirch, Stuttgart, 1936) and *Völkrrecht* (Berlin, 1931). Vanselow's role in attempts after Brest-Litovsk to seize the Russian fleet is described by Gehrhard Ritter in *The Sword and the Scepter;* ironically he does not connect Vanselow with the armistice in the West.

Foreign Minister von Rantzau is quoted on reparations and the blockade in Charles Mee, Jr., *The End of Order: Versailles 1919* (New York, 1980). Louis Botha is quoted from the same source.

The 1940 British propaganda manipulation of Hitler's armistice appearance in France is reported by Len Deighton in *Blitzkreig.* The telephone conversation about the *wagon-lit* between Generals Huntziger and Weygand is from William L. Shirer, *The Collapse of the Third Republic* (New York, 1972), where Weygand's insistence on cavalry over tanks is also quoted. The Nazi refusal to give the French more than twelve hours to sign, and Keitel's speech at Compiègne, are from Maxime Weygand, *Recalled to Service*, trans. E. W. Dickes (New York, 1952). Hitler's November 8, 1943, speech claiming never to repeat "the mistake of 1918" is quoted from Domarus, *Hitler: Reden*, II, in Craig, *Germany 1866–1945.*

LAST SHOTS

The experiences of Harry Truman's battery are related in Jay McIlvaine Lee's *The Artilleryman* (Kansas City, Mo., 1920), while the quotation from Truman is from *Man of Independence* (New York, 1950) by Jonathan Daniels. The November 11, 1954, Truman memo is printed in Robert H. Ferrell, ed., *Off the Record: The Private Papers of Harry S. Truman, 1945–1971* (New York, 1980). John Broaddus wrote to me on Truman and other matters on November 25, 1980.

For Frank Sibley, see notes to "The Stillness." The 1st Gas Regiment's role is described in James Thayer Addison's *The Story of the First Gas Regiment* (Boston, 1919). The German company commander's letter is quoted in Major General Sir Archibald Montgomery's *The Story of the Fourth Army* (London, n.d.). Max Spiegel's reminiscences are reported to me by M. Spencer, Guildford, Surrey, in letters of October 9 and November 4, 1979. A. Velser's story of the mining of the Hamont station is from his letter to me dated November 10, 1979, from Valenciennes. Victor Quelon-Caille's memoir is from his letter to me, Villiers-Plouich, November 15, 1979. Accounts of Major Friebe's death are from German war diaries. The *Punch* cartoon showing recruits awaiting 11:00 A.M. was in the issue of November 13, 1918. General Mangin's cry of concern is quoted in H. Essame, *The Battle for Europe, 1918,* as is the battalion adjutant's observation (Essame was the adjutant). R. Meinertzhagen's experience is from his already-cited memoirs. The scene at Pershing's HQ is described by Lloyd Griscom in his *Diplomatically Speaking* (Boston, 1940).

Published "last shot" accounts also include Frederick Morse Cutler's *The Fifty-fifth Artillery* (Worcester, Mass., 1920) and the anonymous *Official History of the Fifth Division* (Washington, 1919). William Pressey's account is from "All for a Shilling a Day," in M. Moynihan, ed., *People at War* (London, 1973). Brigadier E. E. Mockler-Ferryman's diary is in the IWM. Signaler Billy Harney's reminiscence was broadcast by the Australian Broadcasting Commission, Sydney, in November 1978 and furnished to me in a tape recording by Rob Sharpe, Executive Producer. The fictional Lieutenant Dormer appears in *The Crime at Vanderlynden's,* vol. 3 of Mottram's *The Spanish Farm.* Cecil Lewis's description of the ravaged front is from his *Sagittarius Rising* (New York, 1936).

C. E. Montague's ALS to H. G. Wells is in the Wells Collection, University of Illinois Library. It is postmarked November 15, 1918.

Frederick Taprill's letter to me is dated October 24, 1979. General Haig's November 11 is recorded by John Terraine in his *Douglas Haig* (London, 1963). Then-Colonel Montgomery is quoted in Field Marshal the Viscount Montgomery of Alamein, *Memoirs* (Cleveland, 1958). Lloyd George is quoted on Haig from his *War Memoirs* (London, 1933–36).

W. Anderson Scott's letter to me is dated October 24, 1979; Harry Smith's taped reminiscence is no. 000045/06 in the Department of Sound Records, IWM; John Wedderburn-Maxwell's letter is dated October 10, 1979; Thomas L. Lomax's letter is dated November 26, 1979; A. F. Marshall's letter is dated November 11, 1979; G. Waugh's letter to me is dated November 11, 1979.

Eddie Rickenbacker's memoirs appear in many forms, with slight variations, this account derived from *Fighting the Flying Circus* (New York, 1919) and from his interviews in old age with Boonton Herndon, who ghosted the autobiography, *Rickenbacker*, mss. of which are in the Cabell Library, Virginia Commonwealth University, Richmond. Webb Miller's memoirs are *I Found No Peace* (New York, 1936). Ewart Garland's diary is at the IWM and was referred to earlier.

Quotations from Sol Cohen's letter of November 13, 1918, to his family are used with the permission of Sol Cohen and the Sol Cohen Collection in the Illinois Historical Survey Library, University of Illinois. I am also grateful to George Hendrick for assistance in locating the letter.

Charles Veil's last flight is told to Howard Marsh in *Ninety-Nine Lives* (London, 1934), while other detail about him, including the discrepancy in kills, is furnished in James Norman Hall's and Charles B. Nordhoff's authoritative *The Lafayette Flying Corps*, supplied to me by Philip M. Flammer. Sumner Sewall is quoted about his last day in the air in Harold Buckley's *Squadron 95* (Paris, 1933), and Harold Hartney tells his story in *Up and At 'Em* (Harrisburg, Pa., 1940). Billy Mitchell's reminiscences are from his *Memoirs of World War I*.

Colonel F. O. Cave's diary (entry for 11-11-18) is in the IWM. Lieutenant Colonel L. A. Strange's memoir is *Recollections of an Airman* (London, 1933). The grounding of the Handley-Page flight is told in Anthony Kilburn's October 25, 1979, letter to me. The abortive flight from France over Berlin to Prague is described in the diary of W. R. Read, extracted in "Cavalryman in the Flying Machines," *People at War,* ed. Michael Moynihan (Newton Abbot, 1973). Data on the 8th Squadron is from October 9, 1979, letter from R. N. Bell; on the 217th Squadron from a letter of October 9, 1979, from Stephen Horscroft; on the 40th Squadron from a letter of January 5, 1980, from Ralph J. Donaldson. Data on the 104th Squadron is from Ewart Garland (see notes to "Armistice Eve"). A. C. Reid's memoir is *Planes and Personalities* (London, 1920). He does not identify his squadron.

THE STILLNESS

General Marshall's account is from his *Memoirs*. German official documents and Army orders are from copies with translations at the USMHI. Communications, reports, and war diary entries of German units are also from the USMHI. Otto Brautigam's diary entry is from his *So Hat Es Sich Zugetragen*, previously cited. John Bagot Glubb quoted from his diary in his *Into Battle* (London, 1978). The American version of the Lieutenant Thoma incident is from the official *History of the 89th Division*, by Lieutenant Colonel George H. English, Jr. (n.p., 1920). Data on the 90th Division is from Major George Wythe's *A History of the 90th Division* (n.p., 1920), and unless otherwise credited, data on the 2nd Division is from *The Second Division American Expeditionary Force in France 1917–1919* by Colonel Lyman Spaulding and Colonel John Womack Wright (New York, 1937). 79th Division data is from *The History of the Seventy-Ninth Division, A.E.F.* (Lancaster, Pa., 1922), published anonymously but authored by William Bell Clark.

General Robert L. Bullard's memoir is *Personalities and Reminiscences of the War* (New York, 1925) and General Robert Alexander's is *Memories of the World War* (New York, 1931). Alden Brooks's comments on Bullard are from his *As I Saw It* (New York, 1930). Late notification and cease-fire reports are numerous, and not all are described above. Major Hoffman Nickerson explains the lure of billets and bathing in Stenay in "The Lessons of the Armistice," a typescript prepared for the Army War College, February 1944, USMHI. The 104th Infantry (26th Division) story is told by Colonel Connell Albertine in *The Yankee Doughboy* (Boston, 1968). Orin Fye's recollection of the 26th is from a conversation with him, March 11, 1980. Frank Friedel's *Over There* (Boston, 1964), quotes Frank Sibley, Lieutenant Harry G. Rennagel, and Lieutenant Walter A. Davenport. Frank Sibley's book is *With the Yankee Division in France* (Boston, 1919).

The inebriated French artilleryman is described by William E.

McCarthy in *Memories of the 309th Field Artillery* (n.p., 1920). William March's [pseud. for William Edward March Campbell] novel is *Company K* (New York, 1933). The sound recording of the cease-fire is the frontispiece to Benedict Crowell's *America's Munitions 1917–1918* (Washington, 1919). The account of the 54th Infantry is from George Mabry's *Recollections of a Recruit: An Official History of the Fifty-Fourth U.S. Infantry* (n.p., 1919). That of the 165th Infantry is from *Father Duffy's Story* by Francis P. Duffy (New York, 1919). Robert Joseph Casey's memoir is *The Cannoneers Have Hairy Ears* (New York, 1927), and Harry Croft's story is in Henry Berry's *Make the Kaiser Dance* (New York, 1978). Corporal Dudley's account is from Elizabeth Frazer's "The Last Fight," *The Saturday Evening Post*, February 8, 1919. The story about correspondent Herman Whitaker is from Gregory Mason, "How America Finished," in *Armistice Day* (New York, 1927). Alexander Woollcott's letter to Edmund Devol is from Bar le Duc, November 12, 1918, in *The Letters of Alexander Woollcott* (New York, 1944). Frederick Pottle's diary entry is in *Stretchers*, previously cited. Harold Horne's account to the BBC was furnished to me by Alan Haydock, and other data about the 63rd Division is from Douglas Jerrold, *The Royal Naval Division* (London, 1927). Extracts from R. F. Delderfield are from his *A Horseman Riding By* (New York, 1966). J. W. Muirhead's diary is in the IWM. The memories of Victor Senez appear in "Le 11 novembre vécu par un enfant de huit ans, Victor Senez," *La Voix du Nord* (Valenciennes), November 11, 1978. Desiré Bontelle's memoir is *Vingt ans après: Les cahiers d'un sergent d'Infanterie, 1914–1918* (Paris, 1935).

Mons accounts include J. F. Livesay's *Canada's Hundred Days*, from which comes the story of the final Canadian artillery salvo and the last officer casualty; the official *Canadian Expeditionary Force 1914–1919* by G. W. L. Nicholson (Ottawa, 1962), which gives the divisional reports on casualties; Will Bird's account is *Ghosts Have Warm Hands;* Howard Vincent O'Brien's anonymously published diary is *Wine, Women and War* (1926); Arthur W. Boyd's letter to me is dated October 13, 1979. Mavor Moore made his play, *The Man Who Caught Bullets*, available to me in CBC scenario form, along with Toronto *Globe* transcripts of the 1928 Currie trial.

Acting Brigadier General Bernard Freyberg's letter to Winston Churchill, apparently written November 11, 1918, is quoted in John Terraine's *To Win a War* (London, 1918).

Sir Harold Parker's letter to me, undated from London, is from about November 1979; the Norfolk Regiment's encounter is described in Colonel (Ret.) E. J. S. Bonnett's letter to me dated October 19, 1979. Cyril Flin's letter to me is dated October 10, 1979; D. O. Dixon's letter to the BBC is dated March 8, 1978; Alfred Bille-quez's to the BBC is dated March 13, 1978; John Vincent's to me is dated October 17, 1979. W. O. Duncan's letter to me is dated October 12, 1979; Olivery Lyttleton's *The Memoirs of Lord Chandos* (London, 1962) describes his experience at Maubeuge. Captain L. W. Lee's letter to the BBC, undated, is stamped "acknowledged 19 April 1978"; Guy Chapman's account is in his *A Passionate Prodigality.*

The *"Im Krieg"* motto is quoted in *Udet: A Man's Life.* Lieutenant Schröder's memoir is *An Airman Remembers* (London, 1936). "Hauptmann Hermann's" memoir is *The Luftwaffe: Its Rise and Fall* (New York, 1943). Rudolf Stark's memoir is *Wings of War;* M. E. Kahnert's is *Jagdstaffel 356;* Ernst Udet's is *Udet: A Man's Life.* The diary of Captain Erhard Milch is quoted in David Irving's *The Rise and Fall of the Luftwaffe: The Life of Field Marshal Erhard Milch* (Boston and Toronto, 1973). Accounts of Hermann Goering differ in details. The most credible are Charles Bewley's *Hermann Goering and the Third Reich* (New York, 1962) and Leonard Mosley's *The Reich Marshal* (New York, 1974). Some accounts have Goering surrender to the Americans (which may reflect a later war); others garble French and German geography, perhaps because the boundaries would change.

Ben P. Simpson's letter to me is dated October 9, 1979; John Ventham's letter to the BBC is undated but about March 1978. James Bertram Davidson's letter to the BBC is dated March 31, 1978. The story of the German machine gunner, repeated in Montgomery's book, is first told in novelist John Buchan's *The History of the South African Forces in France* (London, 1920). Walter Kempowski's "last shot" reminiscence is from his *Days of Greatness,* trans. Leila Vennewitz (London, 1982). Arthur Wrench's unpublished diary was made available to me by the author, while Frederick Nicolson's unpublished diary was furnished to me by his nephew, Nigel Nicolson. Vivian de Sola Pinto's memoir, quoted earlier as well, is *The City That Shone.* Leslie Walkinton, who has written a memoir, *Twice in a Lifetime* (Devon, 1979), described his experience of November 1918 to me in a letter dated October 15, 1979.

A JOYFUL NOISE

The exchange with Jean Piot is in Alexander Werth, *The Twilight of France, 1933–40* (New York, 1942); Marcel Proust's observation is from George Painter, *Marcel Proust*, II (New York, 1959). Michel Corday's comment is from his *The Paris Front: An Unpublished Diary: 1914–1918* (London, 1933), while the Mayor's entire proclamation is reprinted in James G. Harbord, *Leaves from a War Diary* (New York, 1925). Major Scott Button's letter to his wife is dated November 18, 1918. John MacKay Shaw's letter to me, enclosing pages from his unpublished memoirs, is dated November 16, 1979. Marianne Hancock's letter to me dated November 12, 1979, includes copies of letters home from her father, Lieutenant J. Harrison Heckman. Brigadier General George van Horn Moseley is quoted from his unpublished *One Soldier's Journey*, Hoover Institution, Stanford.

Mrs. J. Borden Harriman's memoir is *From Pinafores to Politics* (New York, 1923). Dorothy Canfield [Fisher]'s "Armistice Day" is reprinted in A. P. Sanford and R. H. Schauffler, ed., *Armistice Day* (New York, 1927). The memoirs of Albert Leon Guerard (1880–1959) are from his unpublished diary, photocopies of which were furnished to me by his son, Albert J. Guerard, author of *The Past Must Alter* (London, 1937) and of a memoir of the period in which his novel was written, "Paris: 1928. A Nostalgic Journey," *The Southern Review*, 16 (1980). Edward Knoblock's memoir is *Round the Room* (London, 1939).

Elliot White Springs's novel is *Contact: A Romance of the Air* (New York, 1930). Edith Wharton is quoted in R. W. B. Lewis, *Edith Wharton* (Harper, 1975) and Mary Roberts Rinehart in Jan Cohn, *Improbable Fiction* (Pittsburgh, 1980). Eve Curie writes about her mother in *Madame Curie* (London, 1938).

Clemenceau at the Chamber is reported in newspaper accounts, in H. M. Hyndman's *Clemenceau* (New York, 1919), and in Jean Martet, *Georges Clemenceau* (London, 1930). Ex-Empress Eugénie on Clemenceau is from Jasper Ridley's *Napoleon III and Eugénie* (New York, 1978). Most of the Monet allusions are in Martet. The Appollonaire story is from the diary of Paul Léauteaud, quoted by Francis Steegmuller in his *Apollonaire* (New York, 1963) and Steegmuller's *Cocteau* (New York, 1970). The legend that the poet was alive when the *"À bas Guillaume!"* shouting was heard under his window appears to have begun with Robert Motherwell in 1949 in a preface to an exhibition catalogue. It has been repeated often since. René Gimpel is quoted from his *Diary of an Art Dealer* (New York, 1966).

Romain Rolland's *The Soul Enchained* includes two volumes touching upon Armistice Day. *Mother and Son*, trans. Van Wyck Brooks (New York, 1927), ends in the Rivière flat with the news of the Armistice. *The Death of a World,* trans. Amalia de Alberti (New York, 1933), continues the narrative of the day. René Naegelen's memoir, "Recollections," is published in *Promise of Greatness.* Emma Dickson's letter to her mother dated November 18, 1918, is in Special Collections, Pattee Library, The Pennsylvania State University. Joseph Paul Boncour's memoir (including the Mangin episode) is *Recollections of the Third Republic,* trans. George Marion, Jr. (New York, 1957). The Teilhard de Chardin letter is quoted in *The Making of a Mind,* trans. René Hague (New York, 1965). Kathleen Scott's diary is *Self-Portrait of an Artist,* published by her as Lady Kennet (London, 1949).

Gertrude Stein and Alice Toklas are quoted in James Mellow, *Charmed Circle* (New York, 1974) and Alice B. Toklas, *The Alice B. Toklas Cook Book* (New York, 1960). Eleanor Dulles is quoted in Leonard Mosley, *Dulles* (New York, 1978).

The account of the Boulogne bordello riot is from Eric Hiscock, *The Bells of Hell Go Ting-a-Ling-a-Ling* (London, 1976). The Mottram quotation is from the first volume of *The Spanish Farm* trilogy. Jacques-Émile Blanche's memoir is *More Portraits of a Lifetime* (London, 1939) and John Dos Passos's novel (from the *U.S.A.* cycle) is *1919* (New York, 1932).

Edouard Vasseur de la Sostee's letter to me is dated February 19, 1980. Paxton Davis's letter relaying his father's reminiscence is dated October 23, 1979, and John H. Nixon's memory of the *Aquitania* is dated October 16, 1979. Ronald Drive's letter to the BBC is dated March 25, 1978, and R. L. Haine's oral reminiscence was taped by the IWM as No. 000033/06. Charles Carrington's memoir is *Soldier from the Wars Returning* (London, 1959), an augmented version of his earlier *A Subaltern's War* (1929), published under the pen name "Charles Edmonds"; J. B. Priestley's memoir is *Margin Released* (New York, 1962). John B. Troxell's letter to me is dated November 27, 1979, and William M. Seuter's saga of the *Kermoor* is from his letter to me dated November 16, 1979, with an attached unpublished memoir. Frank R. Smith's memories of being spirited from a French hospital were related to Lynnell Mickelsen for the Knight-Ridder newspaper chain's Sunday release of November 7, 1982, as "A Veteran Looks Back at World War I." The Trouville hospital "eating" episode was described to me by Charles Bowers in a letter dated October 29, 1979. Willy Coppens de Houthulst's memoirs are *Days on the Wing,* trans. A. J. Insall (London, n.d.). Oscar Ludmann's reminiscence is from his *Stepchild of the Rhine.*

How Marcel Bloch (Dassault) spent November 11, 1918, is described in Pierre Assouline, *Monsieur Dassault* (Paris, 1983).

"How 'Ya Gonna Keep 'Em Down on the Farm" (1919) was written by Sam M. Lewis and Joe Young to music by Walter Donaldson. Copyright © 1919 by Mills Music; renewed 1947 by Mills Music, Inc. and Warnock Music, Inc.

HAVING A KNEES-UP

Newspapers of the eleventh, twelfth, and thirteenth furnish some of the details in this section. Balfour's letter to Stamfordham appears in Harold Nicolson, *King George the Fifth* (London, 1952). Nicolson's "Strumnitza" account is in his *Peacemaking 1919* (New York, 1933). Mary Veronica Wauchope's letter to me is dated November 12, 1979; Grace Emily Brightman's is dated October 12, 1979. Edward Marsh's involvement is cited by Christopher Hassall in his *A Biography of Edward Marsh* (New York, 1959); Churchill's is told by him in his own *The World Crisis*, V (New York, 1930) and by Martin Gilbert in *Winston S. Churchill*, IV, *1916–1921* (Boston, 1975). Maurice Hankey's memoir is *The Supreme Command*, II (London, 1961); Chaim Weizmann's is *Trial and Error* (New York, 1949); Margot Asquith's is her *Autobiography*, II (London, 1922). The Fisher quotation is from Alan Clark, ed., *"A Good Innings": The Private Papers of Viscount Lee of Fareham* (London, 1974); the Baldwin quotation is from Keith Middlemas and John Barnes, *Baldwin* (London, 1969).

David Kneebone's schoolboy memory is from a letter to me dated October 14, 1979. The late Lord Snow recalled his Armistice Day in a letter dated March 5, 1979. Alan Elphick wrote to me on October 10, 1979, and Stephen Usherwood on October 13, 1979. A. J. A. Lunghi's letter to me is dated October 9, 1979. Victoria Smith wrote to me on October 17, 1979, and Edward C. Doughty on October 9, 1979. Sheilah Graham tells her story as *The Late Lily Shiel* (New York, 1978). Malcolm Muggeridge's memoir is *The Green Stick* (New York, 1973); Francis Chichester is reported by E. S. Turner in *Dear Old Blighty* (London, 1980); V. S. Pritchett's memoir is *A Cab at the Door* (New York, 1968); and Louis MacNeice's is *The Strings are False* (London, 1965). Barrie's letter from Paris is quoted in Andrew Birkin's *J. M. Barrie and the Lost Boys* (New York, 1979) and Brian Howard's in Marie-Jacqueline Lancaster's *Brian Howard* (London, 1968). Kenneth Clark's memoir is *The Making of an Aesthete* (London,

1974). Evelyn Waugh's autobiography is *A Little Learning* (Boston, 1964), and his *Diary* was edited by Michael Davies (Boston, 1976). Christopher Fry's memoir is *Can You Find Me: A Family History* (Oxford, 1978) and Rupert Hart-Davis's is *The Arms of Time* (London, 1980). John Straker's letter to me is dated October 11, 1979; that of R. J. Johnstone is October 18, 1979.

Dora Carrington's letter, November 12, 1918, to Noel Carrington, is quoted in Michael Holroyd, *Lytton Strachey: A Biography* (London, 1971). Conan Doyle is quoted from his *Memories and Adventures* (Boston, 1924) and from a letter to his wife, Jean, in John Dickson Carr's *The Life of Sir Arthur Conan Doyle* (New York, 1949). Ezra Pound's letter to John Quinn is quoted in Noel Stock's *Life of Ezra Pound* (New York, 1973). The *Canto* is No. 105. The King's diary is quoted by Harold Nicolson in his *King George the Fifth* (London, 1952). The *Punch* cartoon appeared on November 20 and 27, 1918. H. W. Yoxall sent me extracts from his diary entry for November 11 on November 17, 1980. Kingsley Martin's memoir is *Father Figures* (London, 1966).

The Sons of Cain is by Robert Bellah (New York and London, 1928). Robert Sherwood's letter to his mother is quoted in John Mason Brown's *The Worlds of Robert E. Sherwood* (New York, 1965) and his own memories appear in his Preface to *Waterloo Bridge* (New York and London, 1930). *Random Harvest* is by James Hilton (New York, 1941). Osbert Sitwell's description of Trafalgar Square is from his *Laughter in the Next Room* (Boston, 1948). The "battle of vegetables" is described by R. E. W. Johnson to me in a letter dated November 1, 1979. The Trafalgar Square bonfire is described in letters from C. J. Mumford (October 10, 1979) and H. F. Forth (to the BBC October 25, 1978). Edward Doughty's letter is referred to earlier. C. H. Rolph's memoir is *London Particulars* (London, 1980). Hettie Bundock Mullis wrote to me on October 24, 1979, and September 16, 1980; Noel Wisdom on November 10, 1979; A. S. Warren on October 25, 1979.

Ford Madox Ford's final volumes of *Parade's End* are *A Man Could Stand Up* (1926) and *The Last Post* (1928), the latter containing Marie Léonie's memories quoted. Agatha Christie is quoted from her *Autobiography* (1977) and Aileen McKenna from her letter to me of November 20, 1979. Sir Charles Petrie's reminiscence appeared in *Promise of Greatness*. Arnold Bennett's *Journals* (New York, 1933) contain Armistice Day recollections on November 12 and 14, 1918. Sir Oswald Mosley's recollection is from *My Life* (London, 1968) and from Nicholas Mosley, *Rules of the Game: Sir Oswald Mosley and Lady Cynthia Mosley 1896–1933* (London, 1982). Noel Coward is quoted from Sheridan Morley, *A Talent to Amuse* (New York, 1969). The meeting of Cedric Morris and Arthur Lett-Haines is from the catalogs of their posthumous shows at the Tate Gallery and the Redfern Gallery, London, 1984.

The Vauxhall ambulance story is in a letter to the BBC from Mrs. B. M. H. Caradose, undated but sometime in 1978. Adela Hill's letter to me is dated October 10, 1979; Patrick Havelock Ellis's letter is in Phyllis Grosskurth's *Havelock Ellis* (New York, 1980). Patrick Ludlow's is October 15, 1979. Vera Brittain's memoir is *Testament of Youth* (London, 1934). Charles Ricketts' diary is *Self-Portrait*, ed. T. Sturge Moore (London, n.d.). Virginia Woolf's letter to Vanessa Bell is in *The Letters of Virginia Woolf*, II, eds. Nigel Nicolson and Joanne Trautmann (New York, 1976); her diary entry is from November 12, in *The Diary of Virginia Woolf*, I ed. Anne Olivier Bell (London, 1977). The East End reminiscence is in a letter to me from E. S. Seals dated October 10, 1979.

Mrs. R. G. Taylor's letter to me is undated but about October 1979. Dan Walker's letter is dated October 24, 1979. Wyndham Lewis's memoir is *Blasting and Bombardiering* (Berkeley, 1967). John Brooks's letter to the BBC is dated July 19, 1978; Vernon Smythe's letter to the BBC is April 28, 1978; and F. N. Scaife's letter to me is undated but about October 1979. H. H. Balfour's memoir is *An Airman Marches* (London, 1933). Ethel Simmonds' letter about Canadian troops with whom her husband was stationed is dated October 12, 1979 (when Mrs. Simmonds was ninety-nine!); Percy W. Hubbard's is October 9, 1979. Frank Honeywood's story is told by Eric Partridge in "Frank Honeywood, Private," *Three Men's War* (New York, 1930).

The unidentified (at his request) lieutenant's Newtownwards letter to me is dated October 9, 1979. Robert Graves is quoted from his *Good-Bye to All That*, 2nd ed. rev. (New York, 1957) and Siegfried Sassoon from his *Siegfried's Journey, 1916–1920* (London, 1946).

James Logan's recollection of Sunderland is in Gordon Reid, ed., *Poor Bloody Murder* (Oakville, Ontario, 1980), while Gerald Brenan is quoted from his autobiography, *A Life of One's Own* (Cambridge, 1962) and Joseph Conrad from Frederick Karl's *Joseph Conrad: The Three Lives* (New York, 1979). E. R. Cooper's Southwold chronicle is found in M. Moynihan, ed., *People at War* (London, 1973) and Rider Haggard from his *Private Diaries*, ed. D. S. Higgins

(London, 1980) and Peter B. Ellis, *H. Rider Haggard* (Boston & London, 1978). The Cromer vignette is from a letter from H. Crowther to me dated October 22, 1979. John Silber's story is told by Ronald Seth in *The Spy Who Never Was Caught* (New York, 1967), based on Silber's own memoir, *Invisible Weapons* (London, 1932). The Girton account is from Phyllis Taylor's letter to the BBC dated October 30, 1978, while the Lady Margaret Hall account is from Annette R. Kennedy-Cooke's letter to me dated October 22, 1979. Elinor Pike's letter to the BBC is dated March 8, 1978.

Herbert Morrison's memoir is *An Autobiography* (London, 1960); Storm Jameson's is *Journey to the North* (New York, 1978). Sidney Webb's letter to Beatrice is in Norman Mackenzie, ed., *The Letters of Sidney and Beatrice Webb*, III (Cambridge, 1978); Beatrice's journal entry is in *Beatrice Webb's Diaries, 1912–1924*, ed. Margaret I. Cole (London, 1952). Stanley Downing wrote to me in an undated letter from about October 1979. *Punch's* "Armistice Day in the North" appeared on November 27, 1918. Maria Marks's letter to the BBC is dated March 19, 1978. Joseph Holloway's diary was edited by Robert Hogan and Michael J. O'Neill as *Joseph Holloway's Abbey Theatre* (Carbondale, Ill., 1967). *The Life of Field Marshal Sir John French* (London, 1931), by Gerald French, quotes his Armistice Day telegrams.

The Glasgow situation is described to me by Jean T. Pithie in a letter dated October 8, 1979, and by Glasgow newspapers furnished to me by Miss Pithie. Aberdeen was described to me by Winifred M. Deans in a letter dated November 11, 1979, and Penicuik by W. W. Black (November 30, 1979), who furnished photocopies of pages from his father's town chronicle.

Churchill described the setting of the Downing Street dinner in *The World Crisis,* and the substance of the dinner in *The Aftermath.* The basic document of the Shearman party is Osbert Sitwell's *Laughter in the Next Room.* Michael Holroyd discusses Augustus John's presence in his *Augustus John* (London, 1975) and quotes his letter to John Quinn. Carrington's letter describing the party is in Holroyd's *Lytton Strachey.* Bertrand Russell's Armistice Day is described in his *Portraits from Memory* (New York, 1956); Galsworthy's diary is quoted in Catherine Dupre, *John Galsworthy* (New York, 1976). D. H. Lawrence's presence is described by David Garnett in *The Flowers of the Forest* (New York, 1955). Huxley's letter to Juliette Baillot (November 25, 1918) is in Grover Smith, ed., *Letters of Aldous Huxley* (New York, 1969), in which another letter, October 25, 1918, to Ottoline Morrell, includes the pre-Armistice anti-Semitic description of Mond. That Huxley is referring to Mond, whose name is expunged from the Juliette Baillot letter, is explained to me by Grover Smith (April 16, 1980), who cut the identification for reasons of law and taste. Mond's military service is reported by Sidney Rogerson in "Lord Melchett. Services of Two Wars," *The Times*, February 3, 1949.

THE REAL THING

Material not otherwise identified comes from newspaper stories in dailies from coast to coast. The *Nansemond* story is from *Stars and Stripes*, November 22, 1918. The *Mentor* story is from T. N. Jackson's letter to me, undated but about November 1979. William Faulkner's correspondence with Malcolm Cowley is in *The Faulkner-Cowley File*, ed. Malcolm Cowley (New York, 1966). Scott Fitzgerald's whereabouts are described in Arthur Mizener, *The Far Side of Paradise* (New York, 1951) and Zelda Fitzgerald's in her *Save Me the Waltz* (New York, 1932). John Dos Passos's letters quoted are in *The Fourteenth Chronicle*, ed. Townsend Ludington (Boston, 1973). Milton Lowenthal's reminiscence is from conversation with him on September 6, 1980. Malcolm Cowley's description is from his *Exile's Return* (New York, 1934). Charles Baldwin's letter to me is dated November 15, 1979; Sigmund Sameth's is November 16, 1979; Alfred Knopf's is May 4, 1979. Irving Berlin's reminiscence is via conversation with his secretary, May 11, 1979. Edison's statement is transcribed from his "Peace Record." Arch Whitehouse's memoir is *The Fledgling* (New York, 1964).

Edith Bolling Wilson's reminiscence is *My Memoir;* Eleanor Roosevelt's is *This Is My Story.* The Samuel Gompers story is from Frank L. Grubbs, *The Struggle for Labor Equality: Gompers, the A. F. of L., and the Pacifists, 1917–1920* (Durham, N.C., 1968).

The War Department employees' song is extracted from the diary of the late Pansy Myers Rader, who was working there in November 1918. The Fred Waring interview by Betty Bechdel appeared in *Town and Gown* (State College, Pa.) August 1979. William Walk's letter to me is about December 1979 but undated; Walter Morgan's is dated February 19, 1979, and Raymond McKeever's, about his uncle John McKeever (with a photocopy of the induction notice), is dated December 11, 1979.

Ernest Erber's story of Chicago is from a letter to me undated but about February 1980. William L. Shirer's Iowa reminiscence is from his *20th Century Journey* (New York, 1976). John Harrison's experience was related to me in a letter from Serrell Hillman, dated February 20, 1979.

The story of John Schrag is told in Frederick C. Luebke's *Bonds of Loyalty* (De Kalb, Ill., 1974) from James C. Juhnke, "John Schrag Espionage Case," *Mennonite Life,* July 1967. Henry Ford is quoted in Allan Nevins and Frank E. Hill, *Ford: Expansion and Challenge, 1915–1933* (New York, 1957). The Clifford Morrow story (newspapers reported his name as Carl Morrow) was checked out by Dolores Veitz, who reported to me (February 22, 1980) what was published in the *Punxsutawney Spirit* on November 12, 1918.

Harry Onken's letter to me is dated March 20, 1980; Emanuel Gebauer's is November 15, 1979; Elliott Barker's is December 21, 1979; Kenneth Wiggins Porter's is November 21, 1979; Edna La Moore Waldo's is November 11, 1979; Dorothy B. Aspinwall's is February 14, 1980. Will Irwin's account of the French colonel on a train in Nevada is from his *The Making of a Reporter* (New York, 1942). Harry T. Moore reminisced to me about Los Angeles on Armistice Day in Houston, Texas, on December 29, 1980.

Omar Bradley's recollection of Des Moines on Armistice Day is from his *A General's Life,* written by Clay Blair (New York, 1983); Dwight Eisenhower's reaction is in Stephen E. Ambrose's *Eisenhower,* I (New York, 1983). The boyhood memories of Elburt Osborn and John Ferguson come from conversations with them.

AFTERMATH: THE FRONT LINES

The *Punch* cartoon "The Final" appeared on November 27, 1918. Quotations from George Seldes in this chapter are from his unpublished memoir, "Adventures with People," furnished to me on June 9, 1979. S. N. Preece's letter to me is dated October 9, 1979; A. C. Wilkinson's letter is October 15, 1979, and forwarded by H. A. F. Radley on November 5, 1979. Birge Clark is quoted from his typescript *World War I Memoirs* in the Stanford Library by David M. Kennedy in *Over Here: The First World War and American Society* (New York, 1980). Harry Dadswell is quoted by Patsy Adam-Smith in *The Anzacs.* Thomas Robbins is quoted from his letter to me dated November 11, 1979. R. H. Mottram described the anticlimax of the armistice in *Ten Years Ago: Armistice & Other Memories* (London, 1928). F. P. Crozier's memoir is *A Brass Hat in No Man's Land* (New York, 1930). Dudley Meneaud-Lissenburg wrote to me on October 22, 1979. Will Judy is quoted from his *A Soldier's Diary*. George C. Marshall is quoted from his *Memoirs*. George S. Patton, Jr., is quoted (diary) from Martin S. Blumenson, ed., *The Patton Papers* (Boston, 1972) and (poem) from the original in the Manuscript Division, Library of Congress.

The London Rifle Brigade's night at Erquennes is described in Aubrey Smith's "The Armistice Was No Fun in France," in Hammerton. Robert Airey's undated letter to me is from about December 1979. A copy of William A. Percy's *Lanterns on the Levee: Recollections of a Plantation Man* (New York, 1941) was furnished to me by W. Gerow Schick, Jr. "Doc" Harrison's unpublished memoir has been referred to earlier. Christopher Marsh's letter to me is dated October 24, 1979. The refugee account is from James W. Howard, *The Autobiography of a Regiment: A History of the 304th Field Artillery in the World War* (New York, 1920).

The "rather inaccurate" flags are described in Alan A. Maude's *The History of the 47th (London) Division* (London, 1922). Bernard A. Bergman's letter to me is dated November 13, 1979. W. Beach Thomas's memoir is "Glimpses of a Vanquished People," in Hammerton's *The Great War;* Philip Gibbs's novel is *Wounded Souls* (New York, 1920). Will Bird's memoir is *Ghosts Have Warm Hands.* Stuart Whibley wrote to me on November 7, 1979. Edmund Wilson's journal entries for November 1918 were published by him in *A Prelude* (New York, 1967). The Scottish RAMC officer is quoted by John Brophy and Eric Partridge in *The Long Trail* (New York, 1965). B. A. Lewis's letter to me is dated October 10, 1979. Frank Richards's memoir is *Old Soldiers Never Die* (New York, 1966). Harry Day's letter to me is dated October 9, 1979. W. R. Read's memoir, "Cavalryman in the Flying Machines," is in *People at War, 1914–1918* (Newton Abbot, 1973), ed. Michael Moynihan.

Marc Bloch is quoted in his *Memoirs of War* (Ithaca and London, 1980), in Carole Fink's Introduction. The unidentified French soldier is quoted from his anonymously written *Le 9e Bataillon de Chasseurs à Pied* (Paris, 1921). The Drieu la Rochelle reference is from Frank Field's *Three French Writers and the Great War* (Cambridge, 1975). Darlan data is from Alec de Montmorency's *The Enigma of Admiral Darlan* (New York, 1943). Jean de Pierrefeu's *French Headquarters 1915–1918* (London, 1924) is translated by C. J. C. Street. André

Maurois's *Memoirs* (New York, 1942) are translated by Denver Lindley. Henry Waite's letter to the BBC is dated March 29, 1978. Cecil Lewis's Chinese Labour Corps story is from his *Sagittarius Rising*. Horatio Rogers's memoir is *World War I Through My Sights;* Frank Sibley's is *With the Yankee Division in France.* Private Slack's experience is related in Edward M. Coffman, *The War to End All Wars* (New York, 1968). Henry Pitts appears in R. F. Delderfield's *A Horseman Riding By.* Sam Van Tries was interviewed on WPSX-TV (Clearfield/University Park, Pennsylvania) on January 24, 1980. Otto Brautigam's memoir is *So Hat Es Sich Zugetragen.* George Leach's *War Diary* was privately printed (Minneapolis, 1923). *The History of the Seventh Field Artillery* (New York, 1929) is anonymously written. Gregory Mabry wrote *Recollections of a Recruit. An Official History of the Fifty-Fourth U.S. Infantry* (n.p., 1919). Wainwright Philips edited *The History of the 101st Machine Gun Battalion* (Hartford, 1922). Harry Truman's 1954 memo is cited in detail in the notes to "Last Shots." Colonel Richard Meinertzhagen's memoir is *Army Diary 1899–1926* (Edinburgh and London, 1960). Stanley Butcher's letters to me are dated October 10, 1979, and November 6, 1979. The Aulnoye festivities are described in the anonymous *History and Memoir of the 33rd Battalion, Machine Gun Corps* (London, 1919). *General Jack's Diary* is edited by John Terraine (London, 1964). Geoffrey Keynes's memoir is "A Doctor's War," in *Promise of Greatness.* Leslie Walkinton's letter to me is dated October 15, 1979.

PRISONERS OF WAR

The Berne prisoner exchange treaty is described in Samuel Shartle, *Spa, Versailles, Munich* (Philadelphia, 1941). The *Stars and Stripes* misdelivery is described by John T. Winterich in his *The Stars and Stripes: Squads Write!* (New York, 1931). The Armistice episode in *The Spanish Farm* in which the Germans insist on surrendering is in Part 3, *The Crime at Vanderlynden's.* General George C. Marshall's reminiscence of the Russian PWs is in his *Memoirs.* Cecil Roberts on a Russian PW burial party is in *The Years of Promise* (London, 1968). Aladar Kuncz's account of Hungarian PWs in France is from his *Black Monastery* (New York, 1934). Herman Reese's memoir of German PWs in France is *Kriegsgefangen!* (Berlin, 1930), while Karl Wilke's autobiographical novel is *Prisonnier Halm* (Leipzig, 1929). Runs of the *Orgelsdorfer Eulenspiegel, Die Baracke,* and the *Kriegsgefan-*

genen Zeitung were made available to me by Agnes Peterson, Hoover Institution, Stanford. Erich Dwinger's *The Army Behind Barbed Wire* is translated by Ian Morrow (London, 1930). Jean Bourdon wrote to me on December 9, 1979, furnishing me an account of his father's PW experience as well as copies of his father's diary and relevant photographs. Charles de Gaulle's PW experience has been described sketchily many times; one of the most detailed is Brian Crozier's *De Gaulle* (New York, 1973).

James Norman Hall's accounts of PW life are (memoir) *My Island Home* (Boston, 1952) and (novel) *Falcons of France* (Boston, 1936). Battle and Tucker appear in Norman Archibald's memoir, *Heaven High and Hell Deep* (New York, 1935), while the account of A. L. Gates is in *The First Yale Unit: A Story of Naval Aviation* by Ralph D. Paine (Cambridge, Mass., 1925). Guy Brown Wiser's letters to me dated October 22, 1979, and November 12, 1979, included photographs of Landshut and reproductions from his diary. Herbert Empson's letter to me is dated December 7, 1979; J. A. Chester's is October 9, 1979; George W. Barrow's is October 17, 1979; Wilfred Stevens's is October 15, 1979; Thomas Johnston's is undated but about October 1979. Philip Jenkins wrote Alan Haydock of the BBC on March 8, 1979.

Joseph Price's letters to me are dated October 15, 1979, and November 19, 1979. These supplement a memoir, "A P.O.W. Escapes," in *Red Fox Magazine* [The Journal of the Fifth Army Old Comrades Association], March 1973.

John Balfour's letter about Ruhleben is dated October 9, 1979. A detailed account of Ruhleben is by J. D. Ketchum, *Ruhleben. A Prison Camp Society* (Toronto, 1965). George Waymark's diary is extracted in "Dreaming of Cream Buns," *Black Bread and Barbed Wire*, ed. Michael Moynihan. Alec Waugh's accounts of Mainz are *The Prisoners of Mainz* (London, 1919) and *The Early Years of Alec Waugh* (London, 1962). Hugh Kingsmill's memoirs of Mainz are *Behind Both Lines* (London, 1930) and *The Progress of a Biographer* (London, 1949). E. C. Pattison's "The Long Way's End" appears in *A Martial Medley* (London, 1931).

John Cummings wrote to me about the Volkenroda mines on October 17, 1979. Tom Easton wrote to me on December 10, 1979, about his return to his PW pit. W. H. Somerset wrote to Alan Haydock on March 9, 1978, about his mining experience as a PW. E. G. Williams wrote about his experiences and those of his brother Tom on October 24, 1979, and December 31, 1979, and also narrated his memories on a tape recording for me. Accounts of Schweidnitz are those of J. B. Sterndale Bennett, "Prisoner's Last View of Germany," in Hammerton; A. D. M. Lewis's twelve-page letter to me dated September 28, 1979; Harold M. Gray's letter of October 22, 1979, with photograph of *Lager* II; and Lieutenant Colonel A. D. M. Lewis's letter September 28, 1979. Cecil Bacon's letter about the PW hospital at Czersk was written to Alan Haydock on May 23, 1978.

THE OTHER FRONTS

Emperor Karl's proclamation appeared in *The Times* (London) on November 12, 1918. The future Admiral Canaris's final 1918 U-boat voyage is described in Heinz Hohne's *Canaris,* trans. J. M. Brownjohn (New York, 1979).

Mussolini's *Il Popolo* editorial is quoted in Richard Collier, *Duce!* (New York, 1971). Edward M. Sturm's letter to me is undated but approximately January 1980. John Clark's is dated November 4, 1918. Alfred Kubin's memoir was published to accompany the 1926 edition of his novel *The Other Side* and added to thereafter. The translation by Denver Lindley is from the New York edition. Gino Speranza is quoted from *The Diary of Gino Speranza: Italy, 1915–1919,* II, ed. Florence Colgate Speranza (New York, 1941). Ernest Hemingway's letter to "Dearest Family," dated November 11 [1918], 4 P.M. from Milan, is 3 leaves, 6 pages, ALS. It is quoted by courtesy of the Lilly Library, Indiana University, Mrs. Madelaine ("Sunny") Hemingway Miller, and the Hemingway Estate. Additional background for the Hemingway experience, including several small quotations from the November 11 letter, can be found in E. R. Hagemann, " 'Dear Folks . . . Dear Ezra': Hemingway's Early Years and Correspondence, 1917–1924," *College Literature,* VII (Fall 1980).

General Franchet d'Esperey is quoted in Alan Palmer, *The Gardeners of Salonika* (New York, 1965). William Mather wrote to Alan Haydock on March 8, 1978, and to me in December 1979. His memoir, *"Muckydonia"—1917–1919,* was privately published (Ilfracombe, Devon, 1979). T. W. White's account of his escape from a Turkish prison is *Guests of the Unspeakable* (Sydney, 1932). Gerald Evans wrote to me on October 9, 1979; F. A. Baker on October 12, 1979. E. G. Middlecote's letter to Alan Haydock is dated March 9, 1978.

Franz von Papen told his story in *Memoirs,* trans. Brian Connell (London, 1952). Anthony Brand's letter to me is dated November

12, 1979. Ronald Storrs's memoir is *Orientations* (London, 1937). *Mark Sykes: Portrait of an Amateur* (London, 1975) is by Roger Adelson. The Alexandria riot is described to me by Leonard Francke in a letter dated October 9, 1979. The Cairo riot is described in Laurence Grafftey-Smith's *Bright Levant* (London, 1970). The Australian Remount Depot war diary is in the Australian War Memorial in Canberra. Sergeant Wood's account is "I Fought with Persians, Armenians and Russians," in Hammerton. Alexander J. Booth wrote to me around October 1979; John R. Millburn wrote to me about his father on October 11, 1979, quoting from Bowness John Milburn's diary. Lieutenant Colonel S. Bull wrote to Alan Haydock on March 9, 1978, and to me on December 10, 1980.

A. P. Herbert is quoted in Reginald Pound's *A. P. Herbert: A Biography* (London, 1976). The Königsberg/Lettow-Vorbeck saga is told by Edwin Hoyt in *The Germans Who Never Lost: the Story of the Königsberg* (New York, 1968) and by Lettow-Vorbeck himself in *My Reminiscences of East Africa* (London, 1920). Harold Owen's memoir is *Journey from Obscurity*, III (New York, 1965). Monica Wareham's letter to me is dated November 2, 1979.

The war in the Archangel area is described in *The Midnight War: The American Intervention in Russia, 1918–1920* by Richard Goldhurst (New York, 1978). Louis de Robien is quoted from *The Diary of a Diplomat in Russia, 1917–1918,* trans. Camilla Sykes (New York, 1970). William Gerhardie is quoted from *Memoirs of a Polyglot* (London, 1931) and Raymond Massey from *When I Was Young* (Toronto, 1976). Lenin's comment to Philips Price is quoted by John Toland in *No Man's Land* (New York, 1980). Gustav Becvar's memoir is *The Lost Legion: A Czechoslovakian Epic* (London, 1939). John Fenchak was interviewed by Brian Fenchak for me in December 1981. Admiral Kolchak's reign at Omsk is chronicled in George Stewart's *The White Armies of Russia* (New York, 1933). Newton Baker is quoted by Dixon Wecter in *When Johnny Comes Marching Home* (Boston, 1944). Nellie May Gray's letter to her husband, Alfred John Gray, from Evesham, November 11, 1918, was sent to me in photocopy by their daughter, Thelma M. Hayward, on October 26, 1979.

BEHIND THE RHINE

Henry Landau's memoir is *All's Fair: The Story of the British Secret Service Behind the Enemy Lines* (New York, 1934). For the Kaiser's first day in Holland, see Michael Balfour, *The Kaiser and His Times* (Boston, 1964). For the Crown Prince see Klaus W. Jonas (trans. Charles W. Bangert), *The Life of Crown Prince William* (Pittsburgh, 1961). Lieutenant Colonel Kriebel is quoted in *Putsch!* (New York, 1970) by Richard Hanser. For Werner Beumelburg see notes to "Armistice Eve." Heinrich Brüning's autobiography is *Memoiren 1918–1934* (Stuttgart, 1970). Ludwig Renn's reminiscence, "The Retreat from Belgium," is in *Vain Glory.* Friedrich Sieburg is quoted from Eric Leed, *No Man's Land,* and Ludwig Lewinsohn, from *Die Revolution an die Westfront* (Charlottenburgh, 1919). General von Einem's report is in Ralph Lutz, ed., *The Causes of the German Collapse.* "Schlump" is quoted in *Vain Glory.* Stephen Wustman is quoted from his *Surgeon with the Kaiser's Army* (London, 1968). For *Prisonnier Halm* see notes to "Prisoners of War." The description of the German officer at Bende is from Stephen Graham, "We Marched to the Skirl of the Pipes into a Silent, Conquered Country," in Hammerton. The story of revolutionary sailors purchasing railway platform passes was told to me by Professor Heinz Kosok of the University of Wuppertal. The Italian soldier's remarks on the departing enemy come from Emilio Lussu, *Sardinian Brigade* (New York, 1939).

The American military attaché's report from Holland is at the Hoover Institution. Hermann Goering's protest is quoted in *Before the Deluge: A Portrait of Berlin in the 1920s* by Otto Friedrich (New York, 1972.) The lines from *Deutschland als freie Volksrepublik* are reprinted in Waite, *Vanguard of Nazism;* also the quotation from Friedrich Wilhelm Heinz. The American agents reporting back to Holland are from the military attaché's report (Hoover). Paul Cohen-Portheim's memoir is *Time Stood Still* (London, 1931).

Gustav Regler's *The Owl of Minerva* (London, 1959) is translated by Norman Denny. Ernst Toller's account of where he was at the time of the revolution is in his *I Was a German* (London, 1934). Joseph Goebbels's letter to Fritz Prang (written November 13, 1918) is in Victor Reimann's *Goebbels* (New York, 1976), trans. Stephen Wendt. Erna Pustau's reminiscence is in Pearl Buck's *How It Happens: Talks about the German People, 1914–1933* (New York, 1947). Rilke's letter to a Dr. Burschell is in *Wartime Letters of Rainer Maria Rilke, 1914–1921* (New York, 1940), trans. M. D. Herter Norton. The description of Eisner at work is from Paul Gentizon, *La Révolution allemande* (Paris, 1919), in Waite. Heinz Guderian's letter to his wife (written November 14, 1918) is in Kenneth Macksey's *Guderian: Panzer General* (London, 1975). Einstein's two-postcard letter to his mother is quoted in Nathan and Norden, eds., *Einstein on Peace* (London, 1963). Ludendorff's letter to his wife is quoted in D. J. Goodspeed, *Ludendorff: Genius of World War I* (Boston, 1966). For Princess Blücher's diary see notes to "The Dining Car in the Forest." For Theodor Wolff see his *Through Two Decades*, trans. E. W. Dickes (London, 1936); also *The Limits of Reason: The German Democratic Press and the Collapse of the Weimar Democracy* by Modris Eksteins (Oxford, 1975). Hjalmar Schacht's autobiography is *Confessions of "The Old Wizard"* (Boston, 1956), trans. Diana Pyke.

The November 11 decree of the Executive Committee of Workers' and Soldiers' Councils is printed in translation by C. B. Burdick and R. H. Lutz in *The Political Institutions of the German Revolution, 1918–1919* (New York, 1966). General Staff machinations to apply pressure upon Ebert are detailed, with documentation, in F. L. Carsten's *Revolution in Central Europe* (Berkeley, 1972). Dittmann's *Errinerungen*, in the Institute of Social History, Amsterdam, is also quoted by F. L. Carsten. Ernst von Salomon's description of the troops returning to Berlin is from his *Die Geächteten* (Berlin, 1930), quoted in Waite. Hans von Plessen's letter to Princess Daisy is quoted in her own *Daisy, Princess of Pless: By Herself* (New York, 1920).

EPILOGUE: A BEER HALL IN MUNICH

Basic sources for the *Putsch* are Richard Hanser, *Putsch!* (New York, 1970); Joachim C. Fest (trans. Richard and Clara Winston), *Hitler* (New York, 1974); William L. Shirer, *The Rise and Fall of the Third Reich* (New York, 1960); Eugene Davidson, *The Making of Adolph Hitler* (New York, 1977). Where these accounts differ in detail (especially in translation) I have tried to reconcile such elements.

The quotation from *The Man Without Qualities* (vol. II, 1932) is from the translation by Eithne Wilkins and Ernst Kaiser (1954). Rainer Maria Rilke's letter to Clara, dated November 7, 1918, appears in Wolfgang Leppmann's *Rilke: A Life,* translated by Russell M. Stockman (New York, 1984).

INDEX